An Introduction to
THEORIES
of
HUMAN
DEVELOPMENT

To EKM for his friendship
and to all the cool sharks in lane 5

NEIL J. SALKIND

University of Kansas

An Introduction to
THEORIES
of
HUMAN
DEVELOPMENT

SAGE Publications
International Educational and Professional Publisher
Thousand Oaks ■ London ■ New Delhi

For information:

Sage Publications, Inc.
2455 Teller Road
Thousand Oaks, California 91320
E-mail: order@sagepub.com

Sage Publications Ltd.
1 Oliver's Yard
55 City Road
London EC1Y 1SP
United Kingdom

Sage Publications India Pvt. Ltd.
B-42, Panchsheel Enclave
Post Box 4109
New Delhi 110 017 India

Printed in the United States of America

Library of Congress Cataloging-in-Publication Data

Salkind, Neil J.
An introduction to theories of human development / Neil J. Salkind.
       p. cm.
Includes bibliographical references and index.
ISBN 978-0-7619-2639-9 (pbk.)
     1. Developmental psychology—Philosophy. I. Title.
BF713.S245 2004
155—dc22

                                            2003017477

08   09   10   11   12   13   9   8   7   6   5   4   3   2

Acquiring Editor:	Jim Brace-Thompson
Editorial Assistant:	Karen Ehrmann
Production Editor:	Diana E. Axelsen
Copy Editor:	Judy Selhorst
Typesetter:	C&M Digitals (P) Ltd.
Indexer:	Teri Greenberg
Cover Designer:	Michelle Lee Kenny

BRIEF CONTENTS

DETAILED CONTENTS

INTRODUCTION

In my 30 years at the University of Kansas, I've had some significant professional good fortune in that I've been able to teach introductory classes on theories of development and I've had colleagues who have been supportive and interested in my work. Both of these circumstances have allowed me to pursue the writing of this book, and in doing so I have had the opportunity to put some of my thoughts about development down on paper and share these ideas with you.

Professors and students have many different books of this type available to them, but I think this book is special, for a variety of reasons. First, it provides a comprehensive overview of the major developmental perspectives without going into a great deal of detail or using unnecessarily technical language; it is intended as it is titled—as an introduction. I focus here on the basics, without talking down or condescending to you, because it is essential for students in the behavioral and social sciences, the helping professions, and other disciplines to have a fundamental grasp of what the most important theorists have said about the development process over the past 100 years. I believe this book is the perfect introduction to theories of development for students in such fields as human services, nursing, sociology, education, and social welfare, among others.

Second, this volume is special in that it briefly addresses the applications of the developmental theories discussed, not only in the text itself but in featured boxed material, in annotated lists of suggested further readings, and in descriptions of some of the related materials available on the Internet. Information about these resources is included to help you learn more about the nature of the different theoretical positions introduced. Finally, this book reinforces learning with pedagogical aids, featuring important summary points in the margins and providing lists of suggested additional readings.

HOW THIS BOOK IS ORGANIZED

This volume is organized into five major parts. Part I, "An Introduction and Important Ideas," consists of two chapters. Chapter 1 introduces some of the primary concepts associated with the study of human development, such as the scientific method and the importance of theory in the study of behavior; provides an overview of the different theoretical perspectives covered in this volume; and briefly addresses the evaluation of theories. Chapter 2 focuses on trends and issues in the study of human development and sets the stage for the discussion of different theoretical perspectives presented in the rest of the book.

The chapters in Part II, "The Maturational and Biological Approaches," deal with theories that have as their basis the importance of biological processes, examining how these processes contribute to different theories. Chapter 3 focuses on Arnold Gesell and his maturational model. This preeminent child development expert's extensive work in documenting normal physical development has contributed a great deal to our understanding of emotional and psychosocial development. Chapter 4 addresses two relatively new and very exciting views about the singularly important role biology plays in the process of development and, hence, in the creation of culture.

Following Part II's introduction to the major biological approaches, you will be ready for Part III, "The Psychodynamic Approach," which moves into the discussion of psychodynamic theories. Chapter 5 focuses on Sigmund Freud, and Chapter 6 addresses the contributions of Erik Erikson. Both of these men brought to life a new view of the human condition, one of conflict and tension. In their work, they were concerned with how conflicts can lead to change and maturity over time.

The two chapters that make up Part IV, "The Behavioral Perspective," discuss the work of scholars in the tradition that emphasizes the importance of environmental influences. Chapter 7 focuses on B. F. Skinner's landmark work on operant conditioning, and Chapter 8 further elaborates many of the same ideas in a discussion of social learning theory that emphasizes the important roles that both individual traits and the environment play in shaping human behavior.

In Part V, "The Cognitive-Developmental View," Chapter 9 focuses on the well-known theorist Jean Piaget and his contribution to our understanding of children's cognitive development. Chapter 10 is devoted to Lev Vygotsky's increasingly attractive ideas about cognitive development, as well as a brief discussion of the differences between Vygotsky's and Piaget's theories.

Part VI, "A Comparative Analysis," contains the volume's final chapter, which compares the theories presented in the preceding chapters using Murray Sidman's (1960) model for what types of question we should ask about theories and what kinds of answers we should expect. It also includes a summary table that will help you to compare the various theories directly with one another.

SPECIAL FEATURES OF THIS BOOK

This volume includes several teaching features that are intended to help you remember what you have read and to encourage you to read more about the topics that interest you. The following features appear throughout the book:

- *Highlighted important points:* Some pieces of information are just too important to mention only once, in passing, so throughout the book, particularly important and basic points are featured in the margins around the text to encourage you to remember them.
- *Text boxes:* No book on theories of development should be without some material that focuses on the more applied nature of the theories discussed; throughout, such material is featured in boxes that stand out clearly from the rest of the text.
- *Suggested further readings:* The materials in the annotated lists of suggested further readings presented throughout this volume include brief articles on original research, reviews, and books. Many of the readings suggested are classic articles that are very important to this field; perhaps your teacher will assign one or more of the suggested readings for classroom discussion. In addition, the appendix consists of a long list of other related readings (without annotations) that you might find useful as reference material.
- *Suggested Web sites to visit:* Each chapter includes a list of several Web addresses and brief descriptions of the sites, which you can visit to find out more about the topics covered in the chapter. The Web sites listed are informative, and some are even entertaining. For the most part, they contain relatively unbiased information, and all of them can lead you to other sites that may be just what you are looking for.

MY THANKS

No book happens with just the author's words on paper (or on-screen, as the case may be). In this case, many people were very helpful and had a vision of what this project could be if guided correctly. A project like this takes the commitment and efforts of many people in addition to the author.

First, I want to express my deepest appreciation to David and Sherry Rogelberg and the fine people at Studio B who represent me in my writing. They're the best.

Without Jim Brace-Thompson, senior editor at Sage Publications, this idea would not have reached fruition. He guided and advised me when I needed it, and I thank him for his efforts, patience, advice, and the terrific lunch in Tampa. Sage has the best editors in the business, and Jim is one of them.

Thanks also to Sage production editor Diana Axelsen and copy editor Judy Selhorst for seeing the manuscript through the production process, and to Steve Kurth for the quick and excellent job he did on the graphics in this book.

If you, the reader, whether student or professor, would like to make suggestions about how this book could be improved or would like to offer other comments, please contact me via e-mail at njs@ku.edu.

—Neil J. Salkind

PART I

AN INTRODUCTION
AND IMPORTANT IDEAS

CHAPTER 1

THE STUDY OF HUMAN DEVELOPMENT

If I have seen further . . . it is by standing upon the shoulders of Giants.

—Sir Isaac Newton

Science is built up with facts, as a house is with stones. But a collection of facts is no more a science than a heap of stones is a house.

—Jules Henri Poincaré

Science is best defined as a careful, disciplined, logical search for knowledge about any and all aspects of the universe, obtained by examination of the best available evidence and always subject to correction and improvement upon discovery of better evidence. What's left is magic. And it doesn't work.

—James Randi

WHAT IS DEVELOPMENT?

This is a book about human development, some of the different theories that have been proposed to explain how development takes place, and, perhaps most interesting, how we might apply these theories to our everyday lives. If you made a list of all the things you did and all the things you thought about in the course of one day, it would probably end up including thousands of items. Such a list of thoughts and events, recorded over a period of days or months, could be called a description of your developmental repertoire—a sort of picture of what you are like as a person.

On a grand scale, your behavioral repertoire represents the developmental process; it helps to explain how you got from point A to point B and what happened along the way. Throughout this book, you will find questions about this process. What different accounts have theorists proposed to help us understand how this developmental process happens? Why might people's behavior in adulthood be so different from their behavior when they were infants? Does individuals' behavior change from the time they are newborn infants to when they are preschoolers, middle school–age children, teenagers, and on into adulthood because of biological programming or because of environmental factors, such as the influence of parents and peers? Are the changes that we experience abrupt in nature or smooth and predictable? Do people change because of the amounts and kinds of stimulation they receive in their schooling? Are you what your environment made you, or is your behavior an expression of your biological inheritance?

—— On the Web ——

Despite its name, the National Institutes of Health (at http://www.nih.gov) does not focus exclusively on "health." In fact, the NIH includes 28 institutes, offices, and research centers devoted to many directly and indirectly health-related subjects, ranging from the National Library of Medicine (at http://www.nlm.nih.gov) to the National Institute on Aging (at http://www.nia.nih.gov) to the National Institute of Child Health and Human Development (at http://www.nichd.nih.gov). These Web sites provide access to a good deal of information about biomedical science, but they also will lead you to a vast amount of information on the social, physical, and psychological aspects of development throughout the life span.

Regardless of the terms we use to pose these and other questions, we can think of **development** as a progressive series of changes that occur in a predictable pattern as the result of interactions between biological and environmental factors. But how is it that one set of factors predominates in certain domains (such as intelligence) and another set of factors predominates in others (such as personality)? Are the percentages of the contributions of biological and environmental influences fixed, or are they variable? How important are people's early experiences? What role does age play in development? How can we explain novel behaviors? Why are most children able to walk alone when they are somewhere between 10 and 15 months of age? Why and how does one stage of development follow another? Why do most children acquire language in the first few years of life? Why is it that some children learn quickly whereas others learn slowly? Are most aspects of development inevitable in a "normal" child? How are theories of development different from each other? How are they the same?

> Development is the result of complex interactions between biological and environmental influences.

All of these questions are examples of problems addressed by the field of developmental psychology and the study of human development. Answers to these and many other questions are likely to come from the research efforts of psychologists, educators, pediatricians, linguists, sociologists, and others who use the tools and knowledge of their own disciplines to understand the developmental process. The answers to these questions (or the best answers available at this time) are valuable to scholars and practitioners in these and other groups because they lead to greater understanding of the process of development and how positive developmental outcomes might be maximized.

The different theoretical accounts of development you will read about in this book have all had significant influence on many of the answers to these questions. The theoretical perspectives discussed here are differing and sometimes complex points of view formulated by scholars who have attempted to account for the factors that control and explain the developmental process.

A DEFINITION OF SCIENCE

Whatever is known today in any given scientific discipline is the cumulative result of the efforts of people who have devoted their lives to seeking out truth, separating fact from fancy, and trying to understand what happens around them. All of these efforts, and more, are what science is about. Jacob Bronowski (1977), the well-known mathematician and writer, defines **science** as "the human activity of finding an order in nature by organizing the scattered meaningless facts under universal concepts" (p. 225). Science is the process through which we organize bits of information. This process lends meaning and significance to otherwise

Science is
the process
through which
humans organize
information and
knowledge.

unrelated and obscure particles of knowledge. Science is also a process through which ideas are generated and new directions are followed.

Science is the way in which we bond facts or knowledge together to form something different from what was there before the process began. In fact, by "doing" science, we give coherence and integrity to the fragmented events we observe in the world. It is not sufficient to study an isolated fact (such as "children walk at around 9 to 12 months of age"); one must pursue information about how this fact might be related to other events (e.g., in a child's life, the fact that a certain level of physical maturity is critical before the child can begin walking). Science is very much like the blueprint that a builder uses to understand how the many different parts of a structure fit together to form something that is more than the sum of the individual parts.

In addition to its dynamic qualities (describing how things happen), science also has static qualities (describing what happens). The static and the dynamic qualities of science go hand in hand because, in part, each determines the other. When people do science, they are taking a logical approach to solving some kind of problem as well as producing a product. For example, through intensive research and experimentation (the process), scientists developed a vaccine (the product) that effectively immunizes children against polio.

"Doing" science
consists of asking a
question, defining
the elements of the
question that will
be studied, testing
the question, and
accepting or
rejecting the
assumptions on
which the question
is based.

Finally, science is also a self-correcting process; advances and setbacks all contribute and help to refine researchers' subsequent efforts at answering certain questions or understanding certain issues. Through the nature of the process itself, science generates answers that provide scientists with valuable feedback. In a pure sense, scientists do not set out to prove certain ideas correct or incorrect, because they are constantly asking, answering, and reformulating questions. Instead, scientists test ideas or hypotheses. They evaluate the outcomes of their experiments and reflect on how new information might modify their original questions.

For example, we might observe a series of interactions between a parent and child and notice that the two of them are talking to each other and generally "having fun." We can further understand the developmental significance of "having fun" by examining the parent-child interchange in more detail and looking, perhaps, for a pattern of behavior. We might then look to see if there are similar behaviors between parents and their children in other groups, thereby lending more or less strength to our ideas about the dynamics of human interaction.

The scientific method is important in any field that includes among its goals the organization of knowledge and the generation of new ideas. It is important to remember that the principles involved in doing science are applicable in all scholarly disciplines, whether the focus is developmental psychology, history, biology, or some other subject. In the next section, I discuss some of these principles and how they relate to each other.

A MODEL OF SCIENTIFIC INQUIRY

Science can be seen as a four-step process:

1. Asking a question

2. Identifying the factors or elements of that question that need to be examined

3. Testing the question

4. Accepting or rejecting the premise on which the original question was based

> The four steps of the scientific method help us to ask and answer questions about development systematically.

The first step, *asking a question,* involves recognizing that something of interest or potential value needs further investigation. What might be a source for such a question? These "first" questions most often do not originate in laboratories, in discussions around conference tables, or in any other highly controlled environment. Some important questions may be identified in or referred to such places, but they are not usually where the questions initially surface. Instead, everyday experiences and events are the sources of most first questions, and thus of most scientific inquiry. These experiences and events can (and do) include art, music, literature, and, of course, events in the lives of individuals. For example, the development of a smallpox vaccine was prompted by Edward Jenner's personal observation that the only people who did not seem to be vulnerable to the disease were women who tended cows. In turn, this observation led to Robert Koch's development of germ theory, a basic and important principle of immunology. Another example is the popular version of Isaac Newton's "discovery" of gravity when he was hit by an apple that fell from a tree. Even if the story about Newton is an exaggeration, it still makes the point: The personal experiences of individuals play a vital role in the development of valuable research questions.

> It is impossible to overstate the importance of formulating and asking the right question—it is the first step toward getting a useful answer.

Another example, and one that is more central to the theme of this book, is the observation that children's cognitive development occurs in a series of different and distinct stages. Many developmental psychologists have made this observation informally and then studied the stages they identified systematically.

Clearly, not everyone has the skill to identify those aspects of an experience or to ask the kinds of questions that might lead to new knowledge. From what the untrained mind sees as confusion and disarray, the trained mind selects important events. As Louis Pasteur noted, chance favors the prepared mind, and the knowledge base from which most scientists operate (as a result of long and intensive training) provides this necessary advantage.

The second step in the process of scientific inquiry is *identifying what factors are important and how they will be examined.* For example, one of the theorists discussed later in this book, Robert Sears, examined the wide range

One of the ways a researcher identifies important factors is by conducting a search of the previous literature, including reports on the work of other researchers.

of differences in the ways parents raise their children. A psychologist might begin such an examination by identifying factors that could be involved in these differences, such as the number of children in the family, the children's sexes, the order of their birth, the family's social class, and the educational status of the parents. In other words, the developmental psychologist would identify the critical factors that are possibly related to the question asked. At this point, the investigator is no longer speculating ("Isn't this interesting!"); rather, he or she is beginning to ask pointed questions about the importance of certain factors and the nature of the relationships between those factors.

This is also the point at which the researcher must make decisions regarding how the questions will be answered. This part of the process involves the design and completion of the research. For example, if one is interested in the effects of environmental stimulation on intellectual development, one could design an experiment to compare the intellectual development of children who were reared in an enriched environment (perhaps beginning school at an early age) with that of children who have not experienced an enriched environment (perhaps having spent time in an institution). This is the step in the model where the scientist asks, How do I go about answering my question? At this point, he or she must operationally identify important factors (or variables), state the possible relationships among them, and determine what method he or she will use in doing the actual research. (If you are interested in an examination of the different research methods and techniques used in developmental psychology, see Overton, 2000.)

The third step, *testing the question,* is the most hands-on part of the scientific process. In this step, the scientist actually collects the data necessary to answer the question. For example, at this point a chemist conducts tests to see which of three compounds most effectively acts as a catalyst; a developmental psychologist at this point might conduct a survey of the problem-solving skills of children with learning disabilities. Once the scientist has gathered the essential information (reading scores, X-ray analyses, responses from an interview), he or she applies some kind of tool (such as a statistical test or an objective criterion) to determine an outcome, and then compares that outcome with what he or she proposed in the original question to see if the two are consistent.

For example, a teacher may be interested in knowing whether students learn to read with more comprehension when he uses programmed instruction than they do when he uses a more traditional teaching method. One way the teacher could test this question would be to compare the scores of groups of students taught using the two methods on a test of comprehension. The tool the teacher might use in making this comparison could take the form of a statistical test that assigns a probability that any difference between the groups results from either chance or exposure to one of the two reading programs.

The last step in the scientific process is *accepting or rejecting the premise on which the original question was based* (and perhaps questioning the accompanying theoretical rationale). Regardless of the outcome, however, the scientific process does not stop here. If the original question the scientist asked (for example, Does early enrichment influence a child's intellectual development?) is answered yes, the scientist continues asking additional questions and pursuing each question through the four steps just outlined. If the results do not support the predicted outcome, the scientist returns to the premise of the original question and reformulates the research accordingly. This may not result in a change to the question itself, but it will perhaps have some effect on the scientist's approach to the question and the meaning of the results. For example, the first method the scientist chose may not have been appropriate to the question asked. It is the scientist's responsibility to decide which parts of the process he or she may need to reconsider. This is why scientific research is an always ongoing process. Scientists are continually redesigning their experiments to accommodate new information, new technologies, and, of course, new findings.

The four steps involved in scientific inquiry discussed above are summarized in Table 1.1, which also provides an example that illustrates the progressive and focusing nature of the scientific process. As you can see, the scientist begins with a personal observation and works toward a specific test of a clearly defined question that results in a decision as to what the next question should be.

TABLE 1.1 A Model of Scientific Inquiry

Step	*Example*
1. Asking the question	Do children who are raised in different types of homes develop different levels of intelligence?
2. Determining what factors are important and how they will be examined	The important factors are parents' child-rearing style, home environment, and child's intellectual ability. Differences in children's intellectual ability will be examined through comparisons of groups of children from different homes.
3. Testing the original question	A test will be done to determine whether any differences exist between the two groups and whether any differences found are the results of parenting styles or some other factors (such as chance).
4. Accepting or rejecting the premise	Depending on the outcome of Step 3, the original question will be reconsidered, and, if necessary, more specific questions will be asked.

TOOLS OF SCIENCE

The model of scientific inquiry discussed above and illustrated in Table 1.1 requires a set of tools or concepts to make it work. In the following subsections, I discuss the different tools or mechanisms of science: theory and its elements, hypotheses, constructs, and variables.

Theory: Definition, Function, and Criteria

A **theory** can be defined as a group of logically related statements (for example, formulas, ideas, or rules) that explains events that happened in the past as well as predicts events that will occur in the future. A theory has three general purposes:

A theory is a group of related statements that explains what happened in the past and helps to predict what the future might bring.

- It provides a guide that scientists can use in collecting the kinds of information they need to describe some aspect of a phenomenon (e.g., development). For example, a theory of language acquisition might allow a researcher to describe the process of babbling and then the use of one-word sentences (or holophrases) in great detail.
- It serves to help scientists in integrating a set of facts into general categories. A theory of decline in aging, for example, might aid a researcher in organizing and better understanding otherwise unrelated occurrences of falls and loss of balance in older adults.
- It helps scientists to present material and information in an organized and coherent way, so that subsequent efforts at answering the same or related questions are not just random, groundless efforts.

—— On the Web ——

The *Skeptical Inquirer* bills itself as "the magazine for science and reason," and many people believe that is an accurate description. You can access *Skeptical Inquirer* articles online at http://www.csicop.or/si. The magazine's entertaining and informative content, written for the most part by scientists, includes reviews of research into scientific phenomena and discussions of important issues in various fields (such as the "nature versus nature" debate in developmental psychology).

TABLE 1.2 Sidman's Six Criteria for Judging a Theory

Criterion	Question
Inclusiveness	How many different phenomena does the theory address?
Consistency	How well can the theory explain new things without having its basic assumptions changed?
Accuracy	How well can the theory predict future outcomes and explain past ones?
Relevance	How closely is the theory related to the information collected within that theory? That is, how well does it reflect the facts?
Fruitfulness	How well does the theory generate new ideas and directions for inquiry?
Simplicity	How simple or unencumbered is the theory? That is, how easy is it to understand?

Evaluating Theories

To evaluate the utility of a theory, we need to apply suitable criteria, asking questions about the theory so that we can understand its usefulness. Murray Sidman (1960) identifies six such criteria: inclusiveness, consistency, accuracy, relevance, fruitfulness, and simplicity (see Table 1.2). Although some of the definitions and uses of these criteria may overlap, each is an important indicator of how well a theory measures up. I address Sidman's criteria in more detail in Chapter 11, where I present a comparison of the different theoretical perspectives discussed in this book and how they compare to one another on each of the criteria. I describe each criterion only briefly below.

The criterion of **inclusiveness** concerns "the number and type of phenomena [a theory] encompass[es]" (Sidman, 1960, p. 13). For example, Einstein's theory of relativity deals with many different types of events, including the relationship between time and space, the nature of light, and the speed of objects. In the study of human development, some theories (such as general theories of development) attempt to explain a great number of different events, whereas others attempt to explain only relatively small segments of particular phenomena (such as theories of play).

The criterion of **consistency** concerns whether a theory can explain new discoveries without the need for any changes in the assumptions on which it is based. A theory tends to become more consistent the more it is tested, because it is constantly being refined—over time, the assumptions become more consistent with new findings. Newton's theory of gravitation is highly consistent: It is applicable to many different situations, all of which illustrate the basic principle that all bodies in nature have a mutual degree of attraction to one another. When a theory is highly consistent, new discoveries tend to be consistent with its basic assumptions.

The **accuracy** of a theory is the degree to which it correctly predicts future events or explains past ones. This criterion is all about how "good" a theory is— how well it does what it says it can do. In a given situation, one theory may be so accurate that it predicts almost every outcome, whereas another theory may be so inaccurate as to be almost useless. The accuracy of any theory depends, of course, on the question being asked. In other words, some theories are better suited to addressing concerns (and answering certain questions) in one area of development than in others.

The criterion of **relevance** concerns the directness of the link between the theory itself and the data collected within that theory. For example, if you are interested in the influence of mother's prenatal nutrition on a child's later intellectual development, you would examine variables such as mother's eating habits and developmental quotient (DQ), not the weight of the baby at birth.

The criterion of **fruitfulness** concerns how productive a theory is in generating new ideas and directions for future research. Many developmental theorists have produced work that is known not for its immediate application, but for its generative qualities. Such theories serve to stimulate further research. Perhaps the best example of this is the profound influence of Sigmund Freud's ideas on the generation of subsequent ideas about the developmental process (even if Freud acknowledged that he was not successful in convincing his peers to accept his theory of psychosexual development).

Sidman's final criterion addresses a general goal of all science: simplicity. The **simplicity** criterion is concerned with whether the degree of detail in a theory makes the best use of the information available. An ideal theory is simple (or *parsimonious*); that is, it is both prudent and efficient. In science it is generally true that the simpler a theory, the more parsimonious it is. Some theories are simple and straightforward in their presentation, whereas others are so encumbered with assumptions that their usefulness is restricted. In general, these latter theories are very difficult to use in anything other than highly specific situations. One generally accepted theorem of science is Occam's razor (a principle put forth by the philosopher William of Occam during the Middle Ages), which states that one should not make more assumptions than the minimum needed. In other words, given two explanations for an outcome, usually the simplest one is correct. This rule is called a razor because it "shaves off" ideas and such that are not really needed to explain outcomes.

We can evaluate any developmental theory by measuring it against the criteria of inclusiveness, consistency, accuracy, relevance, fruitfulness, and simplicity.

It is doubtful that any theory meets all of Sidman's criteria, although a theory that meets some of them might almost certainly meet others. It would be surprising, for example, if a theory that is highly inclusive (applicable in many settings) is not also fruitful, given its wide range of applicability and its generation of new directions for study. Perhaps it is best if we view each criterion as a separate goal, something worthy of consideration but not absolutely necessary, as we evaluate how well various theories increase our understanding of development.

Theories both explain and predict. In addition to organizing already established bodies of information, they serve as road maps for future inquiries. In many ways, tables of contents and indexes in books serve a purpose similar to that of theory in that they organize information. Imagine how difficult it would be to locate specific information in a book without a table of contents or index. Theories make phenomena more intelligible, make the existing knowledge about phenomena easier to assimilate, and provide frameworks within which questions can be asked.

Although a theory is often the final product of an effort to organize information, a theory can be a responsive and changing tool. According to the model of scientific inquiry presented above and in Table 1.1 (page 9), new information stimulates a theory's evolution, either by supporting its basic assumptions or by triggering reconsideration and refinement of those assumptions. A theory is as much a changing tool used by scientists as it is an end unto itself.

Elements of a Theory:
Variables, Constructs, and Hypotheses

As discussed above, the first two steps in "doing science" are asking a question and deciding what factors the investigation will focus on. In other words, what "things" does the scientist need to measure, assess, or examine to increase the likelihood that the answer reflects the real world?

For example, if a psychologist wishes to study the interaction between a mother and her child, she must decide what to study about this interaction. The "whats" that she decides to study are called *variables*. In this context, a **variable** is anything that can take on more than one label or value; it usually represents a class of things. Examples of variables that are often of interest to researchers are College Board test scores (which can range from 200 to 800), biological sex (male or female), and occupation (lawyer, construction worker, home economist, and so on). In the example of the psychologist studying mother-child interactions, the number of times the mother makes contact with the child per minute is an operational measure of a variable the psychologist might call parent-child interaction.

A variable is anything that can take on more than one value, such as height, weight, or intelligence.

Constructs, or groups of variables that are related to each other, are important elements of theories. In some developmental theories, for example, a construct called "attachment" consists of a number of different behavioral variables, including eye contact, physical touching, and verbal interaction between parent and child. It is important to note that a construct's name can determine its usefulness. The same set of behaviors that make up the construct of attachment could be arbitrarily called many different things, such as "affection," "familial interaction," or "visual contact." If the terminology used to define a construct is so narrow that it defines a very limited set of behaviors (such as "visual contact"), the construct may become no more descriptive than a variable and so may be severely limited in its usefulness.

A construct is a group of variables that are related to one another.

Using a construct is more efficient (or parsimonious) than dealing individually with each of the variables that make up the construct. For example, it is more efficient to discuss the construct of intelligence than it is to discuss the individual components of intelligence, such as memory, comprehension, and problem solving.

In developing constructs, scientists must consider many different variables, some of which may eventually be included in constructs and some of which may not. Constructs, then, are made up of variables that are related to one another on some theoretical level. Scientists often disagree with one another regarding which variables should or should not be included as part of particular constructs and what various constructs should be called.

The last component of theory development is the **hypothesis,** an "educated guess" that posits an "if . . . then" relationship between variables or constructs. Hypotheses are statements that represent the questions scientists ask when they want to gain a better understanding of the influences that variables have on other variables (or constructs). For example, a developmental psychologist might be interested in understanding the factors that influence moral development in young children. Through some informal contact with children, he has noticed that children at different developmental levels approach moral dilemmas in different ways. The psychologist might then formulate the following statement as a hypothesis: "There is a significant relationship between the developmental level of the child and the method the child uses to solve a moral dilemma." Implicit in this statement is an "if . . . then" proposition: If the developmental level of the child changes, then the way the child approaches moral dilemmas will change as well. The hypothesis becomes a direct test of a question.

A hypothesis is a statement that posits an "if . . . then" relationship between variables or constructs.

How does a scientist know whether a proposed hypothesis can be accepted as true or must be rejected as false? By collecting relevant data and applying some external criterion (such as a statistical test), the scientist can assign some level of confidence to the outcome. That is, the scientist can determine how confident he or she can be that the outcome of the research is a result of the variables that were examined (or manipulated) and not some other, extraneous influence. For example, a child's moral development might be a function of the society in which he or she grows up as well as of the child's level of development. For the psychologist in the example above to have confidence in the outcome of his experiment, he must not only take such factors into account, he must control for them.

The Relationship Between Science and Theory

The four-step model of scientific inquiry presented earlier in this chapter conveys the essence of how the scientific process operates. The development of a theory operates in a parallel way. Although the natural phenomena that theories represent (such as gravity or learning) may have been operating for eons, theories themselves are artificial, developed by scientists through a series of systematic steps that involve variables, constructs, and hypotheses. Theory development is a microcosm of the scientific process itself, and any progress that developmental psychologists might make in advancing specific theories is progress in the general science of developmental psychology as well.

Theory is the backbone of science; without it, scientific advancement could not be possible. Theories provide the frameworks within which scientists become aware of what questions are important to ask and what methods they should use to answer those questions. Without a theoretical context within which to operate, new information is nothing more than a quantitative addition to an already existing body of knowledge. However, when scientists are aware of where new data may or may not fit within a given framework, the premise under which they operate becomes infinitely more useful and moves closer to that abstract goal of truth, and the relevance of the new findings to applied settings can increase dramatically.

> In many ways, science and theory follow parallel courses of development and serve the same purposes.

THEORIES OF DEVELOPMENT: AN OVERVIEW

All of the theories of development discussed in this book have different contributions to make to our understanding of the developmental process. Different theories are in agreement on some points and differ on others. Before I present these theories in detail in the following chapters, I want to summarize the characteristics that differentiate them from one another. In the following overview, I answer five important questions about each theory:

1. What are the basic assumptions of the theory?

2. What is the philosophical rationale for the theory?

3. What are the important variables most often studied in relation to the theory?

4. What is the primary method that proponents of the theory use to study development?

5. In what areas has the theory had its greatest impact?

The answers to these questions should prepare you for the in-depth discussions that begin in Chapter 3 and also provide you with a framework that you can use in comparing and contrasting the different viewpoints presented. Table 1.3 presents a summary of important points across the four different theoretical perspectives that this book covers: maturational, psychodynamic, behavioral, and cognitive-developmental.

Maturational and Biological Models

The maturational model stresses the importance of biological influences on development and has had its greatest impact on child-rearing practices.

The work of Arnold Gesell, the foremost maturationist in developmental psychology, represents a unique approach to the study of human development. As a physician, Gesell believed that the sequence of development is determined by the biological and evolutionary history of the species. In other words, development of the organism is essentially under the control of biological systems and the process of maturation. Although the environment is of some importance, it acts only in a supportive role and does not provide any impetus for change.

While working with G. Stanley Hall within the tradition of Darwinian influence that was very popular during the 1920s, Gesell applied the tenets of recapitulation theory to the study of individual development (or ontogenesis). Recapitulation theory states that the development of the species is reflected in the development of the individual. In other words, the child progresses through a series of stages that recount the developmental sequence that characterizes the species.

Gesell believed that the most important influences on the growth and development of the human organism are biological directives. He summarized this theory in five distinct principles of development, which he later applied to behavior. All these principles assume that the formation of structures is necessary before any event outside the organism can have an influence on development. It is interesting to note that Gesell was not alone in pursuing the notion that "function follows structure"; designers, architects, and engineers have also found a great deal of truth in this idea.

Gesell also believed that behavior at different stages of development has different degrees of balance or stability. For example, at 2 years of age, the child engages in behavior that might be characterized by a groping for some type of stability (the so-called terrible twos). Shortly thereafter, however, the child's behavior becomes smooth and consolidated. Gesell believed that development is cyclical in nature, swinging from one extreme to another, and that by means of these swings, the child develops and uses new structures.

TABLE 1.3   An Overview of Major Theories of Development

	Maturational and Biological	*Psychodynamic*	*Behavioral*	*Cognitive-Developmental*
What are the basic assumptions of the theory?	The sequence and content of development is determined mostly by biological factors and the evolutionary history of the species.	Humans are conflicted beings, and individual differences as well as normal growth result from the resolution of those conflicts.	Development is a function of the laws of learning, and environment has important influences on growth and development.	Development is the result of the individual's active participation in the developmental process in interaction with important environmental influences.
What is the philosophical rationale for the theory?	Recapitulation theory, preformation, and predeterminism	Embryological	Tabula rasa (blank slate)	Predeterminism
What are the important variables most often studied in the theory?	Growth of biological systems	Effects of instincts on needs and the ways instincts are satisfied	Frequency of behaviors	Stage-related transformations and qualitative changes from one stage to another
What is the primary method used in the theory to study development?	Use of cinematic records, anthropological data, normative investigations, and animal studies	Case studies and the indirect examination of unconscious processes	Conditioning and modeling paradigms	Observation of social and cognitive problem solving during transitions from stage to stage
In what areas has the theory had its greatest impact?	Child rearing, the importance of biological determinants, aspects of cultural and historical development	Personality development and the relationship between culture and behavior	Systematic analysis and treatment of behavior and educational applications	Understanding of how thinking and cognition develop in light of cultural conditions and demands

Because he placed such a strong emphasis on the importance of biological processes, Gesell focused in the majority of his work (as did his colleagues, most notably Frances Ilg and Louise B. Ames) on biological systems as a beginning point for understanding development. Through Gesell's use of cinematic (moving picture) records, stop-action analysis provided the foundation for his extensive descriptions of "normal" development. This technique allowed Gesell to examine the frame-by-frame progression of certain motor tasks, from their earliest reflex stage at birth through a system of fully developed and integrated behaviors. For example, his detailed analysis of walking provided the first graphic record of the sequence this complex behavior follows.

Gesell also made a significant contribution with his development of the co-twin method for comparing the relative effects of heredity (nature) and environment (nurture) on development. In this method, one child in a pair of identical twins would receive specific training in some skill (such as stair climbing) and the other would receive no training in the skill. The rationale for this strategy was that, because identical twins have identical genetic makeup, any difference found in the two children's abilities in the skill that was taught to one and not the other must be the result of the training. This is the basic paradigm that Gesell used to question some very interesting and controversial statements about the nature of intelligence.

Unquestionably, Gesell's greatest contribution has been to the understanding of the development of the "normal" child. His detailed cinematic records, their analyses, and their translation into books for the popular press have influenced child-rearing patterns in the United States as much as have the books of the famous Dr. Spock (who incorporated many of Gesell's principles into his philosophy).

Gesell's ideas and theoretical approach never entered the mainstream of current thought about developmental psychology. Perhaps this is because many observers saw much of his work as too biological in nature and not sufficiently theoretical. From both historical and applied perspectives, however, Gesell's contribution was and still is an outstanding one.

Over the past few years, developmental psychologists have demonstrated heightened interest in other maturational approaches, most notably ethology and sociobiology (both of which I discuss in Chapter 4). These approaches, even more than Gesell's, emphasize the importance of biological and evolutionary principles as determinants of behavior.

The Psychodynamic Model

The psychodynamic (or psychoanalytic) model, developed initially by Sigmund Freud, presents a view of development that is revolutionary in both its content and its implications for the nature of development. The basic assumption of this model is that development consists of dynamic, structural, and sequential components, each of which is influenced by a continuously renewed need for the gratification of basic instincts. How psychic energy (or the energy of life, as it is sometimes called) is channeled through these different components constitutes the basis of the developmental process and individual differences.

The dynamic or economic component of Freud's tripartite system characterizes the human mind (or psyche) as a fluid, energized system that can transfer energy from one part to another where and when needed. The structural or topographical component of the theory describes three separate, yet interdependent, psychological structures—the id, the ego, and the superego—and the ways in which they regulate behavior. Finally, the sequential or stage component emphasizes a progression from one stage of development to the next, focusing on different zones of bodily sensitivity (such as the mouth) and accompanying psychological and social conflicts.

It is difficult to identify the philosophical roots of psychoanalytic theory, because most psychoanalytic theorists would consider their roots to be in embryology, the biological study of the embryo from conception until the organism can survive on its own. This identification with a biological model has a great deal to do with Freud's training as a physician, his work in neuroanatomy, and his belief that biological needs play a paramount role in development. Some people believe that the philosophical tradition of preformation (which in its extreme form holds that all attitudes and characteristics are present at birth and only expand in size) is basic to the psychoanalytic model, but this may be untrue. Preformationists stress the lack of malleability of the developing individual, whereas the psychoanalytic model describes a flexible character for the individual and the potential for change.

Freudian theory places important emphasis on the resolution of conflicts that have their origins at an unconscious level. It states that the origins of these conflicts are biological and passed on from generation to generation. Development (and the development of individual differences) is an ongoing process of resolving these conflicts.

If the roots of behavior are located in the unconscious, how can they be accessible to study? Through a series of historical accidents, Freud was introduced to hypnotism as a method of treatment. This technique, in turn, gave birth to his now famous method called free association, in which individuals are encouraged to say freely anything that comes to mind in response to certain words or phrases. Freud believed that such exposition of underlying needs and fears is the key to understanding typical behavior. Free association is a highly subjective method of collecting information, and a large part of the criticism leveled against Freud and many of his followers has been directed at this practice. The theory itself, however, is based on abstract and subjective judgments, and the fact that the behaviors under study are not easily amenable to scientific verification has caused controversy for years.

> The psychodynamic model assumes that development is the result of a continuing need for the satisfaction of instincts.

However, the richness and diversity that Freud brought to a previously stagnant conception of development started a tradition that is healthy and strong even today. Perhaps Freud's most significant accomplishment was the first documentation and systematic organization of a theory of development.

The psychoanalytic model and the work of such theorists as Freud and Erik Erikson have undoubtedly had their greatest impacts in the study of personality and the treatment of emotional and social disorders. Erikson focused mainly on the social dimension of behavior, unlike Freud, who focused on the sexual dimension. The impact and significance of both men's contributions cannot be overstated.

The Behavioral Model

The behavioral model contends that development is the result of different types of learning as well as imitation and modeling.

The behavioral model characterizes a movement that is peculiar to American psychology and distinct from any other theoretical model. The behavioral perspective views development as a function of learning and as something that proceeds according to certain laws or principles of learning. Most important, it places the major impetus for growth and development outside of the individual—in the environment, rather than within the organism itself.

The importance placed on the environment varies among the specific theories within this general model, but in all cases the organism is seen as reactive instead of active. Almost every behavioral theory incorporates the assumption that behavior is a function of its consequences. If the consequences of a behavior (such as studying) are good (such as high grades), that behavior is likely to continue in the future. If the consequences of a behavior (such as staying out past curfew) are not good (such as loss of privileges), the behavior will change (perhaps the person will come home at an earlier hour or not go out at all on weeknights).

In the behavioral model of development, the laws of learning and the influence of the environment are paramount. Through such processes as classical conditioning and imitation, individuals learn what behaviors are most appropriate and lead to adaptive outcomes. Given that this model views development as a learned phenomenon, it allows for the breaking down of behaviors into their basic elements. This has led some people to view the behavioral model as "reductionistic."

The behavioral perspective views the newborn child as naive and unlearned. John Locke's notion of tabula rasa best exemplifies the philosophical roots of the behavioral tradition. Literally, *tabula rasa* means "blank slate." From this perspective, the newborn child is seen as a blank page waiting to be written on, with only the most fundamental biological reflexes (such as sucking) operative at birth. The organism is malleable, and behavior develops and changes as a result of events or experiences. This is a more open view than that of the maturational model or the psychodynamic model, because it sees human potential as unlimited by internal factors. The behavioral model does acknowledge that sometimes biological endowment (an internal factor) can limit developmental outcomes, as in the case of genetic disease or familial retardation, but it holds that even in the case of severe retardation, a restructuring of the child's environment can greatly affect his or her basic competencies and ability to perform such self-care functions as eating and using the toilet.

Given that the behavioral perspective emphasizes events that originate in the environment and their effects on the organism, it is no surprise that the variable of primary interest to behaviorists is the frequency with which (or number of times) a behavior occurs. For example, if a researcher is interested in studying an aspect of sibling interaction, he or she must make sure that the behaviors of interest are explicitly defined (or operationalized) and objective enough to be measured reliably. A construct such as "nice feelings" would not meet such criteria, but the construct "number of times brother touches friend" would.

Using frequency of behavior, the traditional way of studying development is to examine what effects certain environmental events have on behavior. Researchers most often do this by identifying and observing those events in the environment that control behavior and then, if necessary, manipulating the events to see if the behavior under observation changes. For example, if a child's speech is delayed, a psychologist might want to observe what the events are that surround the child's verbalizations when left to run their course. The psychologist might then suggest some intervention—for example, encouraging the child's parents to respond more directly to the child—and then conduct additional observation to see if there is any change. This type of research design, which behavior analysts use frequently, illustrates one way in which researchers can isolate and identify the effects of certain contingencies.

Most interesting, however, given behaviorists' lack of emphasis on biological age or stages of development, is the behavioral model's viewpoint that the sequence of experiences is the critical factor in development. In other words, when behaviorists discuss developmental status, experience—not age—is the important factor. Although age and experience are somewhat related, from a behavioral perspective age is not thought of as a determinant (or cause) of behavior; rather, it is only a correlate (a simultaneous outcome).

A more recently popular approach to understanding development (within the past 50 years or so) involves social learning theory and the work of such people as Robert Sears and Albert Bandura. The social learning theory approach to development is based very much on the same assumptions as the more traditional behavioral approach. A major difference, however, is that the social learning theory model incorporates ideas not found in the behavioral model, such as vicarious (or indirect) reinforcement (i.e., the individual does not need to experience something directly to learn it). This approach reflects the importance of the environment while at the same time suggesting that individual differences contribute something as well.

The most significant impacts of the behavioral model can be seen in advances in the systematic analysis of behavior, in changes in the treatment and management of deviant behaviors, and in educational applications such as programmed instruction.

The Cognitive-Developmental Model

The cognitive-developmental model focuses on the transitions between different stages of development and views the human being as an active participant in the developmental process.

The cognitive-developmental model of human development stresses the individual's active rather than reactive role in the developmental process and the individual's role in the social and cultural context within which he or she develops. The basic assumptions of the model are as follows:

1. Development occurs in a series of qualitatively distinct stages.

2. These stages always follow the same sequence, but they do not necessarily occur at the same times for all individuals.

3. These stages are hierarchically organized, such that later stages subsume the characteristics of earlier ones.

Another characteristic of the cognitive-developmental model that sets it apart from other theoretical models is the presence of psychological structures and the ways in which changes in these underlying structures are reflected in overt changes in behavior. The forms these changes take depend on the individual's developmental level. Many people categorize the cognitive-developmental model as "interactionist" because it encourages the view that development is an interaction between the organism and the environment.

The philosophical roots of this perspective are found in the predeterminist approach, which views development as a "process of qualitative differentiation or evolution of form" (Ausubel & Sullivan, 1970). Jean-Jacques Rousseau, the noted 18th-century French philosopher, wrote that development consists of a sequence of orderly stages that are internally regulated, and that the individual is transformed from one into the other. Although Rousseau believed that the child is innately good (and most of the early predeterminists believed that the environment plays a very limited role), modern cognitive-developmental theorists would not tacitly accept such a broad assumption.

Although the environment is decisive in determining the content of the stages of development, the important biological or organismic contribution is the development of structures within which this content can operate. For example, all human beings are born with some innate capacity to develop language and to imitate behavior. Human beings are not born with a capacity to speak a specific language, however, or even to imitate particular behavior. Children born in the United States of French-speaking parents would certainly not be expected to speak French (or any other language) without exposure to that language. Within the organismic model, the capacity for development emerges as part of the developmental process. Although the environment is an important and influential factor, the biological contribution is far more important, because it is the impetus for further growth and development. The sequence and process of development are predetermined, but the actual content of behavior within these stages is not.

Of primary interest to the cognitive-developmental psychologist is the sequence of stages and the process of transition from one stage to the next. It is for this reason that researchers have focused on the set of stage-related behaviors and their correlates across such dimensions as cognitive or social development. For example, a psychologist might be interested in examining how children of different ages (and presumably different developmental stages) solve a similar type of problem. After observing many children of different ages, the psychologist can postulate the existence of different types of underlying structures that are responsible for the strategies children use.

A great deal of Jean Piaget's work has been directed toward reaching a better understanding of the thinking processes that children at different developmental levels use to solve problems. In fact, much of the Piagetian tradition emphasizes that these different ways of solving problems reflect, in general, different ways of seeing the world. Another cognitive-developmental theorist, Lev Vygotsky, also placed a great deal of importance on the accomplishments of the individual in his or her own actions, but unlike Piaget, Vygotsky emphasized the role that culture and outside influences play in leading the individual toward the next level of development.

Considering cognitive-developmental psychologists' interest in the concept and use of stages, it is not surprising that the primary method these scholars use to study behavior is the presentation of problems that emphasize differences in structural organization. An infant might depend on purely sensory information (such as touch or smell) to distinguish among different classes of objects, whereas an older child might place the items in a group of objects into categories based on more abstract criteria (such as "these are all toys, and these are food"). The "how" of development is seen to be reflected in the strategies that children use at qualitatively different developmental levels to solve certain types of problems. More important for cognitive-developmental psychologists, however, is *why* these differences are present. Studies examining this issue have resulted in a model that hypothesizes that different underlying structures are operative at different stages.

Undoubtedly, the greatest impacts of the cognitive-developmental approach have been in different areas of education. Given that much of the research conducted over the past 50 years by cognitive-developmental theorists has focused on the general area of "thinking," this may come as no surprise. The educational philosophy and practices that have arisen out of this theoretical perspective emphasize the unique contributions that children make to their own learning through discovery and experience. Children are allowed to explore within environments that are challenging enough and interesting enough to facilitate the children's growth within their individual current stages of development.

WEB SITES OF INTEREST

- "Internet History and Philosophy of Science," at http://www.humbul.ac.uk/tutorial/hps: You can't really have a good understanding of science and its important role in humankind's understanding of the process of human development without knowing something about the philosophy of science. This Web site will provide you with an introduction.
- "The Scientific Method," by Paul Johnson, at http://paedpsych.jk.uni-linz.ac.at/internet/arbeitsblaetterord/wissenschaftord/faqsscience.html: Johnson provides an excellent introduction to the scientific method, discussing, among other things, what the method is; the distinctions between a fact, a theory, and a hypothesis; and Occam's razor. This Web site is very informative and even a bit fun.
- "Thomas Kuhn," at http://www.emory.edu/EDUCATION/mfp/Kuhnsnap.html: Thomas Kuhn's *The Structure of Scientific Revolutions,* published in 1962, continues to have profound effects on the definition and study of science. It should be on any scientist's reading list. This Web site provides some information about Kuhn and his influence.

FURTHER READINGS ABOUT HUMAN DEVELOPMENT

Ciarrochi, Joseph, Forgas, Joseph P., & Mayer, John D. (Eds.). (2001). *Emotional intelligence in everyday life: A scientific inquiry.* Philadelphia: Psychology Press.

Emotional intelligence (EI) is defined here as the ability to perceive, understand, and manage emotions, and this book is a good example of how theory is developed and can be applied to everyday situations. It provides an informative and interesting review of scientific research in the field and the ways in which EI is important to everyday life.

Hatfield, Gary. (2002). Psychology, philosophy, and cognitive science: Reflections on the history and philosophy of experimental psychology. *Mind and Language, 17,* 207–232.

This article presents some history of psychology with which any psychology student should be familiar. Hatfield discusses psychology's birth as a discipline and the relationship between psychology and philosophy.

Meltzoff, Andrew N. (2002). Elements of a developmental theory of imitation. In Andrew N. Meltzoff & Wolfgang Prinz (Eds.), *The imitative mind: Development, evolution, and brain bases* (pp. 19–41). New York: Cambridge University Press.

For years, scientists have examined the phenomenon of imitation during infancy. In this chapter, Meltzoff describes his work on imitation in human infants and proposes that infant imitation precedes the development of empathy toward others and theory of mind, a relatively new and important construct that psychologists are now studying. (In Chapter 8, I discuss the importance of imitation in social learning theory.)

White, Sheldon H. (2002). Notes toward a philosophy of science for developmental science. In Willard Hartup & Richard A. Weinberg (Eds.), *Minnesota Symposium on Child Psychology: Vol. 32. Child psychology in retrospect and prospect: In celebration of the 75th anniversary of the Institute of Child Development* (pp. 207–225). Mahwah, NJ: Lawrence Erlbaum.

In this chapter, White, a well-known developmental psychologist, discusses the contributions of three important periods during the establishment of what he calls "developmental science." The first, around 1895, created a cooperative naturalistic study of children. The second, the child development movement, which began in the 1920s, was based in a number of child development institutes and centers. The final period that White discusses began in the 1960s and continues today. Read this chapter along with the article by Hatfield described above, and you'll be both a philosopher and a historian.

CHAPTER 2

TRENDS AND ISSUES IN HUMAN DEVELOPMENT

It is not true that life is one damn thing after another—it's one damn thing over and over.

—Edna St. Vincent Millay

Human action can be modified to some extent, but human nature cannot be changed.

—Abraham Lincoln

We have to believe in free will. We've got no choice.

—Isaac Bashevis Singer

One of the most interesting things about the process of development is how different individuals are from one another. Older people, although they are supposedly "set in their ways," still vary widely, not only physically but emotionally and psychologically. Even among newborn babies there are many differences: Some are more active than others, some are less irritable than others, and some are even more attractive to adults than others. And each infant looks distinctly different from all others—just ask any new parent.

Despite this diversity, similar developmental processes occur in all human beings. Although theorists may differ in their explanations regarding how development happens, they all recognize a number of common influences on the developmental process, certain directions or trends that are stable and reliable indicators of the changing nature of the individual. Theorists disagree, however, about other aspects of the developmental process. These disagreements are often framed as choices between the extremes on particular continua, such as whether the process of development is controlled primarily by hereditary influences or by influences found in the individual's environment. As I will show in this chapter, however, neither end of any one of these continua represents the "correct" view, nor are the two extremes even separable. In any science as young and complex as the study of human development, it is not unusual to find scholars raising such seemingly irresolvable issues and focusing on them in their research. These points of contention serve a very useful purpose: They help to generate new questions and directions for study that go far beyond the significance of the original questions.

Although I cannot possibly cover all of the trends and theoretical issues in human development in this chapter, I believe that the discussion I offer here will provide you with a broad base that you can use to begin to compare theories with one another and to get a feel for how they differ. Each of the issues discussed in this chapter gives rise to a general question that we might ask about the nature of development. These questions, which are listed in Table 2.1, are valuable not only because they can help you to understand the position that any given theory represents but because they allow you to compare theories with one another, which we will do throughout this book. You might find it useful to review these questions before you begin reading each chapter. Think of them as organizational tools that will help you to understand the material presented. At the conclusions of selected chapters, I will refer again to these questions to help clarify the view that each of the theoretical models presents, and in the final chapter I will use these questions to organize a comparison across the different theories.

> Theories of development differ on many different dimensions, and by understanding these differences we can understand the basic assumptions underlying each theory.

COMMON TRENDS IN HUMAN DEVELOPMENT

From Global to Discrete Response Systems

One common trend in human development is the transition from a global system to discrete systems. A global response is a generalized one, such as the cry

TABLE 2.1 Important Issues in Development

The Issue	The Question We Ask
The nature of development	What is the major force that influences the course of development?
The process that guides development	What is the underlying process that is primarily responsible for changes in development?
The importance of age	What role does age play as a general marker of changes in development?
The rate of development	Are there certain sensitive or critical periods during development, and, if so, how are they related to the rate of change?
The shape of development	Is development smooth and continuous, or do changes occur in abrupt stages?
The origins of individual differences	How does the theory explain differences in development between individuals of the same chronological age?
The methods used to study development	What methods are used to study development, and how do they affect the content of the theory?

of a newborn infant, that can have many different meanings. A discrete response is a highly specific behavior that can easily be distinguished from other behaviors in terms of its intent or usefulness. An infant's crying, which begins as a global behavior, soon becomes differentiated into sounds that have specific meanings, such as hunger, discomfort, or pain. As development progresses, crying becomes increasingly discrete, eventually leading to the next stages of vocalization and intelligible speech.

All humans share certain developmental trends.

Another example of a global response is the way young children grab haphazardly at anything and everything as they begin to learn about their world. Eventually this indiscriminate grabbing becomes more refined, and children use their hands to explore their environment more effectively. Young children first propel themselves by using gross pushing movements; these eventually become more refined into crawling and then walking. In time, the relative simplicities of childhood lead to the well-defined responsibilities of adolescence (getting a job) and young adulthood (starting a career or perhaps a family).

Development progresses from general or global systems of responding to specific or discrete systems of responding.

Increase in Complexity

As development progresses, most systems become increasingly complex.

As development progresses, the individual becomes more complex. Biologically, the one cell that was present at conception divides and subdivides to form more than a million separate yet interdependent units. There is an increase in psychological complexity as well: The number of emotions increases, and the strategies the individual has available for solving problems become more sophisticated. Not only does behavior become more quantitatively discrete, but qualitative changes occur as the complexity or multidimensionality of behavior increases. Most theories of development consider both qualitative and quantitative changes as increases in complexity and hallmarks of development.

Increase in Integration and Differentiation

Biological and psychological systems become increasingly differentiated (or separate) from each other as well as increasingly integrated (or entwined) with each other as development progresses.

For an individual to survive, his or her behaviors can't function alone; rather, they must become part of a coherent, organized system. When behaviors become differentiated, they are more articulated, or distinct, from one another. When behaviors become integrated, they become enmeshed with or incorporated into one another, often forming something that is qualitatively different from what was there before.

The dual processes of differentiation and integration involve a refinement of behaviors and the combination of those behaviors into a unified whole. Within the cognitive-developmental model, for example, both psychological and physical systems become differentiated yet remain in communication and coordination with one another. Although in psychological systems (such as thinking and feeling) separation and integration are not as apparent as they are in biological systems (such as respiration and circulation), the processes are parallel as larger, more inclusive systems are developed. For example, young children use basic sensory information, such as seeing or touching, to explore their environments. As children develop, they begin to organize these basic strategies into a more efficient and adaptable system that combines both seeing and touching.

Decrease in Egocentrism

During the early years of development, a child tends to believe that his or her own perspective on the world is the only one possible. This preoccupation with one's own view of the world, or **egocentrism**, assumes different forms as development progresses, but in almost all theories of development it is understood to become less and less of an influence as the individual develops. This may occur because of changing social conditions (that is, people tend to become less self-centered when they begin socializing with others) or even because of biological changes (that is, when the body needs to direct less effort toward self-growth, the individual is able to devote greater energy to reaching out and exploring the world).

> Egocentrism is an individual's preoccupation with his or her own perspective. It is characteristic of development at all levels.

Development of Social Autonomy

The last general trend I will discuss here is the development of social autonomy—that is, the growing human being's increasing independence and ability to provide for his or her own needs. Initially, the infant is dependent on others for basic care. In contrast, the older child is much more self-sufficient, and the young adult even more so. Some anthropologists (and psychologists as well) believe that the immature status of the newborn human infant relative to newborns of other species reflects the long period of dependence that characterizes human beings and allows for intense socialization to take place.

> The expression of autonomy, a critical part of developmental change, can take many different forms.

Eventually, most children show varying degrees of independence from their primary caretakers. In addition, as individuals become increasingly autonomous, other things begin to happen as well. One of the most important of these is that they begin to accept the standards of society as they interpret these standards from their own viewpoints rather than from, say, the viewpoints of their parents.

ISSUES AMONG THEORIES

The Nature of Development

From the perspectives of both history and science, no issue concerning development has been more pervasive than that of whether development is a function of the genetically transmitted codes we now know as the rhythm of DNA (heredity, or nature) or the result of external influences (i.e., influences found in the individual's environment). This "nature versus nurture" question has long been the focus of heated debate and voluminous research conducted by people who have usually assumed that these two factors are independent of one another. Unfortunately, their actions have confused the issue instead of clarifying it.

> The issues raised by theorists in developmental psychology generate new questions and new directions for study.

Nature versus nature? Heredity versus environment? Jeans versus genes? This is the major issue that characterizes almost every discussion concerning the factors that most influence growth and development.

Most theories have some basis in philosophical thought, and that is the case with theories that take on this important issue as well. In the past, **preformationists** posited that an individual is fully formed in the sperm of the male (those who took this position were referred to as *homunculists*) or in the ovum of the female (*ovists*). Given this premise, these theorists expected that only very limited quantitative change could take place at conception and believed that environment had little effect on developmental outcomes. In contrast, theorists who subscribe to ideas such as John Locke's notion of tabula rasa assume that the newborn's mind resembles a blank slate and that environmental influences are responsible for all developmental changes that are not biologically based. As a philosopher, Locke left the details of studying the specific elements of the environment that might influence development to those who followed in the tradition of American empiricism and the behavioral perspective.

Over the past half century, developmental psychologists have devoted a great deal of research and thought to the issue of nature versus nurture, and many have come to believe that it is not a question of the greater importance of environmental influences or hereditary factors, or how much of each is present; rather, what is important is the way in which these two elements interact (Anastasi, 1958). One possible way to examine this interaction is to view both hereditary and environmental forces as potentially having both positive and negative effects on development. For example, a positive environmental influence might be good prenatal care, and a negative environmental influence might be lack of adequate socialization during the early years. Genetically transmitted diseases such as Tay-Sachs and sickle-cell anemia are clearly negative influences, as are inherited predispositions toward certain types of mental disorders.

——— On the Web ———

At http://www.wikipedia.org/wiki/free_will_and_determinism you'll find a terrific discussion of free will and determinism that, in many ways, parallels a primary point of discussion in this chapter—that concerning the relative influence of nature and nature. Do you think that everything you do is a result of your own choosing and design? Do you think that everything you do is somehow predetermined by hardwired genes or other forces? Read all about it here—and think again.

One way to organize this discussion is by separating two fundamental viewpoints: the **nativist model** and the **nurturist model.** A nativist views hereditary factors as the primary influence on development, regardless of the effects of the environment. A nativist believes that children who inherit some undesirable characteristic will benefit little from the restructuring of their environments, because, regardless of environment's potential effects (negative or positive), those effects are preempted by the effects of hereditary influences. A nurturist, on the other hand, believes that environment shapes behavior and is the ultimate influence, regardless of an individual's genetic inheritance. Consequently, a nurturist believes that where the environmental influence is positive, regardless of the influence of genetic factors, the final outcome will be positive.

Both the naturist and nurturist main-effect models seem extreme from a commonsense perspective, especially given the results of research that has been completed in recent years. It is generally accepted today, for example, that certain children identified as being at high risk (developmentally) at birth, such as low-birth-weight infants, can be helped dramatically by some course of intervention that will improve their chances for healthy development. Likewise, it is understood that negative environmental influences can affect a potentially normal child in such a way as to prevent him or her from making the transitions necessary for healthy development. Of course, if both environmental and hereditary influences are simultaneously positive (or negative), the outcome will probably be positive (or negative) as well.

> The important question is not to what degree heredity and environment influence development, but rather how they interact.

Another way of examining the relationship between hereditary and environmental influences is through the **interactional model**. In this model, the potential outcomes are the same as those noted above in the main-effect models when both influences are simultaneously positive or negative, but the discordant interactions provide an interesting contrast. More than 50 years ago, Donald Hebb (1949) discussed the interactive relationship between heredity and environment, stressing that both operate 100% of the time and noting that we cannot possibly understand the influence of one without considering the influence of the other. For example, children who are born with genetic abnormalities (such as certain types of mental retardation) can be taught to function at much higher levels than was once believed possible. If such children are not given appropriate opportunities in supportive environments, they might always function at subnormal levels.

The interactional model can help to explain the relative effects of genetic and environmental influences on development. Unless one set of influences, environmental or hereditary, is clearly dominant, there is a subtle interplay (or interaction) between the roles of heredity and environment. An individual's **genotype**, or genetic inheritance, sets absolute limits for that person's **phenotype**, or the observable, physical characteristics that result from the interaction between the individual's

> Most developmental psychologists favor the interactional model because it places importance on both hereditary and environmental factors at each moment in development.

genotype and factors in the individual's environment. Innate characteristics, however, define the lower and upper limits of potential change, and the upper limits cannot be fully actualized unless the surrounding environment is supportive.

Through the mechanism of evolution (which I address in Chapter 3), all animal species maintain characteristics that are adaptive for them and lose characteristics that are less adaptive. It is fascinating to observe the way in which the limits of human beings' genotypic qualities have forced us to seek out and to construct an environment that is suitable to our innate qualities. The environment in turn then influences the potential of the genetic contribution. Anthropologists recognize that apes descended from the trees and became tool users before their brains increased in size; this illustrates the complex and circular interplay involved in the heredity-environment (or nature-nurture) issue.

In general, the relationship between genetic and environmental factors is one of mutual interaction. On one hand, the genotype sets absolute limits of growth that rarely can be exceeded (for example, regardless of how much we eat or how much growth hormone we take, we can never grow to be 10 feet tall). On the other hand, environmental factors set absolute limits on the degree to which an individual's genetic potential can be realized. A society should strive to maximize the genetic potential of its members by providing a wide range of environmental settings in which development can take place.

Scarr's Triarchic Theory of Experience

Sandra Scarr (1993), a developmental psychologist, has set forth yet another point of view concerning heredity and environment that is very interesting in that it considers both environmental and genetic influences in a way that goes beyond even the interactional model discussed above. Scarr presents a theory of experience that takes into account a third possibility—that in the organism-environment interaction, the "environment" can have different meanings for different people. In this triarchic theory, Scarr asserts that people "create" their own environments in three different ways:

Sandra Scarr theorizes that individuals create their own environments, given their own characteristics and the demands of the world around them.

1. An individual's genes and their surrounding environment are correlated with one another.

2. Individuals evoke responses that are related to the individuals' characteristics.

3. Individuals actively select environments that are related to their interests.

What might all this mean? It means that human beings take an active role in creating environments that best suit their own interests and needs, and that reflect their individual differences. Examples range from the child who enjoys music asking her parents if she can take piano lessons to the introverted adult who refuses an invitation to go dancing because he prefers to stay home—within the environment he has created for himself. Although there are hints of this possibility in the interactional model, Scarr's triarchic theory is really the first to identify individuals as taking such an active role in creating their own environments.

An Ecological Model of Human Development

Another theorist, Urie Bronfenbrenner, has also tried to deal with the important role of the environment in development without ignoring the uniqueness of the individual. He has developed what he calls an experimental **ecology of human development**. Within this model he stresses the importance of the developing person in his or her surrounding environment. He defines the ecology of human development as the study of "the progressive, mutual accommodation, throughout the life span, between a growing human organism and the changing immediate environments in which it lives" (Bronfenbrenner, 1977, p. 519; see also Bronfenbrenner & Morris, 2000).

Bronfenbrenner's basic argument is that traditional studies in human development are very rigorously and tightly controlled. Although this control can be a benefit, such studies are also often very limited in scope, given that many take place in settings that are artificial in their construction and so are unfamiliar to the participants. In other words, they don't represent what the real world is about very accurately. As Bronfenbrenner and Morris (2000) put it, developmental research has been "the study of the strange behavior of children in strange situations for the briefest possible period of time" (p. 994). Because he is so concerned with the qualities and characteristics of the environment, he includes in his ecological model definitions of a series of structures that all "fit" or "nest" within one another (much like, Bronfenbrenner points out, Russian nesting dolls). In his earliest works, Bronfenbrenner describes four such structures: the microsystem, the mesosystem, the exosystem, and the macrosystem.

> An ecology of human development stresses the importance of "mutual accommodation" by the individual in a changing environment.

The *microsystem* is the immediate setting that contains the person. Just as our immediate settings change throughout the day, the microsystems in which we find ourselves change as well. For example, you might find yourself in the microsystem of the library late at night and in the microsystem of an office or classroom during the day. Every microsystem has three different dimensions: the *physical space and activities* within the microsystem, such as the lighting over your desk or the temperature of the classroom in which you are taking a test; the *people* who are part of the microsystem (and their roles), such as your roommate or your classroom teacher; and the *interactions between the individual and the other people* in the microsystem, such as angry or friendly exchanges with your roommate.

Applying Ideas About Human Development

Heredity Versus Environment: The Proof Is in the Early Experience

One of the points stressed in this chapter is the importance of understanding the complexity of the heredity-environment interaction. Whereas scientists used to think that one or the other of these two forces is dominant, with development influenced a certain amount by one versus the other (such as 40% environment and 60% heredity), it is now more apparent than ever that the most important influence is produced by the nature of the interaction between the two. As you will read in this chapter, as Donald Hebb (1949) noted, it is both, all of the time.

Yet developmental psychologists know for sure that early experience is critical to later development. They reached this conclusion by examining the effects of early intervention. Craig Ramey and Sharon Landesman Ramey provide an exhaustive and informative review of these effects in their 1998 article on early intervention and early experience. These authors define *early intervention* as a collection of activities "designed to enhance a young child's development." Probably the best known of the many early intervention programs currently in operation is Head Start,

which was launched in the mid-1960s to improve school readiness among disadvantaged children.

The rationale behind early intervention is based in an understanding of the importance of children's early experiences for their later development. Children who are not well prepared to begin school, for example (and there are still thousands of such children in the United States), are also prone to a wide variety of negative outcomes, from poor school performance to placement in special education programs and dropping out of school. It is clearly in our best interest, as a society, to establish public policies that will ameliorate the effects on children of early educational disadvantage. Legions of studies have shown that Head Start and similar programs work, and that they work well. We know that, in certain circumstances, early intervention works. And what's more important is that we know *why* it works.

Ramey and Ramey identify six principles that help us to understand why early intervention programs such as Head Start are effective. The first of these is the principle of *developmental timing*. Simply stated, the sooner

Bronfenbrenner's second level, the *mesosystem*, is made up of the relationships among the different settings in which the person spends time during different periods of development. That is, the mesosystem consists of the interrelations among microsystems. For example, a college freshman's mesosystem might consist of the campus dining hall, various classrooms, his or her family home, a dormitory room, and the intramural softball field.

Bronfenbrenner describes the third structure, the *exosystem*, as a set of specific social structures that do not directly contain the individual but still have impacts on interventions begin, the more effective they are. The longer we wait to introduce a disadvantaged child to an enriched environment, the less effective this enrichment will be. Second is the principle of *program intensity*—that is, if you want to maximize the effects of an early intervention program, you need to make it as intense as possible: Have the children attend for many hours each week, encourage lots of parent involvement, have program personnel make many visits to the children's homes, and arrange for the children to participate in many different activities. The greater the program intensity, the better the outcomes.

The third principle is that of *direct provision of learning experiences.* Any program that includes family support and parent training can have some impact, but programs that involve direct participation by trained staff (in addition to the less direct involvement of the children's family members) have been shown to be especially successful. The fourth principle is that of *provision of support services and parent training:* The more support services a program provides, and the broader the parent training, the better the outcomes. Researchers have found that early intervention programs that provide health and social services as well as individualized attention to clients' family crises (along with other services), in addition

to direct and intensive learning experiences, have the best outcomes.

The fifth principle that Ramey and Ramey identify is that of *individual differences.* That is, individual differences in the children in a program result in individual differences in outcomes. The level of benefits that children in a program receive depends on their initial level of risk. Thus, all other things being equal, programs that are targeted primarily at children with relatively great needs show more benefits than do programs that are targeted at children whose needs are not so great.

The sixth principle is that of *ecological dominion and environmental maintenance*—in other words, for a successful early intervention program to have lasting effects, it must maintain important aspects of the intervention over time. Programs can't just hit and run—be there to start children on a normal or upward trajectory and then end.

The research that has been conducted on early intervention is fascinating as well as important for an understanding of the nature of development. We know that both heredity and environmental forces are important, and the effectiveness of early intervention programs, as explained by the six principles described above, tells us why.

that person's development. These structures "influence, delimit, or even determine what goes on" in the microsystems of the developing individual. For example, one person's exosystem might be made up of his or her doctor's office, the teachers' lounge at his or her school, and grandma's house. Included in an individual's exosystem are all the places that have indirect impacts on his or her development.

The last element or structure in Bronfenbrenner's model, the *macrosystem,* consists of all the elements contained in the individual's micro-, meso-, and exosystems plus the general underlying philosophy or cultural orientation within which the person lives. Bronfenbrenner (1977) describes macrosystems as the "overarching institutional patterns of the culture or subculture, such as the economic, social, educational, legal, and political systems of which local micro, meso, and exosystems are the concrete manifestations."

This early model of the ecology of human development can help us to understand human development in two primary ways. First, it places the interaction between nature and nurture in a very clear and easily definable context of one of the four systems described above. Second, it encourages us to move away from laboratory-based settings and begin to examine development in the "natural stream" of when and where it occurs. Today, scientists who study human development are placing increasing emphasis on the qualitative nature of changes and are using research methods that reflect this emphasis—that is, they are moving away from the use of tightly controlled laboratory studies.

Like all good scientists, Bronfenbrenner has continued to develop his theories. Working with Pamela Morris, he has taken the next step suggested by his earlier work, emphasizing several new concepts that complement his earlier ideas. Bronfenbrenner and Morris's (2000) revised model of human ecology includes bioecological factors that influence the individual's contribution to his or her own environment. The primary addition these scholars have made to the ideas Bronfenbrenner presented more than 20 years ago (now referred to as part of the **bioecological model**) is the concept of *proximal processes* (that is, interactions in the individual's immediate environment), which can be described as follows:

1. In order to develop, an individual needs to be an active contributor to his or her environment.

2. The individual's contributions, or activities, have to take place on a regular basis and over an extended period of time.

3. These activities also need to become more complex over time—activities that do not change will not act as the "engine" of development.

4. The process of development is reciprocal; that is, each member of a dyad or group influences each other member.

5. An individual's interactions with people are very important, but his or her interactions with objects are influential as well.

6. The importance and role of these processes change over time as the individual and environment change as well.

Clearly, Bronfenbrenner has expanded his original model to place greater emphasis on the importance of the environment and the interaction between the individual and his or her environment.

The Process That Guides Development

Another issue often raised within different theories of development concerns the role ascribed to the mechanisms of maturation and learning. The "maturation or learning" debate parallels the arguments about hereditary and environmental influences discussed above. In this case, however, instead of focusing on the source or origin of the influence, the debate addresses the mechanisms through which changes take place.

Maturation is a biological process in which developmental changes are controlled by internal (or endogenous) factors. Events that result from maturation (such as walking or secondary sex changes at puberty) are characteristic of the species; they never take place because of specific practice or exercise—that is, they are not learned.

But just because maturation is a process that all humans go through, does that mean that we can't gain greater understanding of individual differences by examining maturation? The process does indeed seem to be very important. Waber (1976) conducted a fascinating study of the relationship between maturation and sex differences. Noting that previous research had shown that males tend to score higher than females on tests of spatial abilities and females tend to score higher than males on tests of verbal abilities, Waber asked the following question: Are these differences in performance the results of differences in maturation or differences in sex? She set out to answer her question by testing both early- and late-maturing males and females. She found that the early maturers in her sample, regardless of sex, performed better on tests of verbal abilities, and that the reverse was true of late maturers (thus confirming her hypothesis). Findings such as Waber's do not mean that we should discount the importance of sex as a variable for explaining differences in performance; rather, from such findings we can see that maturational processes have a broader influence than scholars might previously have believed.

Maturation is controlled by biological processes and dictates species-specific behaviors, whereas learning is specific to the individual.

Learning is a function of direct or indirect experience. The term refers to developmental changes that result from exercise or practice, and the outcomes of learning are highly individualized and specific. Examples of learned behaviors that depend on highly specific training include speaking a second language and driving a car. There are many different types of learning, from the ability to draw simple relationships between events in the environment to complex systems of imitation, or modeling. This diversity of learning paradigms provides a foundation for the set of developmental theories based on principles of learning, which I discuss in other sections of this book.

Learning is a function of experience or exercise and is idiosyncratic.

The work of Mary Ainsworth (see Ainsworth, Blehar, Waters, & Wall, 1978) and John Bowlby (1969) on attachment behavior between children and their caretakers provides excellent examples of the synthesis of learning and maturation. Ainsworth asserts that very early in life, a child has a developmental predisposition to form an attachment to some caretaker. This predisposition, according to Ainsworth, is part of the general maturational process and results from genetic programming. The choice of the person to whom the child forms the attachment, however, is highly idiosyncratic, often situationally determined, and the entire process is probably the result of learning.

As a result of social forces and expectations within American culture, females are usually the primary caretakers of infants and thus the primary "targets" for attachment. Females may make the best "mothers," but there is ample reason to believe that "mothering" (or parenting) is a learned set of very complex behaviors rather than a set of traits genetically transmitted from generation to generation. Our society also often seems to assume that simply having a child qualifies a person to be a parent and endows the knowledge necessary to rear a child. As any new parent knows, however, this is not the case—and babies do not come with instruction manuals.

The Importance of Age

Chronological age has historically been the most convenient and readily available guideline for estimating an individual's level of development. Because age can be determined easily and accurately, an individual's development has often been evaluated through the measurement of that person's performance against criteria based on expected performance at a certain age. The most frequently used normative or comparative standards have been the ages at which a certain number or percentage of children can perform at certain levels. For example, 7-year-olds are expected to know the meanings of a given number of words on general intelligence tests. There is a good deal of debate, however, concerning whether age is a reliable measure for evaluating development. For example, differences that exist between groups of children of different ages may not always be caused only by age. Indeed, factors such as sex, social class, and intelligence might explain more (and allow us to understand more) than age alone.

Age is a wonderful descriptive variable, but not a very useful explanatory one.

One of the problems with using age in measuring development is that age tends to be related to almost everything about a person (because so many things have age in common) and yet explains very little. We all know, for example, that as children get older, they grow taller. Their height, however, is only incidentally related to their age; it is much more a function of factors such as diet, quality of health care, and heredity. Chronological age is nothing more than an indicator of how much time has passed between two events (between an individual's birth and the present time). It does not help us understand what might cause differences in development. Thus developmental psychologists must systematically study the events that occur over time in a developing child's life (both internal and external to the child) to understand all the factors that affect developmental outcomes.

Donald Baer (1970) presents a unique perspective on this issue—the thesis that age is irrelevant to development. Baer draws a distinction between an age psychology, which is dependent on *products,* and a developmental psychology, which is characterized by *processes.* He argues that age is a convenience, providing a continuum along which change can be noted, but it is not very useful for explaining why developmental change occurs; that is, age has descriptive but not explanatory power. What is crucial, Baer asserts, is the sequencing of events in the individual's environment and their subsequent effects on behavior. This view is representative of theories that emphasize learning and other environmental influences as fundamental to the developmental process.

Other theories of development do incorporate age as an important landmark, however. Aside from using age as a general indicator of when change should occur, some theorists use age as an index of development. When researchers use age alone in evaluating development, the only method of study open to them is that of making relative comparisons of children with other similarly aged children.

Such evaluations can be problematic, especially when the data **overlap**—that is, when a child who is associated with one group on the basis of one variable (such as age) is at one extreme on another variable relative to that group. For example, a tall 10-year-old in the fifth grade may be as tall as, or taller than, a child in the seventh grade. The overlap between the distributions of children in the fifth and the seventh grades occurs in the area common to both classes, as shown by the shaded section in Figure 2.1. Those children who fall within the shaded area are either extremely tall fifth graders or extremely short seventh graders (relative to their peer groups).

Normative measures such as this, in which some children are short, some tall, and some located in between, describe relative rather than absolute levels of development. It is difficult to evaluate extreme cases (or outliers) using normative measures, and one needs to be very cautious about attributing the characteristics of other members of a given group to these individuals. Hence the argument that we need to look at variables other than age alone when making judgments.

Rate of Development and Critical or Sensitive Periods

One characteristic of the developmental process—regardless of one's theoretical viewpoint—is that it involves constant change. Some changes seem to occur more rapidly during certain periods and less rapidly during others, and developmental psychologists often focus on differences in rates of change as a major variable of interest. In infancy and adolescence, for example, rapid rates of physical change are accompanied by subtler psychological changes.

A critical period is a span of time during which the organism is maximally susceptible to internal or external influences.

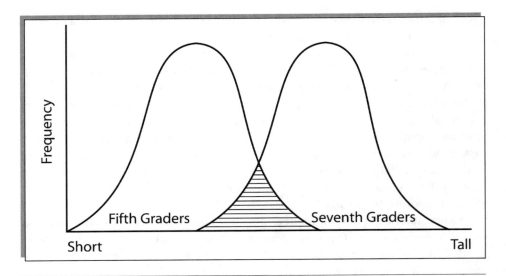

FIGURE 2.1   An Example of Overlap

Change often appears as a cyclical phenomenon. For example, at 2 years of age, children are usually somewhat cooperative and generally pleased with their accomplishments, whereas at 2½ they might seem uneasy and argumentative (Ilg & Ames, 1955). Similarly, throughout the early years of development, periods of fluctuating extroversion and introversion occur. Although the ages at which these cycles begin and end vary for different children, this fluctuation, or periodicity, is the result not of genetic or environmental factors alone, but of the interaction between the two.

According to Benjamin Bloom (1964), the greatest effects on development take place when these changes are occurring most rapidly: "Variations in the environment have greatest quantitative effect on a characteristic at its most rapid period of change and least effect on the characteristic during the least rapid period of change" (p. vii). The faster the rate of change, the greater the potential external and internal events have for affecting subsequent development. Bloom also stresses (as do Ilg & Ames, 1955) that for each dimension of human behavior there is usually a period of rapid change and a period of slow change. This variability in rates of change over the life span forms part of the basis for some theorists' argument that 50% of an individual's intellectual development is completed by 4 years of age, as a result of the rapid biological and social changes that occur during those early years.

An issue closely related to rate of development is that of whether critical or sensitive periods exist. A critical period is a span of time during which internal or

Critical periods used to be widely seen as "do or die" windows of opportunity for influence and potential change, but today they are viewed more as sensitive periods during which outcomes and changes are not so dramatic or limited by time.

external events have maximum impacts on development. During such a period, the individual is more susceptible to certain influences than at other times. For example, the research literature on animals (e.g., Hebb, 1947; Levine, 1957) and some research on humans (e.g., Bloom, 1964; Hunt, 1961) suggests that the optimal time to intervene in order to help individuals avoid potential developmental problems is during the first 3 years of life, when the rate of change is fastest across many dimensions.

Psychologist Robert Havighurst (1952) views critical periods from within a framework of what he calls **developmental tasks**, each of which should be completed during a certain stage of life or time span if the healthy development of the individual is to be ensured. He describes a developmental task as a task that arises "on or about a certain period in the life of the individual, successful achievement of which leads to his happiness and success with later tasks, while failure leads to unhappiness in the individual, disapproval by the society, and difficulty with later tasks" (p. 2).

The completion of successive developmental tasks lays a foundation on which later developmental progress is based. For example, in American society, one developmental task faced by adolescents is to gain increased independence or autonomy. It is worth noting, given the above discussion, that an individual's successful completion of a developmental task is often the result of the combined influences of maturation and environment. The developmental tasks associated with various times in the life span differ from one culture to another; it is interesting to speculate about these differences, as well as about what types of developmental tasks (and changes) may be universal.

> Critical or sensitive periods may well exist, but we must view these periods in the light of many other factors that also influence development.

Researchers have had difficulty studying critical periods in humans because of ethical and moral concerns that prevent them from artificially depriving human subjects of stimulation, physical contact, or food during certain hypothetically "critical" periods. On occasion, naturally occurring events have provided situations in which scholars have been able to test the critical period hypothesis. An example is the case of Victor, a 12-year-old "wild boy" who was captured in the French countryside during the early 19th century. After being declared an incurable idiot and treated as an animal, the boy was placed in the custody of Dr. Jean-Marc Itard. Although Itard recorded making some progress with Victor through intensive daily training sessions, Victor consistently failed to learn language. If Victor was not retarded (and Itard believed he was not), then his failure to learn language at the late age of 12 could support a critical period hypothesis for language development. According to linguists such as Lenneberg (1967), language development spans the period from 2 years of age to the onset of puberty. Lack of adequate instruction in language during those critical years could have been responsible for Victor's inability to communicate verbally. (For an interesting description of Itard's experiences, see Harlan Lane's book *The Wild Boy of Aveyron,* 1976. The 1970 film *The Wild Child,* directed by François Truffaut, also tells Victor's story.)

Another example of a critical period is the timing of sex role assignment for the young child. John Money and Anke Ehrhardt (1973) have studied children who were reared as the opposite of their genetic sexes because of hermaphroditism or some type of disfigurement. They found that during the first 18 months of life there is a great deal of latitude in the assignment of psychological sex roles. For example, biological males can be socialized to become social females if the socialization takes place early and is intense. After 18 months, this pliability decreases sharply, and by 3 to 4 years of age there is little chance of significant sex role change taking place.

Some theorists who argue against the existence of critical periods do so because they don't accept the idea that any developmental component can be susceptible to great change during (and only during) a relatively narrow span of time. This group includes those theorists who believe that development is a process controlled by environmental (or exogenous) forces rather than by biological imperatives.

The use of the term *critical period* can be misleading, because it can be understood to imply a restricted time period and a viewpoint that seems to ignore other factors (such as experience) whose effects may be more noticeable at other times in the developmental cycle. A better way of thinking of a critical period is as a range or span of time during which an individual is most susceptible to a certain kind of change. Undoubtedly, critical periods for some aspects of development do exist, but the extent to which events during these periods result in alterations in future outcomes is still open to speculation.

It may be best to think of these periods as *sensitive periods,* during which the individual may be susceptible (or sensitive) to the effects of particular biological or environmental influences. From this perspective, the individual's sensitivity to influences during these periods would not be viewed as critical.

The Shape of Development

Development can be characterized as either continuous or discontinuous; the characterization one chooses depends on one's view of how developmental processes occur.

Although change in behaviors over time (one way to define development) does not have any physical form, we can describe such change as having a "shape." Depending on one's theoretical orientation, one can see the shape of the course of development as smooth and continuous or as abruptly changing and discontinuous.

Those who view development as a **continuous process** believe (a) that changes occur in small, gradual steps; (b) that the outcomes of development are "more of the same" and not qualitatively different from what was present earlier; and (c) that the same general laws underlie the process at all points along the developmental continuum. Theories of development that tend to stress the

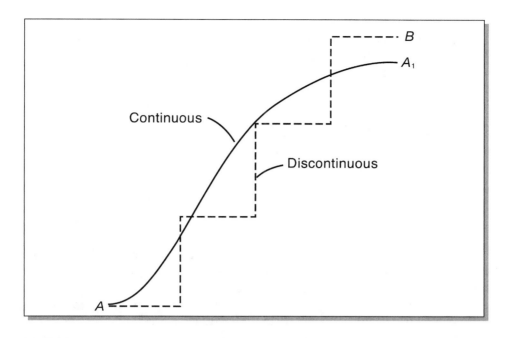

FIGURE 2.2   Comparison Between Continuous and Discontinuous Change

importance of environmental factors, such as behavioral approaches, view development as continuous.

Those who view development as discontinuous believe (a) that developmental changes are abrupt and represent qualitative differences from what existed before and (b) that different general laws characterize various developmental changes. Theorists who believe that development is characterized by a series of independent, qualitatively different stages (such as Jean Piaget) view development as a **discontinuous process**. Figure 2.2 illustrates how continuous and discontinuous change differ, showing continuous change as a smooth, gently curving line (from A to A1) and discontinuous change as somewhat variable and advancing in a steplike manner (the dashed line from A to B).

Similar to the heredity/environment debate, the continuity/discontinuity issue represents a somewhat artificial choice between alternatives. Some theorists who believe that development is influenced primarily by environment see development solely as a continuous process, whereas other theorists consider development to be completely discontinuous. An examination of the actual shape of change over time, however, reveals that developmental changes are of both types.

One of the key questions for any developmental psychologist is whether early behaviors predict later ones— the question of continuity over time.

TABLE 2.2 Different Types of Continuity with Similarity in Behavior Between Time 1 and Time 2

Overt Behavior	Underlying Psychological Process	Type of Continuity or Discontinuity
Identical	Identical	Complete continuity
Different	Identical	
Identical	Related	
Different	Related	
Identical	Different	
Different	Different	Complete discontinuity

It is also possible to view continuity and discontinuity as a continuum, an idea that Jerome Kagan (1971) has discussed in some detail. Table 2.2 presents a continuum that ranges from complete continuity to complete discontinuity, with gradual changes along the way. For example, sets of behaviors from one point in time to another (Time 1 and Time 2) can be identical to each other or different. The underlying process responsible for these behaviors can also be identical, different but related, or different and unrelated. The table shows the various relationships possible between a behavior and its cause (its underlying psychological process), as well as the type of continuity represented by each relationship.

Take, for example, a case of complete continuity. A young child may be very aggressive because she has learned that this is the most effective way to deal with frustration. When the girl becomes an adult, she exhibits the same pattern of behavior (for the same reason). In this case, the behavior is at the two points in time, and the psychological process that underlies the behavior (frustration) is identical as well. On the other hand, a case for discontinuity can be made if the adult's aggressive behavior is the result of psychological processes that are different from those that drove her childhood aggression. Perhaps she behaved aggressively out of frustration as a child, but as an adult, her aggression is a reaction to her feeling threatened.

Theorists who believe that development is discontinuous usually adopt the view that changes in behavior are accompanied by changes in underlying psychological structures. We can draw an analogy between the presence of the physical structures necessary to walk (sufficient neurological and muscular development) and the presence of the psychological structures necessary to solve certain types of problems. These developmentalists would agree that quantitative changes occur (such as an increase in the number of words a child speaks), but these changes in and of themselves do not reflect the true nature of development.

The opposing point of view is that behavior is the structure of development itself, and that there is no underlying frame or foundation that dictates the sequence of development, or what will occur next. In other words, overt (observable) behavior represents the functional nature of the individual, not the operation of any underlying mechanism. Hence behavior is continuous in nature. For example, some people believe that certain differences that have been observed between males and females in academic performance are not the result of structural differences, but instead are due to social learning and people's desire to fulfill expectations that are imposed on them at an early age. This perspective is called *functional* because it stresses the way in which specific behaviors become functions of specific changes in given settings. This view is characteristic of behavioral approaches, which I discuss in detail in Chapter 7.

Individual Differences

One of the most fascinating things about the study of human behavior is that, although all individuals have a great deal in common, we are all different as well. By understanding how various theories of development explain these differences, one can gain some insight into the differences among these theories. For example, from the earliest days of life, individual differences are in evidence. Some babies cry more than others, and some seem to enjoy physical contact to a greater degree than others. Infants develop their own individual sleep patterns as well. Arnold Gesell, the theorist who is the focus of Chapter 3, recognized differences even in identical twins at birth.

Ausubel and Sullivan (1970) summarize six categories of such differences in infants: irritability; activity level; tone, length, and vigorousness of crying; tolerance of frustration or discomfort and reaction to stress; sensitivity to stimulation; and smiling behavior. There is no question that some developmental psychologists believe these early differences are the results of biological processes. On the other hand, as children grow and the differences among them include differences in more complex behaviors, such as language development or patterns of attachment, it is much less clear that biological processes are responsible for any individual differences.

In the chapters that follow, as I discuss different theories of development, one of my areas of focus will be what each theory views as the source of differences among developing individuals who are at the same chronological level of development.

Even from birth, individual differences are apparent in humans. Why these differences occur and what they lead to are two fundamental issues in developmental psychology.

—— **On the Web** ——

If you want to know more about individual differences, visit the Web site of the International Society for the Study of Individual Differences, at http://issid.org/issid.html. At this site, the society explains its primary mission, which is to support research devoted to examining individual differences in temperament, intelligence, attitudes, and abilities. The society also publishes its own journal, the *Journal of Personality and Individual Differences;* you can find out more about it online at http://www.elsevier.nl/locate/issn/01918869.

How Is Development Studied?

The methods that psychologists use to study the process of development are often determined by the theoretical frameworks within which they ask their research questions.

The methods used to study development are as varied as the theoretical viewpoints on the process itself. In fact, often (but surely not always) the researcher's theoretical viewpoint determines the method used. That is, the method used usually reflects the question of interest (the research question). For example, most behavioral theorists are interested in the behavior itself, rather than in the underlying process responsible for that behavior, and because of this orientation, they are likely to focus on how frequently a certain behavior occurs and under what kinds of conditions. It's no surprise that much of the research work done in the basic analysis of behavior focuses on the *frequency* of behaviors, or the number of times given behaviors occur. The method used by such researchers, which is basically one of counting, reflects the philosophical orientation that behavior itself is what is important, rather than some other process that cannot be directly observed.

In contrast to this focus on counting observable events, researchers working within the psychoanalytic framework initiated by Freud stress the importance of helping the individual reveal unconscious and subconscious thoughts. These thoughts theoretically represent the presence of unobservable processes. Researchers who take a psychoanalytic approach use methods that are less direct than those used by behaviorists as they try to make accessible the kinds of processes that Freud considered important.

To help you understand how particular research methods relate to particular theories of development, throughout this book I provide examples of studies conducted by researchers working within the theoretical orientations discussed. You will see how the assumptions of the researchers often dictate the questions they ask, and how the answers to those questions depend on the methods used.

TABLE 2.3   Longitudinal and Cross-Sectional Methods for Studying Development

Year Born or Cohort	Age				
	25	*30*	*35*	*40*	*45*
1965			**2000**	2005	2010
1970		*2000*	**2005**	2010	
1975	*2000*	*2005*	**2010**		

NOTE: The longitudinal study is represented in boldface type; the cross-sectional study is represented in italics.

Whether or not age is a critical variable in the study of development (as noted above, theorists differ in the importance they place on age), it is still a component of many developmental studies. This leads us to a brief discussion of the two basic techniques used to study development: longitudinal and cross-sectional methods. A **longitudinal study** examines one group of people (such as people born in a given year), following and reexamining them at several points in time (such as in 2000, 2005, and 2010). Longitudinal studies of development look at *age changes*. (See Table 2.3, where a longitudinal study is represented by the dates appearing in boldface type.) A **cross-sectional study** examines more than one group of people at one point in time. For example, a study might look at three groups of people (those born in 1965, 1970, and 1975, for instance) in the year 2000 (when the subjects are 35, 30, and 25 years of age, respectively). Cross-sectional studies of development look at *age differences*. (In Table 2.3, the dates in italics represent a cross-sectional study.)

When should researchers use each of these methods? We'll get to that later, but before we do, let's look at the advantages and disadvantages of each (which are also summarized in Table 2.4).

Longitudinal studies are the best way to study age changes over time, and they generate big data sets that can be used by many researchers. Perhaps the biggest advantage of longitudinal studies is that participants act as their own controls, because they are followed year after year. In other words, many uncontrollable factors in a sample population (such as the individual backgrounds and genetics of participants) don't change, because the researchers are always looking at the same group of people. On the other hand, longitudinal studies are very expensive, difficult to conduct (because the main core of researchers changes over time), and require a lot of training for researchers and research assistants. Worst of all, participants drop out, and with each lost participant the very nature of the sample being studied may change.

Studies of development traditionally use either longitudinal or cross-sectional methods; both techniques have advantages as well as disadvantages.

Longitudinal studies produce rich pictures of individual development over time, but such studies are expensive and difficult to maintain.

TABLE 2.4   Advantages and Disadvantages of Longitudinal and Cross-Sectional Research Methods

Research Method	Advantages	Disadvantages
Cross-sectional study	Inexpensive Short time span Low dropout rate Requires no long-term administration or cooperation between staff and participants	Limits comparability of groups Gives no idea as to the direction of change a group might take Examines people of the same chronological age who may be of different maturational ages Reveals nothing about the continuity of development on a person-by-person basis
Longitudinal study	Reveals extensive detail on the processes of development High comparability of (the same) groups Allows for the study of continuity between widely differing groups Allows modified cause-and-effect speculation about the relationships between variables	Expensive Potential for high dropout rate

Cross-sectional studies are relatively inexpensive and quick to conduct (researchers can test many people of different ages at the same time), and they are the best way to study age differences (*not* age changes). On the other hand, a cross-sectional study cannot provide a very rich picture of development; by definition, such a study examines one small group of individuals at only one point in time. Finally, it is difficult to compare groups to one another, because they can have many basic differences.

Aside from the disadvantages mentioned above, both of these research methods result in another problem: the confounding of age with another variable—either the cohort (usually thought of as year of birth) or the time of measurement (when the assessment took place). **Confounding** is the term used to describe a lack of clarity about whether one or another variable is responsible for observed results. In this case, we can't tell whether the obtained results are due to age

Cross-sectional studies are quick and relatively simple, but they don't provide much information about the ways individuals change over time.

(reflecting changes in development) or some other variable. For example, when you do a longitudinal study, you may find changes in a certain variable that could be due to age or due to the year in which the participants were born (for example, 1970). How can the year in which someone was born conceivably make a difference? Sometimes events take place that can have unexpected effects on members of certain birth cohorts. For example, during the early 1950s infants who were born prematurely were treated with a certain protocol that led to problems with vision in some cases. When the effects of the protocol were discovered, the treatment was changed, and children who were born prematurely in later years did not develop the same vision problems.

> **Confounding** refers to a situation in which the effects of two or more variables on some outcome can't be separated.

Cross-sectional studies confound the time of measurement (year of testing) and age. For example, suppose you are studying the effects of an early intervention program on later social skills. If you use a new testing tool that is very sensitive to the effects of early experience, you might find considerable differences, but you won't know if they are attributable to the year of testing (when that new tool was used) or to age. These two variables are confounded.

What can be done about the problem of confounding age with other variables? K. Werner Schaie (1965), a developmental psychologist, first identified cohort and time of testing as factors that can help to explain developmental outcomes, and he also devised methodological tools to account for and help separate the effects of age, time of testing, and cohort. According to Schaie, age differences between groups represent maturational factors, differences caused by when a group was tested (time of testing) represent environmental effects, and cohort differences represent environmental and/or hereditary effects, or an interaction between the two. For example, Baltes and Nesselroade (1974) found that differences in the performance of adolescents of the same age on a set of personality tests were related to the year in which the adolescents were born (cohort) as well as when these characteristics were measured (time of testing). We can draw another example from our own experiences: College students today are very different from those of 10 or 20 years ago, even though they are, of course, in the same age group.

> **Sequential development designs** help to overcome the shortcomings of both cross-sectional and longitudinal developmental designs. They avoid the confounding of age, time of testing, and cohort.

Schaie proposed two alternative models for developmental research—the longitudinal sequential design and the cross-sectional sequential design—that avoid the confounding that results when age and other variables compete for attention. **Longitudinal sequential designs** compare subjects from different cohorts when they have reached particular ages. So, for example, as shown in Table 2.5, three studies would be conducted in which participants ages 35, 40, 45, 50, and 55 would be tested in the years 2000, 2005, and 2010. **Cross-sectional sequential designs** are similar to longitudinal sequential designs, except that they do not repeat observations on the same people from the cohort; rather, different groups are examined from one testing time to the next. For example (again referring to Table 2.5), the people tested in 2000, 2005, and 2010 would all come

TABLE 2.5 Sequential Designs to Avoid the Confounding of Age With Other Variables

Year Born or Cohort	Age				
	35	*40*	*45*	*50*	*55*
1965			2000	2005	2010
1975		2000	2005	2010	
1985	2000	2005	2010		

from different sets of participants born in 1965. Both of these designs allow researchers to keep certain variables (such as time of testing or cohort) constant while they test the effects of others.

Qualitative Methods of Studying Development

The traditional ways of doing developmental research described above, cross-sectional and longitudinal studies (and the quantitative methods for analyzing data associated with them), have in recent years been augmented (and in some cases replaced) by qualitative methods. In the simplest terms, **qualitative developmental research** is research that is conducted within the context in which the developmental phenomenon being studied occurs.

Although developmental scholars have been using qualitative methods to help answer their research questions only for a relatively short period, the use of such methods to answer questions about behaviors is by no means new. In fact, qualitative methods have been around for thousands of years, one of the best examples being the oral transmission of histories from one generation to the next.

Table 2.6 lists and provides brief descriptions of some of the information sources that qualitative researchers use. One important thing to remember is that among these different sources there is often overlap in the methods used and the kinds of information obtained. For example, case studies can involve interviewing, and historical research can often rely on historical artifacts.

An example of a recent qualitative research effort within the area of human development is Cardon's (2000) study of at-risk students and technology education. Noting that little is known about why at-risk students might want to take technology education courses, how these students value such courses, and whether the value they place on the courses has any influence on their staying in school, Cardon designed a study "to explore, describe, and examine how at-risk students experience and interact with the technology education curriculum." Using case-study and

TABLE 2.6 Information Sources Used by Qualitative Researchers

Source of Information	Brief Description	Example
Documentation	Records of private and public transactions	An important manuscript written by a noted developmental psychologist
Archival records	Stored documents	Budget documents from the early meetings of a professional society
Physical artifacts	Objects or elements that are open to interpretation	Eye-movement-tracking monitors
Direct observation	Real-time viewing of behavior	Observation of three different groups of children playing in three different settings
Focus group	Assembling a group of people to sample ideas and attitudes	A group interview with older people about their preferences for residential versus in-home medical care
Interview	Accessing information directly from study participants through verbal exchange	One-on-one questioning of adolescents about their preferences for particular types of foods
Case study	Intense study of a single event or individual	An assessment of a school district's policy toward adult education

participant-observation methods, he performed a pilot study to develop his research questions as well as his observation techniques. He found that the students in his sample gained new knowledge and created new sets of skills as a result of the technology courses they took, and that they reported increased motivation. He also confirmed that the students preferred hands-on learning experiences over traditional book and lecture teaching methods. Of the eight students in Cardon's sample (qualitative research usually involves the intensive study of relatively small numbers of participants), five reported that they would have dropped out of school had they not had the technology curriculum available to them.

Perhaps the most important distinction between quantitative and qualitative research methods is that they are useful for answering different types of questions; one type of method is not always better than the other. For both beginning and experienced developmental psychologists, the research questions asked dictate the methods of investigation used—not the other way around.

WEB SITES OF INTEREST

- "Heredity and Pre-Natal Influences: An Interview with Dr. Alfred Russel Wallace," by Sarah Tooley, at http://www.wku.edu/~smithch/wallace/S737. htm: Charles Darwin made great contributions to our understanding of the evolutionary process, and Alfred Wallace did the same, only a bit later. This interview, which was conducted in 1894, gives us a historical perspective on the development of such ideas.
- "Do Parents Matter? Judith Rich Harris and Child Development," by Malcolm Gladwell, at http://www.gladwell.com/1998/1998_08_17_a_harris. htm: In her 1998 book *The Nurture Assumption,* Judith Rich Harris makes some very bold statements about the role that parents play in the child's development. In this article, Gladwell provides a readable and informative summary of Harris's position and a very interesting ending to this story of scholarship and ideas.
- "Urie Bronfenbrenner," at http://people.cornell.edu/pages/ub11/index. html: One of the ways in which the heredity-environment interaction has been conceptualized is through Bronfenbrenner's ecological model, as discussed in this chapter. This Web site provides more information about Bronfenbrenner, who is currently an emeritus professor at Cornell University, and includes samples of his work. You can even e-mail him from the site.

FURTHER READINGS ABOUT
CONCEPTS IN HUMAN DEVELOPMENT

Ehrnstrom, Colleen Margaret. (2002). Individual differences in the relationship of work experience to adolescent behavior and development. *Dissertation Abstracts International, 62*(8B), 3797.

What does an understanding of individual differences contribute to our understanding of work and adolescents? In the research Ehrnstrom conducted for her dissertation, she examined whether adolescents' work experience can account for differences in problem behavior, mental health problems, health behaviors, and family involvement. She also looked at whether work experience and individual differences in psychosocial characteristics can predict changes in these four areas of behaviors over a year's time. Her results showed that knowledge of an adolescent's work experience is important for an understanding of the development of the adolescent.

Loehlin, John C., Horn, Joseph M., & Willerman, Lee. (1997). Heredity, environment and IQ in the Texas Adoption Project. In Robert J. Sternberg & Elena L. Grigorenko (Eds.), *Intelligence, heredity, and environment* (pp. 105–125). New York: Cambridge University Press.

In this chapter, the authors report on one of several well-known studies of the relative effects of genetics and child rearing on the development of intelligence. They conclude that the major contributor to familial resemblance is genetic in nature, but that the effects of environment are sizable, no matter what type of environment family members share. However, environmental effects are significant only when children are young; by the time they are adolescents, environment plays a much smaller role.

Pulkkinen, Lea, Nurmi, JariErik, & Kokko, Katja. 2002. Individual differences in personal goals in mid-thirties. In Lea Pulkkinen & Avshalom Caspi (Eds.), *Paths to successful development: Personality in the life course* (pp. 331–352). New York: Cambridge University Press.

In this chapter, the authors report on a study that examined the life themes of individuals who were successful or less successful in their development. The participants were first tested at 8 years of age and then followed through the age of 36. The discussion focuses on how the successful or unsuccessful developmental paths of the individuals were rooted in personality and emotional characteristics that were evident in childhood.

Satre, D. D., & Knight, B. G. (2001). Alcohol expectancies and their relationship to alcohol use: Age and sex differences. *Aging and Mental Health, 5,* 73–83.

Satre and Knight examined levels of alcohol consumption and frequency of drinking in two groups: 92 older adults and 83 younger adults. They found lower total alcohol consumption in the older adults than in the younger group, but also higher frequency of drinking in the older group (that is, they drank alcohol more often). The researchers also found significant differences between the age groups and within genders by age. These findings are important because they may help alcoholism treatment program designers to identify the kinds of treatment models that might be most effective.

PART II

THE MATURATIONAL AND BIOLOGICAL APPROACHES

CHAPTER 3

ARNOLD GESELL AND THE MATURATIONAL MODEL

The purpose of learning is growth, and our minds, unlike our bodies, can continue growing as we continue to live.

—Mortimer Adler

There is nothing permanent except change.

—Heraclitus

Every generation rediscovers and re-evaluates the meaning of infancy and childhood.

—Arnold Gesell

Arnold Gesell's long life of 81 years (1880–1961) included an enormously productive career that saw him become a psychologist and then an educator, physician, and writer. In all these endeavors, he focused on the development of children and the importance of biological controls. After working in the field of education, Gesell (pronounced ge-ZEL) completed his Ph.D. at Clark University, where he was influenced by G. Stanley Hall's interest in **recapitulation theory**. According to this theory, the development (or ontogenesis) of the child occurs in a sequence of stages that replicates the evolutionary history of the development of the species. In other words, **ontogeny** (the development of the individual) recapitulates **phylogeny** (the development of the species). Much of recapitulation theory, as well as Gesell's early work, was influenced by Darwin's theory of evolution as presented in *On the Origin of Species* (1859). It is interesting to note how much influence the biological sciences (such as biochemistry and physiology) had at that time on newer disciplines such as child development.

Gesell studied for his medical degree at Yale University and then, with his training in education, psychology, and medicine, he devoted his life to the scientific and practical concerns of the field of child development, especially child rearing. In 1911 he became the director of the Clinic of Child Development, and by the time he retired from the clinic in 1948, his work and the work of his students constituted an impressive contribution to the field of developmental psychology. Although Gesell's work can be reviewed in terms of his theoretical orientation or the innovations he introduced in methods for studying children (such as the use of motion pictures), its most lasting effects have been in the area of child-rearing practices. Because Gesell was well versed in many different fields, he could speak knowledgeably to different constituencies. In addition, because he wrote for scientific, professional, and popular audiences, his influence was widespread. However, even though the impacts of Gesell's work are still apparent, many practitioners who reflect those impacts today are not directly familiar with Gesell's contributions.

> Because Gesell studied education, medicine, and psychology and wrote for scientific, professional, and popular audiences, his impact was, and still is, widespread.

GESELL'S THEORETICAL VIEWPOINT

Gesell did not arrive at his theory through the successive testing of a formal set of hypotheses or postulates as part of a process of theory development (as discussed in Chapter 1). Instead, he placed heavy emphasis on biological forces, which he believed are responsible for both the impetus and the direction for development. As noted above, Darwin's theory of evolution had a significant impact on Gesell's developmental work. Gesell was also influenced by the work of Coghill (1929) concerning the role that structure plays in relationship to function. Coghill believed that structure determines function. This is still a very popular thesis, especially within the theoretical view that hypothesizes how the operations of underlying structures account for behavior. Simply put, physical structure must be present and developed before function can occur, and particular behaviors are simply not possible if the structures necessary to support them are not yet developed. For

> Structure must be present and developed before function can occur.

example, a child cannot walk until he or she has the structural equipment to do so (including the maturational development of certain muscles and the necessary neural organization).

Basing their argument on the huge body of information they had collected, Gesell and his colleagues maintained that human development progresses through an orderly sequence and that this sequence is determined by the biological and evolutionary history of the species. The rate at which any given child progresses through the sequence, however, is individually determined by the child's own genotype (i.e., the child's heredity background received from his or her ancestors). Although the rate of development can be artificially altered, it cannot be fundamentally changed. Thus a child who is developing more slowly than the average child cannot be deflected from his or her course, just as the faster-developing child is similarly set on a course. On the other hand, the environment can temporarily affect the rate at which a child develops. For example, malnutrition or illness may affect the rate of development, but biological factors are ultimately in control. This is analogous to the way biological characteristics of the species control the sequence of development. Frances Ilg and Louise Bates Ames (1955), two of Gesell's colleagues, effectively summarize the essence of this position in one of their many popular books: "A favorable environment (home or otherwise) can, it appears, permit each individual to develop his most positive assets for living. An unfavorable environment may inhibit and depress his natural potentials. But no environment, good or bad, can so far as we know change him from one kind of individual to another" (p. 64). This statement stands in dramatic contrast to the viewpoints of other developmental theorists, such as that of the more literal behaviorists (discussed in Chapter 7).

> The environment may temporarily affect the rate at which a child develops, but individual biological factors ultimately control development.

BASIC PRINCIPLES OF DEVELOPMENT

Gesell made his most comprehensive statement about development several years after he retired. In a well-known (and widely read) chapter titled "The Ontogenesis of Infant Behavior" (1954), he described his views of the developmental process. In this work, Gesell sought to unite the basic principles of morphological (or underlying structural) growth with those of behavioral growth, to show how "psychological growth, like somatic growth, is a morphogenetic process" (p. 338). He stated five basic principles of development that he described as having "psychomorphological" implications—that is, they represented developmental processes that occur on both a psychological level and a structural level. Also, Gesell based many of these principles on the biological functions he observed in the large sample of normal infants he studied. I discuss each of Gesell's five principles in turn below.

> The developmental processes addressed in Gesell's five principles are considered characteristic of every child's growth pattern.

—— On the Web ——

The University of Michigan's Center for Human Growth and Development is considered one of the outstanding research institutions of its kind in the United States; you can visit the center's Web site at http://www.umich. edu/~chgdwww. Established in 1964 with a mission "to further the understanding of the complex processes by which human beings grow and develop," the center has produced some very important research findings about these processes through the multidisciplinary collaboration of biomedical, behavioral, and social scientists. The center's long-range goal is to optimize children's physical, cognitive, and socioemotional development through research and training.

The Principle of Developmental Direction

Gesell's **principle of developmental direction** states that development is not random; rather, it proceeds in an ordered fashion. The fact that development systematically proceeds from the head to the toes is a good example—at any point, a developmental trend will be more advanced in the head area than in the foot area. Thus the newborn infant is relatively more mature in neuromotor organization in the head region than in the leg region, and coordination of the arms precedes coordination of the legs. This is described as the **cephalocaudal** (or head-to-tail) **trend.**

According to the principle of developmental direction, development has direction, and this direction is basically a function of preprogrammed genetic mechanisms.

Development also progresses from the center of the body outward, toward the periphery. For example, movements of the shoulders show considerably more organization early in life than do movements of the wrists and fingers. This **proximodistal** (or near-to-far) **trend** can be seen in the child's grasping behavior. At the age of 20 weeks, this behavior is quite crude and dominated by upper-arm movements, but by 28 weeks, as the child gains increasingly sophisticated use of the thumb, it involves much finer motor skills. Both the cephalocaudal and proximodistal trends support Gesell's contention that *development (and behavior) have direction* and that this direction is basically a function of preprogrammed genetic mechanisms.

The Principle of Reciprocal Interweaving

Gesell derived the **principle of reciprocal interweaving** of behavior from a principle of physiology called *reciprocal innervation,* which was proposed by

Sir Charles Scott Sherrington, winner of the 1932 Nobel Prize for medicine. Sherrington's physiological principle states that inhibition and excitation of different muscles operate in complementary fashion to produce efficient movement. Gesell asserts that a parallel phenomenon operates in the developmental process—that is, behavioral patterning requires complementary structural growth. Thus Gesell describes the developmental sequence that results in walking as a series of alternations between flexor (bending) dominance and extensor (extending) dominance that involves the arms and legs in a kind of neuromuscular coordination and integration that takes place over an extended period of time. He employs this principle in describing the development of walking as well as the development of right- or left-handedness. He summarizes the principle as follows: "The organization of reciprocal relationships between two counteracting functions or neuromotor systems is ontogenetically manifested by somewhat periodic shifting of ascendancy of the component functions or systems, with progressive modulation and integration of the resultant behavior patterns" (Gesell, 1954, p. 349).

According to the principle of reciprocal interweaving, opposing sets of forces are dominant at different times during the developmental cycle.

Through such complementary processes, opposing sets of forces are ascendant (or dominant) at different times during the developmental cycle. The work of these opposing forces results in integration and progression toward a higher level of developmental maturity. As you will see in upcoming chapters, this idea of oppositional forces operating simultaneously to facilitate the move toward more sophisticated development comes up often; it is a characteristic common to many models of development that emphasize the role of biological factors as well as cultural factors.

The Principle of Functional Asymmetry

Although many aspects of development can be described as the balancing and constant reorganization of opposing tendencies, a special case of reciprocal interweaving, the **principle of functional asymmetry**, is the exception to that rule. According to this principle, behaviors go through periods of asymmetric (that is, unbalanced) development to enable the organism to achieve a measure of maturity at later stages. The primary physical example that Gesell offers to illustrate this complex principle is a basic response called the tonic neck reflex. This reflex is present when an infant assumes a position like that of a fencer, with the head turned to one side, one arm extended to that side and the leg on that side straight, and the other arm folded across the chest and the other leg bent at the knee. This asymmetrical behavior is the precursor of the later development of symmetrical reaching, in which the child's two arms come together to grasp a suspended object. This is an important step in the child's efforts to master and understand the environment.

According to the principle of functional asymmetry, behaviors go through periods of asymmetric development that allow the organism to achieve a measure of maturity at later stages.

Gesell also asserts that the principle of functional asymmetry has a great deal to do with the development of handedness and other forms of psychomotor dominance. It also helps to prevent the infant from suffocation (by turning the head) and is part of the reserve of reflexes that contributes to certain acts, such as throwing a ball and even aggression.

The Principle of Individuating Maturation

According to the principle of individuating maturation, development involves predetermined sequential patterning that is revealed as the organism matures.

Within Gesell's theoretical framework, development is conceptualized as a process of predetermined sequential patterning in which the patterning is revealed as the organism matures. Maturation is a process controlled by endogenous or internal factors; it cannot be influenced on a basic level by exogenous or external factors, such as teaching. In other words, as the **principle of individuating maturation** summarizes, the results of maturational processes cannot be learned. This principle stresses the importance of a growth matrix, an internal mechanism within the individual that establishes the direction and pattern of his or her development.

Gesell (1954) sums up the relationship between maturation and the environment as follows: "Environmental factors support, inflect, and specify; but they do not engender the basic forms and sequences of ontogenesis" (p. 354). Consequently, learning can occur only when structures have developed that permit behavioral adaptation, and no amount of specific training prior to the development of those structures will be effective. Gesell places heavy emphasis on the role of biological factors. It is important to note that although he does not discount the influence of the environment, he asserts that its effects on the final outcomes of development are probably quite limited.

The Principle of Self-Regulatory Fluctuation

According to the principle of self-regulatory fluctuation, every stage of disequilibrium or imbalance in development is followed by a stage of equilibrium.

Gesell's **principle of self-regulatory fluctuation** proposes that developmental progress fluctuates in seesaw fashion, between periods of stability and instability, and between periods of active growth and consolidation. These progressive fluctuations, as part of a give-and-take much like that described by the principle of reciprocal interweaving, culminate in a set of stable responses. These fluctuations are not undesirable or irregular; rather, they are definite efforts on the part of the organism's system to maintain its integrity while assuring that continued growth occurs.

In fact, according to Gesell, a distinct sequence of stages occurs repeatedly as the child matures, and stages of disequilibrium or unbalance are always followed by

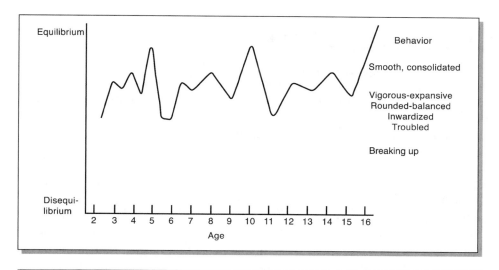

FIGURE 3.1   The Cycles of Development
SOURCE: Adapted from Ilg and Ames (1955).

stages of equilibrium. Figure 3.1 shows the levels of balance in development from ages 2 through 16, illustrating how development occurs in cycles that range from relative equilibrium to relative disequilibrium. The trend line in this figure represents hypothetical characteristics of behavior in general, not the behavior of any one child.

THE IMPORTANCE OF INDIVIDUAL DIFFERENCES

Although all of the five principles described above are considered to be observable in the growth patterns of all children, Gesell also emphasizes the importance of wide-ranging and stable individual differences. One of the unique contributions Gesell made to the field of developmental psychology was the use of motion pictures to record children's development for study. Gesell and his colleagues first used these "cinema records" to study five infants during the first year of life; they then studied these same children 5 years later.

During the first year, the researchers rated each child on 15 behavior traits (including energy output, social responsiveness, and self-dependence) and then ranked the five children in the group on each trait. They repeated the process 5 years later. A comparison of the rankings of the children between the first year and at age 5 showed remarkable similarity on traits such as laterality (handedness), self-dependence, sense of humor, and emotional maladjustment. These findings indicate a certain degree of stability in the development of individual differences,

Applying Ideas About the Maturational Model

It's the *Individual* Differences That Count

One of the mainstays of Gesell's research was the observation and recording of physical growth and change. Although a great deal of this work (as noted throughout this chapter) has implications for our understanding of domains of development other than the biological, such as personality and cognitive development, it was most thoroughly grounded in the physical realm, so it's no surprise that Gesell often felt that, just as each child has individual needs, different stages of development have their own types of individuality as well.

In an interesting and very cleverly designed research study, Michelle Lampl and her colleagues undertook an examination of individual differences in growth (Lampl, Veldhuis, & Johnson, 1992). Their study was implicitly suggested by a comment made by a friend of Lampl about how fast Lampl's young baby was growing (as in your mother's report to your grandmother, "He shot up overnight!"). Doctors usually check infants' height and weight every month in the beginning and then every few months as they get older. These researchers decided to see if babies really do grow particularly quickly at certain times, or in spurts. To do so, they measured growth in a sample of babies over an extended period of time.

You may be amazed to learn that some of the infants in Lampl et al.'s study, who were assessed at ages from birth to 21 months, grew as much as a full inch in a 24-hour period (just one more piece of data attesting to the individual differences that exist among young children and, by extension, at all levels of development). To put this in perspective, say that an infant was 20 inches in length; that would mean that growing an inch would represent about a 5% increase. If you are an average American adult male (about 5 feet, 10 inches tall) and you were to grow 5% in a day, you would suddenly be about 6 feet, 2 inches tall; if you are an average female (about 5 feet, 4 inches tall), you would grow to about 5 feet, 7 inches.

There is another important lesson to be learned from Lampl et al.'s findings. In the past, most scientists have believed that during the first 20 or so years of life, steady and smooth rates of growth are the norm. The general consensus was that the stages of infancy, young childhood, and adolescence could be characterized as entailing smooth and gradual transitions from one point along the growth continuum to the next. Thanks to studies like the one described above, however, we now know that smooth and even rates of change may not be found in every case.

a characteristic that, according to Gesell, has its source in some kind of biological mechanism.

In another study of 33 infants who were observed at intervals from infancy through the teenage years, Gesell and his colleagues found a remarkable degree of stability in what Gesell refers to as "trends in mental development." Those infants whose mental development was found to be below normal continued to show the same trend as teenagers. Similarly, children who were superior as infants were also superior as adolescents.

Gesell breaks down individual differences in behavioral development into four different areas: motor behavior (locomotion, coordination, specific motor skills), adaptive behavior (alertness, intelligence, different forms of exploration), language behavior (all forms of communication), and personal-social behavior (reactions to persons and to the environment). Indeed, in the popular books that Gesell and his colleagues wrote for parents, they described the behaviors that parent should expect to see in their children at various ages in terms of these four domains. These domains also formed the basis for a screening test widely used by parents to determine the developmental status of infants from 1 month through 6 months of age, the Denver Developmental Screen Test (or DDST-II), created by Frankenburg and Dodds (1992). This test, which a parent can complete in about 10 minutes, gives a very general overview of the child's status in fine motor-adaptive, gross motor, personal-social, and language skills.

> Gesell breaks behavioral development down into four areas: motor behavior, adaptive behavior, language behavior, and personal-social behavior.

In each of these four domains, the five general principles of development described above continue to function, with individual differences in the rate of development dominating. The child is an integral whole within which the four domains interact while under the control of biological forces expressed through the five principles of development. To summarize Gesell's theoretical point of view: The development of the child is controlled entirely by biologically determined principles of development that produce an invariant sequence of maturation. In turn, this maturational process makes behavioral expression possible. Although individual children progress at their own rates (and these rates are not directly responsive to environmental manipulation), the sequence of development is the same for every child.

Gesell was a tireless empiricist, and he collected a great deal of information about children, particularly during infancy. He continually sought new and better ways of measuring and recording behavior, and he made several important contributions to the field of development in terms of methodologies. As I have already mentioned, he was among the first to use moving pictures in development research, both for recording the growth of behavior patterns in children and for studying the postural development of infants (which he did by examining film footage frame by frame).

> Gesell showed early concern for such methodological issues as reliability of measurements and the importance of the repetition of observations.

Gesell was actively involved with children in other ways as well. One of the earliest educational documentaries ever made in the field of child development, a two-reel film titled *Life Begins,* features Gesell presenting his point of view, stating that science has a contribution to make in safeguarding the successful development of the child. Gesell also was concerned about such methodological issues as standardizing the materials used in research and the reliability or consistency of measurements. Although the database he amassed does not demonstrate much diversity—most of the children who served as subjects in his studies were from white, middle-class families in New Haven, Connecticut—it does represent one of the earliest and most carefully collected normative reference groups. He was able to organize all this information into a description of growth and development that allowed him to devise a series of tasks to be used in evaluating an individual child's development relative to that child's age group. He then incorporated these tasks into the Gesell Development Schedule, from which a child's "DQ," or developmental quotient, could be derived. Although this schedule is no longer used in many research or evaluation settings, it became the prototype for most of the infant assessment techniques developed in the years since.

Gesell's normative approach relied on repeated testing of the same children over long periods of time (a longitudinal strategy) to obtain characteristic age descriptions and to test the stability or continuity of individual differences. (Individual differences are said to be stable if an individual maintains the same relative position over time on some measure in comparison to his or her peers.) Gesell and Thompson (1929, 1941) introduced the now classic **co-twin control research method**, in which they studied sets of identical twins (two children who developed from the same fertilized egg, and so have identical genotypes, or genetic histories) to shed light on the question of whether biological forces (maturation) or experience (learning) represents the major force in development.

In a study using this method, both twins are initially tested on some criterion behavior, such as walking or stair climbing. Then, one twin is given specific training in the behavior, and the other twin (who acts as the control) is left to the natural opportunities of the environment (see Figure 3.2). Both twins are then again assessed on the behavior at a later point.

Gesell and Thompson found in their studies that the twin receiving the training (Twin 1) would show slow, incremental gains in the behavior of interest, while the control twin (Twin 2) showed no gains. Then, when Twin 2 reached the age where, maturationally, he or she would be expected to be able to begin learning the behavior, the researchers would begin intensive training with that twin. Their results indicated that with a short period of training, the Twin 2 achieved the same level of mastery as Twin 1—at the end of the experimental period there was no difference in competence between the two children. Based on the results of such studies, Gesell and his colleagues concluded that early training, before a child is physically mature enough to make significant gains in given behaviors, is of little consequence to the ultimate outcome. Maturation is such a predominant factor in development that learning is possible only where the maturational, or structural, apparatus necessary for learning to take place is functioning.

Development makes learning possible; learning does not foster basic development.

Gesell and his colleagues introduced the co-twin control research strategy, in which they studied identical twins to clarify the importance of maturation versus learning.

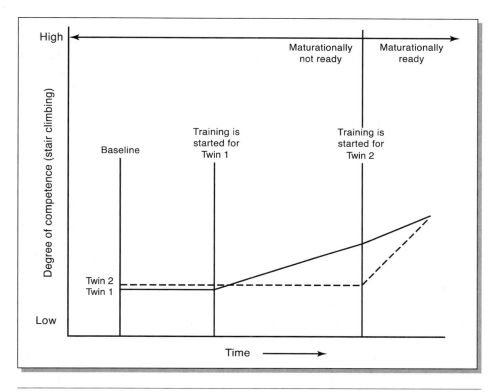

FIGURE 3.2 Results of Gesell and Thompson's Co-Twin Control Studies

We need to understand the immediate and long-term effects of such training (or learning), however. Myrtle McGraw (1935), who conducted some of the early studies using the co-twin control paradigm, made a series of films recording her research. In these films, the trained twin (who received training in a variety of motor skills) is seen to have developed into a lean, athletic, graceful individual. The control twin, however (that is, the twin who did not receive training), did not become lean, grew to be decidedly unathletic, and was quite ungraceful. Gesell believed that training could not modify characteristics that are biologically set, but he did not seriously consider the cumulative effects of environmental variables as a major part of his research program. In considering the impacts of early training, we should be aware that cumulative as well as sleeper effects (effects that show up much later in an individual's life) may be very important even when immediate effects are not strong or durable. In fact, sleeper effects may have been operating in the Head Start programs initiated during the 1960s. Follow-up evaluations of these programs have found that many benefits to individuals of preschool participation in Head Start surfaced only many years later, when the participants reached maturity as adolescents or young adults.

Given Gesell's strong emphasis on the biological basis of many characteristics, it is not surprising that developmental researchers working from a Gesellian orientation leaned toward the idea that each individual has a fixed level of intelligence. In opposition to this point of view, Harold Skeels and Harold Dye (1939) set out to demonstrate that environmental enrichment can significantly raise IQ levels. They chose an orphanage in Davenport, Iowa, for their experiment, in which they planned to give one group of children specially enriched preschool experiences while another group received no special experiences. In preparation for the experiment, the researchers gave each child in the orphanage an IQ test, and they found that two little girls were severely retarded—at 13 and 16 months of age, they were functioning at the levels of 7 and 8 months, respectively. Skeels and Dye recommended that these two children be placed in an institution for the retarded. Six months later, Skeels (who happened to serve as a consultant to the institution where the girls were placed), visited the institution. There he saw the two little girls, now 19 months and 21 months old, running around and acting quite normal for their ages. A formal test of the girls' developmental levels confirmed this impression. Because the investigators did not believe that such dramatic changes (that is, bringing retarded infants into the "normal" range) could actually have occurred, the girls were left in the institution. However, when they were retested several months later, the results were the same. These two little girls were functioning at a normal level of intelligence and were no longer considered retarded.

Further investigation revealed that when the "retarded" infants were originally brought to the institution, there had been no infants' ward in which to put them, so they were placed on a ward with retarded older women who, it was assumed, would care for them. Indeed, these women cared for the girls very well. In addition to playing with them and treating them as special, the women had bombarded the children with affection. The nurses had also taken a liking to the girls and often took them on outings. As a result of the high degree of stimulation the girls received, remarkable changes occurred.

To find out whether the changes in the girls were really the result of their changed circumstances and not some chance occurrence, Skeels and Dye began a formal experiment in which they placed a group of low-normal children from the orphanage on the ward with the retarded women. At the same time, they selected a control group of children (who tested initially somewhat higher in intelligence than the experimental group) who remained in the orphanage. The children in the experimental group remained in the institution for the retarded for varying amounts of time, and, like the original two girls, they showed dramatic increases in intelligence levels over the course of their stay. Many of them returned to the orphanage only briefly when the experiment concluded and were either adopted

---

—— On the Web ——

Gesell spent so much of his professional life at the Yale Child Study Center that it would be worth your time to make a quick visit to the center's Web site (at http://info.med.yale.edu/chldstdy). The center's range of research interests is very broad (from Tourette's syndrome to neuroimaging), and scholars there are involved in training practitioners in many areas, including developmental psychology, pediatrics, and even law and law enforcement.

---

or returned to their biological parents, who had not previously been able to care for them. Follow-up testing that took place 2½ years after the conclusion of the experiment revealed that (a) some of the dramatic gains shown by the experimental children were maintained, and (b) some of the control children who had remained in the orphanage had shown dramatic declines in intelligence.

It appears, then, that a brief and somewhat unsystematic intervention produced remarkable changes in intelligence. These results might be seen as strong support for the environmentalist position regarding the malleability of intelligence and as evidence against Gesell's claim that mental development is biologically rather than environmentally determined. For a number of reasons, however, Skeels and Dye's findings did not have much effect on the debate. One problem was the way the research was done. Too many elements of the research were not well controlled; for example, the amount of time in the experiment and the initial levels of tested intelligence varied widely among the children. Further, the persons who administered the intelligence tests were aware of each child's status as an experimental subject or a member of the control group, and this knowledge may have affected their objectivity. In addition, it was not clear that any increases in IQ resulted solely from the experimental conditions because many of the children in the experimental group did not remain in the orphanage during the period between the end of the experiment and the beginning of follow-up testing. All these factors made it impossible for anyone to tell whether the changes in the children were attributable to any specific cause.

Furthermore, Gesell's contention that development is controlled primarily by biological factors assumes a normal environment. In his own work, Gesell did not address the issue of seriously deprived environments, perhaps because his subject population came primarily from average middle-class homes. Given that the orphanage involved in Skeels and Dye's research could be considered a seriously

---

Applying Ideas About the Maturational Model

Maturation: The Process That Can't Be Ignored

Gesell didn't focus on maturation just because he was a physician and it was a process he observed and studied every day. Rather, he identified maturation as a central process because he believed that it had implications for every aspect of human development. He also speculated about the role depression might play in resilience as well as the role maturation might play in insulating individuals from the effects of depression.

In a very interesting study, Lisa Miller and Merav Gur (2002), two psychologists from Columbia University, examined the impact of physical maturation on how well religiosity can protect adolescent girls against depression. The 3,356 girls who participated in the study (average age was 16 years) were interviewed as part of a much larger study, the North Carolina Adolescent Health Study. To assess maturation, Miller and Gur recorded self-reports of secondary sexual characteristics and age at onset of menstruation; they assessed religiosity on the basis of personal devotion, personal conservatism, institutional conservatism, and level of participation in religious community.

The researchers' statistical analyses showed that, regardless of age and ethnicity, personal devotion and participation in religious community were associated with decreased likelihood of depression in non-highly mature girls and with a higher decrease in highly mature girls. Also, other variables showed some relationship to depression as well. Personal conservatism and institutional conservatism were associated with a decrease in depression among non-highly mature girls, but these variables were not associated with depression in highly mature girls. Miller and Gur conclude that physical maturation may be associated with the protective qualities against depression that religiosity has for adolescent girls. Their findings suggest that, to gain a better understanding of what factors might pose serious threats during development, we should look at level of maturation and, more important, how reaching a particular level of maturation acts to insulate children and young adults from the effects of certain negative circumstances.

---

nonnormal environment, it is not even clear that Gesell would have interpreted the findings from that research as being counter to his position.

By the time Skeels and Dye published the last of their data in the early 1940s, the nature/nurture debate had effectively been defused. The fury on both sides of the argument had largely ceased, and the advent of a world war diverted attention from the issue as well. The debate was widely thought to have reached an impasse because of researchers' admitted inability to separate environmental factors clearly from biological factors in assessing human traits such as intelligence.

In the early 1960s, when Skeels was on the verge of retiring from his position at the National Institutes of Health, he set out to see what had happened to the children who had participated in the experiment almost 30 years earlier. He published the story of his search, what he found, and a review of all of the earlier data in a 1966 monograph. Skeels's long-term follow-up revealed that the two sets of people who had been part of his research as children had gone on to have remarkably different life histories. Those who had been in the experimental group (who had initially scored lower than control group members in intelligence) went on to lead relatively normal, productive lives. Those who had been in the control group, in contrast, either remained in institutions or were employed in menial jobs. Skeels is cautious in interpreting his findings, urging readers to be careful about concluding that the experimental treatment was responsible for the differences in outcomes. Nevertheless, it is worth noting that if one looks at the initial performance of the members of these two groups from the Gesellian position on the stability of mental growth, one is likely to predict outcomes far different from what Skeels actually found.

Whether scholars support or oppose Gesell's theoretical viewpoint depends on how they interpret the data that Gesell and his colleagues present. Gesell firmly believed that these data support the maturationist position. On the matter of growth patterns for all children, Gesell's data in the area of motor development have stood the test of time and have seen frequent replication (a hallmark of scientific credibility). Gesell was also among the first to document individual differences in rates of growth, and these data have also been verified repeatedly. Gesell stressed the idea that there are individual differences in personality patterns, and he presented numerous case histories to support his point of view. The findings of other studies that have examined individual differences from birth onward echo some of Gesell's major themes in this area (e.g., Chess & Thomas, 1977; Escalona, 1968; Mayer, 1999; Pawlik, 1998).

APPLICATION OF GESELL'S THEORY TO HUMAN DEVELOPMENT

Gesell and his colleagues wrote three books aimed at the general public: *The First Five Years of Life* (Gesell, Ilg, & Ames, 1940), *The Child From Five to Ten* (Gesell, Ames, & Bullis, 1946), and *Youth: Years From Ten to Sixteen* (Gesell, 1956). These books detail, year by year, the behaviors that parents should expect to see in their children in the four domains of motor, personal-social, adaptive, and language performance. The books also stress the principle that growing children are true to their biological nature, and thus any attempts to push or force their development are doomed to failure. Maturational forces will always win out in their own good time.

When a child does not seem to be doing what other children are doing, Gesell and his colleagues tell parents not to despair; given sufficient time for the necessary maturational development, the child will develop the appropriate behavior. Thus children who are not learning are simply not ready to learn; when they are, learning will happen. Attempts to intervene before the child is ready will be fruitless and frustrating and can create disharmony among parent, teacher, and child.

Thousands of pediatricians, teachers, and parents have been influenced by Gesell's philosophy that time (or the process of maturation) takes care of most problems in behavioral development. Proponents of this philosophy generally advise parents, many of whom are anxious to see their children achieve early in life, not to push their children. They believe that readiness is the key, the explanation for any child's learning or not learning, rather than other factors in the child's world, such as instruction or nutritional needs. If one leaves the child alone, most behavioral development will happen by itself as the necessary physical structures come into being and enable that development to take place. Most normal children achieve behavioral development without any special treatment.

> Thousands of pediatricians, teachers, and parents have been influenced by Gesell's philosophy that time takes care of most "problems" in development.

Unfortunately, the advice that grows out of Gesell's theory can lull us into thinking that, because no treatment is necessary, no treatment of any kind is taking place. We should, however, consider the normal environment as an influential treatment in itself. Changes may occur in a child's behavior without any obvious intervention related to those changes, but that does not mean that the natural environment was not important in fostering the developmental outcomes. In fact, the normal environment itself is a stimulating and active factor, encompassing many different events. Only recently have developmental psychologists looked to the ecology of child development to gain a better understanding of the role of the environment in "normal" development (for more on this, see Bronfenbrenner & Morris, 2000). And in the same article in which she presents her triarchic theory of intelligence, discussed in Chapter 2, Sandra Scarr (1993) also emphasizes the fact that the parenting behaviors of the vast majority of parents are within the "normal" range—that is, they are likely to lead to healthy children.

Although the advice that proponents of Gesell's theory give to overanxious parents may help to remove the unnecessary and sometimes harmful pressures some parents tend to put on their children, such advice may be relevant only for the parents of certain children in certain kinds of settings. The problem is that Gesell's theory can lead to a mind-set in which the normal environment's contribution to normal development is ignored. The theory stresses the dominance of maturational forces in development, and it places the normal environment in a supportive, rather than causative, role. One problem with this is that the theory never addresses what a "normal" environment is, or how one might alter a nonnormal environment to make it normal.

It is likely that in many instances when a child's development is not progressing as expected, the child's parents adopt some intervention strategy without even knowing it. For example, take the case of a healthy 2-year-old girl who does not talk but communicates her desires by pointing. The concerned mother consults a pediatrician, who examines the child, finds nothing wrong, and says to the mother, "Don't worry, she'll talk when she's ready." The mother asks if there is some special treatment that might help, suggesting that perhaps she should take her daughter to see a speech pathologist. Confident that time will take care of the problem, the doctor dissuades the mother from seeking any special treatment. Six months later, the mother reports, and the doctor can see, that the child is now talking: She uses words appropriately and has a respectable vocabulary for a child of 2½. The doctor might believe that the advice she gave to the mother was valid, that no special treatment had been necessary, and that time resulted in (or caused) the changes in the child's language behavior. The mother may even agree with that assessment and be glad that she did not subject her child to needless further examination. Yet probably the mother provided some sort of subtle and effective treatment herself, without even realizing it. Concerned about the child's not talking, she might have done a number of things: When she talked to her daughter, she may have slowed down her own speech, repeated words and phrases more frequently, or made her speech more distinctive; she also may have made it clear to her daughter that some events were contingent on the child's use of words. In other words, the mother may have altered her own behavior and so inadvertently altered some dimension of the child's "normal environment."

In this example, the doctor's advice and the subsequent events were not harmful to the child's development. But consider another case that starts out the same but in which the reassured mother does not provide subtle treatment. After 6 months, there is no appreciable change in the child's language, and the doctor begins to entertain the hypothesis that the child's language development is somewhat below normal. If the doctor believes that behavioral development is controlled by maturational factors, she may see her proper role to be that of helping the parent to accept the fact that her child is developmentally delayed. The danger here is that when development is significantly delayed or retarded, recourse to the maturational explanation can become a self-fulfilling prophecy.

In the realm of popular belief, and in the arena of advice to parents, Gesell's work has had and continues to have enormous impact. For years, Gesell's colleagues Frances Ilg and Louise Ames wrote a syndicated daily newspaper column titled "Know Your Child," in which they stressed the powerful natural impetus to growth and change that is contained in the biological system of the developing child. Gesell never said that normal development was likely to be fostered in seriously adverse environments, and he was a great advocate of providing children with healthy environments in which to grow and develop, believing fervently that such positive environments lead to what he referred to early on as "good mental hygiene" (what we today call good mental health). Yet he was not concerned with a detailed analysis of children's environments, perhaps because he trusted that most parents would provide environments appropriate for fostering the good development of their children.

Arnold Gesell's legacy is significant. His basic contributions to the methodologies used in the study of development and the large amounts of data he gathered will always stand as significant advances for the field of developmental psychology.

Applying Ideas About the Maturational Model

How Early Is Too Early for School?

A great deal of Gesell's work, along with that of his colleagues Louise Bates Ames and Frances L. Ilg, focused on the application of knowledge about child development to the educational process. In a study published in 1964 (long after Gesell had died), Ames and Ilg examined whether results from Gesell's developmental tests would be a better indicator of a child's readiness for school admission than the child's chronological age. School readiness, which is a huge issue for parents and educators, has been linked to everything from the content of television shows that children watch (Wright et al., 2001) to parent-child relationships (Lamb-Parker, Boak, Griffin, Ripple, & Peay, 1999) and motivation (Carlton, 2000).

In their study, Ames and Ilg hypothesized that a child's school readiness is best indicated by the child's developmental, or behavioral, age rather than chronological age alone. Their thesis was that children should behave at age levels consistent with their years. To answer their research question, they looked at test data for 52 boys and girls who were tested when they first entered kindergarten and again when they were in the sixth grade. The researchers enlisted three experts to evaluate each child's readiness for kindergarten using the child's

scores on three tests: a behavior examination, two personality tests, and a vision examination. All of the children were of the correct chronological age for admission into kindergarten.

Ames and Ilg found that by the time the children in their sample were in the sixth grade, those who were judged to have been ready for kindergarten (by at least two of the three judges) were in the top two groups in academic performance. Those children who had been judged as not ready for kindergarten did not perform as well, scoring in the lower half of the class. The relationship between later school performance and how ready the children were for school was fairly strong, indicating that the criteria the researchers used for selecting children were quite reliable.

Here we have a classic test of Gesell's hypothesis concerning the importance of biological forces and their influence on development. Because chronological age reflects a variety of things in addition to maturation (see the discussion above), one might expect it to be a less reliable predictor of educational success than more direct measures of maturational development such as Gesell's behavior tests, which did indeed predict school success more accurately than age.

WEB SITES OF INTEREST

- Yale Child Study Center at http://info.med.yale.edu/chldstdy: Arnold Gesell spent 50 years of his career at the Yale Child Study Center, developing a set of guidelines so that parents and educators could understand how the process of maturation translates into the everyday growth events they see in children. The center is still the focus of important research in areas such as autism and early childhood education.
- "Guide to Developing Grade-Level Brochures for Parents," at http://www.dpi.state.wi.us/dpi/dltcl/bbfcsp/doc/grade.doc: In listing the characteristics of children at different ages, this publication of the Wisconsin Department of Public Instruction shows the strong influence that Gesell's associates Louise Bates Ames and Frances L. Ilg have had on practices and philosophies in public education.

FURTHER READINGS ABOUT THE MATURATIONAL MODEL

Ames, Louise Bates. (1989). *Arnold Gesell: Themes of his work.* New York: Human Sciences Press.

Ames and her colleague Frances Ilg have helped to disseminate Gesell's philosophy; at one time, they wrote a very popular syndicated newspaper column about Gesell's work and its implications for child rearing. In this book, Ames presents a summary of 20 themes in Gesell's research and invites readers to judge and evaluate his contributions.

Benefice, Eric, Garnier, Denis, & Ndiaye, Gnagna. (2001). Assessment of physical activity among rural Senegalese adolescent girls: Influence of age, sexual maturation, and body composition. *Journal of Adolescent Health, 28,* 319–327.

In the study of development, age and maturation can often be looked at as separate and equally important variables. In the research reported in this journal article, the authors examined the relationship between level of habitual physical activity and age, maturational stage, and growth status in a group of adolescent Senegalese girls. They found that the girls' activity levels declined during the course of study, that schoolgirls in the sample were less active than other girls, and that there was a weak but positive correlation between body mass index and activity during the day. During the night, there was a positive correlation between activity and body mass.

De Bellis, Michael D., Keshavan, Matcheri S., Beers, Sue R., Hall, Julie, Frustaci, Karin, Masalehdan, Azadeh, Noll, Jessica, & Boring, Amy M. (2001). Sex differences in brain maturation during childhood and adolescence. *Cerebral Cortex, 11,* 552–557.

Maturation is a fascinating element in the development of any aspect of human behavior. This article reports on a study that examined age-related sex differences in the maturation of the human brain. The researchers collected magnetic resonance imaging (MRI) data on the subjects in their sample along with information on age, gender, handedness, socioeconomic status, and IQ. Their primary conclusion is that there are important age-related sex differences in brain maturational processes.

CHAPTER 4

THE IMPORTANCE OF BIOLOGY

Ethology and Sociobiology

The general theory of evolution . . . assumes that in nature there is a great, unital, continuous and everlasting process of development, and that all natural phenomena without exception, from the motion of the celestial bodies and the fall of the rolling stone up to the growth of the plant and the consciousness of man, are subject to the same great law of causation.

—Ernst Haeckl

Evolution is not a force but a process; not a cause but a law.

—John, Viscount Morley of Blackburn

Man with all his noble qualities . . . with his godlike intellect which has penetrated into the movements and constitution of the solar system . . . still bears in his bodily frame the indelible stamp of his lowly origin.

—Charles Darwin

In Chapter 3, I discussed how Arnold Gesell's training and interest in the biological sciences led him to emphasize the role of biological processes in development. This is best illustrated by his belief that certain fundamental forces encourage development to proceed in a specific direction. The cephalocaudal (or head-to-toe) trend in neurological development is only one example of these forces.

Other scientific theories also stress the role of biological processes in the development of individuals and their cultures. These include ethology and sociobiology (also referred to as **evolutionary psychology**), both of which are relatively new contributors to theorists' ongoing discussion of human development. Our understanding of the biological bases for many human behaviors has grown in recent years, and the theoretical perspectives of ethologists and sociobiologists are becoming increasingly relevant to the study and understanding of human development in general.

Another term for sociobiology is evolutionary psychology.

ETHOLOGY: UNDERSTANDING OUR BIOLOGICAL ROOTS

Ethology can be defined most simply as the study of behaviors that are rooted in humans' evolutionary background and in individuals' biological backgrounds. This definition suggests that we inherit tendencies to behave in certain ways from earlier generations. Within this framework, the transmission of behaviors and traits through genetics plays a significant role in the development of even complex behaviors, such as emotion and thinking. Another implication of this definition is that learning holds a somewhat less important position than biological and "evolutionary" influences.

To date, no one has fully explored the application of the basic principles of ethology to human development. Even so, it is possible to look at development from an ethological point of view, at the relative effects that genetics and evolutionary history might have on the process of development. In effect, this entails looking at how certain patterns of behavior often serve the same functional purposes for humans and animals alike.

The Theoretical Viewpoint of Ethology

The ethological approach may be one of the first ever used by scholars attempting to study behavior systematically; it is at least the earliest documented approach. Most popular theories of human development had their beginnings in the early to middle 20th century, but early evolutionists, such as Charles Darwin and Andrew Wallace, began their work around 1830 in their explorations of distant parts of the world. In that year, Darwin, then 22 years old, set out on a scientific expedition to South America aboard the ship HMS *Beagle.* It is interesting to note that Darwin's grandfather, a well-known poet, had published a poem titled *Zoonomia* in 1794 that included discussion of the concept of evolution; it is possible that his grandfather's thinking had some impact on Darwin's work.

Darwin's extensive observations of the animals of the Galápagos Islands led him to conclude that all living creatures must compete with one another in their natural habitats, and that it is the "natural order" of things that those who cannot compete will eventually die. Likewise, these who survive will adapt to changes around them and eventually pass these adaptive characteristics and behaviors on to their descendants. Darwin formulated these ideas as he was reviewing Thomas Malthus's famous 1798 thesis on population growth. He did not express them in published form, however, until 1859, almost 2 years after he returned from his voyage on the *Beagle.*

It was a very close race between Darwin and Wallace as to whose view of "evolution" would be published first and capture the interest of the scientific world.

As is the case with most great discoveries in all fields of science, Darwin was not alone in his speculation regarding how new species of animals might have originated and how they might survive through various changes demanded by hostile environments. Around the same time Darwin was formulating his theory, Andrew Wallace (working in an entirely different part of the world) developed a theory of evolution as well. In addition, in 1843 Robert Chambers also anticipated some of Darwin's thoughts about the role of evolution.

It was not until 1857 that both Darwin and Wallace formally presented their thoughts about evolution to the London Lineage Society. In 1859, Darwin published his now famous book *On the Origin of Species,* which greatly offended many religionists, who believed that humans did not evolve from animal ancestors but instead were created whole by God in one glorious moment. As you probably recognize, this debate (evolution versus creationism) is alive and well today in classrooms and courtrooms in some parts of the United States.

Evolution: A Definition

Evolution is the complex process through which organisms change in response to the pressures placed on them by a changing environment. Those that cannot change and adapt eventually die as they become increasingly ill equipped to handle the new challenges in their environments. Those that change become stronger and more adaptable. One simple example of this is the way human beings became more erect in physical posture over millions of years: Walking upright allowed humans to defend themselves more effectively against attacks by other humans and animals, to see farther into the distance (and thus better detect threats), and to develop and use tools with their hands.

The process of natural selection, which underlies ethological theory, focuses on how organisms increase their chances for survival through the adaptation of certain characteristics.

——— On the Web ———

You can find out all you may ever want to know about evolution at the Nova/WGBH "Evolution" Web site, at http://www.pbs.org/wgbh/evolution. On this site, which was created in connection with a 7-part series on evolution that was aired on PBS stations in September 2001, you can find out about Darwin and extinction, search through an extensive library on evolution, and even take a look at clips from the series. Videotapes of most of the series episodes are probably available at your public library.

At the heart of the process of evolution are two essential factors. The first of these is that the genes of parents combine at random to produce offspring; this variation is an absolute necessity for evolution to take place. The second factor is that without change, survival is impossible. As for the first, you may remember from your basic course in physiology that the genetic makeup of any organism (or the genotype) is passed from the parent (or parents) to the offspring through reproduction. The genetic makeup of any new organism with two parents, however, is highly dependent on the chance alignment of the parents' genes with one other. There are all kinds of possibilities for eye color, but an offspring's eye color depends on the chance combination of certain genes inherited from the parents.

Genotype refers to a person's genetic configuration; *phenotype* refers to the way a genotype expresses itself physically.

All of the genes (and chromosomes) that control the expression of certain traits, behaviors, and appearance in animals (including humans) are contributed by previous generations in a given family line. With each new offspring, however, there is no way of knowing which combinations of genes will occur. Sometimes genes combine to produce blue eyes or tallness; at other times, they produce mutations that are not adaptive, such as tragic birth defects. One way in which nature controls the transmission of undesirable traits to future generations is by making it impossible for defective organisms to survive long enough to pass the traits on.

It was Darwin's contention that when chance is allowed to operate, and when there is a need for change, the process of **natural selection** (later termed *evolution*) can operate. He based his theory of natural selection on three assumptions, all of which relate to the factors of chance and necessity just noted above. His first assumption was that through reproduction, organisms vary, and this variation is inherited over time. With each successive generation, a new combination of genetic material results. One reason many organisms (such as humans) reproduce sexually (rather than asexually, as do some animals and many plants) is that sexual mating increases the likelihood of such variation's being introduced into the mix.

Darwin's second assumption was that organisms always produce more offspring than can survive. This tends to be less true for humans and other relatively "advanced" species, but we must remember that such species are only a small minority among the vast numbers and types of animals that exist on the earth. Among certain species that have developed sophisticated and complex systems for caring for their young, such as humans, the per parent birthrate is low because the likelihood is very high that the offspring will reach maturity and reproduce themselves.

Finally, Darwin assumed that offspring that vary in ways that allow them to meet the demands of the environment will live to reproduce. In addition, the selection of traits and behaviors that are favorable for the survival of the species will tend to accumulate in these groups.

Note that all these assumptions relate to the organism's having a survival advantage over others—an advantage that can result in the organism's passing its favorable traits on to its offspring, who in turn will modify their behaviors and traits so that new, even more adaptive changes can again be passed on. This process, which Darwin called "descent with modification," is at the heart of evolution and classical ethology. Darwin emphasized the use of the phrase *descent with modification* instead of the term *evolution* for a very good reason: He believed that an organism's place along the phylogenetic ladder should not necessarily be taken as an indication that it is more or less advanced than an organism at some other place along the same ladder. We might like to think of humans as being more "advanced" than other animals, and perhaps in some ways we are. Darwin's point, however, was that we should not equate evolution with social progress.

Another term for evolution is *descent with modification.*

As you may know, since Darwin's time, many people have been resistant to the idea that human beings are an extension in evolutionary terms of earlier animals. Most of these objections have been voiced by people whose religious beliefs have made it difficult, if not impossible, for them to accept that "man" is not something special, unique, and separate from other animals. However, religious belief and the theory of evolution are not necessarily contradictory. For example, one might believe that human behavior is strongly influenced by the evolutionary history of the species, but that human beings hold a position above that of other organisms because of our spiritual and moral capabilities.

Interestingly, scientists in disciplines other than ethology have incorporated the notion that humans (and human behavior) are continuous with nature. One of these was Sigmund Freud (the subject of Chapter 5), who believed that humanity had to endure two "insults" brought on by scientists. The first of these was when scientists showed that the earth (and therefore humankind) is not at the center of the universe. The second was the result of work by scientists like Darwin, when "biological research robbed man of his particular privilege of having been specially created, and relegated him to a descent from the animal world" (Freud, 1920; quoted in Gould, 1977).

Applying Ideas About Ethology and Sociobiology

Having Babies Early and Often

Fortunately, the birthrate among single adolescent women (teenagers) in the United States has decreased over the past 10 years. Unfortunately, it is still very high—about 485,000 babies are born each year to teenagers from 15 to 19 years old (Ventura, Curtin, & Mathews, 2000).

Many different observers have proposed many possible reasons why the rate remains so high, ranging from the presence of health or sex education in the schools to the absence of the same. In any case, a new viewpoint has been added to the discussion—that of the sociobiologist. Daniel Goleman summarizes this viewpoint in a 1991 *New York Times* article headlined "Theory Links Early Puberty to Childhood Stress," in which he reports on the research of Belsky, Steinberg, and Draper (1991).

Remember that most sociobiologists believe that all animals adopt reproductive strategies that maximize the animals' genetic legacy. Thus most human females give birth (more or less) around the time they want to and under the conditions they want to as well. According to the perspective Goleman describes, young women, especially those who live in inner cities and under other conditions of stress, attempt to "boost the chances of having their genes survive into the next generation by choosing earlier sex, earlier motherhood and more children."

These young women, according to the theory that is the subject of Goleman's article, probably experience the onset of puberty (when they can conceive) earlier than do young women who are not under such stress. Indeed, scientists who have tested this proposition have found that in families with unusually high levels of stress, this is the case. For example, Goleman mentions one study that found that girls in families where divorce was present (which was assumed to be a source of stress) tended to reach puberty significantly earlier than girls in less stressed households. Another study he cites showed the same result—girls who lived in homes where there was fighting or divorce between parents reached menarche earlier than did girls in homes without such sources of stress. The more stress girls are under, and the more threatened they feel, the greater the urgency for them to adopt a reproductive strategy that ensures their preservation—that is, giving birth as early as possible and multiple times.

As always, however, there's another point of view. Many developmental psychologists would contend that early puberty is as much a function of when the girl's mother reached puberty (a biological or genetic link) as it is of any other factor. It might also be that girls from single-parent homes become sexually active early because they are unsupervised, or that girls who live in depressed inner cities have few job hopes and believe that the future holds little else for them but motherhood.

In any case, as this brief example shows, the theories and ideas discussed in this chapter have fascinating applications to many different social issues.

Basic Assumptions of Ethology

The most fundamental tenet of ethology as it applies to our understanding of human development is that human behaviors are like biological organs—they are structural parts of a living and developing organism. Just as the structure of the body is passed from one generation to the next through the genetic code, so are certain classes of behaviors and tendencies to act in certain ways. In other words, some classes of behaviors are biologically based; people do not have to learn them formally in order for them to accomplish their intent. Ethologists refer to these classes as *innate behaviors,* of which there are several types: reflexes, taxes, and fixed action patterns. Before I discuss each of these types of innate behaviors below, I offer a definition of innate behavior in general, emphasizing the role such behavior might play in development.

> Ethology differs from sociobiology in that it is concerned with culture as well as with biology.

Innate Behaviors: Definition and Function

Eckhard Hess, an ethologist who has extended the work of other researchers with animals to humans, believes that innate responses are of ultimate importance in the course of development. His primary reason for this belief is the survival value of these responses; for new organisms of any species, survival is the highest order of business. If an organism can't survive as an individual, it can't pass on its "good" qualities, and those qualities will, of course, vanish.

Stated most simply, innate behaviors are behaviors that occur without the individual's having to learn them. Remember from our discussion in Chapter 2 that learning is defined as a change in behavior that occurs as the result of exercise or practice. In general, learning is not the result of any biological process and is highly specific to the individual. Learned behaviors (such as memorizing a list of words) are specific to the individual, whereas innate behaviors are specific to the species. For example, mammals have among their many innate behaviors a sucking reflex that has the obvious survival advantage of providing a means of getting nutrition. Sucking is not a learned behavior; a baby not more than minutes old may exhibit this response when placed at the mother's breast.

> Ethology is the study of those behaviors that are rooted in our evolutionary and biological backgrounds and that seem to serve the same purposes across species.

In many species of birds, an innate response of following the mother (or whatever figure is present when the young bird hatches) is imprinted into the genetic code, thereby ensuring that the offspring will follow the adult. This innate behavior serves the survival advantage of protection from predators, among other things.

Three Kinds of Innate Behaviors

The most basic innate behavior is the **reflex**, which is a simple response to a stimulus. Reflexes account for a great deal of early behavior. Some 25 basic reflexes

Reflexes, or unlearned responses, form the bases for many behaviors.

have been identified in newborn humans, from simple sucking and grasping to a reflex that looks like walking, which is stimulated when the infant is held up and his or her feet are allowed to make contact with a flat surface. An ethologist might contend that many of these early reflexes, some of which are rather primitive, are passed down from our early ancestors, for whom they once served very important functions. For instance, the strong grasp of the newborn child might be a carryover from a time when newborns had to cling tightly to their mothers for survival. Likewise, the aversion that newborns show to having their faces covered may be a reflex that early humans developed to help ensure a free and uninterrupted flow of air to the lungs. The presence of these reflexes, and others, has clear implications for the survival of the species.

Many of the reflexes found in newborns do not last very long. Instead, they are replaced and supplemented by more sophisticated learned behaviors. It seems likely that the reflexes disappear because, after a certain point, they no longer serve any kind of survival or evolutionary function. In fact, the presence of some of the reflexes found in newborns later in early development can be a sign of some kind of neurological imbalance or developmental delay.

Innate behaviors, which are biologically based and not susceptible to the influences of learning, can be divided into three types: reflexes, taxes, and fixed action patterns.

Another kind of innate behavior identified by ethologists is a **taxis**, which is an orienting or locomotory response to some stimulus. Examples of taxes in the animal kingdom would be the postural stance that a dog assumes when it smells another animal and the arched back of a cat when it is threatened. Certain events in an animal's environment prompt it to assume a particular position, whether the animal is seeking food or defending against some threat. Such functions clearly have survival value. One locomotory response in human infants is the way they tend to "cuddle" or fold into the arms of the adults who hold them. A baby who does this might be seeking shelter or anticipating a feeding, but in either case, the behavior is unlearned.

I want to emphasize here that these orienting responses are unlearned; they are transmitted from one generation to the next through genetic material via reproduction. A taxis partially consists of one or more innate reflexes. In some ways, taxes might be described as complex reflexes.

The last of the three types of innate behaviors is the **fixed action pattern**. This is by far the most complex of the three as well as the most significant for our understanding of the application of ethological principles to human behavior. A fixed action pattern can be thought of as a genetically programmed sequence of coordinated motor actions. As you might expect, because such sequences are genetically programmed, they do not vary within a species. One example of a fixed action pattern in dogs is their tendency to continue to hunt, if given the opportunity, even if they are not hungry. In relation to human behavior, fixed action patterns can be represented as very complex sequences of actions, such as nurturing a small child's growth.

Fixed action patterns, whether simple or very complex, form the bases for sets of adaptive coordinated motor actions.

TABLE 4.1 The Components of a Fixed Action Pattern and Their Locations

The Environment	*The Organism*	*Environment-Organism Interaction*
Stimulus 1 ⟶	No response	—
Stimulus 2 ⟶	No response	—
Signed stimulus ⟶	*Innate releasing mechanism (IRM)* ⟶	*Fixed action pattern*
Stimulus 3 ⟶	No response	—

Fixed action patterns are more complex in nature than either reflexes or taxes, and they include additional components. Table 4.1 illustrates the relationship between a resulting fixed action pattern and the other components: the innate releasing mechanism (IRM) and the signed stimulus. In any organism's environment, a host of stimuli are present. Some of these have direct impacts on the organism's behaviors, whereas others do not and are generally ignored. For example, you stop your car at a red light, but you probably ignore the colors of the cars that pass by while you wait for the light to change. An infant may ignore the comings and goings of other children in the room yet may become quite agitated when his or her mother leaves, even for a moment.

A stimulus such as a parent's withdrawal may elicit a response of despair or anxiety in an infant. Stimuli that have such "power" or significance are called **signed stimuli**, so named because they have valences attached to them that give them a value to the organism that other stimuli do not have. There are also stimuli that have such power as a result of learning rather than as a result of some biological or evolutionary perspective. A signed stimulus in turn activates an **innate releasing mechanism** that initiates a fixed action pattern. In Table 4.1, you can see that only one of the four stimuli in the environment has the "power" to set off an IRM, which in turn stimulates some fixed action pattern.

Konrad Lorenz, one of the most famous of all ethologists, believed that one such IRM, or "trigger," is common across a wide range of animals (further illustrating the commonality of form and function that many species share): the "babyish" appearance that characterizes many animals during early development. No doubt you've observed that many people find the young of any species much more attractive (much "cuter") than the adults of the same species. Have you ever noticed how hard it is to walk past a new puppy without stopping to pet it?

Lorenz (1965) took this idea a step further, speculating, based on the characteristics of dolls, that the toy industry tries to attract adults rather than children to

An innate releasing mechanism initiates a fixed action pattern, or a biologically based set of behaviors that is social in nature.

A signed stimulus acts as a trigger that activates an innate releasing mechanism, which in turn produces a pattern of motor behaviors.

its products. After all, the parents make the purchases, not the children. Lorenz asserted that some of the physical characteristics that toy makers try to incorporate into the design of a doll to make it attractive to adults are "a relatively large head, predominance of brain capsule, large and low lying eyes, bulging cheek region, short thick extremities, a springy elastic consistency, and clumsy movements" (quoted in Gould, 1980, p. 105). It's no surprise that this description also applies to the human baby. Babies need the attention and care of adults to survive, so they exhibit features that make them attractive to adults.

In an essay titled "A Biological Homage to Mickey Mouse," Harvard scientist Stephen Jay Gould (1980) presents a humorous but accurate application of this idea. He shows how over the course of three decades, Mickey Mouse's features became increasingly juvenile. Gould measured the characteristics listed above on drawings of Mickey that were produced over a 30-year period. In all cases, from one year to the next, head size, eye size, and the size of the cranium became larger. In effect, Mickey came more and more to resemble a younger and younger child. Such "progressive juvenilization," as Gould terms it, is called *neoteny*. Gould applies this argument to human development as well. Through our own evolution, juvenile characteristics have become enhanced in adults, as evidenced by the fact that our ancestors had the more "adult" features of protruding jaws and small craniums. In Hollywood movies, aliens who are members of advanced civilizations (such as those in *Close Encounters of the Third Kind*) are often depicted as large-headed and bald, physically much like the newborns of our species.

It is important to remember that the innate releasing mechanism is internal to the organism; it acts almost as a switch that is activated by the presence of a signed stimulus. If the signed stimulus is not there, the IRM will not be activated, and the fixed action pattern will not occur. Ethologists would say that if a signed stimulus is not present, it is probably because it is not necessary.

Let's extend a bit further our example about the infant who is separated from his or her mother. The slightest presence of a signed stimulus, or provocation, probably does not result in a fixed action pattern. For example, if the mother simply leaves the room but the baby can still hear her voice, the mother's absence alone might not be sufficient for the baby to begin crying.

In addition, innate releasing mechanisms become operative only under certain conditions involving a combination of several factors. Ethologists believe that one of these conditions is the presence of sufficient **action-specific energy**, which is much like the notion of "readiness" discussed in earlier chapters. The more action-specific energy a signed stimulus has, the easier it is for the stimulus to elicit or release the corresponding fixed action pattern through the IRM. Ethologists have found that the amount of action-specific energy is related to the length of time since the last response, with a longer time lag resulting in more action-specific energy to activate the IRM and, in turn, the fixed action pattern.

A certain level of action-specific energy must be present for a stimulus to be powerful enough to trigger an innate releasing mechanism, which in turn leads to a fixed action pattern.

Another example of a fixed action pattern is a parent's response to a distressed child. In the everyday course of parent-child interactions, both parent and child are exposed to many stimuli that they do not attend to because the stimuli hold no inherent value for them. For example, although what the baby is doing in the playpen might be pleasant to watch, the child's mother might feel perfectly comfortable attending to a letter or paying the bills instead. In this case, the child's playing alone holds no value as a stimulus for the mother. The child's behavior is only one of many stimuli, all of which may have similar levels of meaning at that moment in time.

Let's assume, however, that the child gets a sharp pain from an earache and begins to scream. Most parents would respond quickly to such a stimulus, dropping whatever they are doing to rush to the child and try to find out what the problem is. In this example, the signed stimulus is the scream from the child, which "sets off" whatever innate releasing mechanism operates for that kind of parental behavior. This in turn eventually results in a pattern of behavior that we might call "caring," in which the parent begins a routine of aspirin, calling the pediatrician, and so on. The complex set of behaviors that began with the child's shriek of pain is a fixed action pattern. The content of the pattern is not fixed by evolution or biology, but these factors determine when and how the pattern is activated.

Another example illustrates how fixed action patterns are species specific rather than specific to individuals. At parks and playgrounds, adults will frequently come to the aid of any children, not just their own, who are injured or in some other kind of trouble. That is, like other animals, human adults tend to "adopt" any of the young of their species who need help. Also, when young children in a crowd are seeking security, they often attach themselves quite securely to the legs or hands of adults they don't know.

> Fixed action patterns are species specific and very selective for particular adaptive behaviors.

Not all signed stimuli and fixed action patterns are related to some kind of stress on the part of parent or child. The ethological perspective explains the origins of many parenting behaviors in terms of fixed action patterns. For example, the young child's smile attracts the attention of adults, who in turn provide that child with attention and nurturance. Similarly, the parent who encourages the "almost talker" to keep trying, telling the child how nice his or her attempts at speaking sound, might also be playing the role of encouraging the kinds of behaviors that are essential for the child's later adaptation and survival.

The Ethogram: Looking at Behavior in a Natural Setting

Scientists who study development always try to answer their research questions by using methods that reflect some of the basic assumptions of their theoretical perspectives. One of ethologists' basic goals is to understand the influence of environmental factors on genetically based behaviors. They study such behaviors by observing their subjects, for the most part, in "natural" settings rather than in laboratory experiments. This means that if ethologists are interested in how families adapt to stress, they are likely to observe families under actual stressful situations rather than in laboratory settings within which the researchers have set up hypothetical situations. Ethologists aim to establish the ecological validity of the behaviors they study by observing those behaviors in natural settings. In other words, by observing behaviors as they occur in natural settings, ethologists can best understand the flow of natural events that surround the adjustments that their subjects need to make.

This concept is related to one of the basic assumptions discussed earlier: Although behavior is genetically based, all behaviors take place within certain environmental contexts. One cannot appreciate the significance of a given behavior without understanding the context or setting in which it occurs. Remember, from the ethological perspective, the selective pressures of the environment, not individuals' genetic makeup, are responsible for changes in behavior. Without such pressures for change, no modification of internal or external structures would be possible, and, theoretically, the species would perish.

The primary tool that ethologists use in their study of behavior is the **ethogram**, an inventory or description that the researcher creates while recording an observed organism's behavior. An ethogram is usually organized by behaviors over a specific number of time periods. The rationale for using such an inventory lies in the nature of ethology. If we agree that the environment exerts selective pressures that help to shape behaviors, then the logical place for us to look to understand the origins and modifications of behaviors is in the organism's natural surroundings. Figure 4.1 provides an example of the beginnings of an ethogram for an adolescent male observed over a 24-hour period. Many more behaviors would be explicitly defined in a full ethogram; this figure is intended only to illustrate how an ethogram is typically organized and visually presented.

> The primary tool that ethologists use in their study of behavior is the ethogram.

Ethologists who are studying the behaviors of animals across different species find ethograms to be especially valuable tools. By examining the ethograms created during their observations, such ethologists can often identify "links" between and across species based on behaviors and the assumptions that at least some of the behaviors serve the same functions and that the species observed share some (no matter how little) genetic similarity.

Ethology and Attachment

There is no question that scholars are just beginning to apply the various principles of ethology to the understanding of human development. However, a major part of the conceptual and empirical work in at least one area of human development research is grounded in some of the ideas and methods related to ethology

Sample Data Sheet

Species: Human being (adolescent)   *Observers:* DeRuk and Nash

Date: 23 October 2002   *Time*: 8:00-18:00

Conditions: At various locations in and around home and school

Comments: Normal adolescent male, aged 15

Behavior Category

Time	School Work	Resting	Eating
8–9	X		
9–10	X		
10–11	X		
11–12			X
12–1	X		
1–2	X		
2–3	X		
3–4	X		
4–5		X	
5–6			X

FIGURE 4.1   The Beginnings of an Ethogram for an Adolescent Male

discussed above. This is the study of **attachment** between human infants and their caretakers.

The person who is most responsible for relating ethology and the issue of attachment is John Bowlby, who, in a 1958 article titled "The Nature of the Child's Tie to His Mother," first discussed contemporary attachment theory within an ethological framework. In this work as well as in his later extensive writings, Bowlby places great emphasis on the biological functions of behavior and contends that certain behaviors are present because they offer definite survival advantages. For Bowlby, the primary function of the complex system of behaviors that we call attachment is to protect infants from harm while they are nurtured toward adulthood (where they can then reproduce and be responsible for the next generation).

It is important to understand that Bowlby does not believe that human infants are genetically predisposed to becoming attached to particular persons. Rather, the processes of learning and experiences that take place shortly after an infant's birth determine to whom that infant will form an attachment. This is not unlike the "imprinting" that Lorenz observed in ducklings, which followed him rather than their mother if he was the first animal they saw during some critical or sensitive period shortly after they hatched. In much the same way, human babies might

The concept of attachment may be the best example of the application of ethology to human behavior and the ways in which innate behaviors are modified by environmental influences.

imprint by following the movements of their caretakers with their eyes, as they are not yet equipped to follow by walking.

The Phases of Attachment

Over the years, Bowlby has developed a model of attachment that includes four separate phases. The first of these, the *preattachment stage,* takes place during the first few weeks of life and is characterized by the infant's readiness to respond to stimuli produced by other members of the species. At this stage, the infant is ready to react to any "friendly" or inviting stimulus, regardless of its origins. It appears that some inborn mechanism helps to orient the infant to where and how he or she should react in the presence of a potential caregiver. In effect, eye following, noises, and even early precursors of smiling are all efforts on the infant's part to encourage and increase proximity and contact between the child and his or her caregiver, usually the mother. These behaviors are somewhat gross in nature, and they are not directed toward any one person in particular.

With time, the infant's behavior becomes more discriminative, and the second phase, *attachment in the making,* begins. During this phase, which starts after the first month of life and lasts well into the second 6 months, the infant forms an attachment to some specific figure. The specificity of responses in this phase is demonstrated by the infant's smiling more in the presence of the "target" of attachment (for example, the mother) and smiling significantly less in the presence of others.

The next phase that Bowlby describes is that of *clear-cut attachment,* which begins when the infant can walk. This greatly increased mobility allows the child to distance him- or herself when necessary from the target of attachment, yet the child is able to maintain a mental image of that person when not in the person's presence. (This ability to form a mental image is one of the changes in cognitive skills that take place in the developing child; I discuss cognitive developmental theory in Chapters 9 and 10.) By this stage, the child has developed a diverse array of well-integrated and directed attachment behaviors.

The last phase of attachment, which takes place during the child's second year, is the *goal-corrected partnership.* In this stage, the child begins to understand the attachment target's behaviors more fully and consequently adjusts to those behaviors, initiating attempts to influence what the target does. From an ethological standpoint, the child employs his or her increased physical and cognitive competence to try to anticipate the caregiver's behavior in order to maximize the contact and nurturance the child receives.

By definition, ethology takes into consideration a multitude of factors that may influence behavior, and in the ethological approach—perhaps more than in any other theoretical approach—the influences of hereditary and environmental factors are understood to be mixed. Unlike many other approaches, ethology does not take the extreme view that one or the other of these forces is dominant; rather, it asserts that heredity and environment have mutual impacts on the development of the organism. For this reason, it is likely that some of the most exciting discoveries yet to be made about human behavior will come out of this theoretical framework.

Studying Attachment

As noted above, one of the ethologist's most useful tools is the ethogram, a running description of an observed subject's behavior in as "natural" or uncontrived a setting as possible. I've also discussed above the study of attachment (and particularly the work of John Bowlby), which represents the most widely applied use of ethological principles in the field of human development. One researcher who has studied attachment extensively within an ethological framework, Mary D. S. Ainsworth (1973), developed a technique for studying attachment (and the effects of separation) called the **Strange Situation Procedure**, in which a baby, the baby's parent (traditionally the mother), and a stranger (a confederate or colleague of the psychologist using the procedure to study attachment) all interact in a highly structured setting.

Ainsworth's Strange Situation Procedure is used to explore how attached children are to their parents.

The Strange Situation Procedure is divided into eight episodes that take place over a 22-minute period (Episode 1 takes about a minute, and all other episodes are 3 minutes long). Before the procedure begins, the baby's mother is given complete instructions concerning how she should behave and is informed about how the stranger in the procedure will behave.

- In Episode 1, the baby and mother are shown the experimental room, which is filled with toys and has places for the mother to sit and for the baby to play.
- In Episode 2, the baby and the mother are alone together in the experimental room. The mother responds to the baby's requests for interaction, but she may not initiate any on her own.
- In Episode 3, a stranger is introduced into the room with the baby and mother. The stranger enters the room, sits quietly for 1 minute, talks to the mother for 1 minute, then interacts with the baby for 1 minute.
- In Episode 4, the mother leaves the room. The stranger, who is still in the room, watches the baby and interacts with him or her if the baby indicates an interest. If the baby cries, the stranger tries to comfort him or her. This episode is stopped if the baby cries hard for 1 minute or if the mother requests that it be stopped. At the end of this episode, the stranger leaves the room.
- In Episode 5, the mother calls the baby from outside the room and then comes back into the room. The mother comforts the baby if necessary and

then sits in the room. Again, she is responsive toward the baby but may not initiate any interaction.

- In Episode 6, the mother again leaves the room and the baby is alone. If the baby becomes very distressed, or if the mother requests it, this episode is ended.
- In Episode 7, with the mother still out of the room, the stranger returns and sits in the room with the baby. Again, the stranger interacts with the baby only if the baby initiates some kind of interaction. If the baby is very upset, the episode is ended.
- In Episode 8, the procedure is the same as that in Episode 5.

What can a researcher learn about attachment and separation by watching a mother and child go through this series of episodes? Most directly, the Strange Situation Procedure allows the researcher to view the child under a set of conditions in which the degree of security of attachment varies a great deal. By observing the child's behavior under varying conditions, the researcher can learn what kinds of attachment behaviors accompany particular kinds of environmental conditions for that child. This in turn can shed some light on the nature of attachment as it relates to familiar and unfamiliar surroundings.

The researcher can then test a variety of factors as to their relationships to or effects on attachment (measured in a variety of ways at different times across the life span) on current or later outcomes. For example, recent studies have included examinations of the relationship between attachment and compliance in toddlers (van der Mark, Bakermans-Kranenburg, & van Ijzendoorn, 2002); the relationships among attachment styles, interpersonal trust, and the marital attitudes of college students (Brown, 2002); and the relationship between attachment and coping with chronic disease (Schmidt, Nachtigall, Wuethrich-Martone, & Strauss, 2002).

SOCIOBIOLOGY: GENES AND DEVELOPMENT

Sociobiology focuses on genes as the direct causes of human behavior.

In the discussion above, I have noted that within the ethological perspective, behavior is seen as a product of the interaction between heredity and environment. Ethologists emphasize the influence of ecological factors on genetically based behaviors. That is, although genetic endowment takes precedence, environmental factors and selective pressures to change are critical influences as well. In this section, I discuss the relatively recent extension of some of the principles of ethology into the new discipline of **sociobiology**. A major difference between ethology and sociobiology is that sociobiologists view all aspects of development as being controlled and caused by specific genes;

unlike ethologists, they place very little importance on factors that originate outside the organism.

To date, few studies have attempted to apply sociobiological principles to human behavior. Primarily for this reason, we need to keep in mind the limitations of the sociobiological perspective even as we appreciate the suggestions it offers for new, and perhaps better, ways of understanding development.

The Theoretical Viewpoint of Sociobiology

As I have noted previously, one of the ongoing arguments in the field of human development concerns whether we are distinct and separate from our primate ancestors (such as great apes) or simply a continuation or extension of them, only at a more "advanced" level. Most ethologists would agree that our ancestors contribute a great deal to our current repertoire of biological and psychological potentialities. Sociobiologists would agree with this as well, but would take this argument one step further, into the realm of biological and psychological determinism.

> Sociobiology can be defined as the systematic study of the biological basis of social behavior.

Sociobiologists contend that the continuity between an individual's evolutionary status and that of his or her immediate and more distant genetic ancestors is almost unbroken. This means that genetic endowment is paramount in relation to behavior. It also means that humans are not as morally and spiritually unique among animals as some people would like to think. In fact, most sociobiologists believe that even humankind's prized attribute of altruism (our capacity for self-sacrifice) has a genetic basis.

Sociobiology has been popularly defined as "the systematic study of the biological basis of all social behavior" (Wilson, 1975, p. 4), where social behavior is defined as the interaction between organisms. Ardent sociobiologists have no reservations about considering even the most complex of human behaviors, such as the selection of a spouse or the rearing of children, as having a biological basis. They assert that such complex behaviors are the outcome of millions of years of evolutionary "progress," do not result from learning, and are highly similar in form and function to the same categories of behaviors in other animals.

> Sociobiologists have a much more deterministic view of human behavior than do ethologists.

The task of the sociobiologist is to demonstrate, based on observation of the social acts of animals, how particular actions help the developing organism to adapt to its environment. More specifically, sociobiologists assert that an organism's "prime directive" is to develop patterns that contribute to the successful reproduction of its species, often at any cost to the parent generation. That is, the most important task for the organism is the evolutionary well-being of its species, which requires the sharing of the organism's own personal genetic legacy; then, an important but secondary element is the organism's sharing of the culture that supports that legacy. For example, it is not uncommon in the animal world for parents to give up food and shelter themselves in order to provide these things for their young; at times, parents literally die to protect their offspring. For sociobiologists, all such sacrifices represent the animals' efforts to increase their species' chances of survival by ensuring that the young prosper and reproduce.

In terms of human behaviors, we can find an example of such ultimate sacrifice in traditional Eskimo culture. Among Eskimos today, grandparents retain a position of honor and respect that is based in large part on the legendary sacrifices made by grandparents in the past for the younger members of their families. According to Eskimo tradition, long ago, when an Eskimo family had to find a new home but did not have sufficient supplies of food to carry all family members through to the journey's end, the grandparents would forgo their share, stay behind, and quietly die. A sociobiological interpretation of this behavior would be that the grandparents, who had already lived full and rewarding lives, made the only choice they could. They made this sacrifice on an individual level for the good of the entire tribe, to ensure that the species (and the gene pool) continued to survive. Further, sociobiologists would argue that the grandparents were motivated to make their sacrifice not by any understanding that grandparents in the future would be revered members of Eskimo society, but by their genetic inheritance.

> Sociobiology, or evolutionary psychology, emphasizes the maintenance of an individual's genetic legacy.

The major problem with this argument, however, is that it is impossible to test adequately, let alone prove. We cannot know whether people sacrifice certain things—even their lives—under specific conditions because of some genetic predisposition or because the capacity for sacrifice is learned or culturally acquired. The only way to settle this question would be to manipulate an individual's genetic potential and observe the outcomes in future generations. We might be able to do this with fruit flies in the laboratory, but we certainly can't do it with humans. Perhaps we will have the technical capability to accomplish such manipulation with humans in the future, but today we do not, nor do we have ethical and social mechanisms in place to deal with such experimentation. For the moment, however, let's assume that we can accept the argument that behavior is under the control of genetic mechanisms and continue our examination of sociobiology by looking at the idea of how behavior begins.

The Causes of Behavior

Sociobiologists divide the events that cause, or precipitate, animal behaviors (including human behaviors, of course) into two general categories: first-level

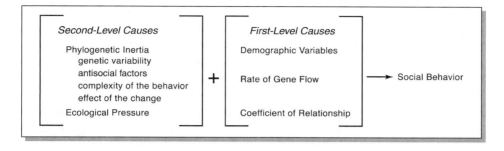

FIGURE 4.2   First- and Second-Level Causes of Behavior

causes and second-level causes. Figure 4.2 shows the relationship between these two kinds of causes and the eventual expression of social behaviors. *Second-level causes,* which are further removed from actual behaviors (or less directly influential) than are first-level causes, consist of phylogenetic inertia and ecological pressure (more about these in a moment). These in turn influence *first-level causes,* which are identified as demographic variables, the rate of gene flow, and the coefficient of relationship (more about these in a moment as well). Together, first- and second-level causes result in what we generally know as social behaviors, which, of course, lead up to the reproduction and sharing of the most adaptive genes. Both these categories of causes are somewhat "removed," or indirect, influences on behavior.

First-level causes are, however, more immediate and more traceable than second-level causes—more closely related to, and perhaps more clearly a cause of, the specific behavior or pattern of behavior under consideration. Because the process begins with second-level behaviors, that's where I begin this discussion.

> According to sociobiologists, the events that underlie all behavior can be divided into two general categories: first-level causes and second-level causes.

Second-Level Causes of Behavior

The concept of **phylogenetic inertia** stems from the strong natural science orientation of sociobiology. As you may remember from your studies in physical science, inertia is resistance to change. Phylogenetic inertia can be defined as the tendency to remain genetically unchanged. An organism's level of phylogenetic inertia determines the ease with which that organism's genetic endowment and tendencies might be alterable. Where phylogenetic inertia is high, change is difficult to accomplish.

Four factors determine the degree of phylogenetic inertia associated with any pattern of behavior (see Figure 4.2). The first of these is the *genetic variability* that

> Second-level causes of behavior are phylogenetic inertia and ecological pressure; first-level causes are demographic variables, rate of gene flow, and coefficient of relationship.

exists in the species. The greater the variability (with an accompanying high level of opportunity for new combinations of genes to take place), the lower the inertia or resistance to change on the part of the organism. This also means that there is an increased likelihood of the organism's generating new and more adaptive behaviors, a very important outcome if species success is to be assured. On the other hand, if there is very little variability, the level of inertia is likely to be quite high. In sum, an opportunity to increase the gene pool decreases phylogenetic inertia, because when new material is introduced, the likelihood of change increases.

The degree of phylogenetic inertia in any pattern of behavior is determined by genetic variability, antisocial factors, complexity of the behavior, and the effect of change on other behaviors.

The second determinant of the degree of phylogenetic inertia is the presence of *antisocial factors,* or anything that encourages the species (as represented by the individual) to isolate itself. When antisocial factors are present, the likelihood of increased genetic variability goes down (because the individual has fewer potential partners to choose from), phylogenetic inertia increases, and chances for adaptive changes are reduced. This is clearly an argument against inbreeding, which not only exaggerates the recessive and often nonadaptive traits and characteristics of a species, but minimizes the chances for genetic variability. A sociobiologist would argue that our social taboos against incest have their origins in this need to avoid isolating individuals from sources of potential variation.

------ **On the Web** ------

An essential part of any discussion of the impacts genes might have on behavior is an exploration of the human genome. The Human Genome Project, which is funded by the U.S. government, provides an introduction to human genome research on its Web site at http: //www.ornl.gov/Tech Resources/Human_Genome/home.html. Features of the site include a primer on the project itself, lots of references, and links to literature about many ethical and social issues related to the research being conducted.

The third factor that determines the degree of phylogenetic inertia is the *complexity of the behavior.* The more elaborate the behavior, the more component parts it is likely to have, and the more component parts there are, the higher the level of inertia needed to keep these parts together and functioning, and hence the more difficult the behavior may be to change. We can see how this works by looking at the complex human behavior of parenting, which consists of a great number of highly interrelated behaviors. A sociobiologist would assert that the reason parents find it difficult to change their parenting practices (as any parent will tell you is the case) is the high level of phylogenetic inertia associated with such complex behaviors.

The last factor determining the degree of phylogenetic inertia is the *effect of the change* in behavior on other traits and characteristics. As I've just noted, if a behavior is complex, the phylogenetic inertia is high—that is, it takes a major effort to alter the behavior. In addition, when one part of a complex system is altered, other parts of the system will probably be altered as well. The more that a change in one part of the system results in changes in other parts of the system, the greater the level of phylogenetic inertia.

The second of the two kinds of second-level causes of behavior is **ecological pressure**, which is defined as aspects of the environment that encourage the organism to change. For the sociobiologist, ecological pressure represents the nurture side of the nature/nurture debate. As one might expect, some ecological or environmental events have no impacts on the social evolution of animals, whereas others are very important. For example, one of the most significant forms of ecological pressure is the presence of predators, because predators threaten the animal's existence and therefore its ability to pass on its most adaptive genes.

> The relationship between phylogenetic inertia and ecological pressure determines the ease with which behavior will change.

Given this pressure, all prey animals have evolved sophisticated means of defending themselves against predators. For example, a primary predator of the brown sparrow is the hawk, which attacks these small birds in flight. When a hawk is flying below a flock of sparrows and the sparrows are not threatened, the sparrows usually fly in a loose grouping. When a hawk is above a flock of sparrows, however, and in position to strike, the sparrows fly close together in a tightly knit group. The hawk is much less likely to attack when the sparrows fly this way, because in trying to penetrate the group it risks injuring vulnerable parts of its body. Consequently, the sparrows' likelihood of survival increases, as does their opportunity to pass on their genetic endowment to a subsequent generation.

Another major source of ecological pressure is the availability of food. Most directly, it is impossible for a species to survive when suitable food is not available. In such a situation, animals are forced to move to new locations in search of nourishment. For example, many African animals move seasonally from location to location, following the growth of certain types of plants on which they feed. Even today, some human groups follow such nomadic herds of animals, relying on the animals for food and other necessities, such as hides for clothing. It is only relatively recently in our history that humans have learned how to make food grow in particular places (sometimes in spite of hostile environmental conditions) and so have been able to settle in those places, making them home.

> Ecological pressure can have significant impacts on the social behavior of humans.

Applying Ideas About Ethology and Sociobiology

Forever Babies

Many changes have taken place on our planet over the past million years or so, and evolution has brought humans a very long way in distinguishing us from other animals: We have language; we create and use tools very effectively (although some other animals do as well); we have much larger craniums, allowing for much larger brains and thus greater intelligence (we at least have the capacity to be smarter than other animals); and (like some other animals) we organize ourselves into groups (such strength in numbers means the young have better odds for survival).

Probably the most fascinating change that has taken place in the human species due to ecological pressure, and the one most applicable to the discussion of sociobiology, is the transition from a tree-based existence to a land-based one. When our ancestors first came down from the trees, they walked on all fours; later, they relied increasingly on their hind legs, eventually assuming an upright posture. Some sociobiologists believe that ecological pressure caused our predecessors to leave their loftier homes to have better access to food, but it is also the case that one of the consequences of a more upright posture is a larger and stronger pelvis, which helps to support the viscera and upper body. A larger pelvis also allowed for another dramatic change in human evolution: the easier delivery of the newborn, with less potential for damage to the infant from coming through a too-small birth canal.

As our ancestors' heads became larger over time (as they developed bigger brains), even more adaptive changes occurred in the structure of female bodies to compensate. In addition, in order for females to survive giving birth, newborns' heads had to be relatively soft and malleable, so that they could pass through the birth canal without causing permanent damage. This means that humans are born in a relatively immature state, which results in the longer period of socialization that human infants need, in comparison with other animals, before they are ready to go out into the world and fend for themselves. Human infants are more plastic, or malleable, than the newborns of other species, and so are better able to adapt to the changing demands of their environments. Also, because human babies are born relatively immature and undergo a long period of socialization before they are ready to be on their own, they are highly influenced by their cultural environments. In addition, their extended period of socialization results in better preparation for, and thus greater chances of, survival and successful reproduction.

Human babies are the most immature of any species. From one end of the phylogenetic scale to the other—that is, from single-cell animals such as amoebae to multicell creatures such as humans—the young at birth are increasingly different from their adult forms. For example, newly hatched ants are ready to go and fend for themselves, calves take some time to get up and running, and human babies remain babies for a very long period, especially relative to their expected life span.

Compared with other species, humans have fewer offspring and give birth less often. Humans also invest more than other species in the offspring they have, providing for their children so that they can reach maturity and ensure their genetic legacy. Thus childhood is both biologically and socially extended—for as long it takes to make sure that children learn the demands of their culture and adapt successfully.

Finally, as E. O. Wilson (1975), a prominent sociobiologist, concludes, "manipulation of the physical environment is the ultimate adaptation." When animals manipulate their environment, it is because they seek to control it, and, as Wilson notes, once animals control their environment, the indefinite survival of their species is almost assured. Humans have made tremendous gains in controlling their environment in a very short period in relation to the evolutionary clock. Once our ancestors discovered the use of tools (softening animal skins by beating them with bones, for instance), they were, in a sense, on their way.

The Relationship Between Phylogenetic Inertia and Ecological Pressure

Both phylogenetic inertia and ecological pressure can be either high or low. Figure 4.3 shows the various impacts that different combinations in the levels of these causes of behavior might have on the development of social behaviors. When ecological pressure is low (that is, when there is little pressure or incentive to change), it is unlikely that the organism will change. When phylogenetic inertia is high, there is increased resistance in the organism to any kind of genetic alteration.

Take, for example, how parents provide nourishment for their young. If there is an abundance of food in the local environment and isolation from related species (that is, low ecological pressure and no phylogenetic inertia), there is not much "biological" incentive to change feeding behavior. On the other hand, if there is opportunity for mating with other animals and thus increasing the diversity of the gene pool (that is, phylogenetic inertia is low) and stores of food have been eliminated through some natural accident, such as an increase in predators (that is, ecological pressure is high), then change in feeding behavior is much more likely to occur. It is difficult to predict what would occur if both ecological pressure and phylogenetic inertia were high. This combination of circumstances would probably result in no change, given the strong biological directive to resist genetic alteration.

> Ecological pressure and phylogenetic inertia work together to increase or decrease the likelihood that a behavior will occur.

First-Level Causes of Behavior

First-level causes of behavior are no more or less important than second-level causes, but they are closer to, or less removed from, the actual behavior. That is, if we are looking for a cause of behavior that is clearly traceable to the behavior itself, the likely candidates would be among the three first-level causes (see Figure 4.3).

The *demographic variables* (or characteristics) of the population are considered to be one first-level cause. Among these variables are birthrate, death rate, and population size. In combination, these three factors directly reflect "quality" of life. This is illustrated by the findings of a good deal of research with animals that has examined the effects of overcrowding. In one set of experiments conducted at the National

| | Phylogenetic Inertia | |
	Low	High
Low **Ecological Pressure**	Low likelihood of change	Very significant resistance to change
High	High likelihood of change	Significant resistance to change

FIGURE 4.3 The Relationship Between Phylogenetic Inertia and Ecological Pressure

Institute of Mental Health, white mice lived in their own "city," where they were allowed to reproduce and socialize without interference. As the population increased, the researchers observed a corresponding increase in aberrant social behaviors. Death rates increased as well, and some of the newborn mice were genetically less well equipped than those of previous generations. That is, they were more susceptible to disease and stress, and hence passed on less adaptive traits when they reached adulthood. Conditions such as those in this mouse "city" are highly conducive to some kind of change in social behavior, for otherwise the animals have no direction in which to grow but toward their own extinction (in such a limited society, anyway).

Another first-level cause of behavior is the *rate of gene flow,* or the rate at which genes from genetically different individuals are introduced into or shared with a new population. The rate of gene flow has a great deal to do with how quickly animals can adapt their behavior to a change in the environment. When the rate of the introduction of new genes is slow, change is much less likely than when the rate is high. Gene flow is one of the most direct ways in which behavior becomes adaptive, because genetic changes can take place within relatively few generations. A high rate of gene flow is almost an artificial way of speeding up the process of natural selection, which can take many generations and, often, thousands of years.

The third first-level cause of behavior is the degree of genetic similarity that exists within species as a function of relatedness, or the *coefficient of relationship.* The more genetically similar groups are to one another, the higher this coefficient is. The higher the coefficient, the more likely the social behavior directed by a set

First-level causes of behavior are closer to, or less removed from, the actual behavior than are second-level causes.

of genes is to be stable within that species. Finally, the more stable the behavior is, the less likely it is to change as a function of other factors. This stability might be encouraged, because it ensures the continuity of presumably adaptive behaviors. However, species that share their own genes (and hence have a high coefficient of relationship) must be careful of the consequences of inbreeding, as discussed earlier. Although inbreeding does help to ensure stability, it also increases the likelihood of the expression of maladaptive traits.

It is important to remember that none of the first-level causes operates in isolation. Like the various elements that make up the second-level causes of behavior, the three first-level causes always operate in conjunction with one another.

Applying Sociobiology to Human Development

For sociobiologists, human behavior is a reflection of first- and second-level causes. These theorists assert that, in effect, human beings are an extension of the animal kingdom, governed by the same rules and principles. This viewpoint has made sociobiologists' attempts to apply their theory to human behavior controversial, because many people feel that human beings are distinct from other animals not only spiritually and intellectually, but biologically. Many people are also offended when sociobiologists reduce humans' "sophisticated" behaviors to simple biological acts. For example, a sociobiologist might say that a person who moves to a new city for a better job is comparable to a predatory animal that follows a group of animals and waits for a chance to single one out for the kill. Many people would argue against this analogy, but a sociobiologist would argue that both animals are attempting to improve their chances for survival.

The primary argument that sociobiologists use to substantiate their claims is that of universality: The same behaviors are found among both humans and other primates, so these behaviors must be related to genetics. The problem with this logic is that the same outcomes do not always result from the same cause. Also, as some have put it, humans are animals, but that does not mean we are nothing but animals.

Most of the above discussion of sociobiology points to one conclusion: Everything an animal does, whether fighting off a predator or foraging for food, is done in service of the animal's goal of reproducing itself. One of the major functions within this reproductive purpose is that of parenting. David Barash (1977) discusses parenting within a sociobiological framework, defining "parental investment" as behaviors that increase the likelihood of survival of and reproduction by offspring at the cost of investment in other offspring. According to Barash's logic, parents who have their first child later in life (at, say, age 40) rather than earlier (at, say, age 20) should invest more in their offspring, because they have fewer years left in which they will be biologically suited for reproduction. Also, when new offspring arrive, they take away resources from the first offspring, who had previously been the one "hope for the future." Perhaps this concept of parental investment accounts in part for the particularly strong emotional attachments parents typically have to their firstborn children and explains why, in general, parents are much less absorbed in every nuance of their later children's childhoods. It also may relate to significant differences among children in families as a function of birth order, explaining why, compared with later-born children, firstborns are usually higher achievers and more successful in their lives.

The sociobiological viewpoint has also been applied to the area of parent-child interaction and conflict. Children, like their parents, seek to maximize their level of fitness and potential to reproduce. Given this goal, it follows that children would demand of their parents a maximum level of investment in the children, which would increase the competition for resources. From this perspective, we might expect that infants would not be easily weaned from their mothers, or that children would not easily accept parental encouragement of their independence. In addition, we might conceive of sibling rivalry as a manifestation of competition for available resources.

Sociobiology, like ethology, is a relatively new and untried discipline as it applies to human behavior. Many people, however, believe that the next advances we will see in humankind's understanding of the development of human behavior will be preceded by increased understanding of biological and psychobiological processes. Sociobiologists have a great deal of room for future research and for more fascinating speculation about the nature of development.

WEB SITES OF INTEREST

- *The Origin of Species,* 6th ed., by Charles Darwin, at http://www.literature. org/authors/darwin-charles/the-origin-of-species-6th-edition: Read the original! This edition of Darwin's classic volume is brought to you by the Online Literature Library, which is sponsored by Knowledge Matters, Ltd.
- "Against Sociobiology," by Tom Bethell, at http://www.firstthings.com/ftissues/ ft0101/articles/bethell.html: In this essay, which appears in the online version of the journal *First Things,* Bethell presents some of the arguments against sociobiology. He also discusses some of the main characters in the history of sociobiology, including Edward Wilson and Richard C. Lewontin.
- Applied Ethology, at http://www.usask.ca/wcvm/herdmed/applied-ethology: This Web site, which is maintained by the Western College of Veterinary Medicine at the University of Saskatchewan, offers links to a significant collection of resources about ethology, including archived articles and a discussion list.

FURTHER READINGS
ABOUT BIOLOGICAL APPROACHES

Barash, David P., & Lipton, Judith Eve. (2002). *Gender gap: The biology of male-female differences*. New Brunswick, NJ: Transaction.

This interesting book explores male/female differences in sexual inclinations, propensities for violence, parenting styles, and childhood experiences, using work from the fields of psychology, anthropology, and sociology. The authors discuss how the new field of sociobiology, or evolutionary psychology, can help us understand human behavior and what it means to be male or female.

Fridlund, Alan J. (1997). The new ethology of human facial expressions. In James A. Russell & José Miguel Fernández-Dols (Eds.), *The psychology of facial expression* (pp. 103–129). New York: Cambridge University Press.

In this chapter, Fridlund examines human facial expressions from an ethological standpoint, discussing how they evolved, what they mean, how they function, and the important roles they play in our everyday lives.

Lieberman, Leonard, Reynolds, Larry T., & Friedrich, Douglas. (1992). The fitness of human sociobiology: The future utility of four concepts in four subdisciplines. *Social Biology, 39,* 158–169.

The main tenets of sociobiology are highly controversial. In this article, the authors report on a study in which they examined the rates of acceptance of four sociobiological concepts (kin selection, reciprocal altruism, male-female reproduction strategy, and the genetic basis for altruism) and the usefulness of each concept for future research. Participants in the study were 1,631 scholars in four disciplines: animal behavior, biological anthropology, cultural anthropology, and developmental psychology. The researchers found the highest degree of acceptance of the four concepts among biologists and the lowest acceptance among cultural anthropologists.

Meyer, Peter. (1999). The sociobiology of human cooperation: The interplay of ultimate and proximate causes. In Johan M. G. van der Dennen, David Smillie, & Daniel R. Wilson (Eds.), *The Darwinian heritage and sociobiology: Human evolution, behavior, and intelligence* (pp. 49–65). Westport, CT: Greenwood.

The main thesis of this chapter is that human culture operates in a frame apart from that of the evolution of animal societies. Meyer explores human social systems that have as a central characteristic reciprocal patterns of interaction between members.

Ristau, Carolyn A. (1998). Cognitive ethology: The minds of children and animals. In Denise Dellarosa Cummins & Colin Allen (Eds.), *The evolution of mind* (pp. 127–161). London: Oxford University Press.

This chapter examines the question of how children come to attribute minds to others, much like some of the "theory of mind" research that has become popular in the past 10 years. Ristau also addresses the question of whether any aspect of children's development of understanding is applicable to the development of understanding in various species of animals and discusses the implications of the answer to this question for the evolution of mind.

PART III

THE PSYCHODYNAMIC APPROACH

CHAPTER 5

SIGMUND FREUD'S PSYCHOSEXUAL THEORY

Everyone is a child of his past.

—Edna G. Roston

The child is father of the man.

—William Wordsworth

Give me the children until they are seven and anyone may have them afterwards.

—Saint Francis Xavier

When making a decision of minor importance, I have always found it advantageous to consider all the pros and cons. In vital matters, however, such as the choice of a mate or a profession, the decisions should come from the unconscious, from somewhere within ourselves. In the important decisions of our personal lives we should be governed by the deep inner needs of our nature.

—Sigmund Freud

HISTORY AND BASIC ASSUMPTIONS OF FREUD'S THEORY

Few psychologists have been responsible for formulating entirely new perspectives on human behavior. What Mendel is to the study of genetics and what Einstein to physics, Sigmund Freud is to the study of the underlying forces that influence human development. Freud's main emphasis was on the study of unconscious psychological processes, which he saw as the primary source of mental illness. His theories were a clear departure from those of other thinkers who maintained that all mental disorders have an organic basis (Munroe, 1955). More important, Freud's work represents the first attempt to formulate a systematic and global theory of human development. Because Freud's training and experience in his chosen profession of medicine had profound effects on his development of psychoanalytic theory, a brief review of his life and times is especially important to a full appreciation of his contributions.

> Freud's work represents the first attempt to formulate a systematic and global theory of human development.

Sigmund Freud was born in 1856 in Moravia (which is now part of Croatia). He received his early education in Vienna, and he began his scientific training as a medical student at the University of Vienna in the fall of 1873. During his first year as a medical student, he enrolled in a basic physiology course taught by Ernst Brucke, a German physiologist who was to have a significant influence on Freud's professional and personal life. Because of his relationship with Brucke and his interest in research, Freud decided to pursue a career as a neurologist and became an investigator in the Institute of Cerebral Anatomy. Even in the early days of his formal education, Freud expressed an interest in helping people and was especially intrigued by emotional and "nervous" disorders.

During this same period, he became interested in the properties of cocaine as a treatment for anxiety and depression (Byck, 1974). At Freud's suggestion, Carl Koller, a colleague, amplified Freud's basic experimental work and as a result received recognition for the discovery of cocaine's usefulness as an eye anesthetic. Although he felt that Koller deserved the credit for this discovery, Freud remained disturbed by this incident, as shown by his frequent references to it in his later writings. Freud felt that had he made such an important contribution early in his career, it would have gained him recognition from his peers and a secure financial future, making it possible for him to marry earlier. In spite of the magnitude of Freud's contribution, he never did realize either financial security or unqualified support from his peers.

> Like any theorist, Freud was a product of the social context in which he lived and worked.

While at the Brucke Institute, Freud became intrigued with what was becoming the most important theoretical development in quantum physics, the principle of conversion of energy. This principle states that energy is a quantity, like any other physical substance, and that it cannot be created or destroyed but only transformed from one state to another. Freud's realization that this principle could be applied to human beings was the first and most important step in the development of his theory. He applied this same principle throughout psychoanalytic theory, and many found this new perspective on human development fascinating, although some found it unconvincing.

The publication of Ernst Brucke's *Lectures on Physiology* in 1874 had a strong influence on Freud. Brucke offered the radical proposition that the living organism is characterized by dynamism—that is, it is in a continual state of flux. Freud soon applied this idea to the levels and structures of the unconscious mind and examined the role that dynamism plays in human development.

In 1882, however, Brucke advised Freud to abandon his theoretical career. Brucke found it especially difficult to advise Freud to take this step, given their close personal relationship, but he knew that Freud needed money and would never be able to earn any if he remained in his present position. It was clear that Freud could no longer expect to receive money from home, because his father, who was not a wealthy man, had other children to support. Disappointed and confused, Freud left his work at the institute and his career as a researcher and went to the General Hospital in Vienna for further training in clinical work. This unfortunate time for Freud turned out to be psychology's good fortune, because it led to his later experience as a practicing physician and analyst, through which he was able to complete much of his productive work in psychoanalysis. In Freud's opinion, however, this period was his most unsuccessful, professionally. Because he was in financial need, he was forced to enter private practice—something he had hoped to avoid.

In the beginning of his clinical career, Freud focused on nervous diseases, a relatively new and uncharted domain. Through his reading of the professional literature, he learned of the impressive accomplishments of the French physician Jean Charcot, who had been concentrating on the use of hypnosis as a technique for dealing with hysterical behaviors, such as the loss of feeling in a limb. The technique worked very well, but no one really understood why; Freud's genius would later provide an answer to this question. From October 1885 through February 1886, Freud worked closely with Charcot at the Salpetriere in Paris, then a home for aged women (Jones, 1953–1957).

Freud's experiences in Paris strongly influenced his later thought as well as his abrupt but logical change from neurology to psychopathology, the study of psychological disorders. During the period when he was working with Charcot, Freud's primary focus was on detailing the distinction between hysterical paralysis and organic paralysis. These efforts led him to believe that some disorders, such as hysteria, have causes other than anatomical dysfunction. Some of the cases he worked on involved paralysis that was not caused by any organic damage, and he began to speculate that it might be the result of some imbalance in underlying

> Freud was influenced in his thinking by the principle of conservation of energy.

> Freud's thinking about the role of energy in his psychoanalytic theory was in part influenced by the active study of thermodynamics that was taking place in Western Europe during the late 19th century.

psychological structures. Up to that time, the general feeling among members of the medical community was that every "nonnormal" behavior must be based in some biological irregularity. Freud believed that this was certainly not so in every case, and he felt that this perspective was unproductive.

Freud's time with Charcot was extremely important to the development of psychoanalysis, because it allowed him to observe patients who were suffering from hysteria. These experiences convinced him that forces other than the physical were operating in these cases. From there it was a short step to the hypothesis that certain types of behaviors might be the results of influences other than those we can observe, an assumption that later became a cornerstone of psychoanalytic theory.

Freud returned to Vienna in 1886 for more training at the First Public Institute for Children's Diseases. He was becoming increasingly dissatisfied with hypnosis as a method for studying unobservable or unconscious influences on behavior. Although hypnosis is highly effective under certain conditions, it produces a temporary state during which the therapist must take certain precautions as well as direct the content of the sessions. In addition, Freud found that it left many basic questions unanswered, because the patient was not readily conscious and could not volunteer any information (Fisher & Greenberg, 1977).

At this point, Freud established contact with someone who was to have a great deal of influence over his professional and personal development and, in many ways, the future of psychoanalysis. Joseph Breuer was a Viennese physician who also worked with hysterical patients, but Breuer used an elegant technique that emphasized the patient's "talking out," or overt expression, of any thoughts that entered his or her mind. The immediate advantage of this technique over hypnosis was that the patient could contribute directly to the content of the session. Through the use of this technique, which he later popularized as free association, Freud developed an extensive body of knowledge about the way abnormally behaving individuals view the world and themselves. Freud believed that this new technique opened a previously locked passageway to the unconscious, a part of the mind that he thought held the answers to many questions about human behavior.

Unfortunately, during the later years of Freud and Breuer's association, Freud's concentration on sexual instincts as a fundamental component of his theory resulted in a permanent rift between the two men. In addition, puritanical 19th-century Vienna could not accept Freud's hypothesis that the development of an abnormal personality is the result of some as-yet-unresolved conflict from the individual's childhood, or, especially, his assertion that such conflicts are rooted in sexuality. Freud's primary belief that psychosexual instincts are at the core of all such conflicts made it very difficult for many to accept his theories.

These early days of ongoing struggle left Freud discouraged yet still persistent in his beliefs. During the years prior to his split from Breuer, Freud managed to train a host of highly skilled students, including Carl Jung and Wilhelm Reich, all of

Through his work with Charcot, Freud refined his theory concerning the roles that conscious and unconscious processes play in the origin of mental disorders.

Freud's treatment of emotional illness included free association.

whom eventually also left Freud's theoretical camp and initiated their own schools of psychoanalytic thought. Their reasons for leaving and the bitterness of these separations proved to be a constant source of discouragement for Freud. Experiences such as these, however, seemed to strengthen his desire to develop the discipline of psychoanalysis according to his model. He established a rigid dogma and strict procedures, and he trained his students to use them.

Throughout his professional life, Freud received little recognition from his peers. He did not receive his first honorary academic degree until 1909, when he was invited, at the request of G. Stanley Hall, to visit Clark University. Freud presented five lectures at Clark, which he delivered in his own style, with little reference to notes and hardly any preparation (Jones, 1953–1957). As always, he was a lucid and articulate speaker, qualities that were to remain with him throughout his professional career. Through Freud's association with other psychologists at Clark University, the American Psychoanalytic Society had its beginnings. The American Psychological Association began at Clark University as well, with G. Stanley Hall serving as the organization's first president.

> Freud and his work were introduced to the United States through the now famous series of lectures Freud gave at Clark University in 1909.

Following his time at Clark, Freud's life was filled with a mixture of personal tragedy and professional progress. He endured the deaths of close friends and colleagues, as well as the untimely death of his young daughter in 1920. Shortly after his daughter's death, he was granted a full professorship at the University of Vienna. He considered this an empty honor, because the university had failed to acknowledge his contributions until he had gained international recognition.

With advancing age, he developed a heart condition and cancer, from which he suffered constant discomfort for the remainder of his life. He underwent more than 30 cancer operations, some of them lasting upwards of 4 hours with nothing more than a local anesthetic. He reportedly complained of his discomfort only rarely, and his courage seemed to increase as his condition worsened. He lived with his affliction, and by his example he gave encouragement to others who were similarly ill.

Although his fame reached a new high during the early and middle 1920s, Freud was never to know the extent of his influence. In the years between the world wars, the economic and political atmosphere in Europe became increasingly oppressive, especially for Jews. Freud had experienced anti-Semitism as an adult, when he was excluded from many learned societies. Eventually, life in Vienna became intolerable as the Nazis indiscriminately looted homes, burned books, and undermined professional groups such as those affiliated with psychoanalysis. After the Nazi invasion of Austria, most members of Vienna's psychoanalytic community had little choice but to flee. Initially, Freud refused to leave, but his family eventually persuaded him that it was necessary. In May 1938, after intervention on the part of American as well as German diplomats, Freud fled to London, where he was warmly received and honored. With the Nazis slowly destroying the Jewish population

> ### —— On the Web ——
>
> In many ways, psychoanalytic theory shows how scientists were thinking about human development more than 100 years ago. At http://www.freudfile.org/psychoanalysis/history.html, you can find out about the history of psychoanalysis, including the work of Freud, Charcot, and Breuer. You can also read about the famous case of Anna O., which, if not the start of psychoanalysis, surely gave it some very important support.

of Eastern Europe, Freud left Austria with anxious feelings about the safety of the family members he left behind, but he also mistakenly took solace in the belief that the Nazis in Austria were to provide special laws for minorities. He never learned of the deaths of his four sisters in Nazi concentration camps.

Freud spent the last years of his life receiving the acknowledgments that had been due him all along and working on his final writings. In 1939, after years of suffering, his personal physician gave him the first painkilling drug he received throughout his illness. He died shortly thereafter, on September 23, 1939, with his family and friends close by. Today, followers of Freud's theories and beliefs still meet to honor him annually, on the anniversary of his death.

Some of Freud's personal and professional letters and other writings have only recently been released to science historians and other scholars. We will probably learn a great deal more about the man and his theory when these materials become more widely available.

FREUD'S THEORETICAL VIEWPOINT

Freud's psychoanalytic model of development consists of dynamic, structural, and sequential components.

The basic psychoanalytic model of development, which Freud continually modified over the last 50 years of his life, consists of three major components: a dynamic or economic component that characterizes the human mind as a fluid, energized system; a structural or topographical component that consists of a system of three separate yet interdependent psychological structures that modulate behavior; and a sequential or stage component that stresses the progression from one stage of development to another, focusing on different sensitive bodily zones, developmental tasks, and psychological conflicts. It is impossible to understand the developmental thrust of psychoanalytic theory fully without first understanding these three components.

The Dynamic Component

Psychic Energy

In keeping with the zeitgeist (or thrust) of late-19th-century intellectual and scientific developments, Freud applied the concept of energy to human behavior. He identified this energy as **psychic energy**, or the energy that operates the different components of the psychological system. According to Freud, psychic energy is biologically based and always available in some form, and, because it exists within a closed system, the total amount of psychic energy within the system does not change. The distribution of psychic energy throughout the system depends on many factors, including the individual's biological needs, stage of development, and experiential history, as well as the demands of the current environment.

Freud postulates that **instincts** (unlearned psychological drives) are the primary source of psychic energy. Instincts have their origins in the biological needs and metabolic processes of the organism, and the most powerful instincts, according to Freud, are those related to the creation and sustenance of life, called *Eros*. Within Freud's theory, the sexual instinct is a major life instinct; it differs from other instincts (such as those related to hunger and elimination) in that gratification of the sexual instinct is necessary for the survival of the species, whereas gratification of other instincts is necessary for the survival of the individual. Freud also identifies another powerful class of instincts, those related to death and aggression, called *Thanatos*. The life instincts are maintained and continue to develop through a special form of energy called *libido*.

Instincts have two very important characteristics: They are conservative and repetitive. That is, they always use the least amount of energy necessary to get the job done and then return the organism to an earlier state, and they occur over and over again. In Freud's system, an instinct acts as a stimulus to the mind, impelling the individual to satisfy certain needs. Instincts can also be seen as a psychological representation of a biological process. The majority of psychic energy in the infant, for example, is invested in fulfilling biological needs, such as eating, elimination of wastes, and bodily stimulation.

The fundamental goal of early instinctual behavior is the reduction of tension (or discomfort), which is obtained through **organ pleasure** (Freud, 1905/1959). Examples of such reduction in tension would be filling an empty stomach with food and emptying a full bladder. For the very young infant, instinctual gratification is easily and directly achieved. Gradually, as the individual ages, the great reservoir of initial instinctual energy becomes transformed into energies related to other, more complex experiences of life. A certain amount of energy, however, is always id energy and, according to Freud, other available psychic energy can always be transformed back into id energy (more about the id later).

> Freud's application of the concept of conservation of energy to human behavior resulted in his identification of psychic energy.

> In Freud's theory, instincts, or unlearned psychological drives, provide the energy for the developmental process. They have their origins in the biological needs of the organism.

The Unconscious

One of the significant characteristics of psychic energy is that it is part of, or located in, the **unconscious**. The concept of the unconscious is one of the most important elements in Freud's theory of human behavior. The unconscious is in control of most early behavior and remains in control of some portion of behavior throughout the life span. According to Freud, the bulk of psychic energy in the unconscious influences behavior, but not at a level the individual is aware of or can think about. An understanding of Freud's notions about the different levels of the mind and the development of the structure of the mind is essential to an understanding of how the unconscious functions.

As I have noted above, infants are controlled almost entirely by instinctual energy, seeking pleasure and gratification without constraints. They sleep at will, eliminate automatically, anytime and anywhere, and demand to be fed when they are hungry. The instinctual drive of hunger provides an excellent example of how id energy is shaped by reality. In the human infant, the gratification of hunger—unlike the gratification of elimination and other instinctual drives—requires interaction with another human being. In the normal course of events, the infant's hunger is not automatically gratified; this results in tension, which the infant most often expresses through crying and increased motor activity. These behaviors serve as signals to the infant's caretaker that the infant is in need of food. With the presentation of the bottle or the breast, the infant eats, the hunger drive is satisfied, tension decreases, and the infant becomes content. Through the repetition of this sequence of events, the infant gradually learns that satisfying instinctual drives requires certain external events, and the infant's awareness of these external events becomes associated with some portion of id energy. As the infant becomes aware that his or her own behavior results in the activation of these external events, some portion of id energy becomes transformed into energy associated with the conscious associations of the infant's self. This transformed psychic energy eventually becomes the **ego**, that part of the mind that is grounded in reality.

Once the infant has developed the awareness that he or she can cause events to occur by behaving in certain ways, the elements of the ego have begun to be formed (Hall, 1954). Some of the infant's psychic energy is now associated with the development of a sense of self. As the individual matures, that sense of self undergoes further development and eventually produces another structure, the **superego**, which represents the principles and mores of the society in which the individual lives. Some people equate the superego with the conscience, but the two concepts are not exactly identical.

The function of the superego can be described by means of the following hypothetical example: A young child is hungry, and, knowing that there is a cookie

> The unconscious urges the id to remain active throughout life, but as development proceeds, increasingly smaller proportions of psychic energy become invested in the id.

> The conscious, unconscious, and subconscious all work together to allow the individual to process thought and resolve conflicts.

jar in the kitchen cabinet, she realizes that she can satisfy her hunger by going to the cookie jar and taking a cookie. However, on more than one occasion her mother has told her that such behavior is not acceptable, and the child has thus become aware that there is another set of factors to take into consideration when it comes to satisfying hunger—parental expectations, or social reality, either of which is a force more powerful than the child. The child is aware that her mother may tell her, "No, you may not take a cookie," or otherwise scold or punish her. Although the child wants to take a cookie and satisfy her hunger, she begins to weigh the situation, comparing ego factors (her own desire to go and get the cookie) against superego factors (her wish to avoid social disapproval and punishment). When the child wants a cookie and knows that she can get one but decides not to, that child's behavior is being controlled by psychic energy that has been transformed into ego and superego energy.

> Many theorists believe that the ego acts as a moderator between the superego and the id.

An individual's psychic energy is distributed among the id, the ego, and the superego. During development, this distribution is unequal and in constant flux, depending on the individual's stage of development and whatever needs may be present.

The Structural Component

The three parts of the structural component of Freud's psychoanalytic model—the id, the ego, and the superego—all serve a well-defined purpose: the attainment of goal objects (the things required to satisfy needs), which results in the eventual reduction of tension. These structures, which lack any physical form, are the basis for the different psychological forces that represent the interaction of biological impulses (the id), adaptive and mediating behaviors (the ego), and moral and ethical standards of control (the superego).

> Within almost every dimension of Freud's theory, the goal of any behavior is the reduction of tension, which is achieved through the attainment of the goal object.

The Id

The **id** (Latin for "that thing"), which serves as the storehouse for all the instincts, is present at birth and so is the oldest of the three psychological structures, developmentally. According to Freud, neither the ego nor the superego is active or even formed so early. Initially, all the psychic energy available in the system is invested in the id, which uses this energy to satisfy basic needs through reflexive or reflexlike behaviors. These needs must be satisfied if, first, the organism is to survive (again, self-preservation) and, second, the organism is to move on to higher needs, needs that are less biologically based and more socially based (again, species preservation).

> The id, which is the storehouse for all instincts, contains everything that is passed on from one generation to the next.

The pleasure
principle states
that the primary
goal of mental
operations is the
achievement of
pleasure through
gratification.

In its most basic form, the id is an inborn biological structure that has as its purpose the reduction of tension through immediate gratification. As the initial reservoir of psychic energy, it accomplishes this primary goal of tension reduction through the **pleasure principle** (also sometimes called the principle of lust, the pleasure-pain principle, and the lust-unlust principle) (Jones, 1953-1957), which states that the primary goal of mental operations is the achievement of pleasure through gratification (Freud, 1920/1955).

Controlled entirely by the pleasure principle, id energy is under no constraints and makes no distinction between fantasy and reality. Thought that does not distinguish what is real from what is not real is called **primary process thinking**. For example, an older child or an adult can temporarily satisfy a need by thinking about the drive object (the thing that would satisfy the need), perhaps by picturing it in the mind. Daydreaming is an example of primary process thinking. For instance, you might be able to relieve hunger pangs for a short period by thinking about your favorite food. Although this daydreaming will satisfy you only temporarily, it is an effective way of discharging stored energy and reducing tension so that the tension doesn't dominate your thinking.

Primary process
thinking is thought
that does not
distinguish what
is real from what
is not real.

The psychic energy associated with the id is unconscious in that the individual is unaware of it and cannot talk about it or think about it. All of the psychic energy associated with the id is unlabeled—that is, it has no verbal associations. It is not available to higher mental processes, and the emotions and feelings associated with it cannot be considered on a rational basis. For this reason, some Freudian psychologists believe that a child cannot remember any events that occur when the child is preverbal.

The unconscious urges of the id remain active throughout life, but as healthy development proceeds, increasingly smaller proportions of psychic energy are distributed to the id and increasingly greater proportions are distributed to the more socially adaptive ego and superego.

The Ego

The ego is formed
as a result of the
interaction of the
organism with the
environment and
the eventual
reduction of
tension associated
with certain needs.

The formation of the ego results from the interaction between the organism and the environment and the continued reduction of the tension associated with certain needs. Freudian theory postulates that the ego begins to develop because of the id's inability to satisfy all the individual's needs by itself (Hall, 1954). The course through which the organism begins to employ ego processes to achieve gratification is called **identification**.

The beginning of identification signifies the organism's awareness that goal-directed behavior, as distinct from irrational affective discharges, can result in tension reduction and satisfaction. The organism can now distinguish between reality and fantasy. Ego processes facilitate gratification by distinguishing between "self" and "not self" and then planning with this in mind. This planning is an example of rational thinking, or **secondary process thinking**. Before the onset of secondary process thinking, the organism's primary method of obtaining need satisfaction is through some affective (emotional) discharge. In itself, such a discharge can be an act or sign alerting potential environmental influences (such as a parent) that help or assistance is needed. Affective discharges release tension, but the relief is only temporary. For example, a child's temper tantrum acts as an outlet for a short period of time, but it does not address the basic need that produced the tension that led to the tantrum.

In contrast to the relative helplessness of the newborn infant, who is dominated by the id, the child in the early stages of ego development can act on the surrounding world with intention and thus directly reduce tension. For example, the hungry id-dominated infant cries, but the hungry toddler may smile at his caretaker, try to open the refrigerator, or ask for something to eat. The effectiveness of this behavior further reinforces ego development.

The ego progresses from a pleasure ego in its initial stages of functioning to a rational ego controlled by the **reality principle**, where ego pleasure is realized through adherence to external realities. Here the subjective expression of needs through emotions is separated from the objective state of the real world. The ego receives the energy to perform such functions from the id, which has been channeled into this reality-oriented structure. Thus psychic energy is redistributed. What was previously invested in id functions is now invested in the ego, which mediates all intellectual decision making.

Although the ego does not employ the pleasure principle of the id, it obtains pleasure (tension reduction or the removal of pain) through the reality principle. External realities are represented in reason and thought rather than in emotion.

In addition to the realistic assessment of the environment, the ego serves another important function: It acts as an organizer of mental processes, mediating at times between the id and the superego (a structure that develops later), and controls the level and direction of energy invested in the outside world. According to Freud, the ego is more affected by sensory perceptions than are the id and the superego, and these sensorimotor experiences are as important to the function and content of the ego as instincts are to the id. The ego functions as a decision-making mechanism that acts in accordance with the id's unconscious wishes. The ego could be described as the executive branch of the three-part structural system—it is the arbitrator that takes into account the available energy and balances expenditures of energy within the entire system to ensure need satisfaction as well as the conservation of substantial amounts of energy for future growth.

Once the developing child realizes that emotional outbursts of energy fueled by the id don't result in the satisfaction of his or her needs, secondary process thinking becomes part of the child's repertoire.

Ego processes facilitate gratification through secondary process, or rational, thinking.

The Superego

While the id directs the organism toward gratification and the ego strives for gratification through constructive interaction with the environment, a third structural component, the superego, also has a role. According to Freud, the superego is psychic energy that acts as an opposing force to balance the id's seeking of unbound gratification. It develops in later childhood, as the child internalizes and assimilates first parental authority and eventually the social and ethical standards of the culture (Freud, 1933/1964). The superego has two purposes: to inhibit or prevent the id from expressing impulses that are inappropriate from society's perspective and to stimulate the individual to strive for the ideal (not necessarily the real).

Freud's theory invests the traditional values and ideals of society in the concept of the superego. Consequently, the superego is the representative of the internalized standards to which well-socialized people are supposed to aspire. The development of the superego is influenced by three primary factors: (a) the individual's resolution of certain conflicts with parents; (b) the demands the individual's environment places on the ego, which cannot always be met by the overly rational ego alone; and (c) the experiences the individual has as a child during the long period when parents have authority over the child.

According to Freud, the psychic energy associated with the superego consists of the ego ideal and the conscience. The **ego ideal** represents those judgments that the child thinks of as being morally good, whereas the **conscience** represents those things that the child thinks his or her parents feel are morally good. In his early writings, Freud (1923/1961) relied on the notion of the ego ideal alone to represent this authoritative force. Later, however, through his extensive clinical work, he came to believe that his theory needed another element—what parents think—to represent social and moral restraints.

> The superego represents not only the principles and mores of society but also what the child thinks his or her parents believe is correct.

> One purpose of the superego is to inhibit the id from expressing impulses that are socially inappropriate.

Defense Mechanisms

The dynamic aspect of Freudian theory involves the distribution and transformation of psychic energy. During the formative first 5 or 6 years of life, psychic energy is redistributed, moving from the id into the underlying structures of the ego and superego. The dynamic and structural components of Freud's model interact continually via mechanisms that help the individual remain comfortable and minimize anxiety. The most prominent among these mechanisms, which begin functioning with the emergence of the ego, are **defense mechanisms**, techniques that the ego uses to distort reality when healthy psychological development is threatened.

Defense mechanisms help protect the individual from too much tension or anxiety. Perhaps the best example of a defense mechanism is the repression that occurs when the incestuous feelings of a parent toward his or her child are not allowed to surface from an unconscious to a conscious level. This conflict, which I discuss in greater detail later in this chapter, exemplifies how a very specialized defense mechanism can prevent an individual from feeling a potentially high level of anxiety. All defense mechanisms help the individual to moderate and tolerate discomfort. These mechanisms may be used temporarily or may become stable and durable modes of operation. When they become stable and durable modes of operation for an adult, they become personality characteristics. Defense mechanisms serve to protect the developing child as he or she experiments with handling unpleasant circumstances.

> Defense mechanisms, which are healthy and adaptive, warn us when our anxiety is getting out of control and taking too much of the energy we need to conduct our daily lives.

Defense mechanisms help to restructure the personality—to move or transform psychic energy—and during development they keep the structure of personality fluid as the child experiments. Defense mechanisms, however, also serve a more important purpose: They ensure that all the available psychic energy does not get invested as anxiety, so that a sufficient amount remains to be directed toward growth. In other words, although we are unaware of their functioning (that is, they occur on an unconscious level), defense mechanisms protect us from recklessly discharging the energy that is necessary for future development.

To summarize the discussion above: As a child develops, the relationships among the id, ego, and superego change, and the distribution of psychic energy shifts. A decreasing amount of energy is invested directly into the functioning of the id, and more and more energy is used in the creation and maintenance of the ego. The ego develops later than the id (which is present at birth), and the superego develops even later. Later structures develop from the psychic energy (and in some cases the surplus) that is invested in earlier ones. Eventually, the ego has more psychic energy invested in it than any other structural component, which is necessary because the ego acts for the most part as a mediator between the biological needs of the organism represented by the id and the demands of society and the social constraints represented by the superego.

Applying Ideas About the Psychodynamic Approach

Fairy Tales: The Universal Message

Remember the fairy tales that your parents read to you when you were young, or that you saw in movie or cartoon form? Perhaps you read fairy tales to your own children now. What's the appeal of these stories? Why do children of every generation continue to find them so comforting?

Psychoanalyst Bruno Bettelheim helps to answer these questions in his famous book *The Uses of Enchantment* (1976), in which he discusses the meanings and importance of fairy tales. Bettelheim shows how, for almost every child, such stories reflect deeply rooted fears and then provide solutions to the challenges of being young.

As you probably know, fairy tales have a very long history. They were originally passed down orally from generation to generation, then, in Europe, the Grimm brothers first undertook to write down some of these stories around 1815. The universal appeal that fairy tales have for children might very well be found in their depictions of confrontations between good and evil in which good inevitably wins. This kind of story is especially important for the small child, who feels relatively helpless in a world of much larger, much more powerful adults. According to Bettelheim, fairy tales have hidden messages that appeal to the child's unconscious; they show the child that trials and tribulations are just another part of growing up.

Let's take one example of this very rich form of literature—the story of Hansel and Gretel. Both of these young children overhear their stepmother as she tells their loving (but weak) father that the family doesn't have enough food, and so the parents should lead the children into the forest and leave them there. The father broods over this action but finally agrees, all the while the children are listening to their parents as they lie in their beds at night. Themes of abandonment and desertion (threats of which are very powerful forces in any child's life) are prominent throughout the story, as is the children's id-related behavior, as seen in the uncontrollable candy binge they indulge in when they arrive at the gingerbread house. But this unrealistic gluttony gives way to realistic thinking—Hansel and Gretel are trapped by a wicked woman who wants to fatten them up for her oven. But through their quick thinking, the children quickly defeat the witch and make their way back home again with diamonds and pearls for their father. When they arrive, they find that their wicked stepmother is dead.

According to Bettelheim, young children benefit tremendously from hearing or reading the story of Hansel and Gretel. They learn that through rational thought they can overcome adversity; they can deal with those people in their lives who treat them unfairly, or who torment and frighten them. By basically appealing to children's unconscious, fairy tales like the story of Hansel and Gretel allow children to experience huge victories and thus to take huge developmental steps.

—— **On the Web** ——

You can check on all the fairy tales you could ever want to read at http://hca.gilead. org.il. This site features information about the fairy tales written by Hans Christian Andersen and includes a complete list, with links, to all of Andersen's stories published from 1835 to 1949.

The Sequential or Stage Component

As noted above, the dynamic component of Freudian theory deals with the source, distribution, and utilization of psychic energy, and the structural component addresses the interdependence and interplay among underlying psychological structures and their effects on development. The third and final part of Freud's model, the **sequential** or **stage component**, has as its central emphasis the pattern or progression of the organism through different and increasingly adaptive developmental stages. In preparation for the detailed discussion below of the five qualitatively different stages of the Freudian theory of development, I present first a brief introduction to some of Freud's general assumptions about this component of development.

According to Freud, the gateway to adulthood is the genital stage of development, where lasting and meaningful relationships are formed.

As his training dictated, Freud began his thinking about development from a biological perspective. He proposed that development consists of a series of stages, each of which is characterized by the focusing of psychic energy on a particular area of the body. The areas of the body associated with the different stages are called *erogenous zones*. The stages of development correspond to sequential changes in the dominance of biological and psychological needs. For example, the earliest stage of development involves sensitivity to stimulation in and around the oral area. It also involves the concentration of psychic energy on the basic need of hunger and the behavior of eating. The second stage is focused on increased or dominant sensitivity in the anal and urinary areas, and psychic energy is thus concentrated on the basic need of elimination. It is interesting (and surely not a coincidence) that this second stage occurs around the same time in the child's life that most people in Western society feel it is necessary to begin formal toilet training.

Freudian theory assumes that the psychosexual stages occur universally, for all children.

It is impossible to overstate the importance of the concept of erogenous zones in Freud's theory. According to Freud, infants are born with the ability to experience excitation from skin contact, and that infants build up surface skin tension that needs to be reduced through direct skin contact. Freud likens this excitation to sexual stimulation but notes that it is qualitatively different from the type of sexual stimulation experienced by adults in that it is more generalized and undifferentiated. Freud (1905/1959) calls this capacity for excitation and the need for its reduction *infantile sexuality,* distinguishing it from adult sexuality.

This attribution of sexuality to infants and young children created an extensive popular outcry against Freud in the last days of the Victorian era and the early part of the 20th century. But, basing their stance on their clinical experiences, Freud and his adherents stuck to the theory that psychological-experiential components intermingle with the biologically shifting dominance of the erogenous zones in a sequential manner. Thus these stages of development are called **psychosexual stages**. Freud's theory assumes that these stages occur universally, for all children everywhere.

The erogenous zones, which are the focal points of the psychosexual stages, often influence cultural practices as well (for example, toilet training).

According to Freud, although the stages are not age bound per se, they occur in an invariant sequence and at approximately the same times for most children. A child's successful progression through these stages, however, is not guaranteed. Just as a child might experience some type of developmental delay in physical growth, a parallel delay can happen psychologically as well. An individual can become fixated at a certain stage, so that the normal progression from stage to stage is interrupted. That is, owing to some apprehension or fear, the person (or at least certain characteristics of his or her personality) can remain rooted at an earlier level of functioning. Any fixations that occur during the five sequential stages that Freud describes have direct effects on the formation of later adult personality. In Freud's theory, fixation is classified as a defense mechanism, because it protects the individual from potentially debilitating anxiety.

According to Freud, the onset of each psychosexual stage and some of the forms of behavior occurring in each stage are controlled by genetic or maturational factors, whereas the contents of the stages vary depending on the culture in which development is taking place. This is another clear example of the importance of the interaction of the forces of heredity and environment in the developmental process.

At the time Freud first proposed his model of developmental stages, this contribution was significant for many reasons. It was the first theoretical attempt to describe developmental change as an orderly and predictable process resulting from a combination of maturational and environmental influences. Freud's notion of stages also led to a distinction between quantitative differences within stages and qualitative differences between stages. From Freud's perspective, development is not a continuous, uninterrupted process of more and more, but a process involving differences, reorganization, and sequential restructuring of behavior. This formulation has become the prototype for most stage theories of development, including Piaget's (see Chapter 9) and even some of Vygotsky's work (see Chapter 10).

Perhaps the most significant contribution of Freud's theory of development was his assumption that the early stages provide the foundation for adult behavior, which means that we can understand adult behavior and personality structure only in the light of early developmental experience.

The Oral Stage

The first psychosexual stage is the **oral stage of development**, which occurs during the first year of life. The primary focus of stimulation during this stage is the mouth, and the primary source of gratification is eating. The oral stage dominates the first year of life—that is, during this period all experience is assumed to be mediated by eating-related activities. The oral stage is largely dominated by id energy, although with the onset of language and motor competence the beginning of ego development becomes apparent. However, much of the experience during the oral period is without any verbal labels and is, therefore, likely to remain permanently in the unconscious. For this reason, Freudians believe it is very important that experiences in the oral stage be positive and that oral conflicts be resolved with a minimum of residual tension.

From a developmental perspective, it is the mother (or other primary caretaker) who often satisfies the infant's basic and fundamental needs during the oral period. The sense of satisfaction that a child can experience during the oral period can be a source of gratification throughout life. The child learns to associate satisfaction with the image of the mother in this stage, and subsequently attaches a sense of satisfaction and security to objects that are associated with the mother, or objects that represent the mother's image. In most Western societies, the mother is still the figure most likely to gratify the infant's hunger. The child's association of satisfaction with the mother occurs through repeated pairings of the mother (and her image) with a reduction in tension (from hunger, for example). These repeated pairings result in something called *memory traces,* which help the child in the future to identify appropriate goal objects and eventually to pursue them.

Aside from the biological necessity of eating, other oral activities also provide pleasurable sensations. In addition to the stimulation provided by feeding, the infant receives oral stimulation through sucking, mouthing, and biting.

Freud came to distinguish two separate phases of the oral stage of psychosexual development: the oral passive/oral dependent phase and the oral aggressive/oral sadistic phase. The infant's first behaviors of sucking are characteristic of the oral passive phase of satisfying needs, and the oral aggressive phase, which coincides with the onset of teething (around 6 to 8 months), is characterized by biting and chewing. Both oral phases are considered to end during the early part of the second year of life.

The Anal Stage

The second psychosexual stage of development, the anal stage, lasts roughly from the second to the fourth year of life. It is accompanied by heightened sensitivity to stimulation of the mucous membranes surrounding the anus. As during all stages of development, in this stage tension is generated as a result of an interaction between some basic biological need and heightened physiological sensitivity. The expulsion or elimination of fecal material is a thoroughly pleasurable sensation for the child that reduces tension and discomfort. The young child initially has little control over bowel or bladder functioning.

However, society requires more voluntary control of elimination. In Western societies, toilet training tends to occur sometime during the second or third year of life. The imposition of this training, in Freudian theory, provides a setting for the child to experience the conflict between immediate gratification (and its pleasures) and delayed gratification (and its discomfort), but with the eventual pleasure of social approval when training is accomplished. The child must learn to delay or postpone necessary elimination functions until the appropriate time and place are available. Just as the elimination process can be viewed as pleasurable, so can the temporary retention of fecal material, because it provides for heightened satisfaction when the matter is released and also leads to increased social approval.

> The anal stage is replete with important moments for the child, from the independence gained through bowel and bladder control to the accomplishments of being able to walk and talk and negotiate with parents and other adults.

Like the oral stage of development, the anal stage has two phases: the anal expulsive phase and the anal retentive phase. During the anal expulsive phase, which occurs first, the child derives pleasure from the expulsion of feces. In the anal retentive phase, the child receives gratification through retaining, or holding on to, feces. It is theorized that the child receives pleasure from the retention of feces because excrement has great power as a possession. In the Freudian view, children feel that in eliminating they are literally giving away a part of the body. Another reason for anal retentive behavior is that the greater the tension, the greater the pleasure on its release.

The anal period has some very important psychosocial implications. During this stage, according to Freud (1908/1957), the child begins to deal seriously with separation from the surrounding external reality. This awareness comes to the child through the process of toilet training. The child begins to establish an identity as an individual, a process that is essential to basic ego formation. Because the child has now acquired language skills, experiences are labeled and retained in the conscious. According to Freud, if toilet training occurs before the development of language and the child's ability to be expressive and understand what is being demanded, the child may come to associate the experience unconsciously with tension and anxiety. Premature toilet training—that is, toilet training that occurs without the benefit of language and symbolic representational processes—is also mistimed from the standpoint of the occurrence of biological dominance of the anal area. Freudians saw the restrictive practices of Victorian society (in which toilet training sometimes began at 6 months of age) as a particularly negative influence on healthy psychosexual development. It is likely that Freudian theory (along with the advent of the washing machine) contributed significantly to the trend toward later and more permissive toilet training practices in Western, industrialized societies.

Within Freudian theory, it is during the anal stage that the child first confronts the need for conformity to social expectations as he or she must increasingly consider the wishes and standards of others. During the oral stage, the child can achieve gratification at personal convenience or desire (thumb sucking, mouthing, biting), and even if social standards are imposed in the form of disapproval, the consequences are not momentous. But by the time the anal stage ends, the child is well aware that he or she cannot achieve gratification at will and that there are consequences for ignoring social standards (a lesson that the child probably remembers well into the coming years and perhaps even for a lifetime). With this clear awareness of others and the growing distinction of self, the stage is set for the next developmental stage.

The Phallic Stage

The third major developmental stage, the phallic stage, is thought to last from approximately the fourth to the sixth year. During this period, psychic energy is invested in the genital organs and the pleasure received through their manipulation. Some of the most profound psychological changes in all of the child's personality development take place during the phallic stage.

By this developmental stage, the child has established a fairly sound identity as an individual (understanding that he or she is biologically and psychologically separate from others) and is faced with increasingly sharp conflicts with parents. The child develops feelings that grow in magnitude to form a complex of interrelated and conflicting emotions and behaviors, termed the **Oedipus complex** for the male child and the **Electra complex** for the female. The most important element of this stage of development is the child's resolution, or working through, of the Oedipal or Electra conflict and subsequent development of appropriate gender role identification. According to Freud (1905/1959), the entire dynamic process of child-parent interaction, including the resolution of Oedipal and Electra conflicts, provides the framework for the basic construction and solidification of the superego.

Masculine and feminine children become boys and girls through the creation of gender identity and the resolution of Oedipal and Electra conflicts.

The Oedipus complex takes its name from the Greek tragic play *Oedipus Rex,* in which Oedipus kills his father (not knowing that the man is his father) and marries the man's widow (who is, unknown to Oedipus, his biological mother). When he learns what he has done, he punishes himself by gouging his eyes out. According to Freudian theory, the desire to possess the mother sexually is characteristic of all males during the phallic stage of development. Parallel to the biological changes that take place during this stage, the male seeks the primary and original love object, the mother, and begins to see the father as a competitive force for the love and affection that only the mother can give. The male child's feelings of inferiority are compounded by the results of a comparison between his genitalia and those of his father.

Although the male child's wish to possess the mother physically and psychologically is unrealistic in terms of societal taboos, he pursues this irrational goal and eventually is forced to confront his father over which of them will be the primary recipient of the mother's attention. During this subtle yet profound confrontation, the male child eventually recognizes his father's outrage at his motives and becomes fearful that the father will punish him (through castration) for his incestuous behavior. This fear takes the form of the **castration complex**, which specifically results in **castration anxiety** for the boy. In other words, he fears his father will deprive him of his sex organs, which are now the focal point of his maturational and psychological growth.

> The inconsistency between the concepts of castration anxiety for boys and penis envy for girls has led many developmental theorists to question Freud's analysis of the development of gender identity.

This fear (which remains at the unconscious level) is so strong that the male child eventually abandons his obviously intolerable feelings toward his mother, realizing that he can obtain the gratification he needs only through identification with his father and through vicarious satisfaction, obtained through father-son interaction via mother-father interaction. It is primarily through this process that the beginnings of the superego come into being, because the resolution of the Oedipus complex represents a recognition of societal and tribal mores and values. The child's identification with his father also leads to eventual successful procreation on the son's part and so, indirectly, to the fulfillment of a very general instinct. The Oedipal conflict is thus resolved.

Freud describes a comparable conflict for the female child, the Electra complex, but he does not elaborate to any great extent. Many Freudians believe that the Electra conflict is much more complex than the Oedipal conflict. According to Freud, the young female child does not initially realize that there are any distinct differences between the sexes. Through experience (physical and social/emotional contact with both parents), however, she realizes that she does not possess the same organs as a boy. This results in a sense of inferiority termed **penis envy**. Penis envy amplifies and intensifies the girl's love for and attachment to her father and causes a corresponding rejection of the mother. The girl is assumed to hold her mother responsible, unconsciously, for the girl's lack of a male sexual organ. Eventually, however, the girl realizes that it is physically impossible for her to obtain or incorporate a penis, and the only way she can achieve gratification of her desire for one is through the vicarious satisfaction she receives by identifying with her mother. Compared with his specification of the course of the resolution of the Oedipal conflict, Freud's writings on the resolution of the Electra conflict are much less detailed. (See Table 5.1 for a summary of the psychoanalytic perspective on the formation of gender identity.)

Freud's view of the different experiences for males and females during the phallic stage of development has often been criticized as chauvinistic, given that

TABLE 5.1 How the Oedipus and Electra Complexes Are Resolved in the Development of Gender Identity

	Gender	
	Male	*Female*
Name of conflict	Oedipus complex	Electra complex
Associated anxiety	Castration anxiety	Penis envy
Developmental mechanism for resolution of the conflict	An unconscious fear develops in the male child because of his unacknowledged and unrecognized feelings for the mother. Upon recognition that such feelings are not acceptable, the child develops male behavior patterns (such as those displayed by the father), which provide a way for the child to interact with and "possess" the mother vicariously.	An unconscious fear develops in the female child because of her unacknowledged and unrecognized feelings for the father. Upon recognition that such feelings are not acceptable, the child develops female behavior patterns (such as those displayed by the mother), which provide a way for the child to interact with and "possess" the father vicariously.
Result of resolution	Male gender role	Female gender role

the male is assumed to be concerned with the expression of his sexual desires through the manipulation of his genitals whereas the female is assumed to be pre-occupied with the inferiority of hers. Although individuals of both sexes eventually come through the conflicts they experience with the same developmental outcomes (development of the superego and a gender role), Freud's characterizations of the male and the female through the process have very different connotations.

During the phallic stage (with the central drama focused on the resolution of the Oedipal or Electra conflict), the child experiences a number of major events of possibly lifelong significance. Most important among these are the solidification of the superego, which finally emerges as a significant part of the psychic structure, and the establishment of appropriate gender role identity. The phallic stage is not smooth for any child, and most children experience some difficulty during this time. Resolution of the Oedipal or Electra conflict is likely to be moderately successful rather than completely successful. Some children remain in this stage even past the sixth year of life, when some form of resolution is thought to occur, whether or not it is satisfactory.

Applying Ideas About the Psychodynamic Approach

Gender Identity: Open to Change?

A major area of focus within the psychoanalytic tradition is the development of gender identity: how males become boys (and masculine) and females become girls (and feminine). As the discussion in this chapter notes, the theory tells us that the development from relatively undistinguished, gender-neutral identity takes place through the child's resolution of either the Oedipal conflict (for males) or the Electra conflict (for girls). But what about the child who, through an accident or a birth anomaly, has an intersex condition (that is, is not clearly male or female, physically)? What about the child who is born female and raised as a male, or vice versa? What about adults who elect to have sex reassignment surgery? What do any of these situations have to say about the psychoanalytic perspective, which contends that up until about 18 months, gender

identity is not fixed, yet shortly thereafter (at about 3 years of age) it is? If gender identity is stable, is it likely that a change could take place?

In 1998, Susan Bradley and her colleagues published the results of several interesting studies that examined such questions (Bradley, Oliver, Chernick, & Zucker, 1998). One study that Bradley et al. relate revolved around a case in which the penis of a 7-month-old boy had been accidentally ablated (burned off) during circumcision, and the child's parents made a decision, 10 months later, to raise the child as a girl. The child underwent surgery at the age of 21 months to make his external genitalia appear female. The original researchers collected data on this child's well-being up until the child was 9 years of age and concluded that, indeed, the child had established an identity as a female. However, in further

By the end of the phallic stage, the child's psychic energy has been well engaged. Conflict has been strong, and pressure for resolution has been relentless. The child is psychically tired and therefore, as biological wisdom would dictate, in need of a period of dormancy—hence the period of latency. However, in this next stage the problems associated with the phallic period and the successful or unsuccessful resolution of the Oedipal or Electra conflict are just beneath the surface. Indeed, all the problems of the early psychosexual stages, most particularly the phallic stage, are put in storage, to be revived during later adolescence.

The Latency Stage

The latency stage is characterized by an inhibition of the sensitivity of the erogenous zones. During this period, beginning around 7 years of age, much of the energy formerly invested in sexual desires is displaced or channeled into other behaviors. This stage is a lull or regression of sorts, during which the individual's follow-up, other researchers found that by early adolescence, the child had rejected the female identity and expressed feelings of discomfort at being a female. Eventually, at age 25, this individual married a woman. In this same article, Bradley et al. relate the case of a different child whose initial circumstances were similar to those of the child in the case just described but who "successfully" made the switch from biological male to social female.

Perhaps the most startling case of this kind is the one that John Colapinto recounts in his book *As Nature Made Him* (2001). This is the true story of a baby boy, born Bruce Reimer, whose physical status as a male was compromised during circumcision (indeed, Reimer could be the anonymous child in the first case discussed above). At the time, his parents and physicians decided that "sex reassignment" (as it was called some 25 years ago) was the right course of action.

The outcome? The child, who was renamed Brenda, spent the next 14 years trying to be female. The family had only wanted to do what they thought was right by the child, but Brenda was uncomfortable as a female and at age 14 made the decision to live life as a male, taking the name David. Ultimately, David was successful at creating a normal life for himself, including marriage and significant relationships with others.

Where does this leave us, as students of developmental psychology (and of psychoanalytic theory)? We're back to that troublesome nature/nurture question: What is the primary influence on the development of a child's gender identity? Clearly, despite being raised as a girl, the person who became David Reimer did not feel female; all attempts to change his gender identity (from the outside) were unsuccessful. Yet case studies show that gender identity has been changed very successfully in some children (and adults). Clearly, we need more research, but perhaps we also need a better understanding of biology and its psychoanalytic correlates.

---

development seems to slow down. The huge amounts of psychic energy that were formerly invested in resolving the conflicts of the first three developmental stages are now focused on developing affection for the parents and on the establishment of strong social ties with same-sex peers.

Freud and his closest followers paid relatively little attention to this period of development. They assumed that nothing of significance is happening during this time in the psychic realm of personality organization or development. Although the child is active and learning and deeply engaged in many kinds of activities, from the psychosexual point of view, the latency stage is a period of rest after the rigors of the prior conflicts that also allows the child to gear up for the battles of the next period. Later contributors to psychoanalytic theory, such as Erik Erikson, paid more attention to this period of development; Erikson's views are detailed in Chapter 6.

Latency is thought to be a time of reserve in preparation for the hectic and demanding genital stage, which follows.

The length of the latency period is quite variable. Its onset occurs, as noted above, at about 7 years of age, with the supposed resolution of the conflicts of the phallic stage. The end of the latency period, and the beginning of the genital stage, is triggered by the onset of puberty, the beginnings of adultlike sexuality, and the reopening of earlier conflicts.

The Genital Stage

The genital stage, which begins around the 12th year, is synonymous with adolescence. Although in recent writings some Freudians have sought to differentiate the genital stage into several substages, for our purposes we will consider it as one major developmental stage. The genital stage is in a sense the final stage of development. It is characterized by intense psychic activity and continual redistribution of psychic energy. The resolutions of conflicts that took place in preceding psychosexual stages and their resulting distributions of psychic energy again come up for reconsideration. The genital area of the body becomes associated with adult sexuality, and physical sexual development is accompanied by psychic sexual identity and role playing.

The genital stage is a period of serious decisions. Sex role identity is reconsidered and, according to Freud, some real or fantasized form of homosexuality occurs universally. Freudian theory has traditionally viewed the final election of homosexuality as a form of deviance resulting from the inappropriate resolution of the Oedipal or Electra conflict. However, in recent treatments of homosexuality, some Freudians have taken a more complex view (Fisher & Greenberg, 1977).

The ego and superego face significant tests during the adolescent period, and Freudians point to inadequate development of one or both as the cause of adolescent suicide, delinquency, and serious mental disturbances. The storms and stresses of adolescence are the psychic wars of the genital period. When the genital period comes to a close, the adult's mature personality structure has been set in place. According to Freudian theory, changes in personality structure are difficult to achieve beyond this point, because the redistribution and transformation of psychic energy typical of the fluid character of earlier developmental periods now require a great deal of effort, usually including professional help and intensive therapy.

The genital stage, which begins around the onset of puberty, includes the task of establishing meaningful relationships.

INSTINCTS AND THE DEVELOPMENTAL PROCESS

The fundamental goal of early instinctual behavior is the reduction of tension.

Perhaps the best way to explain how Freud's psychosexual theory can be applied to the processes of development is through an examination of instincts and the cycle of gratification mentioned earlier. Table 5.2 shows the components of this cycle—need or instinct, goal object, action or goal-oriented behavior, and reduction of tension—using the example of the satisfaction of the basic biological need of

TABLE 5.2 The Cyclical Nature of Instincts

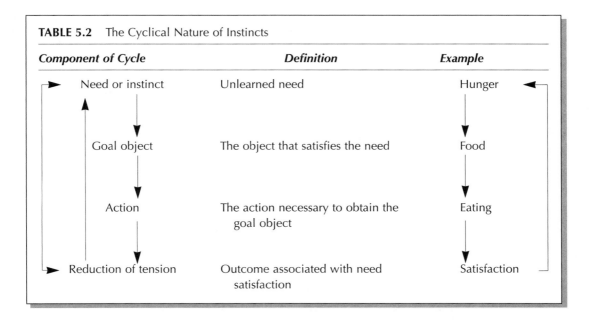

Component of Cycle	Definition	Example
Need or instinct	Unlearned need	Hunger
Goal object	The object that satisfies the need	Food
Action	The action necessary to obtain the goal object	Eating
Reduction of tension	Outcome associated with need satisfaction	Satisfaction

hunger. As the table illustrates, through associations, memory traces are formed between the sensation of hunger and the presence of food; the person "knows" the appropriate action to take (eating) to reduce the tension associated with the need.

This simple table shows how the individual takes an active role in satisfying basic needs. It also illustrates the cyclical or **repetitive quality of instincts**. Hunger occurs again and again, and the cycle continually begins anew. In fact, most needs are satisfied only temporarily; the system eventually returns to its original state of tension, again seeking different ways to satisfy more developmentally advanced needs (such as the need for affiliation or emotional support), thereby ensuring uninterrupted progress. The table cannot illustrate another important characteristic, the **conservative quality of instincts**. As noted briefly above, instincts use the least amount of energy necessary to move toward obtainment of the goal object and satisfaction.

The nature of instincts (and their role in development), however, is much more complex and elegant than the simple reduction of tension. Freud's psychoanalytic theory is often presented only in terms of its implications for personality development, with little attention given to dimensions such as thought (or cognition) or other aspects of development. However, there is a subtle relationship between emotions and thought, and an understanding of this relationship is integral to an understanding of Freud's theory and the role that instincts play. The problem-solving component of development, which is a major part of our everyday behavior, can also be understood within the psychoanalytic model, as shown in Figure 5.1.

Instincts have a cyclical quality in that most needs can be satisfied only temporarily; eventually, the organism returns to the original state of tension.

By their very nature and definition, instincts are both conservative (using the least amount of energy necessary) and repetitive (occurring again and again).

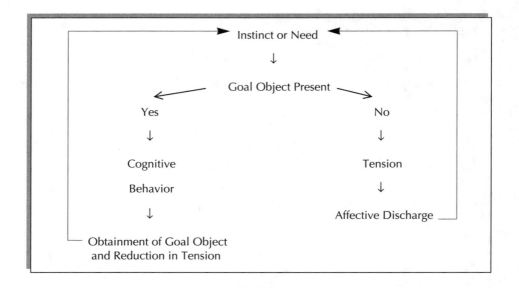

FIGURE 5.1   The Role of Instincts in the Development of Cognition

All thought, whether it is primary or secondary process thinking, results from the need to reduce tension. In the search for a goal object that will reduce tension (such as food or sleep), the individual eventually accepts whatever goal object offers maximum reduction in tension with minimal expenditure of energy. The primary dynamic of development is, however, that the essential goal object is never really obtainable, and this absence is a source of continual motivation to seek satisfaction.

Even when there is no object that can provide complete gratification, there are two possible outcomes. The first involves an affective, or emotional, discharge of energy. For example, the infant, who operates with an abundance of id-controlled energy, cries when he or she is hungry. The infant is not physically equipped to act alone to find food, and the infant has a history of receiving the necessary gratification through some external agent, such as the mother. The very young infant has not yet developed the structural capability to deal with the environment by obtaining goal objects through purposeful thinking. The infant's affective discharge of energy in the form of crying serves the important purposes of (a) reducing tension and (b) alerting someone (usually the mother) to provide for the infant's needs. Although crying is effective (it does release tension), it is only temporarily so, because if the need is not gratified the infant is forced to continue the search. Daydreaming about seeing your significant other, a young child's temper tantrum, and blowing up at your best friend are all examples of

According to psychoanalytic theory, we become thinking beings in part because we have to seek out and incorporate goal objects (or what they represent) without expending too much energy on costly emotional discharges.

discharges of energy that temporarily meet a need but don't provide long-term satisfaction.

The second possible outcome when the goal object is not present results from the interrelationship between memory traces and association with the goal object. As noted above, memory traces (which are links or bonds between goal objects and needs) and images are formed through the satisfaction of basic needs. When the child experiences a need that is the same as or similar to a need that has been satisfied in the past, the child can recall the image of the fulfilling object and use that as a guide in *thoughtful* pursuit of the goal object. Through the establishment of a base of memory traces, the child compiles a wealth of complex associations that allow him or her to identify alternative goal objects when needed. That is, the child learns to satisfy a need through a variety of choices, all of which are expressed as socially acceptable behaviors rather than emotional expressions, which eventually lead nowhere.

In some situations, however, the surrounding world may be structured in such a way that it provides for the satisfaction of the child's needs with the child's having to make only a minimal commitment of energy or no investment at all. For example, some children in wealthy families are quickly provided with everything they desire and are not expected to make any effort or take any action to satisfy their own needs. The outcomes of such situations are potentially tragic, because no investment of energy means no growth. Theoretically, an individual can never develop the higher-order (or secondary process) thinking necessary to obtain goal objects without the presence of tension.

> The most important role that instincts play may be found in their end result: a thinking, problem-solving being who knows how and where to find goal objects (whatever they might be) and how to resolve conflicts.

To summarize: Sigmund Freud was interested in the clinical treatment of people with emotional problems. In the process of developing a theory to account for a treatment technique, he devised the theoretical elements described in this chapter: the energy model, the structural components, and the developmental stages. Freud viewed the process of helping someone regain psychological health as involving a restructuring of the distribution of psychic energy. He understood behavioral problems to be symptoms stemming from the maladaptive distribution of psychic energy. Freud assumed that his patients were motivated by the psychic energy of the unconscious—that is, the motivations for their behaviors were unknown to them. He believed that through therapy, an individual could be helped to transform unconscious motivation to the conscious level, so that he or she could talk about it, deal with it, and reassign and psychic motivation to the conscious level, where awareness (ego and superego) is in better control and theoretically is more adaptive and functional for the individual.

A discussion of psychoanalysis, as therapeutic technique or clinical theory, is beyond the scope of this book. Our interest in Freud's work lies primarily in his development of the clinical dimensions of psychoanalysis that led to the

> In psychoanalytic theory, individual differences result from the ways in which people resolve conflicts.

formulation of a developmental theory. Freud found that when he helped his patients to transform unconscious energy into conscious energy, a frequent result was that they could more clearly recall experiences from early childhood. This consistent finding, along with the similarity in the kinds of experiences and events that patients recalled, led Freud to consider the importance of the events of early childhood and resulted in his proposal of the id, ego, and superego as developmental structures.

WEB SITES OF INTEREST

- "Psychoanalysis and Literature," by John Lye, at http://www.brocku.ca/english/courses/4F70/psychlit.html: One of the reasons psychoanalysis has been criticized is that many psychoanalysts have long claimed that it applies to everything. Lye's article, which addresses how psychoanalytic theory can enlighten the study of literature, seems to provide some support for that claim.
- "The Sigmund Freud and Carl Jung Lectures at Clark University," at http://www.clarku.edu/offices/library/archives/Freud&Jung.htm: Freud delivered his very first lectures in the United States at Clark University during the early part of the 20th century. This Web site provides some information about the lectures as well as about the social and cultural world in which they were delivered.
- "Sigmund Freud: Austrian Originator of Psycho-Analysis, 1856–1939," at http://www.lucidcafe.com/library/96may/freud.html: This Web site provides just about everything you might ever want to know about Freud in a short and informative biography. It also features links to books about and by Freud, videos, and even e-texts you can read on your Palm Pilot on the way to school.

FURTHER READINGS ABOUT PSYCHOANALYTIC THEORY

Curtis-Boles, Harriet. (2002). The application of psychoanalytic theory and practice to African Americans. In Elizabeth Davis-Russell (Ed.), *The California School of Professional Psychology handbook of multicultural education, research, intervention, and training* (pp. 193–209). San Francisco: Jossey-Bass.

Perhaps the tenets of psychoanalytic theory are not as universal as many people think. In this chapter, Curtis-Boles discusses the major limitations of contemporary psychoanalysis for application to the life experiences of African Americans. She argues that the psychoanalytic approach does not address the sociocultural challenges that most African Americans face, such as racism and discrimination, poverty, and violence.

Gedo, John E. (2001). The enduring scientific contributions of Sigmund Freud. In Jerome A. Winer & James William Anderson (Eds.), *The annual of psychoanalysis: Vol. 29. Sigmund Freud and his impact on the modern world* (pp. 105–115). Hillsdale, NJ: Analytic Press.

Gedo asserts that Freud's most important contribution was his development of a method of observation that led to the collection of reliable and valid data about the inner lives of human beings. He also discusses several other important contributions, such as Freud's emphasis on the unconscious, the notion that behavior is characterized by a variety of automatic repetitions, and the importance of the role of early childhood.

Grinker, Roy R. (2001). My father's analysis with Sigmund Freud. (2001). In Jerome A. Winer & James William Anderson (Eds.), *The annual of psychoanalysis: Vol. 29. Sigmund Freud and his impact on the modern world* (pp. 35–47). Hillsdale, NJ: Analytic Press.

This chapter gives an interesting account of the author's father's life, including the man's experience of undergoing psychoanalysis with Freud. Although Grinker's father thought that Freud was a genius when it came to the intellectual side of his theory, Grinker notes that, in his own opinion, Freud was not a very good clinician. This piece provides an interesting view of interesting men.

Jones, Ernest. (1953–1957). *Sigmund Freud: Life and work* (3 vols.). London: Hogarth.

Jones corresponded with Freud and wrote about every aspect of Freud's personal and professional life. This three-volume work makes compelling reading for any student of development.

Taylor, Eugene. (1999). William James and Sigmund Freud: "The future of psychology belongs to your work." *Psychological Science, 10,* 465–469.

If you like to read about history and are interested in William James as well as Freud, both great men who made important contributions to the study of psychology, seek out this article. James and Freud were very different in their approaches to understanding behavior, but recent findings in neurological research shed some light on the validity and utility of the beliefs of both these scholars.

CHAPTER 6

ERIK ERIKSON'S FOCUS ON PSYCHOSOCIAL DEVELOPMENT

The main business of the adolescent is through gentle transaction to stop being one.

—Arthur Koestler

This sense of identity provides the ability to experience one's self as something that has continuity and sameness, and to act accordingly.

—Erik Erikson

The four stages of man are infancy, childhood, adolescence and obsolescence.

—Art Linkletter

BASIC ASSUMPTIONS OF ERIKSON'S THEORY

As Freud's psychoanalytic theory grew in influence, students flocked from all over Europe to Vienna to learn from Freud himself. Some of these students went on to develop specific aspects of Freud's theory, whereas others challenged parts of it. Most of the variations on Freudian theory focus on understanding abnormal behavior and extrapolating from the theory various ideas and principles related to childhood. Two of Freud's students who focused directly on children and on developmental processes were Anna Freud, Sigmund Freud's daughter, and Erik Erikson, an artist and teacher who came under Freud's influence and subsequently turned his attention entirely to children. Erikson eventually extended Freudian theory as he shaped a particular emphasis that is noted for its focus on the ego as a central component in the individual's functioning. Erikson's **psychosocial theory** has had a significant impact on the study of developmental processes because it addresses development across the entire life span. In fact, Erikson is often considered the first true "life-span developmental psychologist."

Unlike many other early psychoanalysts, Erik Homberger Erikson never really "left" the Freudian camp—that is, he never rejected Freud's initial orientation. He did, however, take a unique perspective on Freud's work, incorporating many of Freud's primary assumptions while greatly expanding on them. Erikson broadened the network of factors considered responsible for influencing development.

According to Erikson (1950b), psychological development results from the interaction between maturational processes or biological needs and the societal demands and social forces encountered in everyday life. Given this viewpoint, Erikson's theory places greater emphasis on the dimension of socialization than does Freud's theory. In addition to this distinction, Erikson's theory concerns psychological development throughout the entire life span, rather than just the years from birth through adolescence. Erikson examined the consequences of early experiences on later life, as did Freud, but he went farther, investigating also the nature of qualitative change during the middle and later years of life. For a long time, developmental psychologists tended to ignore these later periods of development, but in the past 25 years or so, trends in fields such as gerontology as well as popular publications such as Gail Sheehy's *Passages* (1976; see also Sheehy, 1995, 1999) and Roger L. Gould's *Transformations* (1979) have stimulated increased thought and research in this area. As a result, interest in Erikson's work has grown.

Like Freud's theory, Erikson's breaks the processes of development down into a series of stages governed by underlying maturational forces and characterized by the presence of conflict. Erikson's theory encompasses eight such stages, each of which is associated with a definite crisis that the individual must resolve in order to move on to the next stage. In Erikson's view, maturational processes might be the

Whereas Freud's theory encompasses psychosexual stages, the stages in Erikson's theory are best described as psychosocial in nature.

Erikson developed the first true life-span theory of human development which breaks down the processes of development into eight stage.

impetus for the onset of different stages, but societal demands, which are present from conception through death, act as powerful mediating and shaping forces.

Erikson never received any formal scientific training before he began his career as a child analyst. Whereas most analysts at that time had degrees in medicine or related areas, Erikson's training prior to his introduction to psychology was in the fine arts. An aspiring artist, he found himself employed in the late 1920s as both a teacher and private portrait painter. Around that period, Erikson came into contact with people who introduced him to the field of child analysis. He then studied for and received a certificate in child analysis, and in 1933 he departed for Denmark, where he practiced for a short time before transferring his studies to the United States.

Whereas Freudian theory is based on the relationship of life energy, or libido, to the psychological functioning of the individual, Erikson's theory stresses the importance of the ego. For Erikson, the ego is a unifying structure, and ego strength is the glue that bonds together the different aspects or dimensions of psychological functioning. Erikson's view of the ego is similar to Freud's: The ego is the executor of realistic goal-seeking actions and the intermediary between the biological urges of the id and the societal constraints of the superego. However, the developmental nature of Erikson's theory makes the ego the structure of prime importance; it is through the ego that certain crucial developmental crises are experienced and eventually resolved. When the ego falters and cannot deal with a crisis, development is thwarted.

Like Freud, Erikson believed that although biological imperatives are of great importance, social pressures and environmental forces have even greater impacts. A detailed examination of such forces in an individual's life provides what Erikson calls a *psychohistory*—that is, a history of those events of a social nature that interact with biological processes to produce behavior. Erikson made extensive use of the technique of relating individuals' past experiences to their present behavior in an effort to understand motivational factors, behavioral outcomes, and the individuals' future needs. Whereas the developmental stages in Freud's theory are called *psychosexual,* Erikson's stages are best described as *psychosocial* in nature, given his serious consideration of these other factors.

> Each stage in Erikson's theory is associated with a conflict that the individual needs to resolve before moving on to the next stage.

> Erikson's theory emphasizes the strength of the ego and its role as intermediary between the id and the superego, or the demands of society.

> According to Erikson, psychological development results from the interaction between biological needs and social demands.

The Principle of Epigenesis

The principle of **epigenesis** (*epi* meaning "upon," and *genesis* meaning "emergence"), which is the theoretical basis of Erikson's work, is related to the embryological model, in which each event during fetal development has a unique time of ascendancy, the plan for which is contained in the organism's genes. Erikson (1950a) explains epigenesis in a general way as follows: "Anything that

Epigenesis is the primary mechanism through which development progresses.

grows has a ground plan, and . . . out of this ground plan the parts arise, each having its time of special ascendancy until all parts have arisen to form a functioning whole" (p. 52). Biologically, the individual has few basic elements at conception, but over time these elements combine and recombine to form new structures. Much in the same way, differing psychological parts come together to form an entirely new and qualitatively unique entity. The functioning whole, by definition, can no longer be reduced to the parts that originally formed it (hence this view is not reductionistic). An analogy might be a building, which on completion is more than simply the concrete, bricks, and wood that went into its construction. As a unique entity it may be a place to work, a place to live, or a place to play. As a functioning unit it serves a new level of purpose that is far more complex than the purposes of the simple structural elements of which it was composed. Similarly, the independent reflexes present at birth become organized in such a way as to produce behaviors that are qualitatively different from the sum of all these reflexes.

According to Erikson, this time plan is controlled by maturational processes by means of the epigenetic principle. During each of the eight stages of Erikson's psychosocial model, a specific conflict has particular significance for development. Given that all these conflicts result indirectly from a struggle between maturation (biological needs) and the social demands placed on the individual, the ego serves as the primary mediating force in the developmental process. In contrast to Freudian theory, which holds that the ego is formed sometime after birth as a developmental by-product of the id (based on surplus available energy), in Erikson's model the ego is present at birth, although in an immature state. For this reason, Erikson is often referred to as an ego psychologist.

STAGES OF PSYCHOSOCIAL DEVELOPMENT

Development takes place through the resolution of crises at successive developmental stages. Erikson first described these eight stages in his influential book *Childhood and Society* (1950a). Table 6.1 lists the stages and shows for each one the associated psychosocial task or crisis, the social conditions that might contribute to or deter successful completion of the stage, and the behavioral outcomes that result from successful or unsuccessful completion of the stage. The psychosocial task or crisis at each stage is stated in general terms in the table. These conflicts are not all-or-nothing situations; rather, they represent continua of psychological functioning. The extremes of each continuum are unrealistic, yet part of each extreme is often present in all individuals at any given stage. For example, no child grows up with complete trust or complete distrust—each individual adapts as social demands dictate.

Societal demands act as powerful mediating forces between biological needs and the total development of the individual.

TABLE 6.1 Erikson's Eight Stages of Psychosexual Development

Stage	Psychosocial Stage	Task	Social Conditions	Psychosocial Outcome
Stage 1 (birth to 1 year)	Oral-sensory	Can I trust the world?	Support, provision of basic needs, continuity Lack of support, deprivation, inconsistency	Trust Distrust
Stage 2 (2 to 3 years)	Muscular-anal	Can I control my own behavior?	Judicious permissiveness, support Overprotection, lack of support, lack of confidence	Autonomy Doubt
Stage 3 (4 to 5 years)	Locomotor-genital	Can I become independent of my parents and explore my limits?	Encouragement, opportunity Lack of opportunity, negative feelings	Initiative Guilt
Stage 4 (6 to 11 years)	Latency	Can I master the skills necessary to survive and adapt?	Adequate training, sufficient education, good models Poor training, lack of direction and support	Industriousness Inferiority
Stage 5 (12 to 18 years)	Puberty and adolescence	Who am I? What are my beliefs, feelings, and attitudes?	Internal stability and continuity, well-defined sex models, and positive feedback Confusion of purpose, unclear feedback, ill-defined expectations	Identity Role confusion
Stage 6 (young adulthood)	Young adulthood	Can I give fully of myself to another?	Warmth, understanding, trust Loneliness, ostracism	Intimacy Isolation
Stage 7 (adulthood)	Adulthood	What can I offer succeeding generations?	Purposefulness, productivity Lack of enrichment, regression	Generativity Stagnation
Stage 8 (maturity)	Maturity	Have I found contentment and satisfaction through my life's work and play?	Sense of closure, unity, direction Lack of completeness, dissatisfactio	Ego integrity Despair

SOURCE: Adapted from Erikson (1950a).

Stage 1: Oral-Sensory

The Psychosocial Issue: Trust Versus Distrust

The first of Erikson's psychosocial stages is the oral-sensory stage, during which the infant experiences the first of many interactions with the immediate environment. The infant needs these outside influences to help regulate basic behaviors.

Massive amounts of stimulation are present in the newborn's environment, and the infant receives information from the sensory modes of touch, taste, smell, hearing, and sight at a rate and intensity that exceed the processing capabilities of the relatively immature organism. The oral component of this stage reflects the biological mode through which the child receives the greatest amount of gratification. In this as in other stages, Erikson nominally combines Freudian terminology with his own. For example, the oral component of the oral-sensory stage maintains an important theoretical connection between Erikson's psychosocial perspective and Freud's psychosexual perspective. In this stage, the psychosocial issue is whether the child can trust the world, and, as you might expect, the focus of this trust is maternal involvement.

The trust-distrust continuum reflects the value of the child's experiences during the first year of life and how the child feels about interactions with outside forces. Erikson emphasizes that it is not just the quantity of trustfulness that is important but the quality as well. For example, if children receive harsh sensory input (loud noises, for example) or they are handled roughly, they may feel a sense of distrust and become defensive in an attempt to protect themselves from a threatening environment. On the other hand, when children experience a supportive and consistent environment, they are likely to be trusting and to develop confidence in their ability to predict what will come next.

The oral stage is typified by the conflict between trust and distrust, which begins with the infant's interaction with the environment.

Erikson (1950b) recognizes that although it is adaptive to be distrustful of certain dangerous things in the environment, too much distrust can lead to excessive cautiousness. Likewise, although trust is important for the formation of a psychologically healthy individual capable of essential human bonds and attachments, excessive trust is naive. Young children often have difficulty discriminating between what is valuable and worth pursuing and what is irrelevant, dangerous, or a threat to their developmental progress.

During the oral-sensory stage, the child's developmental task is to determine whether he or she can trust the world. The child at this stage continually asks this question and receives feedback through social interactions. If these interactions are supportive and meet the child's basic biological and social needs, the child develops trust and a sense of confidence. If the child's social interactions are characterized by lack of support and inconsistency and the child's basic needs are not met, the child will form a sense of distrust that can threaten his or her later developmental progress. The child who does not successfully resolve the trust/distrust crisis at the appropriate time (that is, during this stage) will have a poor foundation on which to resolve later crises.

Stage 2: Muscular-Anal

The Psychosocial Issue: Autonomy Versus Doubt

The second stage in Erikson's model involves the child's ability to regulate or control his or her own physical behavior. Most notably, this includes the eliminatory functions associated with toilet training. Indirectly, however, and just as important, during this stage children learn that they have input into the forces that affect their lives.

The Freudian counterpart of this stage is the anal stage of development, during which emphasis is placed on the control of specific muscles located in the anal region of the body. These muscles are important in the expulsion of feces and in toilet training. In Freud's theory, the developmental task of this stage is to acquire control of these muscles. In contrast, Erikson's view of this stage goes beyond the specific anal area and generalizes to musculature throughout the body. That is, in this stage control of all the muscles becomes the focus of the child's surplus energy. The child is expected to develop control not only of the muscles that deal with elimination, but of his or her impulses in general. This change leads to a successful feeling of autonomy (control over one's behavior) as opposed to feelings of shame (lack of control). Whereas in Freud's theory the psychological and social components are distinct, in Erikson's theory they are more closely intertwined.

The psychosocial issue during the muscular-anal stage concerns the child's growing independence and control over his or her bodily functions. During this stage, children face the task of defining or discovering the degree of control they have over their own behavior. If they are given opportunities to explore their world and their attempts at independent action are encouraged, they will develop a sound sense of autonomy. On the other hand, if they have no opportunities to test their own limits (perhaps because their caretakers are overprotective), they will develop a sense of shame and doubt their ability to deal effectively with the world. This stage is characterized by a dilemma between holding on and letting go. With the successful resolution of this conflict, children learn to control their own behavior and, to some extent, their environment, and thus develop a sense of autonomy.

Stage 3: Locomotor-Genital

The Psychosocial Issue: Initiative Versus Guilt

In Freud's theory, the genital stage of psychosexual development is characterized by conflict resulting from the Oedipus or Electra complex. In a similar fashion, Erikson's locomotor-genital stage involves social expectations for independent movement and motivation as a result of newfound autonomy and control. The formulation of this stage exemplifies the way in which Erikson employed and extended basic Freudian theory.

In Freud's model, this stage is characterized by the focus of energy on the genital areas of the body. Erikson's theory includes this concept but takes the idea one step further, incorporating the psychosocial component as a major part of this biological need. Freud's Electra and Oedipus complexes involve the resolution of a conflict caused by the child's desire to embrace the parent of the opposite sex. This conflict is eventually resolved with the child's realization that societal constraints prevent fulfillment of the desire. The locomotor component of Erikson's third stage of psychosocial development represents the child's movement away from dependency on the parents and toward the ability to meet his or her own personal needs. In this stage, children become capable of initiating more complex actions on their own, resulting in more gratification than was possible earlier when they were more dependent on their parents.

> The child's movement away from dependency on parents increases at the same time the child's feelings of control and autonomy increase.

This initiative is important because the child's autonomy is continually increasing and because the child needs to reject any guilt that might be associated with not moving in an independent direction. This guilt results from the discrepancy between the child's aspirations for certain goals using new locomotor skills and the acts the child initiates to accomplish these goals. As Table 6.1 (page 143) shows, the locomotor-genital stage is characterized by the question, "Can I become independent of my parents and explore my limits?" This is an important beginning step toward independence. If the child is given support for these efforts and encouraged in them, he or she will develop a strong sense of initiative. In contrast, if the child lacks opportunities to explore limits and/or experiences negative feelings because he or she is punished for trying to exceed established limits, the child will develop a sense of guilt. Both ends of the initiative-guilt continuum are probably determined more by social factors than by internal or organismic factors.

Stage 4: Latency

The Psychosocial Issue: Industry Versus Inferiority

The latency stage of Freud's model of psychosexual development is characterized by the child's investment of energy in the pursuit of knowledge and other intellectual and social exercises rather than clear biological needs. In other words, during this stage the available psychic or libidinal energy is not focused on any specific region of the body (as it is in the anal and oral stages of development); rather, it is focused on less concrete needs, most of which are related to social and cognitive development. (As a matter of fact, some observers have asserted that the later developmental stages of Erikson's theory are more concerned with social processes than with biological processes.) For Freud, this period is psychosexually inactive, but for Erikson it is just as dynamic and active as earlier periods.

According to Erikson, the latency stage of development is a crucial time for the child's sense of industry; during this period, the child must master the social skills necessary to compete and function successfully as an adult in his or her society. For example, in an agricultural society, the developmental task (a term also made famous as an educational construct by University of Chicago scholar Robert Havighurst, 1952) that a child must accomplish to complete this stage successfully is to learn the skills associated with farming. At this stage of development, cultural expectations take precedence over other needs, and the child's ability to master certain skills becomes paramount. Erikson describes a child who masters the necessary skills as *industrious,* and he asserts that industriousness leads to feelings of completeness or satisfaction.

When children have no opportunities to learn how to master their own world or have their efforts to do so blocked, these unsuccessful experiences lead to a sense of inferiority, or the feeling that they lack worthiness. Feelings of inferiority result when children perceive that they lack importance or that they are unable to deal with the demands of their world. When a preadolescent child who is striving for recognition finds it unreachable, the feelings of inferiority that result may persist through later stages of development.

This stage of psychosocial development is important to later success for another reason as well. The preadolescent invests a tremendous amount of energy inward, toward the development of such skills as industriousness and the self-help aspects of growth. This period, which precedes formal adolescence, is a time for reorganizing and regrouping energies to handle the tremendous biological and emotional demands that will shortly follow. When the demands of adolescence arrive, the individual who has already acquired useful social skills (whether these are related to fixing cars, caring for siblings, or milking cows) has the distinct advantage of having completed an important step toward the development of a meaningful identity. During the latency stage, the child's question is "Can I master the skills necessary to survive in my community?" If the conditions surrounding the child support the development of these skills—such as good educational institutions and adequate models in the home—the child is likely to develop the industriousness that leads to a sense of satisfaction. Feelings of inferiority are encouraged by social conditions that fail to prepare the child for entrance into adult life by providing the tools the child needs to succeed.

> Unlike Freud, Erikson views the stage of latency as a time characterized by the child's investment of a great deal of energy and effort into mastering the social skills necessary for success in adulthood.

—— On the Web ——

A well-written article by Sharon A. Stringer titled "The Psychological Changes of Adolescence: A Test of Character," which appeared in the *ALAN Review*, is available on the journal's Web site at http://scholar.lib.vt.edu/ejournals/ALAN/fall94/Stringer.html. In her informative discussion of Erikson's interest in adolescence, Stringer details all the facets of Erikson's conceptualization of the puberty and adolescence stage of development. Best of all, she includes a short but terrific glossary.

Stage 5: Puberty and Adolescence

The Psychosocial Issue: Identity Versus Role Confusion

As the individual moves from adolescence toward young adulthood, he or she begins defining ideas and interests about further education, careers, and young adult life.

Puberty is a time when some of the most drastic changes occur in all spheres of individual development. Up to this time, the child has not experienced any changes in either physical or psychological capacities and needs that are as great as those of puberty. Adolescents are expected to begin defining their interests in terms of such areas as career choices (which may involve further education or the need to learn trade skills), marriage, and raising a family. Both biologically and culturally, adolescence is considered the end of childhood and the entrance into adulthood. It is a time of great change and excitement, and it is also the stage at which the individual develops an identity, or a definition of self. The child begins to select and define a role and prepares to handle the chosen position.

If development has proceeded successfully, the adolescent should begin this stage with some sense of security. Through the first four stages, the individual has gained the ability to trust, has become somewhat autonomous, has become capable of initiating behavior toward a defined end, and has become industrious to the extent that he or she is competent in performing certain skills. The next crucial step is the development of a sense of identity. That is, the adolescent asks, "Who am I?" and "What ideas, thoughts, or objects do I feel represent my way of thinking?" If the environment is not supportive and the adolescent finds it difficult to establish a role, he or she may develop an ill-defined identity, a condition that Erikson calls *role confusion.*

Given the turbulent nature of today's world, it is understandable that some adolescents have great difficulty in defining or adhering to a certain role or set of beliefs. Some scholars have attributed much of the social activism in the United States during the late 1960s and early 1970s to young people's not being able to "find themselves" and so developing a kind of "existential guilt"—that is, they felt guilty about their own good fortune while others suffered. According to Erikson, such a lack of role definition (or role satisfaction) can result when a child feels pressure to define a role at an early age to please parents, before he or she has successfully completed the tasks of earlier stages of development.

Stage 6: Young Adulthood

The Psychosocial Issue: Intimacy Versus Isolation

Because Erikson's theory of psychosocial development is based on the epigenetic principle, it holds that development is optimally successful only when the individual successfully resolves the crisis associated with each stage in the developmental process. The stage of young adulthood illustrates the importance of such success at earlier stages. At this stage, for the first time the individual faces new goals and tasks that directly involve other people, and during this period the individual is expected not only to develop and meet career goals, but also to begin the developmental process of forming intimate relationships with others (both of the same and opposite sex). Now, at full biological maturity, one of the individual's primary developmental tasks is the formal inception of a family unit through marriage or cohabitation.

At the young adulthood stage, the focus is no longer on the individual; rather, the individual's relationships with and feelings about others take precedence.

This should not be understood to mean that entering into a monogamous sexual union and producing children are the only forms that intimate relationships can take. The intimacy that forms the goal of this psychosocial stage may simply be closeness between people, regardless of gender or personal arrangements. From Erikson's viewpoint, such intimacy represents commitment on the part of the individual to others, resulting in the establishment of warm and meaningful relationships. The maturing adult is expected to make commitments to others through intimate interactions.

This stage of development is intertwined with the stage of adolescence, because an outcome of role confusion in that preceding stage can lead to a poor sense of identity, which in turn can result in unsuccessful and superficial relationships. The need for intimacy supersedes every other need in young adulthood. According to Erikson, to be successful at this stage the individual must give of him- or herself to another person deemed worthy of trust. To do this, the individual must be able to invest his or her own feelings, belief systems, values, and goals in that other person. To enter into such a relationship, the individual must have a foundation that includes some degree of autonomy and basic trust as well as a clear sense of identity.

When an individual fails to establish sufficient intimacy in relationships, the consequence is a sense of ostracism or isolation. That is, when a person is unable to

Applying Ideas About the Psychosocial Approach

Adolescence: Not as Bad as We All Thought

As you know by now, many theoretical perspectives emphasize the importance of developmental stages—qualitatively distinct periods when behaviors change abruptly along some dimension of development. Certainly Freud's and Erikson's theories are of this kind.

One of the most often talked about stages is that of adolescence, which many see as a time of great upheaval. G. Stanley Hall (1904), one of the founders of child and developmental psychology, called adolescence a period filled with "storm and stress." But in reality, how much storm and stress is there during adolescence? The research findings might surprise you. One scholar who has investigated this subject is Jeffrey Jensen Arnett at the University of Maryland. In a 1999 article in the *American Psychologist*, Arnett notes that there is reason to believe that adolescents go through some storm and stress, but in order to understand the concept of adolescence and what children go through during those years, one has to look at individual differences as well as cultural variations—factors that are much more important than biology.

Arnett focuses on three elements that often appear in discussions about understanding adolescence and that are thought to exemplify the differences between adolescents and younger children. The first of these is *conflict with parents* (and other authority figures, for that matter). You may remember your own adolescence and how difficult this aspect might have been; you may especially remember having embraced a characterization of being antiauthority, rejecting people such as your parents or teachers. The second element is the *mood disruptions* that characterize adolescence; that is, adolescents may

communicate or share feelings with others, he or she is likely to feel left out, and low self-esteem can result. This is harmful to the individual's self-concept and prevents advancement to the next stage. Development in the young adulthood stage is characterized by strong efforts to develop real and meaningfully close physical and psychological relationships. The lack of such relationships results in despair, loneliness, and a kind of isolation that sometimes lasts for the remainder of the individual's life.

Young adulthood is also the time for another interesting change. As the individual becomes increasingly competent, he or she becomes more autonomous and secure, and thus less dependent on external agents for assistance. During young adulthood, the social conditions that characterize probable psychosocial outcomes are more internalized than at earlier stages and less the results of concrete conditions in the surrounding environment. Therefore, in Erikson's theory the social conditions that affect outcomes beyond puberty (in young adulthood, exhibit more extreme mood swings than do younger children or adults. The final element is the tendency of adolescents toward *risk taking*. Perhaps because of their unbridled optimism about what the future holds or their lack of foresight, they take more risks than older or younger individuals.

How true are these perceptions? Just how much storm and stress is there? Arnett found in his research that adolescents and parents surely do have conflicts, but many of these are neither serious nor long lasting enough to affect the foundation of the parent-child relationship. Rather, even when difficult, these conflicts seem to be a part of the adolescent experience— perhaps a way of establishing independence, as many scholars have suggested.

Of the three elements that Arnett discusses, mood disruptions seem to be the one that is most often part of the popular view of adolescence. But again, Arnett found that although mood swings may be real in adolescents, they are not severe, and they may very well reflect environmental and cognitive factors rather than

biological or maturational processes. Arnett notes that factors such as popularity, school performance, and the quality of family relationships can affect the likelihood of mood swings.

Finally, what about those risky behaviors? Car accidents are the number one cause of death in the adolescent age group, and the risky practices we attribute to teenagers, such as unsafe sex and dangerous driving, contribute to our image of them as "wild and crazy." But, as Arnett notes, we cannot generalize to all adolescents from this image. He found that the degrees of risk-taking behavior in different adolescents are due as much to individual differences and individual circumstances as to their age.

So are adolescents constantly weathering storm and stress as they face the future? To some extent, yes, absolutely. However, as Arnett wants us to remember, not all of adolescence is characterized by such feelings. They are only a small part of what individuals must accomplish among the more pleasant aspects of growing into adulthood.

adulthood, and maturity) are described within the context of the individual's needs rather than solely external social factors.

Stage 7: Adulthood

The Psychosocial Issue: Generativity Versus Stagnation

One of the important features of Erikson's theory is that it views development as a continuous, ongoing process. For the young adult who is well on the way to a successful career and intimate personal relationships as a result of successfully completing the stage of young adulthood, the relevant task in the next stage, adulthood, is to generate whatever is necessary to define a style or life role.

Maintaining the continuity of work and life is critical to the stage of adulthood, during which the individual often seeks out fulfilling experiences based on personal or intellectual, rather than financial, goals.

This generativity characterizes the young woman who, after working for 5 years to accumulate some savings, begins graduate school and takes the first step toward becoming a physician or begins to have children and take part in their development. It also characterizes the middle-aged man who feels that he needs to change his occupation to establish greater congruence between his role expectations and his actual behavior. It is not uncommon for individuals to change direction suddenly after 20 years in one profession, taking on new kinds of work, study, or adventure. Frequently, when friends and others ask such people why they decided to make these changes, the response is something like "All my life I wanted to do this, and only now have I realized that I can." What these people may be saying is that although their roles in life before they decided to make a change may have been satisfactory, they were not sufficiently fulfilling.

A major component of the stage of adulthood is its emphasis on continuity with the preceding stages. The sense of generativity that the adult feels comes from the efforts he or she makes to have some part in supporting and encouraging the development of the next generation. An individual who cannot help to lend this continuity to the next generation may become overly absorbed in personal needs, ignoring the needs of others, and may gradually experience stagnation.

Stage 8: Maturity

The Psychosocial Issue: Ego Integrity Versus Despair

Erikson uses the term *ego integrity* to describe the outcome of the stage of maturity for the older individual who has come to recognize, after a lifetime of successfully resolving conflicts, that he or she has led a meaningful, productive, and worthwhile life. This final stage of development includes some mystical elements, with an emphasis on the importance of being "one with your past" and creating and feeling a new love for the human ego and not necessarily for oneself. The older

Developmentally successful older adults can look back on their lives with a sense of satisfaction and accomplishment, especially concerning their own personal growth and development.

person can dispense wisdom to children and younger adults. To gain this wisdom, the mature adult has traveled the long and difficult road from the basic trust/distrust conflict of the earliest stage of development through all the other stages to this final stage of realization. If development has proceeded successfully through the years, in this stage the individual is able to gain some perspective on what has occurred.

According to Erikson, the healthy individual at this stage is able to look back on past years and, regardless of their content, feel satisfied. Such a person views his or her own being as congruent with the purpose, rhyme, and reason of life and develops a great deal of ego strength or ego integrity from this awareness. The strength gained from a high degree of ego integrity also helps the individual adjust to the aging process and the inevitability of death. This is much like the state of self-actualization that Abraham Maslow (1968) discusses. The person at this stage of life who cannot successfully view his or her life as meaningful makes a desperate attempt to compensate for lost time. Such an individual finally realizes that things are not as they should be and that the emptiness that has characterized so many of his or her later years is bound to continue. In such a case, a tragic state of despair can develop.

THE STAGES AND EPIGENESIS

Throughout all of the eight psychosocial stages discussed above, the principle of epigenesis is the primary controlling force that integrates the separate parts of human development to form a unified whole. Although the idea of an epigenetic sequence of stages is most firmly rooted in the work of biologists, Kitchener (1978) points out five essential features of epigenesis from the perspective of developmental psychology:

1. Epigenesis is represented by a causal set of events. This means that development consists of events that operate in a preordered sequence in which each event is related to later ones. This is one reason Erikson's model is referred to as *hierarchical:* The resolution of the crisis associated with each stage is related to the resolution of later crises. The success with which each crisis is resolved has a bearing on later adjustment and developmental progress.

2. The concept of epigenesis implies the existence of a series of stages that are qualitatively different from one another. Erikson, however, is the only psychoanalytic theorist to postulate explicitly a series of stages across the entire life span. His work represents the increasingly popular point of view of the life-span psychologist, who is concerned with the development of the individual from conception through death.

   > Epigenesis, the basic principle on which Erikson's theory is based, assumes that all parts of a system have unique ascendancy within that system.

3. Epigenesis is a process through which behaviors become differentiated to form unique elements or parts of a functioning whole. For example, adolescents who are trying to establish their identities might work toward that goal through the continual refinement of their needs, given the social milieu in which they exist. This is a very important feature of Erikson's theory because it accounts for the way in which new and unique behaviors arise.

4. The parallel process of organization takes place largely as a result of increased differentiation. For the individual to develop successfully, and for

the whole to become functional, each of the independent units must be sufficiently well organized to maintain strong ego integrity. Organization reflects how successful the underlying mechanisms of development are in different individuals. In order for the whole to function, each part of the system must be organized and coherent.

5. Epigenesis is the primary process through which the separate systems, which have become increasingly differentiated from one another and then organized, become integrated and finally produce a new element to be assimilated by the whole.

Many practitioners have adopted Erikson's theory of psychosocial development as a useful framework from which to deal with parents and children. Much of Freud's theory and influence are present in Erikson's model, but it raises very little of the controversy surrounding Freud's work. For example, educators often find Erikson's descriptions of the developmental tasks useful when they are choosing and designing curricula. The commonsense dimensions of Erikson's proposed stages are intuitively appealing, and because in his writings he pays central attention to schools, neighborhoods, cultural values, and social patterns, his readers find examples of experiences they can identify with.

> Erikson's approach to understanding human development can be summed up as respect for the individual and for the individual's expression of freedom.

Erikson's theory has had especially extensive appeal among Americans. Perhaps this is so because some of the central elements of Erikson's characterization of the developmental process were influenced by his own transplantation from European to American society. As a sensitive observer of the American scene, he developed a sharp appreciation for the influence of social factors on development. Erikson's theory of good development is also consonant with the ideals of a democratic society. His concept of development is almost entirely equated with such democratic principles as freedom to choose different options and the right to privacy.

Erikson's major contributions to developmental theory include his popularization of the concept of psychosocial stages and his emphasis on the importance of strong and healthy ego development. Erikson's book *Childhood and Society* (1950a) is still widely read, and many people probably find it easier to accept the basic assumptions of Erikson's theory than those found in Freud's.

> Erikson's theory encompasses the nature of qualitative change during the middle and later years of life as well as the early years.

It is not unusual for educators, physicians, and parents to combine the Gesellian and Eriksonian approaches, applying Gesell's emphasis on the importance of developmental tasks and individual maturational factors as well as Erikson's views on the virtues of a loving and supportive environment. When development is not proceeding well, waiting for the child to catch up (the Gesellian stance) is probably less effective than clinical intervention (the Eriksonian stance). A practitioner working from the Eriksonian framework would direct such clinical intervention toward identifying the problems blocking growth, removing or remediating those impediments to strengthening the ego, and providing the supportive conditions that encourage further healthy development.

WEB SITES OF INTEREST

- "Erik Erikson: 1902–1994," by C. George Boeree, at http: /www.ship.edu/~ cgboeree/erikson.html: Boeree presents an interesting discussion of Erikson's work that focuses on Indian lore and the child's passage through adolescence to adulthood. In addition to providing a biography of Erikson, Boeree comments on Erikson's most influential writings and his theory.
- "Landing on the Moon," by Erik Erikson, at http://www.news.harvard.edu/gazette/2002/06.13/06-eemoon.html: Erikson gave this unusually titled lecture at Harvard University on September 24, 1969, shortly after the first man walked on the moon. Among other things, he notes that he was curious to know why he and a number of other "old men" (and no women) were asked to comment on this occasion. He also says that "the kingdom has always been within each of us, if we can only learn to face it—and to share it."

FURTHER READINGS ABOUT PSYCHOSOCIAL DEVELOPMENT

Kobayashi, Ryuji. (1991). Psychosexual development of autistic children in adolescence. *Japanese Journal of Child and Adolescent Psychiatry, 32,* 1–14.

In this article, Kobayashi explores the establishment of gender identity in nine autistic adolescents (ages 10 to 17 years), focusing on the prime developmental tasks for such adolescents: learning how to deal with the power of the sex drive, establishing relationships with peers or persons of the opposite sex, and becoming independent of one's parents.

Mitchell, Stephen A., & Black, Margaret J. (1995). *Freud and beyond: A history of modern psychoanalytic thought.* New York: Basic Books.

Mitchell and Black present a history of psychoanalytic thinking since Freud in this informative and not overly technical book. They include discussion of the ideas of many of Freud's disciples as well as a historical account of the development of psychoanalytic theory.

Nakata, Yojiro, & Mukai, Tekayo. (1997). Psychosexual development during the second decade of life in the present society. *Journal of Mental Health, 43,* 3–12.

In this article, which focuses on the sexual problems of teenagers, Nakata and Mukai discuss biological development and gender identity as well as parent-child relationships during puberty within a psychoanalytic model. They suggest that more research on male teenagers' gender identity is necessary to shed light on the factors involved in teenagers' delinquent sexual behavior.

Siskind, Diana. (1994). Max and his diaper: An example of the interplay of arrests in psychosexual development and the separation individuation process. *Psychoanalytic Inquiry, 14,* 58–82.

Siskind presents an interesting case study of a 3-year-old boy who refused to give up his diapers. She discusses the factors involved in his treatment, which included separation and individuation issues and the mother's difficulty in allowing the child adequate expression of aggression. When the mother was able to permit the boy to express aggression adequately, the child was freed to use his aggressive drive in a nondestructive way and to progress developmentally.

Snarey, John R., Son L., Kuehne, Valerie S., Hauser, S., & Vaillant, George E. (1987). The role of parenting in men's psychosocial development: A longitudinal study of early adulthood infertility and midlife generativity. *Developmental Psychology, 23,* 593–603.

Snarey and his colleagues prospectively studied 343 men over four decades; within this sample, 52 of the men experienced infertility during their first marriages. The researchers found that the ways in which these men resolved parenting issues could be predicted by their prior infertility coping strategies and parenting outcomes. According to Erikson, parenting during early adulthood is a crucial but not sufficient prior condition for the midlife achievement of psychosocial generativity.

PART IV

THE BEHAVIORAL
PERSPECTIVE

CHAPTER 7

BEHAVIORAL MODELS OF DEVELOPMENT

Heredity is nothing more than stored environment.

—Luther Burbank

With a good heredity, nature deals you a fine hand at cards; and with a good environment, you learn to play the hand well.

—Walter C. Alvarez

I am I plus my circumstances.

—José Ortega y Gasset

THE BEGINNINGS OF BEHAVIORISM

The different theoretical perspectives discussed so far give special attention to maturational or biological themes in development. Freud's psychoanalytic model, Gesell's maturational model, and ethological and sociobiological models all emphasize the way in which development results from complex interactions among biological factors across a wide range of settings. Theorists working from all these perspectives place some importance on the role of the environment, but they do not believe that the environment is the major determinant or shaping force behind developmental change. To them, the environment is caused, not causal. They assume that there are underlying structural components that follow a unique timetable of emergence, and that the presence or absence of these components affects the direction and rate of developmental progress. Although the structures are not directly observable, their presence is inferred based on observation of individuals' performance on various tasks.

Behaviorism (the school of developmental psychology based on behavioral models) offers alternative ways of describing how the developmental process takes place. Like Freudian theory, behaviorism has many variants; that is, there are several different behavioral models, not just one. Behaviorists all share the same basic tenet, however: Development is a process that adheres to principles and laws of learning. Biological givens provide some of the foundation for development, but experiences and opportunities to learn are the central and necessary elements that give direction to the process.

Although much of behaviorism is based on the early work of the Russian physiologist Ivan Pavlov, behavioral models have been characterized as uniquely American because the scientists who have formulated and applied Pavlov's basic model have for the most part been Americans. In addition, the central location for advanced research within this field is still in the United States.

Most behaviorists believe that the large body of information that researchers have amassed in studies of how learning occurs can be applied to the developmental process. Most basic undergraduate-level psychology courses devote a considerable amount of time to the study of learning principles, and many students in psychology laboratories have had experience in reproducing the phenomena described by the principles of learning, such as conditioning (more about this later). Although the original evidence for how learning occurs came from laboratory studies, psychologists have elaborated on the rudimentary learning principles developed in labs to account for the behavioral repertoires of children and adults.

I want to stress one point before beginning a discussion of the behavioral perspective. Whenever different theorists attempt to explain any phenomenon, there is overlap in the variables they study, the methods they use, and (if there is "truth" in science) their findings. Within any theoretical camp, there is always a great deal

Behavioral approaches to development are very different from the other approaches discussed so far. In behaviorism, the emphasis is overwhelmingly on the importance of environmental events in the creation and modification of behavior.

The term *behaviorism* encompasses a wide range of behavioral models that vary in the degree of influence they attribute to the environment.

of variability among the views of different theorists, although they are basically tied to the same philosophical assumptions. For example, within the broad framework of psychoanalysis, some theorists adhere strictly to the teachings of Freud whereas others reject some of the basic tenets of Freud's teachings and develop their own ideas.

For a variety of reasons, this dimension of the behavioral approach to development has been slighted. Students are sometimes taught about only one type of behaviorism, in which developmental processes are understood to be controlled completely by environmental forces. This viewpoint may be representative of one group of behaviorists, but there are others who believe that, along with environment, internal cognitive and/or biological processes play important roles as well. In fact, during the past decade some behaviorists have studied the idea that, in addition to being acted upon by the environment, humans act on the environment as well.

In general, behaviorists do not place greater importance on biological influences than on environmental influences. However, many behaviorists today are incorporating more and more cognitive and social elements of behavior into their theories, making a rich and diverse set of ideas even more useful.

BASIC ASSUMPTIONS OF BEHAVIORAL MODELS

Behaviorism's name comes from the work of psychologist John B. Watson in the early 20th century. Watson rejected introspection, or self-inspection, as a method of studying behavior and declared that only *observable behaviors* are worthy of serious study. Watson believed that psychology is a science, just like physics or chemistry, and as a science it should be based on concepts that can be objectively and reliably observed. Watson used the term *behaviorism* in the sense of a particular methodological approach to the study of behavior that is sometimes called *methodological behaviorism.*

Behaviorism also refers to a set of different theories concerning the developmental process that attribute the control of developmental outcomes more to environmental factors than to biological ones. These theories share some basic tenets that serve as starting points for most developmental behaviorists, which may be the reason some people fail to distinguish among behavioral theorists and theories. This foundation shared by behaviorists provides some continuity between past and present behavioral perspectives. In fact, the links between today's behavioral theorists and the behaviorists of the early 20th century are stronger than similar links found in other theoretical perspectives. Regardless of what specific theory is being discussed, some basic assumptions are common to all behavioral views of development:

According to behaviorism, development results from the organization and reorganization of existing behaviors.

1. Development is a function of learning.

2. Development is the result of different types of learning.

3. Individual differences in development reflect differences in the histories and past experiences of individuals.

4. Development results from the organization of existing behaviors.

5. Biological factors set general limits on the kinds of behaviors that develop, but the environment determines the behaviors in which the individual engages.

6. The development of the individual is not directly related to biologically determined stages.

I discuss each of these assumptions briefly in turn below.

Development is a function of learning. Robert Gagne (1968) defines behavioral development as "the cumulative effects of learning." In this context, learning is defined as short-term changes in behavior. When these short-term changes are combined and are *hierarchically organized* (that is, when they build on each other), the result is development. Development, then, is the result of the linking of accumulated experiences. Development results from learning—learning does not result from development.

Behavioral theorists believe that development is a function of learning.

Other behaviorists believe similarly that development is a function of learning, and many have presented detailed analyses of how this learning takes place. For example, Sidney Bijou (1968) defines learning as the "relationship in the strengthening and weakening of stimulus and response functions" (p. 419). In this paradigm, processes such as reinforcement and punishment (which I discuss later) control, or govern, how and what behaviors are acquired.

Development is the result of different types of learning. To appreciate fully the diversity and richness of human behavior within the behavioral model, it is important to understand each type of learning that governs the developmental process. Some of these different types of learning are associated with particular theorists whom I discuss in this and the following chapters.

Individual differences in development reflect differences in the histories and past experiences of individuals. Differences in individual development result from the past experiences that people have had and the value of these experiences for helping the individuals to accomplish immediate or long-range goals. Behaviorists view the history of the individual as a series of short-term changes that, when linked together, form the foundation for development. The content of these experiences and the way they are organized contribute to the differences between one person's behavior and another's. For example, all children go through something called "child rearing," yet the experiences this entails surely differ for different people. These experiences are part of the individual's history of learning. The dynamics of how people store and recall their experiences, and how they transfer their experiences to new situations, are crucial elements of the behavioral perspective.

Development results from the organization of existing behaviors. That is, development is a process in which simple isolated behaviors are organized into complex patterns. For example, the healthy infant is born with some very sophisticated reflexes, such as the rooting response, in which the infant responds to being stroked on the cheek by turning his or her head in the direction of the stroked cheek. This is clearly an important reflex, because it orients the infant toward the source of nutrition. This reflex and 30 others are the individual elements that form the basis for more complex behaviors. Later development, in all its richness and complexity, is related to these early biological reflexes. This process lends the idea of continuity or consistency over time to behavioral models of development.

> Development progresses from simple behaviors to more complex ones, all subject to the laws of learning.

To understand the progression from simple to complex behaviors, picture a set of building blocks in which each block represents a unit of behavior. All healthy infants have the same basic equipment or biological mechanisms. Over time, their different experiences result in the unique organization of the biological potentials of each child; that is, the building blocks are stacked in different ways for different people. Later in life, the differences among individuals become even greater, because the organization of their experiences undergoes further change. Of course, the developmental process is rather more complex than a process of simply putting blocks or experiences together in different ways.

Biological factors set general limits on the kinds of behaviors that develop, but the environment determines the behaviors in which the individual engages. Within the behavioral perspective, biological influences are considered to be the fundamental systems on which behavior grows. Although biological processes provide a framework, the environment determines the kinds of behaviors an individual will acquire. Even conception is not a purely biological event, because environmental factors—such as the hospitality of the womb and maternal diet, smoking, and alcohol intake—influence it and can affect development significantly. Although the newborn infant displays an impressive repertoire of reflexive, biologically based behaviors, the newborn's behaviors reflect significant environmental influences. Many behaviorists insist that environmental input affects biological as well as behavioral features.

> Biological factors set the limits of development, but the environment determines the kinds of behaviors in the individual's repertoire.

From a behavioral perspective, if biological needs (such as good health care, nutrition, and exercise) are met, developmental progress depends on the sequencing and relevance of experiences. The nature of these experiences plays a large part in determining the content of behavior as well. For example, in some cultures school-age children acquire skills such as reading and writing, whereas in other cultures they learn skills in oral communication.

The development of the individual is not directly related to biologically determined stages. Behavior is not biologically determined, nor is it necessarily tied to or a function of internally regulated biological processes. Behaviorists, however, do not dismiss obvious universal maturational sequences. Being able to maintain balance, for example, is a prerequisite of walking. However, if a child who is capable of maintaining balance is not given the opportunity to learn to walk, walking may be significantly delayed. On the other hand, the provision of certain types of experiences can accelerate development.

> The development of the individual is not fixed by biologically regulated stages.

Behaviorists do not make any a priori claims about the sequence or the presence of stages in development, but they also do not reject the possibility that evolutionary history may predispose an organism toward particular behavioral patterns and sequences. A behaviorist would not endorse the idea that any given behavior belongs to a particular stage of development, as we have seen is the case in theories discussed earlier. Rather, a behaviorist would look at the concept of stages as a convenient way to organize behaviors.

> Behavioral theorists are a highly varied group and have differing opinions concerning the importance of environmental events.

The six assumptions discussed above are not universally held among behaviorists. Because behaviorism is an evolving point of view, some advocates of behaviorist models would qualify these assumptions in various ways. Although they are not hard-and-fast rules, they illustrate the behaviorist viewpoint in general and can be used as a tool for organization.

CLASSICAL CONDITIONING AND IVAN PAVLOV

Along with Sigmund Freud, Russian physiologist Ivan Pavlov is one of the most significant contributors to the growth of the study of human behavior as a science. Pavlov's research on digestion processes in mammals earned him the Nobel Prize for medicine in 1904. As a by-product of his interest in physiology, he questioned the way in which certain biological events become systematically related to changes in the environment that accompany them. Although Pavlov was not a psychologist and was not specifically interested in the study of learning, the results of his research have been applied to further studies aimed at clarifying how certain behaviors come under the control of the environment. Pavlov's examination of two concepts, classical conditioning and the classically conditioned reflex, started this revolution in thinking about development.

> Ivan Pavlov, a Russian physiologist, was the first scientist to study the direct relationship between behavior and events in the environment.

Classical Conditioning and the Conditioned Reflex

Classical conditioning is a type of learning that occurs when two different events happen simultaneously and one of the events takes on the quality of eliciting the other (or the original) event. Pavlov presents a good example of this phenomenon in his influential text *Conditioned Reflexes* (1927): When a hungry dog is given food, it salivates. If the presentation of the food is accompanied or paired (usually more than once) with another event (such as the ringing of a bell), the dog will eventually salivate when that other event alone is presented (in this example, when the bell rings). The learned response of salivation in response to a previously neutral event (that is, one that by itself could not cause the dog to salivate) is called a **conditioned response** (or **conditioned reflex**). The process through which this very specific type of learning takes place is called **classical conditioning**.

In this example, the food the dog receives is an **unconditioned stimulus,** or UCS. According to Pavlov, an unconditioned stimulus is any event that "naturally" produces an unlearned response—that is, the response occurs without the need for previous experience or learning on the part of the organism. Another example of an unconditioned stimulus is the knee-jerk response; any reflexive behavior that is controlled by the autonomic nervous system falls into this category. The dog's salivation (as a response to the unconditioned stimulus) is referred to as an **unconditioned response,** or UCR.

> Classical conditioning is based on the pairing of previously neutral stimuli with autonomic behaviors (that is, behaviors not under the direct control of the individual).

The classical conditioning paradigm contains two important elements: the conditioned stimulus (CS) and the conditioned response (CR). In Pavlov's example of the dog, after the unconditioned response of salivation has occurred, the pairing of the food and the ringing of the bell is begun again; that is, with the introduction of the food, the bell is rung. At this point, the sound of the bell contains no controlling power. After a number of such pairings, however, the bell is presented alone, without the food, and the dog salivates. The bell's role here is that of **conditioned stimulus**, and the salivation is a conditioned response. In this example, the UCR and the CR are identical. This is not always the case, but these responses are often highly similar to one another.

Pavlov's classical conditioning paradigm is illustrated in Figure 7.1. At Time 1 in the figure, the food (the UCS) alone produces salivation, the unconditioned response. After repeated presentations of the food with the bell (Times 2, 3, and 4), the bell alone elicits the response of salivation and hence becomes a conditioned stimulus. Timing is a very important factor in this process—the unconditioned and conditioned stimuli must be presented close to each other for conditioning to occur.

Figure 7.2 illustrates another example of classical conditioning, a case in which a young child comes to pair a frightening experience such as a nightmare with darkness, resulting in the child's fear of the dark. The figure shows how this relationship

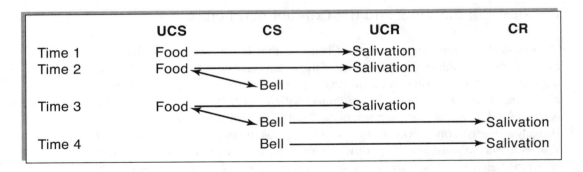

FIGURE 7.1 The Classical Conditioning Paradigm

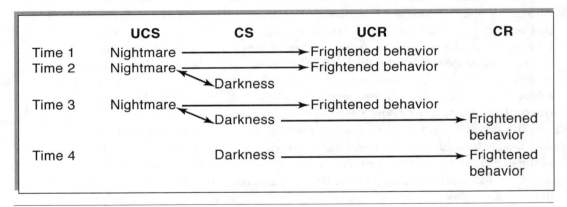

FIGURE 7.2 Classical Conditioning and Fear of the Dark

between the nightmare and the darkness is established and the darkness itself becomes a conditioned stimulus for frightened behavior.

Factors That Influence Classical Conditioning

Some of the important factors that influence classical conditioning are reinforcement, punishment, and extinction.

Our behavior would remain very limited if the simple process described above were all there is to classical conditioning. Because the classical conditioning paradigm is not enough on its own to explain the richness and diversity of human behavior, more elaborate concepts are needed. Pavlov identifies two factors that affect the strength of the conditioned reflex: reinforcement and extinction. He also notes that the degree of transfer of one conditioned reflex to another is influenced by two factors: generalization and differentiation.

Reinforcement occurs when the relationship between the conditioned stimulus and the unconditioned response (for example, the darkness and the fearful response) becomes strengthened through repeated association. This relationship is weakened to the point of disappearing when reinforcement is no longer present. In other words, if the child does not experience more nightmares in the dark room, the conditioned response is likely to disappear. This process is called **extinction.**

Even though the concepts of reinforcement and extinction explain how certain behaviors become more or less likely to occur in the future, they do not explain why individuals' behavioral repertoires consist of many different behaviors of all degrees of strength. To account for this complexity of behavior, Pavlov introduced the complementary concepts of generalization and differentiation.

Generalization occurs when a conditioned stimulus results in a response that is similar to the original conditioned response. For example, the child who has nightmares may refuse to enter any dark area of the house. The complementary process is **differentiation**, or the way in which one stimulus is discriminated from another. Differentiation takes place through the selective reinforcement of certain associations and the lack of reinforcement of others. For example, the child may learn not to be fearful in certain dark settings (such as movie theaters), but may be fearful in others.

The main theme of this chapter is that development results from learning, which in turn reflects the individual's experiences. Pavlov showed his genius when he used the conditioned reflex as a methodology for understanding how a fundamental and important type of learning occurs. In many ways he was the founder of behaviorism, and the essence of his work still continues today in many laboratories around the world. The application of Pavlov's work on the conditioned reflex to the process of development can be summed up by two points: First, learning is governed by relationships between stimuli in the environment and the organism's reaction to those stimuli (responses). These relationships are strengthened by reinforcement and weakened by extinction. Second, the way one response generalizes to other stimuli (and in turn is differentiated from other stimuli) explains how an organism becomes increasingly complex in its multifaceted relationship to the environment.

> Through repeated pairings, previously neutral stimuli become conditioned stimuli and conditioned responses.

> Among Pavlov's important discoveries is that behavior is governed by the relationship between stimuli and environmental conditions.

THE BEGINNING OF BEHAVIORISM IN THE UNITED STATES: JOHN WATSON

The founder of behaviorism in the United States, John Watson, analyzed learning in more detail than did Pavlov and further elaborated some of the principles through which learning occurs. Watson also stressed the necessity of studying behavior objectively as part of detailed analyses of the rules that govern the acquisition of simple behaviors.

Up to the beginning of the 20th century, psychology was characterized by the European tradition of introspection, a technique for focusing on the core of an experience by dealing with the unconscious elements of that experience. The early structuralists, those who used introspection as a technique, believed that this method was highly objective because it consisted of systematic observation and detailed reporting. However, some psychologists disagreed, claiming that anything that relies so heavily on an individual's interpretation is contaminated by unknown and uncontrollable factors.

In much of his work, Watson de-emphasized the importance of mentalistic contributions to the nature of behavior.

Watson was the first student to receive a Ph.D. in psychology from the University of Chicago. He quickly realized the necessity for studying behavior objectively, rejected the use of so-called mentalistic concepts, and dismissed the method of introspection, asserting that it is imprecise. When Watson introduced behaviorism in 1913 as a psychology of objective and observable phenomena, he believed this new brand of psychology should employ the methods of such natural sciences as chemistry and physics. Watson argued that through the use of exacting and rigorous methods, one could eventually document precise cause-and-effect relationships between stimuli in the environment and the behavior of the organism. If these same techniques and standards could be applied to the study of human behavior, Watson felt, the mechanisms of behavior and development could be identified.

—— On the Web ——

B. F. Skinner wrote *Walden Two* (originally published in 1948) to present his ideas about behavior and development and to show how they could be applied in a real-world setting. The book provided the foundation for many real communities, one of which was Los Horcones Community in Mexico. On the Walden Community Web site at http://perso.wanadoo.es/waldencm/ w2en.htm, you can find commentary about the experience by people directly involved in the project, as well as links to several related sites.

The Stimulus-Response Connection

Like Pavlov, Watson believed that the basic component of behavior is the **stimulus-response unit** and that any behavior can be produced (or explained) by the particular sequencing of stimuli and responses. This point of view has far-reaching implications for, and raises some basic questions about, issues of the control and prediction of human behavior. In one of Watson's (1925) frequently quoted passages he discusses this directly:

> Give me a dozen healthy infants, well formed, and my own specified world to bring them up in and I'll guarantee to take any one at random and train him to become any type of specialist I might select—doctor, lawyer, artist, merchant chief and, yes, even beggerman and thief, regardless of his talents, penchants, tendencies, abilities, vocations, and race of his ancestors. (p. 104)

As this quote makes clear, Watson believed strongly in the total malleability of the individual; he asserted that any outcome is possible given control over critical events. Watson studied the work of Pavlov closely and accepted Pavlov's basic findings about classical conditioning and the conditioned reflex. This provided Watson with a firm foundation on which to build a theory that incorporated his own ideas and beliefs in greater detail. In his theory, he felt compelled to deal with behavior of all kinds rather than just the reflexive types of behavior that are biological in nature.

Watson defined a **stimulus** as any form of energy that excites a sensory organ. This is an objective definition that specifies both the source of energy (such as a sound) and the measurability of the stimulation. Internal thoughts and feelings cannot be considered stimuli because they are not clearly identifiable as sources of energy and they cannot be shown to stimulate any sensory organs. In addition, they are impossible to measure directly. Some behaviorists see Watson's definition of a stimulus as extreme, and it is not wholeheartedly adopted by all.

A **response** tends to follow a stimulus and is an observable reaction of some physiological subsystem to a stimulus. The **stimulus-response connection** forms the basis of all behavior, influenced, of course, by the laws of classical conditioning.

Although Watson believed that human behavior is definitely malleable, he also recognized that there are realistic limits to what can be taught and learned.

From Watson's perspective, the analysis of complex behaviors should consist of an analysis of the constituent stimulus-response (S-R) units. The responses are not only reactions to stimuli; they in turn serve as stimuli for further events. This link between responses and stimuli provides the basis for more extended and complex learning. The classically conditioned reflex (a special type of response) acts as a stimulus for a response that may follow. In turn, this provides a linking of one S-R association to the next S-R association and so on, creating a complex chain of interrelated behaviors in which the response from an earlier S-R association becomes the stimulus for the next. This notion of associations was an important step in the advancement of behaviorism, because it goes beyond the simple S-R event and suggests a more complex system of behavior.

Factors Affecting S-R Connections

Watson introduced
two important
concepts that help
to explain how
behavior changes:
the law of recency
and the law of
frequency.

Like Pavlov, Watson believed that it is important to take into account factors beyond the simple S-R association. For Pavlov, these factors were reinforcement and extinction and the complementary processes of generalization and differentiation. Watson introduced the law of frequency and the law of recency, which are elegant in their conception and have far-reaching implications for our understanding of the developmental process.

The **law of frequency** states that the more often a person makes a response in the presence of a certain stimulus, the more likely it is that the person will make the same response to that stimulus in the future. For example, after a person learns that red lights mean "stop," the frequency with which a red light is associated with that person's putting a foot on the brake and stopping the car will increase. The identification of this link in the system (which has many other little links within it, such as picking up the foot from the accelerator pedal, placing it on the brake, and pressing down) is similar to Pavlov's concept of differentiation. When the light turns green, the foot is taken off the brake, placed on the accelerator, and pressed down. According to the law of frequency, the pairing of the act of stopping with the presence of a red light becomes one of many high-priority associations. It is no accident that stop signs are red, because it is the traffic engineer's purpose to alert people to stop through the dual signal of reading "STOP" and seeing the color red. The engineer assumes that from drivers' experience, red represents "take your foot off the accelerator and put it on the brake." The more frequently an association occurs between the same (or similar) set of stimulus and response, the stronger this association becomes. Hence the more likely it is that the same response will result given the same or a similar stimulus or event in the future.

The more
frequently a
connection occurs
between a stimulus
and a response, the
stronger the
association
becomes (law of
frequency).

The **law of recency** states that the more recently a particular stimulus has been associated with a particular response, the more likely it is that the association will occur again. Whereas the law of frequency addresses the number of times something occurs, the law of recency addresses the length of time between the stimulus and the response. For example, the factors associated with certain behaviors are often obscured because these factors occurred so far in the past that it is difficult to attribute any causal role to them. The more time elapses between the stimulus and the response, the less likely that the response will occur again given the same or similar stimulus. This is true because as time passes, more mediating events occur to cloud the picture. Similarly, those events that occur most closely in time following a stimulus are far more likely to become associated with that stimulus than those that occur later. For example, when a young child misbehaves, it makes little sense to wait to punish the child "when Daddy gets home," because so much time will have passed that the child will be unlikely to draw any significant relationship between the behavior and the punishment. To extend this example, think how unfortunate it is for the child to run up to the father on his arrival home, ready with a hug and a "hello," only to be threatened with discipline for misbehaving earlier that day. The only sense the young child can make out of such an incident is that running up to say hello to Dad when he comes home results in punishment.

Because the rules of frequency and recency operate simultaneously, it is important to consider the events that immediately follow a stimulus and to what degree these events recur. For example, children are often not given feedback on their behavior consistently (frequency) or soon enough (recency) for it to be an important influence. Ideally, children should be praised or punished immediately after they exhibit behavior that is praiseworthy or undesirable, or at least as soon after the behavior as possible, to ensure that the associations they form between the praise or punishment and the behavior are as strong as possible. In addition, parents should be consistent in dispensing both praise and punishment, so that a child always receives support for certain things and also learns that other things may be inappropriate or unacceptable. Consistency is the key.

Watson's militant stance regarding the proper methodology for psychology, coupled with his reliance on stimulus-response associations, left a lasting impression on psychology in general and developmental psychology in particular. Watson placed behaviorism squarely on the environmental, or nurture, side of the nature/nurture debate. His position is both extreme in its claims and wildly optimistic that a good developmental outcome is ultimately a matter of appropriate control of critical events, when perhaps it is not. Here's the quote that you read earlier, but this time, I've included additional text from the original at the end that people often leave off when they present this quote to make a particular point (the italics here are added here for emphasis):

> Give me a dozen healthy infants, well formed, and my own specified world to bring them up in and I'll guarantee to take any one at random and train him to become any type of specialist I might select—doctor, lawyer, artist, merchant chief and, yes, even beggerman and thief, regardless of his talents, penchants, tendencies, abilities, vocations, and race of his ancestors. *I am going beyond the facts and I admit it, but so have the advocates of the contrary and they have been doing it for many thousands of years.* (Watson, 1925, p. 104)

So Watson felt strongly, but he surely considered the importance of other factors and admitted that other points of view may have credibility as well. It is ironic that in their rush to criticize such perceived extremism, however, Watson's critics have largely ignored his optimism concerning human potential and the possibilities for fostering optimal outcomes.

The more recently a certain response has been given to a certain stimulus, the more likely it is that the same or similar stimulus will result in the same response (law of recency).

B. F. SKINNER'S EXPERIMENTAL ANALYSIS AND BASIC ASSUMPTIONS

With increased pressure for a "better" and more practical psychology in an increasingly technological world, the field of developmental psychology seemed ready for the work of B. F. Skinner (1904–1990). Over the past 50 years, the contributions of this writer turned psychologist have made his work as controversial today as Freud's was during the early 20th century. For interested readers, I recommend Skinner's (1976a) fascinating autobiography.

Without any doubt, B. F. Skinner's research and writings had profound effects on the popularity and usefulness of behaviorism in the United States.

The basic assumption of Skinner's theory is that behavior is a function of its consequences. In other words, the qualities and characteristics of the stimuli that follow behavior are of primary importance, not the qualities and characteristics of the stimuli that precede behavior. Skinner believed that through the systematic study and analysis of the consequences of behavior, we can understand the effects of environmental events on learning. Because learning is the primary mechanism through which development occurs, we can then also understand development.

Skinner, his colleagues, and other behaviorists have invested a great deal of time in defining the rules and conditions that govern the relationship between a response and the events that follow it. Skinner believed that the consequences of any behavior will cause an increase, a decrease, or no change in the probability, or likelihood, that the behavior will occur again. In his first book, *The Behavior of Organisms* (1938), he proposed many of the basic concepts that have been applied to the everyday concerns of his audience, which has grown larger and larger over time with the increasing acceptance and application of these principles. The broad use across many disciplines of such phrases as *behavior modification* and *teaching machines* reflects the scope of Skinner's influence. His detailed description of behaviorism as a science turned full circle from Pavlov's initial work on the classical conditioning of innate reflexes to the broad conception of a utopia presented in *Walden Two,* Skinner's (1948/1976b) controversial fictional account of communal living. His last book, *Recent Issues in the Analysis of Behavior,* published in 1989, a year before his death, is a collection of papers on human behavior, this one targeted at psychologists and behavior analysts.

Respondent and Operant Learning

To understand Skinner's contribution to developmental psychology fully, it is useful to have some familiarity with the difference between two fundamental types of learning: respondent learning and operant learning. **Respondent learning** is learning that is subject to the laws of classical conditioning (as discussed above), is automatic in nature, and is not under voluntary control. For example, in Pavlov's

---

TABLE 7.1 A Comparison of Respondent and Operant Conditioning

	Respondent Conditioning	*Operant Conditioning*
Origin of the stimulus	Known and important	Irrelevant
Origin of the response	Elicited by stimuli (S^R)	Emitted by the organism
Relationship between stimulus and response	Eliciting stimulus precedes response	Reinforcing stimulus follows response
Examples	Eye blink, digestion	Driving, mowing the lawn, socializing
Synonyms	Classical conditioning	Instrumental conditioning
	Type S learning	Type R learning
	Associative shifting	Trial-and-error learning
	Conditioning	Problem solving

---

work, the dog's salivation was elicited by the presentation of meat. Salivation is no more under the dog's control than a knee-jerk reflex is under an adult human's control or the sucking response is under an infant's control. These responses are not learned, nor can they be "improved" through practice. They are instinctual or species-specific behaviors, such as the grasping reflex in humans or flying in birds. These behaviors are not actively transmitted through teaching or any other cultural process, are not "learned" (in the common meaning of the word), and are elicited or controlled by what precedes them.

Another type of learning, **operant learning**, forms the basis for Skinner's theory of operant conditioning. Operant behaviors are behaviors that are controlled by what follows them, not by what precedes them. Further, operant behaviors are not elicited by stimuli that precede the behaviors, but are emitted and are initially under the control of the organism. Because such behaviors are emitted, little emphasis is placed on the stimuli that precede them. In other words, the stimulus that precedes an operant behavior is not a focus of systematic experimental analysis. Table 7.1 presents a comparison of respondent and operant conditioning across several dimensions.

Why did Skinner choose to study operant rather than respondent behaviors? Respondent behaviors tend to be limited in their variety and in their susceptibility to control by environmental events. In effect, they are simply less interesting than operant behaviors. Humans exhibit many different types of behaviors, and almost all of them are operant in nature. For example, here are just a few operant behaviors you might exhibit (and some of their common consequences): brushing your teeth

> Respondent behaviors are controlled by what precedes them, and operant behaviors are controlled by what follows them.

> In respondent conditioning, behaviors are controlled by what precedes them; in operant conditioning, behaviors are controlled by what follows them.

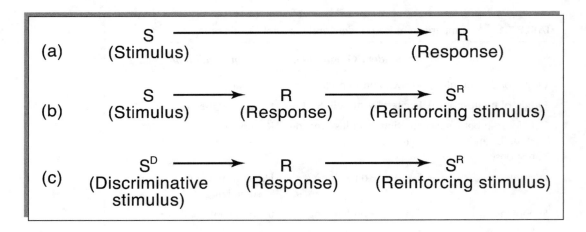

FIGURE 7.3   The Basic Operant Conditioning Model

A positive reinforcer is a stimulus that is added to a situation, and a negative reinforcer is a stimulus that is subtracted or removed from a situation.

In the simplest of Skinner's paradigms, when a behavior is reinforced by a stimulus, the strength of the association between the stimulus and the behavior is increased.

(fewer dentist visits), dressing nicely (attention from other people), cooking a meal (good food to eat), and walking to work (exercise for good health). Given that there are so many different behaviors that are not reflexive and that those behaviors have so many possible outcomes or consequences, it is no wonder that the individual differences among people are so wide-ranging and varied. Skinner devoted a great deal of time and effort to understanding the factors that influence these differences.

Like other behaviorists, Skinner was concerned about understanding behavior (and development), and so he focused on the study of observable behaviors. Figure 7.3 presents a simple model of how the consequences of a behavior become important. As you can see, Figure 7.3a illustrates the simple paradigm of a response (R) following a stimulus (S), characteristic of respondent learning. This part of the model is no different from other learning-based models of development already discussed. The difference between Skinner and other theorists becomes apparent when a new element, the concept of the **reinforcing stimulus**, is introduced (part b of Figure 7.3). This S-R event (the R superscript in the figure represents a reinforcing event) acts to control behavior that has preceded it and determines the degree of certainty (or probability) that the behavior will occur again. If a stimulus that follows a behavior increases the probability of that behavior occurring again, the stimulus belongs to the general class of stimuli called **reinforcers**. For example, when you find a lost wallet and return it to its rightful owner, your behavior may be reinforced by the owner's giving you some money as a gesture of thanks. Because of this reinforcement, you might take the same action in a similar situation in the future.

Sometimes an event that follows a behavior causes a decrease in the probability that the behavior will occur again. Such an event belongs to the general class of stimuli called **punishers**. For example, if you run out of gas and have to walk 3 miles to get some, you are likely to find the experience unpleasant. People learn that the consequences (having to walk 3 miles) of some events (running out of gas) are unpleasant and adjust their behavior to avoid having to face those consequences again.

> A punisher is a stimulus that follows a behavior and decreases the likelihood that the behavior will occur again.

Even if we are aware of the processes through which behavior is affected, how do we know what the consequences of different behaviors will be? Through learning, we accumulate storehouses of experiences, and through these experiences we gain the ability to identify stimuli in the environment that are likely to act as either reinforcers or punishers. Through experience, we learn how events in the environment act as **discriminative stimuli**, signaling that given behaviors will be followed by some type of reinforcer or punisher. With the concept of a discriminative stimulus, something new is added to the model. Figure 7.3c shows basically the same schematic as in Figure 7.3b, but the original S (stimulus) is now an SD (discriminative stimulus). This event acts as a sign or a "flag" for the learner that a behavior will have certain consequences. For example, a discriminative stimulus for the behavior of walking to the nearest gas station because you ran out of gas can be the fuel-gauge needle pointing to "empty." A discriminative stimulus for eating may be the time of day, whether or not the person is hungry. Many different stimuli can take on discriminative qualities, again contributing to individual differences.

> Different stimuli in the environment take on special meaning and assume discriminative qualities; these discriminative stimuli control subsequent behavior.

Factors That Influence Behavior

The idea that behavior is a function of its consequences can be applied directly to everyday experiences. If we examine the contents (and contexts) of behavior, we see that those behaviors that have substantial payoffs are repeated, whereas those that have less attractive payoffs are not. For example, a person might enjoy a high payoff from going to classes, restoring an old house, and managing a business and so repeats those behaviors often. On the other hand, that same person avoids doing things that have a low payoff (for him or her), such as paying bills, cleaning the house, and working at the office past 8:00 P.M. It is important to note, however, that emotions such as enjoyment and discomfort are correlative properties of the reinforcement process. Behaviors, not feelings or people, are reinforced.

To understand and appreciate the operant perspective on human development fully, we need to understand not just how behavior is affected by its consequences but a host of other factors as well. I address some of these factors below.

The Concept of Reinforcement

As noted above, a reinforcer is a stimulus event that follows a behavior and increases the likelihood that the behavior will occur again. All reinforcers are classified as stimuli, yet the reverse is not necessarily true. All stimuli are not necessarily reinforcers because (a) stimuli do not always have the effect of increasing the frequency of the behavior they follow (the primary criterion for a reinforcer), and (b) stimuli are sometimes not easily operationalized or relevant. A Skinnerian psychologist would not spend time searching for stimuli that have minimal effects on behavior.

There are two basic classes of reinforcers: positive and negative. These terms have nothing to do with any kind of value judgment; that is, positive reinforcers are not "good" and negative reinforcers "bad." Rather, they refer to whether a stimulus is added to a situation (a positive action) or subtracted (a negative action). That is, *positive* and *negative* reflect actions (presenting or withdrawing) rather than any state or judgment (good or bad).

Positive reinforcers are stimuli that are added to a situation and result in an increase in the probability that a behavior will occur again. In other words, they strengthen the future probability of an operant response. For example, praising children for cleaning up their rooms (a positive reinforcer) may be a very effective way of maintaining that behavior. Thanking a friend for doing you a favor is also a positive reinforcer. In both examples, a stimulus (praise, affection) added to the situation following the behavior acts to increase the probability that the behavior will be repeated.

Negative reinforcers are stimuli that are withdrawn from a situation, resulting in an increase in the probability that a behavior will occur again. That is, the behavior is reinforced through the withdrawal of an unpleasant or aversive stimulus. For example, the removal of a splinter is negatively reinforcing because something is being taken away that is unpleasant. It is sometimes difficult to tell whether a reinforcing stimulus is acting as a negative reinforcer or a positive one. For example, the removal of a splinter is followed by relief from annoying pain. The key question is whether the removal or the addition of a stimulus increases the behavior it follows. In the splinter example, nothing is added to the situation; the splinter (and its associated pain) is removed. Hence it is a negative reinforcer for the behavior of seeking treatment for painful splinters (rather than, for example, avoiding treatment).

Behaviorists use special symbols to represent reinforcers in their research and writings. Positive reinforcers are represented by the letter S (for stimulus) with a superscript plus sign, S^+. Negative reinforcers are represented by S^-—that is, with a superscript minus sign. The general class of reinforcers is represented as S^R.

Because the environment is so full of potential reinforcers, it is often difficult to distinguish what is a reinforcer from what is not. According to Skinner, the best way to determine what reinforcers are present is to observe what follows a behavior. For example, if we are interested in understanding why a certain child keeps raising his hand in class, we should observe what happens each time after the child exhibits this behavior. We might find, for instance, that the consequence of the child's behavior is the teacher's attention, which reinforces the child's behavior.

Let's apply a more detailed analysis to this same example. A child continually raises his hand in class and, when the teacher responds, appears to have nothing to

---

There are two basic classes of schedules of reinforcement: continuous (every response is reinforced) and intermittent (responses are reinforced according to time or rate).

Whether positive or negative, reinforcers increase the likelihood that a behavior will occur again.

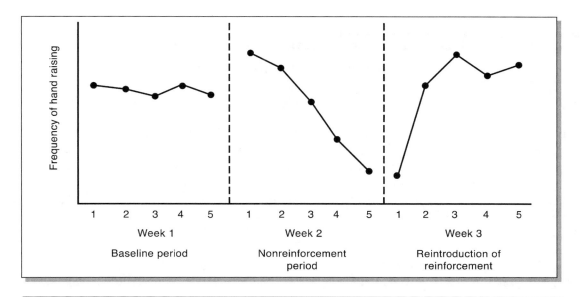

FIGURE 7.4 The Course of an Operant Behavior When Reinforced, Ignored, and Reinforced Again

say. By observing this behavior, we find that every time the child's hand goes up, the teacher provides him with attention. When the child asks a question, the teacher provides some type of response. It soon becomes clear that the teacher may be reinforcing the child's behavior through a combination of attention and verbal support.

To be sure that the teacher's attention is the reinforcer, and not some other factor, we could apply the following strategy. For a fixed period of time (in this example, one school week), we observe and record how often the teacher reinforces or gives attention to the child for his hand-raising behavior. Note that the emphasis here is on the *frequency* of the response. The period of time during which we make these initial observations is the **baseline period**, and the rate of responding (the primary measure of interest here) is the *baseline frequency*. The Week 1 graph in Figure 7.4 illustrates the results of our observations: The points represent the frequency of the behavior on each of the 5 days in the baseline week, and the line connecting the points represents the trend. To test our hypothesis that hand raising is controlled by teacher attention, we next remove the attention (by asking the teacher to stop providing it) and examine the effect that this has on the child's hand-raising behavior. To do this, for the next week we again observe and record the frequency of hand-raising behavior, this time under the new condition of nonreinforcement. Suppose that, as the Week 2 graph in Figure 7.4 shows, we find that the rate of the behavior gradually decreases. (Although a behavior might initially increase right after reinforcement is terminated, eventually the level stabilizes.)

Applying Ideas About Behavioral Approaches

Behavior Modification: S-R Theory Applied

A primary theme of this chapter is the behavioral psychologist's emphasis on the importance of environmental influences as contingencies on observable behaviors. One of the most useful applications of behavioral theories of development has been in the area of behavior modification—the identification and modification of highly specific behaviors through the systematic application of various principles of operant learning. The study described below, which was conducted by Allen, Hart, Buell, Harris, and Wolf (1964), is an excellent example of such an application. The purpose of the study was to determine whether adult attention (used as a social reinforcer) increases children's formation of play relationships with peers.

As in most behavioral interventions, the researchers defined both "adult attention" and "play relationships" in measurable terms. They defined "adult attention" as "a teacher's going to, talking to, smiling at, touching, offering and/ or giving assistance to the child," and "play relationships" as the child's looking at, smiling at, touching, helping, or working with another child.

This study, like many behavioral studies, had only one subject, a 4-year-old preschool girl. The researchers first made an objective record of how much time the child spent by herself (away from other children), with adults or alone. After establishing a baseline frequency of how much time she spent alone, the researchers had the child's teachers begin procedures aimed at reinforcing the child's play relationships with peers. The teachers encouraged the child to participate in groups and praised her when she did so; in addition, they turned away from the child or otherwise ignored her when she sought adult attention.

To ensure that it was the attention of the adults that had originally maintained the child's involvement with other children, the researchers then reversed the situation. Under this condition, the teachers did not encourage her when she did. This reversal resulted in an increase in the child's isolate behavior, as would be expected if the child's behavior was under the control of the social attention. The researchers then reversed the conditions once more, and the child's behavior returned to the goal set by the teachers: high rates of contact with other children and a decrease in the child's seeking attention from adults.

This simple yet very powerful example shows the impact that the systematic application of environmental contingencies can have on a child's behavior. It also illustrates how much of behavior and the process of development can be explained through the application of the principles of behaviorism.

There is one final phase to our test: We reintroduce the reinforcer to examine the effect it has on the behavior. Why is this step important? We need it to be sure that the decrease in frequency of the behavior that we saw when the teacher withheld reinforcement was not caused by some other factor (for example, maybe the child's classmates warned him to stop taking up so much class time). If we find that the rate of the child's hand-raising behavior increases when teacher attention is reintroduced, then we know that teacher attention must be what is controlling the behavior. If we find that the behavior does not increase, we will need to consider the possibility that another stimulus in the environment is controlling the behavior. This research paradigm is called an A-B-A design, where A represents the introduction of reinforcement, B represents the withholding of reinforcement, and the second A represents the reintroduction of reinforcement.

Superstitious Behavior

Out of Skinner's extensive laboratory work another interesting phenomenon was identified: superstitious behavior, or behavior that is accidentally reinforced. This is unplanned learning that takes place when a behavior and a stimulus acting as a reinforcer are inadvertently paired together through coincidence. For example, an athlete may associate winning a game with some behavior he coincidentally performed the same day, and so continue that behavior. One highly successful Major League Baseball player eats only chicken on a game day. Another puts his uniform on in a certain order and wears "lucky socks." He has come to associate the order in which he gets dressed, and his wearing the same socks, with his team's success. In such a case, the socks can even take on the value of a reinforcer, because they are associated with the powerful reinforcing stimulus of winning.

> When behaviors are accidentally reinforced, they can become superstitious in nature.

People are also often reinforced for performing certain kinds of behaviors by what does *not* happen to them. For example, some people insist on sitting in certain seat numbers or in certain parts of the airplane when they travel by air because they have experienced the outcome of safe trips when they have sat in those places in the past; each safe trip further reinforces their behavior, leading them to choose the same seats again. Such behavior is of course not related to the safe flight of the airplane.

The Concepts of Extinction and Punishment

The above discussion of how behaviors are reinforced (that is, how the likelihood that they will occur again is increased) leads naturally to the opposite subject: how behaviors are discouraged or their frequency decreased (that is, the likelihood that they will occur again is lessened). Behaviors decrease in frequency in response to two main influences: extinction and punishment.

—— On the Web ——

If you want to know more about the scientific study of behavior à la Skinner's early, and fundamental, work with animals and learning theory, pay a visit to the Skinner Box at http://www.biozentrum.uni-wuerzburg.de/genetics/behavior/learning/SkinnerBox.html, where you will find a description of the basic hardware Skinner used when he was formulating and testing his ideas about learning. As you have learned in this chapter, much of what he found has direct application to human behavior.

Clearly, individuals do not continue to do the same things over and over again for no reason. Among the factors influencing operant behaviors are some that may cause them to decrease in frequency or even stop altogether. In the example used earlier of the child who was reinforced in his hand-raising behavior by the teacher's attention, the teacher's ignoring the behavior and withholding any type of reinforcement resulted in a decrease in the behavior. The result of such lack of response to a behavior, or nonreinforcement, is called *extinction*. The B part of the A-B-A design discussed above (represented in Figure 7.4 (page 177) by Week 2, when reinforcement was withheld) is an example of extinction.

Many new parents experience another example of extinction when they eventually learn to avoid reinforcing their infants' behavior of crying at bedtime with attention. Young children quickly learn which of their behaviors result in rewards, and new parents frequently reinforce their infants' crying when put to bed or when placed in a playpen by providing the infants with extra attention. The scenario often goes something like this: After the baby has had dinner and a change of diapers, the parents play with the baby affectionately for a little while and then place the child in her crib and leave her room. No sooner is the door of the child's room closed than the familiar crying begins. The parents let the child cry for a few minutes, but, no longer able to stand the noise (or their fear that something is actually wrong with the child), they go in and pick up and cuddle the crying baby. The baby stops crying immediately, and the parents feel they did the right thing—they are reinforced in their behavior by the baby's silence, which they interpret to mean that all is well.

However, when they put the baby back in her crib, the crying begins again. The established cycle is strengthened: The child cries, the parents provide

Punishment and extinction are the two processes by which the likelihood of a behavior's occurring again is decreased.

attention and so reinforce the crying, and the baby learns that the way to gain more attention is with more crying. This is an exhausting routine that benefits no one. Nobody is getting any sleep, and the parents eventually realize that they have to break the cycle somehow. They know that the baby is not crying at bedtime because there is something really wrong; they have checked each time to see if the baby was wet or maybe being jabbed by a diaper pin or had some other source of discomfort. Interestingly, parents learn very early to distinguish among their children's different cries. For parents the child's quality of crying becomes a discriminative stimulus for their going to aid the child (fell-out-of-crib crying) or ignoring the child (attention-getting crying). Although it is very difficult for the parents to do, they realize that they must ignore (or at least not respond to) their child's attention-getting crying; this nonreinforcement will lead to extinction of the behavior. In the beginning of this process, the baby might continue to cry for hours, because she has learned how well the crying usually works—largely because ignoring a crying baby is very difficult.

Punishment is the presentation of an aversive or unpleasant stimulus to decrease the frequency of a behavior. For example, if you park in a no-parking zone, you may receive a parking ticket. The ticket (actually, the fine you pay as a result) acts as a punisher, decreasing the likelihood that you will park in that zone again (if, of course, the fine is high enough to be painful to you). Punishment can be related to the two classes of reinforcers discussed above: It can take the form of withdrawal of a positive reinforcer (negative punishment) or of the presentation of a negative reinforcer (positive punishment). Again, to determine whether a stimulus is acting as a reinforcer or punisher of either kind, we need to examine the effect the presentation or withdrawal of the stimulus has on the behavior. If the effect is to increase the probability of the behavior, the process of reinforcement is occurring. If the result of the stimulus following the operant behavior is to decrease the likelihood that a behavior will occur again, it is a punisher.

Keep in mind, however, that the characteristics of the stimulus are less important than the effect of the stimulus on behavior. For example, some parents use spanking to discipline their children. However, it is impossible to determine the role that spanking plays without knowing the effect that spanking has on the child's specific behavior. For one child in a family, spanking might be an effective way of stopping the child's behavior of running out into the street (that is, the spanking acts as a punisher), whereas for another child spanking increases that behavior (that is, it acts as a reinforcer). Perhaps the second child, unlike the first, receives some degree of reinforcement from the personal attention that goes with the spanking—if that's the case, he will probably come back for more of both.

Even if the consequence of a behavior is unpleasant, the consequence can be considered a punisher only if the associated behavior decreases in frequency.

TABLE 7.2 Effect of Stimuli on Behavior

	Outcome	
Action	*Behavior Increases*	*Behavior Decreases*
Stimulus added to the situation	Positive reinforcement	Positive punishment
Stimulus subtracted from the situation	Negative reinforcement	Negative punishment

Table 7.2 summarizes the relationships between a stimulus in the environment and the various effects the presentation (addition) or withdrawal (subtraction) of that stimulus might have on future behavior. The difference between negative punishment and extinction is that in extinction there is no consequence (nothing follows the behavior), whereas in negative punishment there is a consequence (something is taken away). For example, taking a toy away from a child who is misbehaving is negative punishment if the action results in a decrease in the misbehavior.

Schedules of Reinforcement

Another important factor in changing behaviors is the relative frequency with which reinforcers and punishers occur. Usually, behaviors are not reinforced or punished each time they occur. In the natural world, the contingencies on behavior do not occur on a perfectly regular basis. Sometimes people ignore "No Parking" signs and risk being ticketed to park closer to the stadium. Sometimes they win at poker, and sometimes waiting for the mail carrier pays off with a long-awaited letter. All of these "sometimes" imply that the frequency of many of the stimuli that act as reinforcers and punishers is not easily predictable.

The term **schedule of reinforcement** (or **punishment**) refers to the regularity with which a pattern of stimuli follows operant behaviors and the effects these stimuli have. For example, is there a difference in good manners between children who are given a penny every time they eat nicely and children who receive a penny only every third time they eat nicely? Although researchers have documented more than 900 individual schedules of reinforcement, or ways of delivering reinforcers and punishers (Ferster & Skinner, 1957), all of them fall into two general classes: continuous and intermittent. When a schedule calls for **continuous reinforcement**,

Schedules of reinforcement contribute to the complexity of behaviors and to behaviors' intricate ties to the environment.

TABLE 7.3   Types of Reinforcement Schedules

		Intermittent Reinforcement	
		Interval	*Ratio*
Continuous Reinforcement	*Fixed*	Reinforcer delivered once per unit of time (such as every 10 seconds)	Reinforcer delivered once per number of responses (such as every 10 times)
	Variable	Reinforcer delivered once on the average per unit of time (such as 10 seconds, then 6, then 2, for an average of 6 seconds per response)	Reinforcer delivered once on the average over unit of responses (such as 3 times, then 4 times, then 2 times, for an average of 3 times per reinforcer)

every response is reinforced. When a schedule calls for **intermittent reinforcement**, in contrast, the behavior is reinforced only at certain times, according to criteria such as the number of responses or the amount of time between responses. Table 7.3 shows how these two basic kinds of reinforcement schedules differ.

In a continuous reinforcement schedule, the reinforcer is delivered every time the organism responds, regardless of the number of responses or the amount of time between them. Although this schedule is less complex than any intermittent schedule, it is certainly just as important from a developmental perspective. Many, if not all, early operant behaviors start through such schedules. A continuous schedule of reinforcement is an excellent way to get a behavior going and to strengthen it in its early stages. Such schedules are not, however, especially good for maintaining high rates of behaviors, because they are vulnerable to the effects of extinction and punishment. When an infant begins to babble, that behavior should be reinforced as frequently as possible. Similarly, when a grade school child is learning a new way of adding figures, until the behavior or habit is established, a continuous schedule of reinforcement is most effective.

There are two general classes of schedules of reinforcement: continuous and intermittent.

Intermittent reinforcement schedules can be differentiated along two dimensions: how often the reinforcer is delivered and how much regularity there is in the intervals between deliveries of the reinforcer. The frequency with which the reinforcer is delivered may be based on the number of responses (a **ratio schedule of reinforcement**) or on the passage of time between responses (an **interval**

schedule of reinforcement). For example, if a child's math-problem-solving behavior is reinforced for every five problems the child completes correctly, a ratio schedule is in use. If a child receives reinforcement for every half hour that he or she sits still in class and does not bother other students, an interval schedule is in use.

The second dimension is that of the time that elapses between the deliveries of reinforcers. Reinforcers may be delivered with equal amounts of time or numbers of responses between them (a **fixed schedule of reinforcement**), or the numbers of responses or amounts of time may vary (a **variable schedule of reinforcement**) between deliveries. For example, if office workers' behavior is reinforced every second day they come to work on time, a fixed interval schedule is in use (the amount of time between reinforcers is fixed at two days). If insurance workers' behavior is reinforced for every third claim they settle, a fixed ratio schedule is in use.

Variable schedules are somewhat different. A variable ratio schedule delivers a reinforcer based on the average number of times a behavior or response occurs. For example, an adolescent may receive reinforcement an average of every third time he cleans his room. He might receive a dollar for cleaning his room the first time, and then perhaps receive another dollar the fifth time and the ninth time, so that he averages one reinforcer every three times he cleans his room. On a variable interval schedule, in contrast, the important element is the amount of time between reinforcers. A child who is working well alone might be awarded one point toward a prize on the average of every 5 minutes. This means that she might be reinforced after 1 minute and then after 9 minutes, or at any other intervals, as long as reinforcers are delivered a total of six times over a half-hour period.

Based on laboratory studies with both human subjects and infrahuman organisms (such as rats), Skinnerian psychologists have been to specify very exactly what types of reinforcement delivery systems are best for maintaining certain rates of particular behaviors. Schedules of reinforcement are important elements in these delivery systems, because the maintenance of some kinds of behaviors is dependent not just on the presence of reinforcement but on the manner in which the reinforcement is delivered. In fact, one could say that the method of reinforcement (that is, the schedule of delivery) is as important as the fact that the behavior is being reinforced.

Stimulus Control and Stimulus Discrimination

The patterns with which stimuli are followed by environmental events are as important as the fact that consequences occur. In our daily lives, not all of our behaviors are reinforced, and, depending on a variety of factors, reinforcers are delivered in different patterns.

We have looked at the factors that influence the rates, or frequencies, of behaviors, but one important question remains to be addressed: How do individuals acquire novel or unique behaviors? In other words, how do people develop systems of behavior that are far more complex than the simple stimulus-response association?

The main criterion for developmental change within any behavioral theory is that learning has occurred. Whether classical or operant conditioning is present, the beginning point of change is often found in the characteristics of the stimulus itself. The above discussion demonstrates the importance of reinforcers, but the topic of how stimuli become important to the individual still has to be addressed. For example, why do you act in a certain way in the presence of some stimuli and not others? What is it about the weather that prompts you to take along an umbrella? Such responses to stimuli are, of course, a function of experience. The process through which experiences become valuable to an individual and through which the individual associates particular stimuli with certain outcomes is called **stimulus control**. Through this process, certain stimuli become highly potent as cues or signs for future behavior and serve as indicators of the relationship between a response and whether or not that response will have any important consequences. These controlling or informing stimuli are called *discriminative stimuli* (represented as S^D).

> The process through which experiences become valuable to us and we learn to associate particular stimuli with certain outcomes is called *stimulus control.*

Stimuli take on discriminative power in many different ways. For example, the sound of the car as it comes into the garage can act as a discriminative stimulus for "Mommy's home" and starting dinner. However, some discriminative stimuli signal the absence of any rewarding condition. Behaviorists represent such a stimulus with the letter S (for stimulus) followed by a superscript capital delta (the Greek letter), S^Δ, which indicates no change in the probability of the behavior being reinforced.

The original conditioning paradigm (presented in Figure 7.3) consists of a simple stimulus-response bond. With the introduction of the discriminative stimulus as a powerful component of development, the paradigm is expanded. The progression is from the simple stimulus-response association ($S \rightarrow R$) to the stimulus-response association with a stimulus acting as a reinforcer ($S \rightarrow R \rightarrow S^R$), to the point where the reinforcing stimulus (S^R) assumes discriminative qualities ($S \rightarrow R \rightarrow S^R/S^D$). Remember that the initial stimulus represented by the letter S is relatively unimportant. Eating when we are not hungry just because it is lunchtime is a good example of how, through learning, stimuli (such as the time of day) become discriminative and control subsequent behavior. More important, the concept of stimulus control illustrates the effectiveness of our ability to discriminate between those stimuli that are favorable to our survival and those that are not. We learn which kinds of situations are life threatening and which are not, and we incorporate this knowledge into our behavioral repertoires.

If we examine the history of a behavior, we can identify the stimuli in the environment that have a controlling influence and those that are superfluous. Given that we can identify those events in the natural world that set the stage for particular behaviors (but do not have control over those behaviors), how do behaviors become associated with one another to form the complex set of behaviors known as development? Behaviors become connected and organized, forming an elaborate developmental system, through the processes of chaining and shaping.

Chaining and Shaping

Chaining is the process through which a stimulus that acts as a reinforcer for one event becomes a discriminative stimulus for the next. In other words, a chain of behavior is a series of stimulus-response-reinforcement elements wherein the reinforcing stimulus from the previous event takes on the quality of a discriminative stimulus. In this fashion, very complex behaviors are constructed.

For example, reading is a task that involves the identification and discrimination of certain stimuli and their individual sounds (letters), their sounds as groupings (words), and the relationships between these groupings (context). Each of these steps is dependent on the previous one, and through the establishment of a long and intricate chain of steps, the simple discrimination of a letter eventually leads to the complex behavior called reading. When children learn to swim, they are not expected to be able to coordinate their arm, leg, and breathing movements immediately. Instead, they learn the simplest elements first and then, through practice and experience, the various skills they need to swim well are linked together. As they learn, moving one arm becomes a discriminative stimulus for turning the head and breathing, while placing the head in the water becomes another discriminative stimulus for exhaling.

Thus all of the activities we take part in throughout the day consist of complex chains of behaviors. From the time you wake up in the morning, you are bombarded by stimuli that act as influences on your future behavior. The weather report becomes a discriminative stimulus for what you decide to wear that day. Similarly, your being tired because you got home late the previous night acts as a discriminative stimulus for getting you home early tonight and catching up on your sleep.

Whereas chaining is the process through which individual behaviors become linked together, **shaping** is the process through which novel behaviors are developed. Shaping involves the systematic reinforcement of some responses and not others. Whenever a child or adult receives feedback in response to a question or a behavior, future behavior is shaped.

Skinner developed the concept of shaping based on discoveries he made while conducting experimental analyses of animal behavior. He found that by successively

---

Chaining and shaping are two processes through which behaviors take on qualitatively distinct and complex forms.

reinforcing behaviors that were closer and closer approximations to the responses he desired, he could create almost any behaviors that were within the physical boundaries of the animal's performance. For example, he succeeded in getting pigeons to play a modified game of Ping-Pong as well as to provide navigational feedback for guided missiles.

In shaping, the individual is directly involved as an agent in ongoing changes in his or her behavior. For example, when a young child progresses from drinking from a bottle to using a cup, the child's drinking habits must also change. The child must change the way he or she uses the lips in drinking, and the child must learn to hold the cup upright—unlike a bottle, which can be turned upside down without spilling the liquid it contains. The new behavior of drinking from a cup is shaped by means of the child's gradual and systematic acquisition of behaviors and the process of reinforcement.

Generalization

Through the processes of shaping and chaining, behaviors become complex and sequentially related. The next question is, How does a behavior (or class of behaviors) become functional in settings other than the one in which it was originally learned? A young child might call every female "mommy," possibly because the child thinks that all of these people are actually his or her mommy, but also because the child has generalized what he or she has learned beyond the primary stimulus.

In generalization, the stimulus or the response changes as a function of its similarity to another stimulus or response. In **stimulus generalization**, a response to a new stimulus is similar to the original response. Take, for example, a driver's behavior of applying the brakes on seeing any flashing red light on the road. Here the stimuli are similar (red traffic signal, the stimulus originally associated with the response, and any flashing red light) but not identical. Table 7.4 presents another example of how this phenomenon works. The child has come to associate his or her female caretaker with the specific response "Mommy!" Throughout the process of stimulus generalization, this response also becomes associated with other stimuli that are in the same general class yet different. The stimulus of female caretaker generalizes to any familiar or similar-looking female, and the identical response ("Mommy!") is the result. Stimulus generalization belongs in the same class as stimulus control, because it affects the control that a stimulus has on a learning outcome.

In the parallel process of **response generalization**, the stimulus remains the same but the response to the stimulus changes. For example, as Table 7.4 illustrates, the young child who has previously responded to his or her mother with

> Behaviorism accounts for novel behaviors in part through the concept of the generalization of behaviors to new settings.

TABLE 7.4 Stimulus and Response Generalization

Concept	From Time 1	To Time 2
Stimulus generalization	Female caretaker: "Mommy!"	Any female who provides mothering or caretaking: "Mommy!"
Response generalization	Female caretaker: "Mommy!"	Any female who provides mothering or caretaking: "Mama!" or "Mom!"

"Mommy!" may learn other responses that are functionally equivalent in other settings, such as "Mom!" or "Mama!"

Many operant psychologists feel that stimulus generalization accounts for the development of concept learning, or concept formation, in the young child. Through continual exposure to similar yet somewhat different stimuli, the child forms concepts, defined as classes of objects that have similar characteristics or functions. For example, the young child who at first thinks that all four-legged, furry things are dogs (overgeneralizing) begins to learn that there are other classes of animals as well, such as cats and even lions. Over- and undergeneralizing are not productive, and so the child needs continual feedback from socializing agents such as parents and teachers.

THE APPLICATION OF EXPERIMENTAL ANALYSIS

To understand development through the application of the behavioral model, it is important to realize that the behaviorally oriented developmental psychologist views development not as a stage-related phenomenon but as a process that operates according to the principles of learning. Behaviorists are concerned with understanding how the various laws of learning affect the individual and contribute to different behavioral outcomes. From this perspective, individual differences are the results of environmental factors, not of any inherent biological processes. Skinner helped to develop and refine behavioral laws to a sophisticated degree, and although he did not deal directly with the process of development in humans, he provided the foundation on which later, more process-oriented developmental theorists built.

From the Skinnerian perspective, development is a reorganization of simple, classically conditioned and operantly learned behaviors. Infants are not totally devoid of predispositions, but, in accordance with the assumption of a blank slate (tabula rasa), these inherited tendencies reflect only biological reflexes. Through such processes as stimulus control, chaining, shaping, and generalization, behaviors become related to one another to produce sequences of interconnected stimuli and responses. As a unit, these connections become the stimuli for later development. The behavioral approach assumes that the individual is passively susceptible to factors in the external environment and that the consequences of a behavior may be determined not by what the individual wants, but by what the environment has to offer. For example, few parents want to abuse their children, but, strange as it may seem, the contingencies in the environment are often such that this behavior accrues some kind of benefit to a parent.

Behaviorism began in scholars' efforts to understand human behavior through understanding the principles of learning. The developmental process itself may be intricate and difficult to untangle, but the theory and assumptions of behaviorism that are applicable to development are straightforward and highly operationalized. According to Skinner, individuals reflect the constraints and opportunities that their environment offers; they contribute nothing on their own other than biological functions and preparedness.

The research techniques developed by behaviorists have been highly valuable to scholars interested in the modification and analysis of individual elements of behavior. These applications also have great social relevance. The task now for developmental theorists is to expand on the basic behaviorist perspective further, adding their own insights regarding the process of learning as a long-term, extended process of development rather than only a short-term process of change.

Behavior Analysis: Sidney Bijou and Donald Baer

In 1961, Sidney Bijou and Donald Baer published *Child Development 1: A Systematic and Empirical Theory,* which offered a new perspective on the study of developmental psychology and has had great influence in the field. In the early 1960s, the concepts of operant psychology were just becoming widely popular, and operant applications to the area of child development seemed appropriate and necessary. As Harold Stevenson (1983) points out, Skinner "did nothing to adapt his theoretical position on operant conditioning to encompass variables that are to be important in discussing children's behavior" (p. 227). At that time, Bijou and Baer's book was probably the most comprehensive statement available regarding development from a behavioral perspective. Bijou and Baer further extended their arguments in *Child Development 2: Universal Stage of Infancy,* published in 1965. *Child Development 1,* which focused on explicit and operational systems within the developmental process, was the first step in the presentation of a theory of development using behavioral ideas and terminology that related operant principles to everyday developmental occurrences, such as language development and social interaction. It is also important to note that although Bijou and Baer's books include the term *child development* in their titles, the ideas and principles these books address are appropriate to discuss within a life-span framework, because they are based on laws of learning that are applicable to the behavior of all humans, regardless of age.

Although some critics of the behaviorist approach believe that it is demeaning to view the developing individual as mechanistic and the process of development as reductionistic, Bijou and Baer offer a straightforward and systematic presentation of how events in the environment shape and modify behavioral outcomes. Their most recent statement, *Behavior Analysis of Child Development* (1978), offers an even more comprehensive treatment of the role that learning plays in the developmental process.

> The focus of behavior analysis is on understanding the explicit and operational systems that characterize the developmental process.

According to Bijou and Baer (1961), psychological development is represented by the "progressive changes in the way an organism's behavior interacts with the environment" (p. 1). They assert that behavior is not a function of either environmental or biological factors alone, but the result of an interaction between the two.

The task of the behaviorally oriented developmental psychologist is to explore the nature of the changing interaction between the behavior of the organism and associated environmental conditions. The center of this interest becomes how the environment changes and what effects environmental changes have on the organism. Likewise, the way in which the organism changes the environment and the ever-changing interaction between the two are important concerns as well. For example, if one wants to understand the early adaptive behaviors of the infant, one needs to consider both the behavioral repertoire of the child (such as cooing and smiling) and the conditions in the environment that might affect that repertoire (such as the caretaker's attentiveness).

Bijou and Baer present a broad interactionist approach that expands on earlier behavioral perspectives. Most of the behavioral theorists whose work preceded Bijou and Baer's had envisioned the human being as somewhat passive, acting only as a receptor of influences originating in the external environment. Within Bijou and Baer's behavior analysis perspective, the human organism uses the forces in the environment to determine subsequent responses and behaviors; thus development is defined by interactions. Bijou and Baer's most important contribution to our understanding of the developmental process lies in their specification of the different elements of these interactions and how these elements influence changes in behavior.

Making Behavior Meaningful: Stimulus Functions

In formulating their theory, Bijou and Baer identified a concept that goes beyond the notion that stimulus-response associations are the building blocks of development. Their concept of **stimulus function** addresses the functional relationship between a stimulus and a response—that is, for a certain stimulus, a response tends to serve a specific function. In specific settings, relationships are established between events. For example, the ringing of a school bell is related to a specific response, such as students' going to their next classes. The response—students' getting out of their seats in their previous classes and moving to their next classes—defines the function of the stimulus. Behavior thus becomes a result of which stimuli in the environment take on functional significance.

> A relationship is established between a particular stimulus and a particular response so that the response tends to serve a specific function.

All stimuli cannot be functional, of course; many events go unnoticed and therefore have no functional significance. The term *functional analysis of behavior* refers to the analysis of the nature of the functional relationship between a stimulus and a response (behavior). For example, parents quickly learn to correlate their child's fussy crying with hunger, and that S-R event eventually takes on some functional significance for the parents. In contrast, for people untrained in the skills of automotive repair, there is no functional significance in particular noises coming from a car engine—they are not likely to relate certain noises to burned-out valves or a faulty carburetor.

On the other hand, some stimuli are indeed nonfunctional. For example, because adolescents tend to focus on social and peer pressure, they might find the opinions of adults not only unwarranted but also meaningless in the general context of whatever is occurring. To quote Bijou and Baer (1961), "Stimulus functions concentrate simply and objectively upon the ways in which stimuli control behavior: produce it, strengthen or weaken it, signal occasions for its occurrence or non-occurrence, generalize it to new situations and problems, etc." (p. 19).

> Stimulus events—which can be physical, chemical, organismic, or social—have measurable impacts on behavior.

It is important to note that many different stimuli might have the same or similar stimulus function. For example, talking with a receptive friend, talking with supportive parents, and talking with individuals other than friends or parents might all serve as reinforcing events that strengthen the behaviors that produce them. This is perhaps one of the most important advantages of the concept of the stimulus function: It allows for the formation of a general class of environmental events and defines the functional relationships of these events to present and later behaviors.

The Basic Elements of Behavior Analysis: Stimulus and Setting Events

Within the historical tradition of the behavioral approach to development, Bijou and Baer assert that the laws of natural science can best explain the development and progression of behavior from one level to the next. This natural science point of view is not uncharacteristic of many behavioral theorists. By adopting this viewpoint, they attempt to reduce the general class of environmental influences to more specific classes of **stimulus events**, or changes in the environment

Stimulus events
set the stage
for changes
in behavior.

that have measurable impacts on behavior. The qualifier *measurable* here is very important, because the only real evidence that some change in the environment has occurred is a change in the individual's behavior that can be reliably observed. A **setting event** is a stimulus event accompanied by a certain response.

Stimulus Events

The first class of stimulus events that Bijou and Baer identify are **physical events**—those stimuli that are produced by humans or occur naturally. For example, television sets, rain, automobiles, rock music, and cornflakes all fit into this class. The second class of stimulus events, **chemical events**, includes environmental stimuli that act at a distance from the organism, such as the smell of fish or the stinging of iodine on a cut finger. The class of **organismic events** includes biological or maturational events that provide stimulation for the organism, such as the onset of puberty, dentition (teething), and the action of the respiratory system. The last class of stimulus events, **social events**, involves the appearance, action, and interaction between living organisms, such as daily conversation with a colleague or interaction with a child.

Whether these different types of stimulus events occur alone or in concert with one another, behaviors related to all of these classes either produce or are directly involved in the developmental process. In fact, most environmental events that eventually establish some type of functional relationships with responses include many stimuli from each class of stimulus events, all interacting with one another. For example, an individual's behavior in the morning may consist of a functional relationship between feelings of hunger (organismic), the smell of coffee (chemical), greetings to family members (social), and deciding what to wear (physical). These different classes are by definition separate, but in a practical sense they overlap to form a complex system of stimuli to which the organism responds. By applying this idea of stimulus events, you can probably identify influences within your own environment that affect your behavior. As noted previously, this concept can help us to organize and systematically assess environmental factors, which are the crucial factors in the developmental process. We must keep in mind, however, that many stimuli in the environment never become stimulus events because they hold no discriminative value.

All of the different stimuli in the environment can be classified into one of the four categories described above. Remember, however, that just because we can identify the proper class of stimulus events into which any given event falls, that does not mean that the event has any functional significance. In addition to the content of the classes of stimulus events, two other factors are important. First, we need to look at stimulus events in the here and now; that is, it is important to specify the relationship between the stimulus event and the current behavior. Second, specific stimulus events have histories of occurring in certain situations, so past events should be taken into account as well. Take, for example, the aromas and festivity that surround the Thanksgiving holiday. For most Americans, significant relationships between Thanksgiving-related stimulus events and certain behaviors are established over many years. In sum, the stimulus events that are associated with past behaviors become very important. Both past and present events have significant influence in the development of the individual.

Each of the four different types of stimuli can serve one of three different functions in relation to changes in learning, or development: eliciting a response, acting as a discriminative event, or reinforcing some outcome. The value of stimulus events and the roles these events play in an individual's development depend on the individual's past reinforcement history.

Setting Events

As you might expect, different stimulus events precipitate different kinds of behaviors. For example, people move out of the path of an oncoming car, whereas they approach and greet friends. But what is the mechanism through which different stimuli and their associated responses become part of the developmental process? Bijou and Baer offer the following explanation. A stimulus event accompanied by a certain response becomes a setting event for another stimulus-response interaction. That is, one event, or occurrence, helps to set the conditions for subsequent events, which become related to one another. This adds a sense of continuity to the progression from one stimulus to a response to yet another stimulus, and so on.

> A setting event is a stimulus event accompanied by a certain response.

Development, however, is much more than the basic process of chaining discussed earlier or one setting event after another. It is not just the association or linking of stimuli and responses to one another in a coincidence of time and space. For example, the child who comes home from school and inadvertently slams the door (receiving a mildly disconcerting look from his mother) finds the stage set for subsequent behaviors, such as a short talk from mom about closing the door quietly. This short talk in turn can become a setting event for subsequent behavior. Setting events, then, are occurrences that set up or prepare the individual for subsequent interaction with the environment that is determined by the current state of affairs (e.g., some form of scolding for slamming the door). Whereas a stimulus event is simply a factor that is influential in soliciting a response (whether the stimulus event acts as a respondent or an operant), a setting event unifies a series of stimulus events and helps provide continuity. Setting events give meaning to certain stimulus events, and therefore act as effective influences on development.

Applying Ideas About Behavioral Approaches

Ages and Stages anod Behavior Analysis

At least one question comes up again and again when the developmental process is discussed: Does development occur in a series of well-defined, age-bounded stages (highly related to biological or internal growth mechanisms), or does it occur in a continuous fashion, with sets of changing behaviors unrelated to the psychological variable called *age*?

Developmental scholars' various answers to this question parallel the nature/nurture or heredity/environment debate. Proponents of the theories of Gesell and Freud—representing the maturational and psychoanalytic models, respectively—believe that development is a series of changes related to age, defined as the passage of time, a convenient and easily understood marker. Very few psychologists would argue with the idea that certain changes in behavior become increasingly apparent with time. However, this does not necessarily mean that changes in age are the primary determinant of changes in behavior. Although age might be a convenient (and often the only) variable along which to categorize a child's behavior, it is also imprecise and nondescript. Many people believe that developmental psychology is synonymous with the idea of age-related change, and some even believe that changes in age explain changes in behavior. This viewpoint provides the framework for many traditional child-oriented activities.

Baer (1970), along with many others, finds this explanation both imprecise and impractical. According to Baer, the important factor for understanding the developmental process is the sequencing, or programmatic presentation, of experiences. Baer distinguishes between a *psychology of description* (in which age is of primary importance) and a *psychology of explanation*. In other words, age relates to or correlates with almost every human behavior (over time), but explains very little about the differences that exist between groups and individuals.

Many popular works on child rearing and child development mention such "stages of development" as the "terrible twos" and "troublesome threes," implying that children's behavior is a function of their chronological age. A child may very well have some biological imperative or need that the parents should approach in a manner different from that they would have used to deal with the same need when the child was younger. However, it is often the demands of the situation that encourage a child to behave in a certain way. One child may be encouraged by parents to take advantage of newfound skills by exploring the environment, whereas another child might be restricted from engaging in exploratory activities and so has no opportunity to enlarge his or her behavioral repertoire. The latter child may receive the wrong messages from parents, and his or her behavior may become contingent on those discriminative stimuli that some parents associate with troublesome behavior.

So, to influence the developmental process, at least according to Baer, rather than waiting for maturational processes to have major effects, parents should arrange sequences of experiences for their children that move the children's behaviors toward particular goals.

WEB SITES OF INTEREST

- B. F. Skinner Foundation, at http://www.bfskinner.org/index.asp: The B. F. Skinner Foundation "was established in 1987 to publish significant literary and scientific works in the analysis of behavior and to educate both professionals and the public about the science of behavior"—an ambitious task indeed. This Web site offers a gold mine of information about Skinner, including a list of his extensive publications and even access to video and audio clips about his life and works.

- Lovaas Institute for Early Intervention, at http://www.lovaas.com: The cause of autism is unknown, and a variety of different approaches are used to treat this disorder. This Web site, which provides information on how behavior modification is used to treat autism, is maintained by an institute named for a leading researcher in the field, O. Ivar Lovaas, a professor at the University of California, Los Angeles.

- The Association for Behavior Analysis, at http://www.abainternational.org: If you are interested in behavior analysis as a way of understanding development, you might think about joining the Association for Behavior Analysis. The ABA's mission is to develop, enhance, and support the growth and vitality of behavior analysis through research, education, and practice.

FURTHER READINGS ABOUT BEHAVIORAL APPROACHES

Comunidad los Horcones. (2002). Western cultural influences in behavior analysis as seen from a Walden Two. *Behavior and Social Issues, 11,* 204–212.

In this interesting article, the authors share their thoughts about their community and about the need for greater dissemination of information about behavior analysis and behaviorism. The authors assert that it is important for the general public to learn more about the concepts of behavior analysis and behaviorism because it is primarily members of the public who decide on the content of educational curricula.

Ferster, C. B. (2002). Schedules of reinforcement with Skinner. *Journal of the Experimental Analysis of Behavior, 77,* 303–312.

This is a reprint of a classic article that first appeared in 1970. In it, Ferster recounts the experiences he had working with psychologist B. F. Skinner in the Pigeon Lab at Harvard University.

Goldiamond, Israel. (2002). Toward a constructional approach to social problems: Ethical and constitutional issues raised by applied behavior analysis. *Behavior and Social Issues, 11,* 108–197.

This article (which was originally published in an early journal titled *Behaviorism*) discusses behavior therapy, behavior change, and behavior modification. The author, Israel Goldiamond, is a very well-known and historically important participant in the development of this discipline.

Kazdin, Alan E. (2001). *Behavior modification in applied settings* (6th ed.). Belmont, CA: Wadsworth/Thomson Learning.

Kazdin offers an excellent introduction to behavior modification techniques in applied settings, with major focuses on the application of operant conditioning principles, the implementation of behavior modification techniques, and the assessment and evaluation of program effectiveness.

O'Donohue, William, & Ferguson, Kyle E. (2001). *The psychology of B. F. Skinner.* Thousand Oaks, CA: Sage.

In this book, O'Donohue and Ferguson offer a summary of the work of one of the most influential psychologists of the past century as well as descriptions of Skinner's contributions to psychology, his philosophy of science, and his experimental research program, including the behavioral principles and applications that emerged from it.

Tacon, Anna, & Caldera, Yvonne. (2001). Behavior modification. In Jacalyn J. Robert-McComb (Ed.), *Eating disorders in women and children: Prevention, stress management, and treatment* (pp. 263–272). Boca Raton, FL: CRC.

In this chapter, Tacon and Caldera describe the application of behavior modification to the treatment of eating disorders. They also cover the basic principles of behavior modification, including procedures such as shaping and chaining.

CHAPTER 8

SOCIAL LEARNING THEORY

Experience enables you to recognize a mistake when you make it again.

—Franklin P. Jones

Experience is not what happens to a man; it is what a man does with what happens to him.

—Aldous Huxley

A parent's job is to be the person who can see over the hill.

—James L. Hymes

Imitation is the sincerest form of flattery.

—Charles Caleb Colton

ROBERT SEARS'S DEVELOPMENTAL LEARNING APPROACH

In the first seven chapters of this book, we have seen how theorists who differ with each other on some issues sometimes share certain basic assumptions concerning the process of development. Freud and Erikson, for example, both proposed that each individual passes through a set of developmental stages, although the stages they theorized are not identical. We have also seen that some theories have very little in common with other theories. For many years, psychologists and educators have discussed how different theoretical views might be combined, but more often than not these efforts have resulted in little if any significant advance. The philosophical differences among theorists have often proved too great to allow for meaningful dialogue.

Robert Sears is one of the few theorists who has been able to bridge the gap between two different theoretical perspectives by combining the most interesting and provocative ideas behind those perspectives into a unified theory.

In the work of Robert Sears (1908–1989), however, we can see a genuine (and, most people would say, successful) effort to bridge the gap between the psychoanalytic and behavioral approaches to understanding human development. Sears combined his training and experience in the psychoanalytic domain (with a special interest in the process of identification) with studies of behavioral theory to produce what might be the first and only eclectic view of development to stand the test of time.

Sears's Theoretical Viewpoint

Sears spent the major part of his academic career as a professor of psychology at Stanford University, where his most significant contributions were in the area of the effects of child rearing on personality development. His training as a psychologist took him from Yale University to the University of Iowa's Child Welfare Research Station, where a great deal of the information available about child development at that time was being generated. It was, however, his relationship with one of his instructors at Yale, Clark Hull, and his work with other behavioral psychologists that greatly influenced Sears's own theoretical growth.

Like most behavioral theorists, Hull believed that the basic building block of learning is the simple stimulus-response (or S-R) link, or association. He elaborated on this by postulating that variables intervening between the stimulus and the response have important influences on behavior. A brief review of Hull's descriptions of the major characteristics of these intervening variables will help to introduce Sears's social approach to learning.

The most important of all the intervening variables in Hull's model is **reaction potential**. This is the potential for an individual's making a certain response given the presence of a particular stimulus. For example, a parent's presence or absence when a toddler falls down determines, in part, whether the child cries after falling or not.

The strength of the reaction potential is determined by five factors. The first of these, *drive,* is any kind of primary need, such as hunger or thirst. When a drive is associated with a previously neutral stimulus (such as when a hungry baby sees a bottle used to feed her), the neutral stimulus takes on the characteristics of the original drive and becomes what is known as a *secondary motivator.*

The second factor that contributes to the strength of the reaction potential is the *intensity of the stimulus.* For example, when we are hungry it is much more likely that we will be receptive to one of our favorite foods than to some kind of food about which we are ambivalent. The higher the intensity of the stimulus, the more likely we are to respond.

Incentive motivation, or the amount of reward given for the behavior, is the third factor that determines the likelihood of a response occurring. For instance, a person is less likely to work for a low wage than for a higher one if both are available, because knowledge of the payoff for the work affects the individual's judgment and future actions. Incentive motivation can be a very powerful factor, because it includes the anticipation of rewards and their value.

The fourth factor in the strength of the reaction potential is *habit strength,* or the number of times the behavior has been rewarded in the past. This component has special applications to Sears's theory, where it takes on the name of *experience.* For example, a 1-year-old baby who is beginning to talk makes all sorts of noises at anyone's encouragement because of the rewards (attention, warmth) that doing so brings.

The final factor affecting the reaction potential is that of resistance to repeating responses, known as *inhibitory potential.* This is the degree to which an individual may be motivated not to respond. For example, although misbehaving may bring a reward (attention), there are also reasons not to misbehave (such as punishment).

By summing these five factors together in a mathematical model, Hull was able to make predictions concerning the likelihood, or probability, that individuals would exhibit particular behaviors given particular stimuli. It is clear that Hull's approach to the study of behavior and the factors that lead up to behavior change was an objective one. We can see traces of Hull's influence on the development of Sears's theory, as the discussion below will show.

Although Hull's work had a profound impact on him, Sears was also influenced during the 1940s by the psychoanalytic approach to understanding development. Although he did not find the psychoanalytic model of development completely satisfactory, it contained certain components that led him to try to bridge some of the differences between his own behavioral approach and what psychoanalysis had to say. Perhaps this is one reason Sears conducted the majority of his work in the areas of child rearing and child-parent interaction—areas that have historically been of primary interest to psychoanalytically oriented child developmentalists. During this same period, Sears was also strongly influenced by the application of behavioral principles to social problems by psychologists such as John Dollard and Neal Miller (1950).

Like other behaviorists, Sears focused on the effects that the consequences of behaviors have on future behaviors. He believed that whatever consequences a behavior might have, these in turn become the causes for later behaviors. This cycle, beginning with innate or instinctual needs and tempered or shaped by the child's experiences, is one of the most significant components of Sears's approach. Over time, experiences take on value as secondary reinforcers. Indeed, according to Sears's theory, the differences in behavior that we see among individuals are the results of how the individuals' different experiences affect the values of particular reinforcers. For example, one child may find it "worthwhile" to verbalize at a high rate (because she receives attention for doing so), whereas another child might receive greater rewards for being passive and relatively nonverbal. For the middle-aged man who was recently been laid off from his job, a history of defeat and embarrassment might be enough to discourage him from job hunting no matter what rewards may lie at the end of his search.

> The basis of many of Sears's propositions is that instincts, or innate needs, are shaped by experience.

Some Basic Assumptions

As noted above, Clark Hull was one of the first American behaviorists to propose the idea of intervening variables between stimulus and response. According to Sears, social influences (especially the home environment and parental attitudes) are the most important of these intervening variables. As the discussion below will show, he had a very strong interest in the nature of dyadic (two-person) interactions as well as in the developmental nature of these interactions. Most important to Sears's theory is the fact that social interactions between the members of a dyad go both ways—each party interacts with and has an impact on the other.

> Critical to Sears's theory is the fact that dyadic relationships are reciprocal; that is, each member influences the other.

In preparation for a discussion of the importance of this interaction, let's focus first on the five basic assumptions of Sears's social learning theory approach.

- *Assumption 1.* Initially, every behavior begins as an effort to reduce tension that is associated with some biological need.

This first assumption clearly reflects Sears's training and interest in psychoanalytic theory. As you remember from Chapter 5, Freud's theory of development places major emphasis on the role that biological needs play in the development of the child's affective and cognitive systems. In addition, instincts are cyclical in nature, and their primary role in development is to allow the individual to learn how to reduce tension and then incorporate that learning into a repertoire of behaviors. Although all humans tend to have highly similar biological needs, the ways in which we satisfy those needs vary widely. This variation is a major source of the differences in behaviors exhibited among people.

For Sears, every behavior begins as an effort to reduce tension that is associated with some biological need.

- *Assumption 2.* Behavior (and development) is a function of interactions between people, especially dyadic interactions.

Sears's primary research interest was in the area of child rearing. Perhaps his best-known work, *Patterns of Child Rearing* (Sears, Maccoby, & Levin, 1957), reflects his intense interest in understanding why parents rear their children using one method rather than another. As part of this research, Sears focused specifically on mother-child interactions, which he believed to be the primary source of the child's socialization and training. (During the late 1950s, fathers were not considered to have anywhere near the influence on their children's development that we know about today.)

Children often mimic their parents, but at other times they show original or novel behaviors. In addition, parents, and especially mothers, encourage (or reinforce) or discourage (or punish) certain behaviors in their children, so that the children eventually learn what is acceptable and what is not. Later in life, the family and then society take over these teaching functions, but initially it is child-parent interaction that builds and strengthens the basic course of the child's development. Because the most common form of interaction the young child experiences is in the dyadic relationship with the child's primary caretaker, Sears reasoned that by examining the dynamics of this relationship he could better understand how social forces affect learning.

Sears's theoretical approach is based on five assumptions concerning the importance of the dyad and the reduction of tension, which formed the foundation for social learning theory in the 20th century.

- *Assumption 3.* Drives that are present at birth provide the foundation for later development.

It is difficult to see how any developmental theorist could argue with Sears's third assumption. Surely, our basic behaviors (such as reflexes) must come from somewhere, and the repertoire present at birth in the form of reflexes is as solid and universal a starting point as any. Sears, however, took this assumption one step further: He believed that primary drives (such as hunger) play a major role in that they are "contiguous" (or paired) with other initially neutral events in the environment. Hence these previously neutral events take on the quality of a secondary motivational system. For example, the child learns that controlling his or her bowels can be a pleasant physical and social experience because of the approval the child receives from parents and others in the immediate environment. These drives (called instincts in some theoretical approaches) seem to be among the many building blocks that the developing child uses again and again. They are constantly being linked with social events to form increasingly complex patterns of behavior.

- *Assumption 4.* Behavior is both the cause and the effect of later behavior.

According to Sears, behavior is both the cause and the effect of later behavior.

Behavior, whether simple or complex, does not occur in isolation; it always affects other parts of the individual's behavioral system. When a behavior is established, it is invariably linked with other behaviors. According to Sears, complex patterns of social behavior (such as child rearing) are formed through the constant refinement of behaviors based on some chosen strategy and the observed effects of the behaviors. This process is similar to that of the chaining of behaviors discussed in Chapter 7, in which discrete behaviors become linked together to form a behavioral system. In Sears's social learning view of development, various behaviors take on the power to elicit additional behaviors, which in turn elicit others, and so on. The complexity of the pattern that emerges depends on a variety of factors, the most important of which is experience.

- *Assumption 5.* The quality of a behavior (in terms of the reinforcement value it holds for the child) is determined by experience and learning.

Sears's theory extends a behaviorally based view of development to the social world and all the influences present in that world.

Sears's concept of the reinforcement value of a behavior is very similar to Hull's concept of incentive motivation—that is, the amount of reward that accompanies a certain behavior. In Sears's theory, it is the history of the individual that determines how valuable it is to that person to perform a certain behavior. A teacher might apply this concept, for example, by tailoring the rewards he offers individual students according to the activities that he knows they particularly enjoy. If a child loves jumping rope, the teacher might find that allowing the child time to do so is an effective way of rewarding the child for the time spent at classroom seat work. Similarly, workers will not put forth their best efforts, whether in an office or on an assembly line, if they are not aware of the value of the reinforcer (and not just the reinforcer itself) waiting for them after they've finished their tasks.

Applying Ideas About Social Learning Theory

To Watch TV or Not Watch TV? That Is the Question

Thousands of studies of children's television viewing have produced massive amounts of data on the power of modeling (and imitation). The majority of these studies have found that television viewing has significant impacts, both positive and negative, on the social behavior of children. However, many researchers in this area caution us not to kill the messenger (TV) for what it delivers (often violent and inappropriate messages for children and people of all ages). In fact, they note, TV has the power to enlighten and educate, and many programs do so. However, many don't and, unfortunately, it is children who are often least likely to benefit from TV viewing.

Just how much TV do children watch? By the time the average child starts school, he or she has spent about 4,000 hours watching television. The Center for Media Education (1997) provides these figures:

- On average, an American child watches 3 to 4 hours of TV per day, or approximately 28 hours each week.
- TV watching is the number one after-school activity for children ages 6 to 17.
- Each year, an average American child spends about 1,500 hours in front of the television, compared with 900 hours in the classroom.
- By the time they are 70 years old, most Americans will have spent about 10 years of their lives watching TV.

- By the time an American child completes elementary school, he or she has witnessed more than 100,000 acts of violence on TV, including 8,000 murders.

Research has shown that children often model the aggressive and violent behavior they see on television, and that they are affected by television in other ways as well. For example, the National Institute of Mental Health (1982) found that children who watch a lot of television, compared with those who do not, may become less sensitive to the pain and suffering of others, may be more fearful of the world around them, and may be more likely to behave in aggressive or harmful ways toward others.

Many researchers have looked at the proximate (that is, near-term) impacts on children of observing violence on TV, but many have also examined the long-range effects of televised violence on children. One of the most interesting and extensive longitudinal studies conducted to date has followed subjects in Columbia County, New York, since the subjects were children in the early 1960s. Researchers on this study have concluded that "watching a lot of television violence makes kids more aggressive and that parental child rearing practices influence the child's developing personality" (Columbia County Longitudinal Study, 2000). This sounds like a pretty strong argument for the effects of modeling. Further, the researchers have found that "behavioral patterns

(Continued)

learned early in life tend to persist into adolescence and adulthood and are related to educational, occupational and social success." And even later in life? The study found that those children who watched a lot of TV early in their development were more likely to be arrested and prosecuted for criminal acts as adults (when they were around the age of 30). This study is now in its 40th year, which makes it one of the longest-running longitudinal studies ever done. The results of the researchers' continuing follow-ups are surely to be important and interesting.

Most psychologists recognize that there probably is not a one-to-one relationship between a child's witnessing a violent episode in a television cartoon program and the child's being violent toward a neighbor, friend, or classmate immediately afterward. What most of the evidence points toward, however, is that for a child who may have a predisposition toward aggression or who lives in an environment where aggression is valued as the most useful way of settling disputes and interacting with others, such behavior might very well be precipitated by the child's viewing of violent actions and models on television.

What can a parent do? Among other suggestions, the most common advice that psychologists and other experts give is that parents should monitor the content of what their children watch on TV and talk with the children about content that includes aggression. The American Academy of Child and Adolescent Psychiatry provides terrific guidelines for families with children from infants through teens in its "Facts for Families" series of articles regarding the impact of television violence on children. These can be found online at http://www.aacap.org/publications/factsfam/violence.htm.

THE DEVELOPMENTAL NATURE OF SEARS'S SOCIAL LEARNING THEORY

A major difference between behavioral theories of development and approaches such as psychoanalytic theory and cognitive-developmental theory (which is the subject of Chapters 9 and 10) is that behavioral theories almost never postulate the existence of stages of development. The primary reason for this is that if development occurs in some kind of sequence of stages, it follows that development must be a discontinuous process in which there are plateaus and abrupt changes when the individual reaches certain points. Traditional behavioral approaches view development as a continuous process, in which earlier behaviors are related to and (as we have seen above), to some degree, become causal factors in later behaviors.

TABLE 8.1   Sears's Phases of Development

Phase	Time Frame	Focus
1. Rudimentary behavior	Birth–16 months	Innate needs
2. Secondary behavioral systems	16 months–5 years	Family-centered learning
3. Secondary motivational systems	5 years +	Extrafamilial learning

---

Sears's Three-Phase Model of Social Interaction

Although his approach is behaviorally oriented, Sears incorporated the idea of stages into his theory, proposing a three-phase model in which Phase 1 is a period of rudimentary behavior, Phase 2 is a period in which secondary behavioral systems develop, and Phase 3 is a period in which secondary motivational systems develop. Table 8.1 summarizes these phases, showing the time frame and the focus of each.

Sears's social learning theory includes three distinct phases in which there are progressive increases in the amount of interaction between the child and the world around the child.

Phase 1: Rudimentary Behavior

Phase 1, a period of rudimentary behavior, takes place between birth and 16 months of age. This phase is characterized by the satisfaction of the infant's innate needs and the kind of behavioral learning that takes place as a function of those needs. Through the reduction of tension associated with having basic biological needs met, the infant begins to amass the kinds of behaviors he or she needs to become somewhat independent from a caretaker. The infant also begins to develop a wide range of social and interpersonal skills. Because the child is "inexperienced," a great deal of learning takes place through simple trial and error. For example, if the infant finds that vocalizing in a certain way does not get the desired response from a parent, he or she tries other strategies until one of them is successful.

When the infant finds a strategy that is successful, he or she is likely to repeat that strategy and may also generalize it to other settings when similar needs arise. For example, the child might learn that the most effective way of getting attention from one or both parents is through loud and direct verbalization directed toward them. The child might then also apply this strategy to get attention from workers at the day-care center or from other relatives. This generalization is an important step, because the child develops new skills through interactions with people in multiple settings.

An important characteristic of this phase of development is often overlooked, especially by the child's parents: During this time, a reciprocity is established between parents and child—that is, just as the parents' behavior affects the child, the child's behavior encourages certain parental behaviors as well. For example, it is not just the parents' innate desire to provide warmth for their new baby that encourages them to rock and cuddle the infant; the child's endearing responses and the "cuteness" of the infant's behavior encourages them to relate to the baby in this way. Children in the later part of this phase (around 16 months) are quite mobile, can get around well on their own, and are also increasingly verbal. Children at this age also behave in ways that encourage certain behaviors on their parents' part, all of which are advantageous to the children's growth and development.

Given the reciprocal nature of child-caretaker interactions, it is easy to see how important the dyadic or one-to-one relationship is during this early phase of development. Research has shown that children in this phase who do not have some of their basic needs met are slower to develop, especially in the area of social skills; one explanation for this might be a lack of reciprocity in their earliest relationships.

Phase 2: Secondary Behavioral Systems

The first two phases in Sears's social learning theory focus on the innate needs of children and children's involvement in the family.

The second phase in Sears's theory, the period in which secondary behavioral systems are formed, lasts from about 16 months until about 5 years of age. In this phase, the primary focus is the interaction between the child's developing physical and intellectual skills and the social conventions of the family. Rather than just associating "mom" or "dad" with the appropriate solution to any concern, the child begins to learn to align the satisfaction of primary needs with what the environment has to offer. For the child around this age, school is not usually a full-time activity, but the child is very busy developing a place within the family system. The child's goal is now more than just the satisfaction of needs—the child also seeks the reduction of tension associated with what I have described above as secondary reinforcers. For example, by eating with the family, the child not only satisfies the basic need for food, he or she also begins to learn the correct way to behave at the table, how to ask for certain things, rules of conversation, and so forth. During this phase, the child reaches out to parents and other family members for guidance on how to satisfy needs that are growing more complex every day.

This is also a time of significant socialization, one example of which is the process of toilet training. During this phase almost all children learn to control their bowels. When a child is younger, especially during the rudimentary phase, it is not important or particularly socially valuable for the child to be toilet trained. Parents understand this and treat the child accordingly. By a certain age, however, the child is expected to be out of diapers, and the pleasurable physical sensations and autonomy that the child experienced earlier are somewhat tempered by the demands of the other member of the dyad, as well as by society. This is a perfect example of how a primary need (in this case, for elimination) becomes linked with a secondary source of reinforcement in the environment (here the approval of parents and others).

Phase 3: Secondary Motivational Systems

In addition to all the other things that happen to the child around age 5 or 6, the most important, for both the child and the family, is the beginning of formal education. It is clear to almost every parent that the moment a child begins school, that child's behavior is shaped by an entirely new set of potential reinforcers. The dyadic relationship that the mother or father had with the child is simply no longer possible at the same level. The child enters the world of socialization, where he or she finds many different types of peers to play or have conflicts with, many different behaviors to try, and many different sources of potential reinforcement for all kinds of behaviors.

By Phase 3, the child has progressed from reliance on one person during the very early stages of development through reliance on the family during Phase 2 and is now faced with the prospect of learning self-reliance.

The Relationships Among the Three Phases of Social Learning

In Sears's model, the three phases of social learning are closely related; anything affecting the first two of these phases affects the succeeding phase(s) as well. Figure 8.1 illustrates how the three phases can be conceptualized as concentric circles. For the adolescent, the rudimentary behavior phase (the first to be formed) is represented as the smallest circle, and the secondary motivational phase (the last to be formed), which represents society's contribution, is the largest, reflecting the importance of this last phase of development. This circle is the largest because it is the most encompassing, containing more socializing influences than either of the other two phases. For the child at birth, who has only the parents available as a source for fulfilling basic needs, the rudimentary behavior phase is represented as the largest. As the child ages, the family and society will become critical socializing agents, but they are not yet part of the child's world.

When an event occurs within one of these circles—that is, in one of the phases—like a pebble thrown into a pond it causes ripples or reverberations throughout the phases that follow. For example, if a child experiences the death of a parent during Phase 2, that event will not only have an impact on the child's socialization within the family structure, it will be among the experiences he or she brings into Phase 3, and so will affect the child's more general socialization as well.

No experience in the developing person's life stands alone; rather, all experiences trickle down and affect later parts of the developmental process.

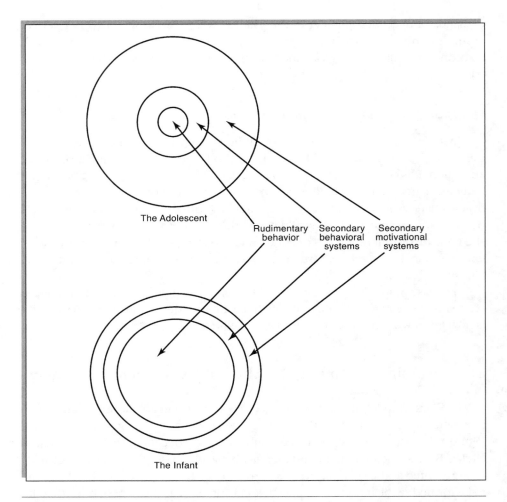

FIGURE 8.1   Sears's Three Phases of Social Learning as Applied to the Infant and the Adolescent

Although Robert Sears's contribution to our understanding of the developmental process is significant, his theory has never become as popular as some of the others discussed in this book. One reason for this may be psychologists' general reluctance to accept any theory that combines aspects of both behavioral and psychoanalytic approaches to development. Or perhaps Sears's approach is not different enough from other approaches that were already available. In any case, we should not overlook Sears's major contributions to the field of human development. By applying psychoanalytic principles within a behavioral model, Sears provided a framework for many of the behavioral theorists who followed him and demonstrated the

---

—— On the Web ——

Albert Bandura and Aletha Stein conducted one of the first studies involving social learning theory in the early 1960s when they looked at the effects of imitation on violent or aggressive behavior in young children. You can read about the original experiment online at http://psychclassics.yorku.ca/Bandura/bobo. htm. Also, at http://academic.evergreen.edu/h/hiljus01/bobo.htm, you can see a photograph of a young boy who participated in the experiment. The photo clearly shows the boy hitting a doll, just as he had seen a model do in a previous episode of the experiment.

---

importance of factors other than those that are directly responsible for change. Among the theorists influenced by Sears is Albert Bandura (1925–), whose work has had by far the greatest impact on the development and acceptance of social learning theory. Grusec (1992) calls Bandura "the intellectual heir of Sears."

ALBERT BANDURA'S SOCIAL LEARNING THEORY

With the theoretical and empirical research undertaken by Sears and others, the behavioral tradition entered an important new era. The idea that individuals are nothing more than passive hosts with little direct control over their fates became less and less acceptable as an adequate explanation for development. With the application of the concept of intervening variables, behavioral approaches were no longer tied to a unidirectional model—that is, the idea that the individual is affected by the environment but the environment is not affected by the individual. With the recognition of reciprocity in the person-environment relationship, a cognitive component was introduced into the behavioral arena for the first time.

Even with Sears's important contribution, questions still existed about how human beings learn so many complex behaviors in relatively short periods of time without obvious practice. For example, the acquisition of language cannot be explained as an arduous process in which the child hears every possible combination of nouns, verbs, and adjectives and is reinforced for copying those combinations. Rather, it is a result of an interaction between predetermined potentialities and a supportive and properly programmed environment. Likewise, people participate in classes of behaviors that do not appear to be the result of direct instruction. For example, parents often employ the same child-rearing practices and philosophies that their own parents employed in raising them. Their parents did not teach them these practices directly. This type of learning takes place through an entirely different process called **vicarious learning** (Bandura, 1971).

Although the value of Bandura's contribution to the formation of social learning theory should not be underestimated, it is important to remember that much of Bandura's early work was an extension of the work of Robert Sears.

Applying Ideas About Social Learning Theory

World Peace Through Social Learning Theory? Not Quite Yet, But . . .

Anyone who reads newspapers knows that the world is full of terrible, and often seemingly intractable, conflicts. In the Middle East, in Ireland, in Africa, even in the cities of the United States, religious, racial, and class struggles continue. Often the original reasons for these conflicts have long been forgotten, and the terrible toll they continue to take stands as a monument to how bigotry and hatred seem to be "passed" from generation to generation. How might this happen, and what can be done about it?

Researchers Muhammad Haj-Yahia and Samia Dawud-Noursi (affiliated with Hebrew University and the U.S. National Institutes of Health, respectively) have examined these questions, and their findings are consistent with many of the observations of the theorists discussed in this chapter; that is, imitation and modeling have great power to shape and reinforce behaviors.

Haj-Yahia and Dawud-Noursi (1998) examined the question of whether children who experience disharmony at home are likely to employ disruptive strategies in attempting to resolve conflicts. They used the Conflict Tactics Scale (Straus, 1979) to measure the conflict-resolution tactics that the subjects in their sample (832 Arab adolescents from Israel) observed in their families of origin and then used the findings to try to predict the tactics these young men and women would use to resolve conflicts with their siblings.

Vicarious learning is learning that takes place through imitation, or modeling.

Albert Bandura and Richard Walters (Bandura's first graduate student and a lifelong colleague) developed a theoretical perspective within which the individual is viewed as an active mediator who operates on the environment in accord with certain expectancies and contingencies, but with foresight or knowledge as to what the consequences of his or her behaviors are likely to be. This is a radical change from the traditional or fundamental S-R conception of learning. Indeed, Bandura and Walters theorized a system in which separate S-R bonds or elements merge into unified patterns of behavior. Further, their theory attributes much of the direction (but not the cause) of behavior to the individual's own internal behaviors, which are referred to primarily as *mediating processes.*

In their seminal work *Social Learning and Personality Development,* published in 1963, Bandura and Walters clearly stated their learning approach to development and at the same time abandoned any type of connection between their theory and psychoanalytic approaches to development (such as that proposed by Sears). In this work, Bandura and Walters made two major contributions: They introduced the idea that the social milieu, or social setting, has impacts on the developmental process, and they argued that developmental theorists had long

As you may know, extensive research has consistently shown that children who experience violence in their homes are more likely than children from nonviolent homes to encounter social and emotional problems later in life, including the possibility of their becoming abusive themselves. Given these findings, and now that you know something about social learning theory, what might you expect Haj-Yahia and Dawud-Noursi to have found?

Here is a summary of their findings in the areas of reasoning, verbal abuse, and physical violence:

- The more often an adolescent had experienced reasoned approaches to solving conflicts (e.g., rational discussion of issues), the more likely it was that he or she would use such tactics with siblings.

- The more often an adolescent experienced verbal abuse and physical violence in his or her family of origin (through observation of his or her parents), the more likely it was that the adolescent would use such tactics with siblings.

With some degree of confidence, we can conclude that these adolescents were likely to use the tactics they had observed at home when they tried to resolve conflicts. We can also probably safely say that few parents want their children to use verbal and physical aggression to resolve conflicts. But, as this study and others have demonstrated, children are much more likely to do as they see and not necessarily as they are told.

placed too much importance on research with animals (very typical of the operant learning tradition).

Bandura's Theoretical Viewpoint

As we have seen, most theories of development within particular general models tend to build on one another. For example, Erikson's theory of psychosocial development is built on the psychoanalytic theory developed by Freud; Erikson's theory differs from Freud's yet embraces many of the same basic concepts. This does not mean that later theories are always logical extensions of earlier ones; rather, some theories incorporate certain concepts and ideas that have already been established. For science to advance and not just keep reproducing itself, this building process is a necessity. This process can be seen in the development of social learning theory, which incorporates the basic rules and terminology of S-R learning along with the fundamental tenets of S-R psychology, including the important concepts of stimulus-response bonds, respondent and operant behaviors, and schedules of reinforcement.

Another important element of social learning theory is the assumption that significant learning takes place through the process of imitation, or modeling. As we have seen, the idea that people imitate, or model, behavior and receive reinforcement for doing so is common to traditional S-R theories. However, in social learning theory the process of imitation is more complex, because the individual is understood to play an active role in determining the classes of behaviors to be imitated as well as the frequency and intensity of the imitation. That is, there's more to the S-R link than just the S and the R. Perhaps the most important difference between the traditional S-R view of imitation and the social learning theory view is that social learning theory allows for the learning of certain kinds of behaviors without the benefit of direct experience. That is, according to social learning theory, for some behaviors vicarious, or indirect, reinforcement is as effective as direct reinforcement for facilitating and promoting imitation. And in order for vicarious reinforcement to be possible, as you will see later, the individual must contribute some cognitive component (such as being able to remember and rehearse) to the operation.

> The single most important element of social learning theory is the concept of learning through imitation, or modeling.

The significance of the assumption that learning takes place through imitation cannot be overstated. For many years, behavioral psychologists worked mostly within a framework that bound the effects of imitation to the temporal qualities of an event. Imitation was thought to be a process tied to the learner (or the person doing the imitating), who received reinforcement as the behavior was taking place. With the development of social learning theory came an entirely new framework, in which reinforcement can occur in an indirect fashion. Thus, although experience might be the best teacher, the experiences of others are important as well. People do not drive through intersections when the traffic signal light is red because they are aware of the consequences of doing so, even though they may never have experienced those consequences directly. Students don't cheat on tests (at least not overtly) because they know what the consequences will be if they are caught.

We often hear parents telling their children, "Do as I tell you!" But from a social learning theory perspective, it is clear that people are more likely to do as they *see* others do than they are to do what others *tell* them to do. Children are often told not to do certain things that they see adults doing (such as smoking, being rude, or displaying bad temper), and when the children revert to these behaviors, adults wonder where they learned them. Parents may be the most powerful models in a child's life, and therefore potentially the child's best teachers. This is true not only because of the high degree of frequency and intensity with which children and their parents interact, but also because of the high regard children have for parents and their desire to be like them. Of course, the easiest way to be like another person is to copy his or her behavior, and such imitation is a process that operates extensively throughout the life span.

Social learning theory ascribes special importance to the operation of internal mediational processes in development. This is a major distinction between social learning theory and other behavioral viewpoints on development. Specifically, social learning theory assumes that internal mediating processes are important to learning. That is, between the sensory input that forms the basis of all learning and the final behavior, internal operations take place that affect the ultimate outcome. If one accepts this assumption, one cannot also accept the unidirectional nature of other S-R theories.

Radical behaviorism's fundamental assumption is that individuals are relatively passive recipients of environmental influences and have little to do with determining the course of their own development. Social learning theory goes far beyond this point of view, assuming that although the impetus for behavior is environmental in nature, the developmental process is bidirectional, characterized by reciprocity between the individual and the environment. Bandura (1977) calls this viewpoint **reciprocal determinism**. At the simplest level, according to this view, sensory input does not automatically produce behavior unaffected by the individual's conscious contribution. In essence, the process of reciprocal determinism can be described as follows: The learner does not acquire a set of S-R bonds, or associations, simply through receiving reinforcement for copying a model. Instead, the individual processes information from the model and develops a set of symbolic representations of the behavior that, through trial-and-error learning, the individual later matches. The learner continues to attempt to match this template, using feedback, until the learner's behavior is on target. Thus learning is not a simple process in which the learner perceives a model and then imitates the behavior, but a much more complex series of steps wherein the learner approximates the model's behavior through the internalization of what the model represents, followed by the learner's attempts to match that representation.

Bandura eventually extended this concept significantly when he began to incorporate ideas of self-value and self-efficacy into his work. He defines self-efficacy as "the belief in one's capabilities to organize and execute the sources of action that are required to manage prospective situations" (Bandura, 1986, p. 87). He contends that as an individual becomes increasingly aware of what "works" (that is, recognizes what can act as a reinforcing event), the more adept the person becomes at using his or her skills and abilities to accomplish what needs to be done.

> The critical difference between Bandura's approach and that of earlier social learning theorists is the importance in Bandura's model of the role that mediation, or cognitive processing, plays in the acquisition of behaviors.

> Social learning theory, as defined by Bandura, places a great deal of importance on the reciprocal relationship between the individual and the environment.

The Importance of Vicarious Learning

A very powerful concept in social learning theory, if not the most powerful, is that of vicarious learning, or learning that takes place without direct reinforcement. This concept is important because it provides an explanation for how we can have the rich behavioral repertoires that we have without necessarily experiencing ourselves all of the things we know about and can do.

One of the most famous and best illustrations of vicarious learning and the effects of modeling is provided by a study conducted by Albert Bandura, Dorothea Ross, and Sheila Ross (1961) that has served as the foundation for many of the social learning theory experiments conducted over the past 40 years. Developmental psychologists have long been interested in the ways in which people acquire, or learn, aggressive behavior, because such behavior is present in some form at all levels of development. How we learn aggressive behavior is also one of the issues often raised as part of the nature/nurture debate. In their study, Bandura and his colleagues were primarily interested in determining whether children's exposure to aggressive or nonaggressive models would make a difference in the rates of aggression the children displayed in situations without the models. The method they used to answer this question has become a hallmark of social learning theory research.

The concept of vicarious learning accounts for our ability to learn various behaviors without direct experience.

Bandura and his colleagues divided the subjects in their experiment, 36 boys and girls enrolled in a preschool, into eight groups. Each child was placed in a room with an adult model; half the children were paired with models who were the same sex as the children, and the other half were paired with opposite-sex models. The child and the model were led into an experimental room, and the model, seated at his or her own table, did one of two things. If the child was in the aggressive condition, the model would first play with some of the Tinkertoys that were available and then begin to act aggressively toward a 5-foot-tall inflated punching doll (affectionately named Bobo) of the kind that returns to an upright position when hit. The model would hit the doll and sit on it while also directing verbal aggression at it. If the child was in the nonaggressive condition, the model would simply play with the toys provided in the room and not pay any attention to the doll.

To test for aggressive modeling, or imitation, the researchers placed each child, after his or her session with the model, in a room containing a variety of toys, including an inflated doll of the same type as described above but only 3 feet tall. Each child spent 20 minutes alone in the room while a judge observed the child from an adjoining room through a two-way mirror and recorded the child's behavior every 5 seconds, using the following predetermined categories: physical aggression, verbal aggression, nonaggressive verbal responses, mallet (or hammer) aggression, sitting on doll, punching doll, nonimitative physical and verbal aggression, and aggressive gun play.

Bandura and his colleagues found that the children who were exposed to aggressive models showed significantly higher amounts of aggression than did those children who had been exposed to nonaggressive models. In addition, the boys in the sample who observed a male aggressive model showed more aggression than did girls who observed a male aggressive model. In recent years, many

---

—— On the Web ——

One of Bandura's important contributions to theories of development is the concept of self-efficacy, or the amount of control an individual believes he or she has over life circumstances. This concept is a very interesting part of Bandura's later work, and as is true for many important constructs, scholars have developed a host of scales and tests to assess and measure self-efficacy in individuals. You can find a description of one such scale, the Generalized Self-Efficacy Scale, at http://userpage.fu-berlin.de/~health/engscal.htm, and you can learn more about self-efficacy in general by following some of the links on this site.

---

people have voiced a great deal of concern about the effects of television viewing on the development of aggressive and antisocial behavior in children. Studies such as this one have helped to increase our understanding of the powerful influence of aggressive models.

The Function of Reinforcement in Imitation

One of the most important concepts in behavioral development concerns the process through which reinforcement acts to influence behavior. Certain factors determine the strength of a reinforcer and its effect on subsequent behavior. One of these is the immediacy with which the stimulus event (or reinforcer) follows the individual's behavior, and another is the schedule of reinforcement, or the frequency with which the reinforcing events occur. As you remember from the discussion in Chapter 7, these are important components of the learning process.

If we examine the traditional S-R perspective, we can see that although reinforcement is a very efficient tool in the modification of behavior, it is not necessarily useful for creating or facilitating the development of novel behaviors. Reinforcement plays an important role in modifying behavior within the traditional behavioral perspective, but social learning theory goes one (very big) step further, ascribing two important and distinct functions to reinforcement: information and motivation.

The Informative Qualities of Reinforcers

Reinforcers have informative qualities—that is, the act of reinforcement and the reinforcement process itself can tell the individual what behavior is most adaptive. People do not grope in haphazard fashion until something in the environment

Applying Ideas About Social Learning Theory

Chance Encounters and Your Life Path

The theorists discussed in this volume can certainly be described as very smart people. Once in a while, a developmental theorist writes an article that is somewhat outside the mainstream of theory but nevertheless has important impacts on other scholars' thinking about the process of human development—sometimes such articles have even greater impact than more strictly theoretical writings.

Albert Bandura's article titled "The Psychology of Chance Encounters and Life Paths" (1982) is a perfect example. In this article, Bandura proposes that chance plays a very important role in shaping how our lives turn out. What's a chance encounter? Bandura defines it as an unintended meeting of persons unfamiliar with each other. We all have chance encounters every day. A chance meeting with a friend of a friend might introduce you to a new topic of study for your graduate work, for example, setting you off on a lifetime of adventure and learning. Or you might receive an e-mail asking you to take part in a certain activity and find that it is signed by a high school friend you have not seen or heard from in years, which leads to a renewed personal relationship.

Bandura discusses the factors that contribute to whether such chance occurrences have significant value for changing a person's life path. He asserts that what makes some of them more important than others in shaping a person's future is in part determined by what these types of encounters have produced for the individual in the past.

He begins by noting that two important psychological processes affect the way in which early development leads into stable patterns of behavior. First, people tend to select environments that are consistent with their personalities (this is similar to Sandra Scarr's [1993] view that people help to create their own environments, discussed in Chapter 2). For example, people who are musically inclined tend to gravitate toward social activities that involve music—they might join school or community choruses or orchestras, for instance. Second, people produce their own environments by constructing settings (such as starting a bike club or having a large family) that are consistent with their own interests and help them to, as Bandura says, "achieve some regularity."

According to Bandura, the power of chance encounters to influence our lives is determined by two sets of factors: personal and social. He names three personal determinants:

comes at the right moment and reinforces a response. They act with intent. In a sense, they learn through experience what to expect in advance, and thus they become progressively better at predicting what behaviors will maximize their chances for success. Before an individual goes to a job interview, for example, she is aware of the potential outcome (getting the position) and, because of this awareness, she engages in behaviors (dressing appropriately, for example) that will maximize her chances of making a good impression.

- *Entry skills:* If any person one meets by chance is to have an influence (good or bad) on one's life, one needs personal skills that will allow one to interact and engage that individual effectively. For example, you might meet by chance a person who can introduce you to someone else who is looking to hire new employees, but unless you somehow engage that person through appropriate interpersonal interaction, it's unlikely the chance encounter will lead to your getting a new job.
- *Emotional ties:* The stronger the emotional ties between people who meet through chance encounters, the more likely it is that those meetings will have significant impacts on later outcomes. For example, you might meet someone who could hold the key to an important shift in the direction of your life path, but if you find that person very unattractive (physically, personally, or otherwise), that would surely put a damper on how long you would want to interact with him or her and pursue that possible lead.
- *Values and personal standards:* The more consistent one's values are with those of the person encountered by chance, the greater the possibility that the relationship will continue. For example, if you find racial prejudice repugnant, you may not want to affiliate with a racist; conversely, if you have racial prejudices of your own, you may be attracted to someone who shares those views.

Bandura describes two social determinants:

- *Milieu rewards:* If a chance encounter leads to a successful outcome, one is likely to pursue again the social conditions that produced the encounter in the first place. For example, if you have had some pleasant chance encounters at a particular hot spot for meeting others, you are likely to find yourself back there again.
- *Psychological closeness:* The more consistent one's beliefs are with the beliefs of those one encounters by chance, the more attracted one may be to those persons or groups and to the life paths they can open. For example, most people who are religiously observant tend to affiliate with churches, mosques, or synagogues where the members' beliefs are consistent with their own.

At the end of this article, Bandura emphasizes that a strong sense of personal agency, or self-efficacy, allows individuals to have important impacts on their own lives by "selecting, influencing, and constructing their own circumstances." In case you haven't noticed, this is a very optimistic view of human nature. Bandura states in the closing paragraph of the article that "human beings have an unparalleled capability to become many things," further confirming his belief that although chance is an important factor in how our life paths develop, what we do with those chance events as they occur is even more important.

Some of the most impressive empirical work based on social learning theory to date has treated this very point regarding expectations. If this idea is valid, one would expect learning to be "better" or faster when some advanced knowledge is present. And, in fact, research has shown that much more effective learning does occur when the individual is aware of what behavior is being reinforced. Thus participants' knowledge of the consequences of certain behaviors can help to optimize the effectiveness of a learning program. If people are informed as to what behaviors will be rewarded under what conditions, the likelihood that they will learn successfully is greatly improved. For example, in a school setting, children are not handed pencil and paper and allowed to make random marks until they produce marks that look like letters of the alphabet. Instead, they are shown models and are instructed what to do. Similarly, adults are informed in their workplaces about how they are expected to complete their work in order to obtain payment or whatever other reward (or reinforcer) is being offered.

The informative function of reinforcers also allows people some insight into the consequences of behaviors before they act. In strange situations or new settings, people often do not have enough information to know what behaviors are acceptable. Without such information, they often find it difficult to know the appropriate behaviors to reach for as a goal. Reinforcers' informative value depends to a large extent on the amount of previous experience an individual has had within a given setting.

The Motivating Qualities of Reinforcers

The second important difference between the traditional S-R view and the social learning theory view of imitation is that in social learning theory, reinforcers are understood to have motivating as well as informative qualities. That is, people learn to anticipate what the reinforcers will be in certain situations, and this initial anticipatory behavior is the beginning step in many developmental sequences. This is one element within the very large context of cognitive, or mediating, operations that occurs within the individual in his or her reciprocal relationship with the environment.

People do not have the power to see into the future, but they can anticipate the consequences of many behaviors based on what they learn from other people's good and bad experiences (and, most important, without directly living through all those experiences themselves). For example, parents have their children inoculated against polio and diphtheria before the children can become infected; they do not have to experience the tragedy of serious illness in their children before they take action. Likewise, people do not park their cars in tow-away zones because they know that if they do, their cars will be towed away and they will be fined. The likely future consequences of behaviors can act as motivators to provide direction to behavior. This notion in itself makes the social learning theory view of development very powerful for helping to explain people's day-to-day behavior.

In addition to social learning theory's concepts of the informative and motivating qualities of the reinforcement process, there are other important differences that distinguish the traditional S-R view from the social learning view. These differences are best described through a comparison of the two viewpoints, which I present in the next section.

TWO LEARNING THEORY VIEWS OF IMITATION

One important distinction between the traditional S-R perspective and social learning theory is found in the role that reinforcement occupies in each. Reinforcement-based theories of imitation postulate the need for direct reinforcement—that is, behaviors must be directly reinforced in order to be learned. In other words, if a person imitates a behavior without being reinforced for that behavior, incomplete learning or no learning takes place. In contrast, according to social learning theory, imitation occurs through the observation of a model; the learner need not necessarily receive direct reinforcement or actually model the behavior. Thus social learning theory takes an observational view of imitation.

As noted in Chapter 7, direct reinforcement is an effective way to facilitate changes in behavior, but this does not necessarily help us to understand how new behaviors are formed. Social learning theory does not consider reinforcement alone to be a sufficient explanation for imitation; rather, it is only one component that facilitates learning, along with covert processes such as attention, organization, and rehearsal.

If one accepts the basic premise of the traditional S-R perspective—that, in order for learning to occur, the individual must directly experience the consequences of his or her action—then the scope of behaviors that can be explained is limited. It is obvious that we could not possibly learn all we know only through those events we directly experience. As noted above, we are indirectly reinforced or punished through the process of vicarious learning. For example, seeing one child being punished for running into the street can deter other children from doing the same. Direct instruction is probably critical for the learning of many skills, such as swimming. We can, however, also learn how to swim by recalling what an instructor has said and the images of the instructor's actions in the water, and by putting these thoughts and images into action.

The understanding that an individual does not need direct reinforcement for a behavior in order to model it was a huge breakthrough in developmental theory.

Individuals do not need to be told or shown all the time that their behaviors are correct or incorrect in order for further learning to take place. It is because of this concept that social learning theory is considered to be so powerful in its explanatory role. It helps to account for the large amount of learning that takes place without direct exposure to models.

Figures 8.2 and 8.3 illustrate the difference between the traditional S-R and social learning perspectives on imitation. From the traditional S-R viewpoint (Figure 8.2), imitative behavior is reinforced as the behavior is taking place and in the presence of the model. This leaves little room for any contribution by the individual other than previous experience, which is represented by a storehouse of earlier S-R associations. Within this model, reinforcement acts to strengthen earlier imitative behaviors in the presence of a model or a modeling stimulus. For example, a child might imitate his or her parents' table manners; if the child is reinforced

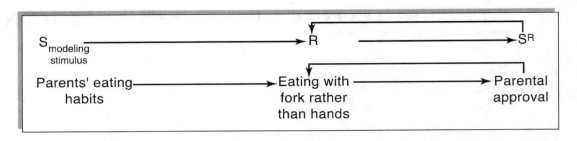

FIGURE 8.2 Imitation From the Point of View of Traditional Learning Theory

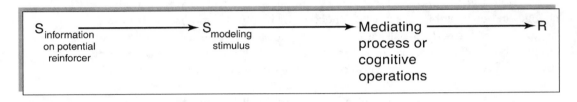

FIGURE 8.3 Imitation From the Point of View of Social Learning Theory

(or punished) for this behavior within a reasonable amount of time, the conditions for simple imitative learning are present. Reinforcement (or punishment) of the behavior and the behavior itself occur in close physical and temporal proximity.

The social learning theory viewpoint (Figure 8.3) is more complex. As before, there is a model that is imitated (modeling stimulus) and a resultant behavior (R). Initially, however, the individual acts on the basis of some awareness of what is and what is not worth imitating and anticipates an outcome that is potentially advantageous. People are frequently in situations in which they choose not to imitate models because the anticipated reinforcers are not worth the effort or hold no value for the individuals. This anticipatory behavior provides much of the motivation for an individual's modeling a specific behavior or class of behaviors. Young children learn the significance of imitating the speech patterns of their parents very quickly, for example, because they often receive a great deal of reinforcement for this behavior.

Another unique component of the social learning theory view is the individual's attention to the modeling stimulus. One crucial way in which social learning theory differs from the traditional S-R view is in its concept of internal, or mediating, cognitive operations through which the individual acts on the information available based on the observation of a model. In this process, information about the model is encoded and stored so that it is available to the individual at a later time, the order of the elements is rehearsed so that the individual can correctly reconstruct them when necessary, and finally these cognitive acts are transformed into actual behavior, or a response. Most social learning theorists describe these internal operations as *mediators* and tend to shy away from such terms as *thinking*. The idea of a mediating influence is much more clearly conceptualized than is some general operation called *thinking*. Social learning theorists are as concerned with operationalizing behavior as are traditional behaviorists, and they find such terms to be nondescriptive.

Although the significance of direct reinforcement from external sources is not a cornerstone element in the social learning theory approach, it is still important. Beyond this, however, vicarious reinforcement is the major force that operates on learning within the social learning theory view (Bandura, 1971). In other words, through a variety of mechanisms, behaviors are reinforced without direct experience. Given this viewpoint, it is obvious that social learning theory does not assume that the organism is passively waiting for the environment to affect its behavior.

> Within the social learning theory view, what goes on inside the individual and what occurs outside in the environment are equally important.

SOCIAL LEARNING THEORY AS A PROCESS

Four processes are necessary for imitation, or observational learning, to occur: attention, retention, motor reproduction, and motivation. Without any one of these, the social learning theory model is incomplete, and successful imitation is less likely to occur.

First, the individual must be capable of attending to, or paying attention to, the event or its different elements. Thus children who have attentional deficits such as poor impulse control may not be able to sit still long enough to learn from the stimulus. They may pick up an element of an experience, but they may be unable to process all the elements necessary to represent the entire event. If an individual does not properly attend to a model, imitation is not possible—thus teachers often contend that if children would only pay attention, they could learn. According to Bandura, factors such as history of reinforcement, sensory capacities, and complexity of the modeled event are also important influences on the attention process.

> Attention, retention, motor reproduction, and motivation are the four processes that must be present for imitation, or social learning, to occur.

The second process that is crucial to imitation is retention, or being able to remember the critical features of an event so that they can be recalled and utilized as necessary. For example, when you have a flat tire, you need to activate the sequence of steps for changing a tire. If you have retained what you learned initially about changing a tire, you recall how to use the jack, how to remove the lug nuts, and so on. If an individual cannot remember the different steps in a sequence of events, he or she cannot successfully model that behavior. Retention involves processes such as symbolic coding and rehearsal. These elements of memory make it possible for an individual to internalize an event and recall its sequencing at a later time.

The third process necessary for imitation is the motor reproduction of modeled behavior—that is, the learner must be capable of physically performing the behavior. For example, to learn how to hit a baseball, you must learn how to watch the ball and swing the bat at it at the correct angle and at the correct time. Swinging the bat and hitting the ball are global behaviors that include many simple steps, such as keeping your eye on the ball, keeping your feet stationary, placing your hands in the proper position on the bat, and maintaining the bat at the correct level while swinging. When batting instructors teach people to hit, they do more than ask their students to watch others hit. They discuss the different constituent behaviors described above and check to see that the learners can at least perform these different individual behaviors before they have the learners make any attempt to combine (or correct) the behaviors. For successful imitation to take place, a learner must be able to perform all the discrete steps that combine to make up the target behavior.

The final component necessary to imitation is some form of motivation. This can take the form of external (direct) or vicarious (indirect) reinforcement. The first of these two motivational influences is the same type of reinforcement present in the traditional S-R model of imitative, or observational, learning, as shown in Figure 8.2. The latter type of reinforcement, as noted above, is what sets social learning theory apart from earlier theories. The concept of vicarious reinforcement means that the individual is more autonomous, less dependent on direct environmental influences, than the traditional S-R model recognizes. The individual does not need immediate reinforcement every time he or she makes a move in the direction of completion of a goal. Behavior is regulated, and the individual finds a comfortable medium between self-generated reinforcement and that received through external sources. Gratification is necessary for a behavior to reach fruition, even if that gratification is self-generated. This ability that individuals have to reinforce themselves is useful in clinical settings, where therapists can teach people to reinforce their own behaviors and increase their self-esteem.

Vicarious reinforcement results when a potential learner increases a behavior that he or she has seen reinforced in others. The existence of this type of reinforcement helps to explain how human beings can acquire so many new behaviors with relatively little direct experience. Experience is a great teacher, but the human organism is very complex, and we cannot learn everything we do as the result of direct experience and direct reinforcement. An adolescent's latest craze may be reinforced by acceptance from peers, for example, which for a teenager is a powerful influence. Or a middle-aged adult may dress and act like a young adult in an effort to recapture past feelings and experiences. Imitating the behavior of a younger generation can be a powerful motivator, with its false promise of bringing with it the feeling of being young again.

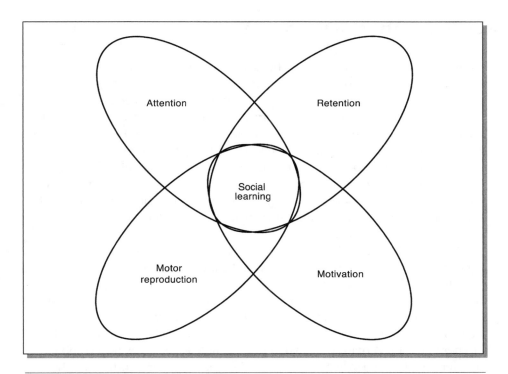

FIGURE 8.4   Interaction of the Four Operations Necessary for Social Learning to Take Place

Like reinforcement, punishing experiences can also be delivered vicariously. People do not have to have the experience of overdosing on sleeping pills or driving a car with an almost empty fuel tank to understand the consequences of their actions. They have learned through other people's experiences what the outcomes of such behaviors are. By watching others, we quickly learn what behaviors are punished (or what behaviors are reinforced) without actually experiencing the pain of punishment ourselves. We raise our hands in class rather than shout, because we know one behavior is rewarded and the other punished.

How do the four operations described above—attention, retention, motor reproduction, and motivation—interact with one another to allow social learning to take place? According to Bandura, the processes take place in an overlapping sequence as shown in Figure 8.4. In any given instance, some of the elements may be stronger than others, but if any one of them is too weak, the entire learning process is disrupted.

For social learning to take place, the learner must be able to attend to, remember, physically perform, and then be reinforced for the behavior modeled.

THE PROCESS OF IMITATION IN ACTION

It is important to note that imitated behavior rarely matches the model's behavior exactly; instead, the learner approximates the model's behavior so that it fits the learner's needs. For example, if an individual learns a certain technique for carving wood by observing an experienced carver, the individual's own personal style is likely to contribute to how he or she implements the borrowed technique. In the same way, imitation can have other effects on behavior. We not only learn new things through the process of imitation, or observational learning; the modeling process may also precipitate behaviors that are already in our repertoires that we had no need for previously. The observation of models can have three distinct effects on a learner's present and future behavior: modeling effects, disinhibitory effects, and inhibitory effects.

The modeling effects, disinhibitory/inhibitory effects, and eliciting effects of the observation of models are important components of social learning theory that can help to clarify the process of imitation.

When the learner behaves in a novel way (that is, does something new), a modeling effect has taken place. For example, a toddler might pick up a rag and use it to dust the furniture as he has seen his mother do, displaying a new behavior that has no clear association with other behaviors he has shown in the past. It should be noted, however, that it is very difficult to say whether any behavior is totally novel, in the sense that no part of it existed previously as an element of another behavior. Perhaps the child in this example is just showing a combination of other established behaviors, such as rubbing a hand over a surface and holding a rag. Together, these become a new behavior called dusting. A new behavior is usually defined as a combination of already existing elements of behavior that the individual has not combined in that fashion before.

When observing a model results in the precipitation of a behavior that already exists in the repertoire of the learner but that previously had not been called on, or actively stimulated, the eliciting effect is present. We have many behaviors in our repertoires that we don't use unless we need them. When the eliciting effect takes place, the learner uses an old (previously learned) strategy in a new and different setting. For example, a person can easily drive a rented car that resembles the car he or she normally drives. Behavior is often an approximation of some target behavior, and for this reason it may be difficult to identify (without any prior knowledge of the individual's history) which of an individual's behaviors are new (resulting from the modeling effect) and which were already established but not active (resulting from the eliciting effect).

The disinhibitory/inhibitory effect is a special case of the eliciting effect. Observing a model can act to disinhibit (encourage) or inhibit (discourage) an individual's imitation of behavior. For a child who has been very aggressive in the past (that is, who has aggressive behavior in her repertoire), for example, a particular set of circumstances might determine whether the child imitates aggressive behavior. If aggression is highly reinforced—in other words, if aggressive behavior is disinhibited through interaction with other models—the child may behave aggressively. On the other hand, aggressive behavior may be inhibited: For instance, the child may decide against aggressive behavior because she knows that aggression will be punished.

The modeling, eliciting, and disinhibitory/inhibitory effects combine with the four processes of attention, retention, motor reproduction, and motivation to provide a framework through which we can understand the acquisition of behavior by means of a series of complex reciprocal interactions between the organism and the environment. The importance of social learning theory's emphasis on the organism's active participation in these interactions cannot be overstated. Aside from distinguishing the social learning viewpoint from the traditional S-R viewpoint, this component of social learning theory represents an important new way of viewing the developmental process.

WEB SITES OF INTEREST

- "Albert Bandura: 1925–Present," by C. George Boeree, at http://www. ship.edu/~cgboeree/bandura.html: Boeree provides a nice biography of Albert Bandura and a review of the highlights of his theory, including some we have not covered in this chapter.
- Information on Self-Efficacy: A Community of Scholars, at http://www. emory.edu/EDUCATION/mfp/effpage.html: This site provides a detailed list of Albert Bandura's writings on self-efficacy, along with links, definitions, and reproductions of some of Bandura's works. It also presents an extensive discussion of different types of research in the area of self-efficacy.
- "Exploration of Fortuitous Determinants of Life Paths," by Albert Bandura, at http://www.emory.edu/EDUCATION/mfp/BanExploration.pdf: This article (originally published in the journal *Psychological Inquiry* in 1998) is Bandura's follow-up to the chance encounters article discussed in this chapter.

FURTHER READINGS
ABOUT SOCIAL LEARNING THEORY

Hagenhoff, Carol, Lowe, Alice, Hovell, Melbourne F., & Rugg, Deborah. (1987). Prevention of the teenage pregnancy epidemic: A social learning theory approach. *Education and Treatment of Children, 10,* 67–83.

In the United States, the incidence of teenage pregnancy has leveled off somewhat and even gone down over the past few years, but it is by no means no longer a problem. Hagenhoff and her coauthors present a social learning model of adolescent sexual behavior and the use or nonuse of contraceptives to explain the high rates of teenage pregnancy in the United States and to suggest what types of interventions might prevent this social problem.

Hogben, Matthew, & Byrne, Donn. (1998). Using social learning theory to explain individual differences in human sexuality. *Journal of Sex Research, 35,* 58–71.

How can individual differences in human sexual expression, perhaps the most complex of all human behaviors, be explained? Using examples and a review of the literature, Hogben and Byrne summarize early and current research in four areas: sexuality development, adolescent sexuality and contraceptive use, health-related sexual behavior, and coercive sexuality.

Maisto, Stephen A., Carey, Kate B. & Bradizza, Clara M. (1999). Social learning theory. In Kenneth E. Leonard & Howard T. Blane (Eds.), *Psychological theories of drinking and alcoholism* (2nd ed., pp. 106–163). New York: Guilford.

One application of social learning theory has been in the study of illnesses that have significant social components, such as alcoholism. In this chapter, Maisto and his coauthors focus on three basic constructs that are critical to an understanding of alcoholism from the point of view of social learning theory: the influence of the social environment, the coping skills and cognitive variables of the individual, and the expected outcomes.

Stuart, Richard B., & Jacobson, Barbara. (1987). Principles of divorce mediation: A social learning theory approach. *Mediation Quarterly, 14–15,* 71–85.

With 50% of all U.S. marriages ending in divorce, researchers are examining alternatives to the traditional legal proceedings associated with divorce, including mediation (in which the parties settle out of court). Stuart and Jacobson discuss the role of social learning theory in divorce mediation, including guidelines for making family mediation work.

Thyer, Bruce A., & Myers, Laura L. (1998). Social learning theory: An empirically-based approach to understanding human behavior in the social environment. *Journal of Human Behavior in the Social Environment, 1,* 33–52.

Social learning theory has been recognized for its importance to social work practitioners. In this article, Thyer and Myers present a theory of normative human growth and development and discuss how social learning theory can improve understanding of the clinical side of psychopathology.

PART V

THE COGNITIVE-DEVELOPMENTAL VIEW

CHAPTER 9

JEAN PIAGET'S COGNITIVE MODEL

Play is child's work.

—Jean Piaget

Action is the basis for thought.

—Jean Piaget

Any subject can be taught effectively in some intellectually honest form to any child at any stage of development.

—Jerome S. Bruner

In addition to the maturational, psychodynamic, and behavioral views of development described in the preceding chapters, there is a fourth general class or family of developmental theories known as cognitive-developmental theories. The cognitive-developmental perspective emphasizes the active role that the individual plays in the developmental process. Cognitive-developmental psychologists assert that development occurs in an ordered sequence of qualitatively distinct stages that are characterized by increasing complexity. They see the role of the developing person in this process as active, not reactive.

The cognitive-developmental view, which is relatively new to the United States, is best represented through the work of Jean Piaget (1896–1980), a Swiss psychologist who wrote extensively about the child's quest for knowledge. Piaget may be described as part philosopher and part biologist, and he combined these two sides of his nature to arrive at his comprehensive and stimulating theory regarding how development happens. No other psychologist has had as profound an impact on our understanding of the developing child's acquisition and use of knowledge. Trained as a biologist, Piaget applied the scientific method to philosophical questions, and through these efforts he helped to bridge the gap that often exists between philosophy and science.

Piaget focused on one special branch of philosophy, epistemology, which is the science of knowledge and how it is acquired. The nature of his contribution to our understanding of the developmental process is best demonstrated by the types of questions his approach encouraged him to ask. For example: What is learning? Is the way things appear really the same as what they are? What is the process through which knowledge is acquired? What roles do direct experience and innate reasoning play in development? How does a child differentiate between an idea and what the idea represents?

Piaget (1950a) developed a new branch of epistemology called genetic epistemology; the term *genetic* in the name denotes the concept that development takes place through progression from one level to the next. Piaget's study of the science of knowledge was focused on the way in which knowledge changes over the course of an individual's development. Epistemology did not so much form the central core of Piaget's theory as it dictated the questions he should ask. Genetic epistemology does not suggest or proscribe particular methods, nor does it define the variables that are important to examine. Rather, it establishes a domain of inquiry to which rigorous and objective methods can be applied.

Piaget was an epistemologist; that is, he studied the origins of knowledge.

A DEFINITION OF DEVELOPMENT

According to Piaget, the developing individual is active rather than reactive. This proposition leads to questions: What is development? How does it differ from learning? Do learning and development occur simultaneously or do they take place parallel to one another? How does the individual and not the environment determine what the individual learns? Development, in Piaget's view, is a broad, spontaneous process that results in the continual addition, modification, and reorganization of psychological structures.

By defining development as a spontaneous process, Piaget (1970) emphasizes the individual's inherent capability of being dynamic, or not remaining static. In many of his works, Piaget relates biology (and its role in intelligence) to the changes that take place in the individual. This interaction between the individual's internal motivational system and the demands of the environment causes a striving for balance that forms the essence of development. Piaget terms this striving for balance, or order, *equilibration*. It can be described as a self-regulatory process that keeps the individual on the right track. This right track is not a genetic predisposition toward a specific behavior (such as laziness, prejudice, or impulsivity) but a characteristic of the entire development of the individual.

> Cognitive-developmental theorists stress the role of the organism as active rather than reactive.

Equilibration as a Model for Development

Piaget was not the first to theorize that living organisms continually seek a state of equilibrium. Just as Freud borrowed his notion of dynamic energy from the work being done in thermodynamics at the time, Piaget borrowed the idea of equilibration from the field of physics. Like Freud and others, he believed that development results in part from conflicts between opposing forces. If there is a common thread uniting many theoretical perspectives on development, it is the concept that development is promoted by conflicts and the ways in which conflicts are resolved.

A simple example of this is the way an individual will avoid or approach a problem until some resolution is established. Physiologists refer to this general phenomenon of seeking resolution as homeostasis. Just as a hungry infant seeks the reduction of tension through the satisfaction of hunger, an adult may seek out companionship to reduce the tension of loneliness. Through the process of equilibration, individuals seek a state of equilibrium between their psychological structures and how well those structures meet their changing needs. According to Piaget, equilibration is the primary motivating force behind development. Sometimes the forces that produce disequilibrium originate in the environment (e.g., the need to do your homework), and sometimes they are internal (e.g., hunger). In either case, the results are the same: the resolution of conflict and some corresponding qualitative change.

> According to Piaget, equilibration is the primary motivating force behind development.

In Piaget's theory, the child is an active agent, seeking out those situations or elements in the environment that will keep him or her in a state of equilibrium. Different things motivate different children. Piaget kept elaborate diaries of the developmental progress of many different children, beginning with his own. He recorded their behavior systematically and used this information to identify the different stages of development through which children pass. This is called the *taxonomic* or *descriptive* task of developmental psychology. If an observer understands a given child's current position in the developmental sequence, he or she can adjust the demands of the environment to ensure that the optimal degree of disequilibrium is present to promote the child's development. If there is too much incongruity between what a child is capable of and the demands of the task at hand, excessive tension results, and the child draws an unfortunate association between unpleasantness and learning.

Piaget's Definition of Development

According to Piaget, development is a broad, spontaneous process that results in the addition, modification, and reorganization of psychological structures.

According to Piaget, development is a spontaneous process in which the organism plays an active role. The process of development entails four factors: maturation, experience, social transmission, and the unifying factor of equilibration (Piaget, 1970).

Maturation, the process through which biological change takes place, is controlled by innate mechanisms. Maturation's primary role in Piaget's theory is to account for the neurological changes that occur through physical growth and for the sequencing of qualitative changes. However, the effects of maturational forces represent a wide range of potential outcomes that depend on other factors.

The second factor is experience, or interaction with the environment, which is necessary for cognitive growth to occur. For development to proceed (that is, for the child to adapt successfully to changing environments and demands), the child must be active, but not necessarily in a physical sense. The child can gain experience from any kind of activity, including mental exercises such as perception and problem solving.

Social transmission occurs when information, attitudes, and customs are transmitted from one group (such as parents) to another (such as children). This is a general factor that accounts for many of the events in the child's world that affect the developmental process.

In Piaget's model, development entails four factors: maturation, experience, social transmission, and equilibration.

The fourth and last factor, the process of equilibration, is, as noted above, the most crucial of the four, because it plays an integrative role as well as a motivational one.

Development results from a combination of biological growth, directed activity or experience, the learning of socially transmitted information, and the individual's inherent tendency to seek a state of harmony or balance. As Figure 9.1

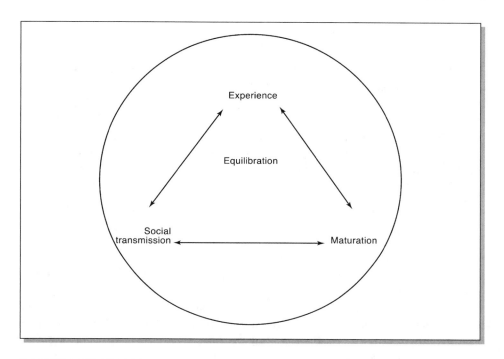

FIGURE 9.1　Equilibration as the Unifying Factor in Development

illustrates, although all four factors together result in development, equilibration acts as a unifying force. The bidirectional arrows in the figure represent the mutual interactions among the factors. Note that no matter how great the influence of any one of these four factors, development is incomplete without the other three. For example, if a child is not biologically mature enough to learn a given task, no amount of experience, whether physical or mental, will be sufficient to enable him or her to learn it.

Clearly, within this model, learning is a necessary but minor component of development. From Piaget's perspective, the most crucial distinction between learning and development is that development is spontaneous (almost automatic) and natural, or inevitable, whereas learning is precipitated, or invoked. Learning is a process that is narrowly defined as the acquisition of certain skills and information (often in response to highly specific stimulus conditions), whereas development is defined broadly, as a general process through which learning takes place. In other words, learning is a function of development.

THE PROCESS COMPONENT

The idea that the child progresses through a set of qualitatively distinct yet interrelated stages of cognitive development is central to Piaget's theory. Before we examine this sequence of events, it will be helpful to look first at some of the basic processes of development. These processes are not characteristic of any one stage or period of development; rather, they operate continuously.

We begin with discussion of Piaget's concept of the schema (this term may be pluralized as either *schemata* or *schemas*) and then go on to the processes of organization and adaptation.

Schemata

A schema is the primary unit of mental organization; it is a flexible structure that can change qualitatively and quantitatively.

It is Piaget's contention that the individual acts on the environment in such a way as to construct his or her own concept of the world. The changes that occur through this process are structural ones, and they are reflected in what Piaget calls schemata. A **schema** is the primary unit of mental organization and the structure through which a person adapts to the environment. Schemata are flexible in both quality and quantity; they have been described as the "mental blueprints" of experience (Kagan, 1971). The earliest schemata (such as sucking and grasping) are reflexive in nature. However, even these behaviors change in response to the demands of the environment. For example, sucking changes in form when the child is fed with a spoon. Here the schema for sucking changes in structure but not in the function it performs. The infant is born with many schemata and, through the processes of organization and adaptation, develops new ones and changes existing ones.

Organization

Organization is the tendency to combine physical and/or psychological processes into a coherent whole. Even in a newborn child, a sophisticated system of communication operates among different biological systems. For example, the circulatory system circulates blood to capillaries in the air sacs in the lungs, where the respiratory system exchanges carbon dioxide for oxygen. Similarly, touching a hot stove acts as a signal to the nervous system to pull the hand away, an act that requires the cooperation of the skeletal and muscular systems. Without these coordinated systems, the child could not survive. All living things have an inherent tendency to organize and synthesize their independent systems. Failure to do so results in biological death.

There are counterparts to organization in the cognitive domain as well. The infant comes into the world with a set of limited but functional schemata, such as

——— **On the Web** ———

Piaget calls his approach to understanding cognition in young children *genetic epistemology.* You can find more out about genetic epistemology, which forms the general framework for Piaget's theory, at http://tip.psychology.org/piaget. html.

sucking, tracking with the eyes, grasping, and some 25 other primary reflexes. As maturation occurs and biological and psychological structures begin to change, organization tends to relate different schemata to one another, expanding the individual's potential for successful intellectual growth. One of the early signs that the young child is beginning to act on the environment (rather than the environment acting on the child) is the child's rudimentary coordination of different schemata (such as grasping and looking). With such coordination, successful behavior begins.

The importance that Piaget places on organization as a process reflects his experience and training as a biologist.

Organization, which is not learned, is a functioning, vital component of the living system. Organization is an important life force that acts as one type of mortar to bond the materials of development together.

Adaptation

Adaptation, or the individual's adjustment to the environment, takes place simultaneously with organization. Like organization, adaptation is a process that has its theoretical roots in biology. The plant and animal kingdoms abound with examples of adaptation. Although the male cardinal is bright red, the female cardinal is a dull brown, so that she is minimally conspicuous and thus in less danger of being killed by predators (a threat to the survival of the species). The beautiful colors of spring and summer flowers attract insects that are part of the reproductive process that takes place through pollination.

Adaptation is a complex process that involves the modification of the individual or the environment to fit the needs of the individual. It can be broken down into two complementary processes: assimilation and accommodation. These operate simultaneously, yet one may take precedence over the other at times, depending on the demands of the environment or the developmental level of the individual.

Assimilation

Assimilation is the process through which the individual incorporates new experiences into already existing schemata, or structures. It is the transformational component of Piaget's theory, the process through which all knowledge is acquired. An example of assimilation can be seen in very young children's common behavior of putting everything they touch into their mouths, whether or not it is food. When they do this, they are using one schema regardless of the demands of the environment. They are changing the environment to fit their internal needs.

When assimilation occurs, the schema into which the new event or experience is being assimilated grows (gets larger) but does not change qualitatively. For example, when a young child classifies lions, tigers, and foxes into the same general class of "kitties," he or she is adjusting an experience (seeing lots of animals that look like "kitties") to fit a preexisting notion, or schema, of four-legged furry animals.

Assimilation is such a pervasive process that Piaget (1952) identifies three different kinds, each of which facilitates development in a particular way. *Reproductive* or *functional* assimilation is the tendency to repeat certain actions. It is as if the child is repeating things for the sake of practice until the behavior is sufficiently integrated into the schemata that are already available. In fact, the behaviors that are repeated most frequently are those that are immature or under-developed. This type of assimilation accounts for young children's repetitive behaviors, which to the untrained eye may seem to be only repeated random movements. The saying "Practice makes perfect" characterizes even the beginnings of intellectual development. In *generalizing* assimilation, specific schemata are generalized to other objects. For example, the child will grasp a finger, a rattle, and a clump of hair to exercise a particular schema, broadening that schema's utility to new objects. *Recognitory* assimilation involves discrimination between those stimuli that are adaptive, or useful, and those that are not. For example, any child will suck repeatedly on a variety of objects (indicating reproductive and generalizing assimilation), but the child will focus more intently when that sucking has a useful purpose (such as during feeding).

These three different types of assimilation correspond to three important outcomes: repetition of patterns of behavior, generalization of those patterns of behavior to new objects, and differentiation among objects depending on the individual's needs. All three of these outcomes are critical to the developing child's successful transition from stage to stage.

Accommodation

Accommodation, the counterpart of assimilation, is the process of modifying existing schemata to satisfy the requirements of new experiences. That is, accommodation is the process through which new schemata are formed. When a child accommodates, a qualitative change takes place in the relevant schema. When a child says "kitty" while looking at a picture of a lion, for example, he or she may be corrected by some adult who says, "No, it is a lion." The child can then do one of three

---

Assimilation is the process through which the organism incorporates experiences into already existing schemata.

Piaget identifies three types of assimilation: functional, generalizing, and recognitory.

things: reject this explanation and employ his or her own rules of logic (even if they seem illogical to the adult), form a new schema called "lions," or expand the already existing schema of "kitty" to include other types of kitties, thereby making it qualitatively different from the previous schema. Accommodation is the process through which changes in the child's intellectual development correspond to reality.

The Relationship Between Assimilation and Accommodation

Assimilation and accommodation are inextricably bound together. It is an outstanding characteristic of the very young child that these two functions are not yet complementary; rather, they are almost indistinguishable from one another. The child at a very early stage of development does not possess even a rudimentary ability to separate the object of a certain activity from the activity itself. For example, the two functions of grasping a new object and adjusting the grasp to fit that object are initially fused with one another. This state of affairs corresponds with what Piaget calls the beginning of egocentrism, or the individual's preoccupation with his or her own views.

Another important characteristic of the relationship between assimilation and accommodation is that one does not occur earlier (in a developmental sense) than the other. Although it might seem logical that the individual first tries to fit a new experience into an already existing structure (assimilation) and then, if this is not successful, tries to change the existing schema to meet the demands of the environment (accommodation), but this is not the case. Assimilation and accommodation are not sequential processes but simultaneous ones. An individual assimilates and accommodates elements of a new experience simultaneously. There is usually something familiar about a new experience that allows the assimilation of some part of that experience, and there is usually something unfamiliar as well that places new demands on already existing structures. People generally do not attend to those things that have little inherent interest for them, nor do they understand those that are too far removed from already existing patterns of behavior.

Finally, as noted above, assimilation and accommodation together constitute the process of adaptation. Piaget (1952) refers to adaptation and organization as *functional invariants* (or *invariant functions*); that is, these processes are operative at all levels of development and never vary in their general purpose.

Accommodation is the process through which existing schemata are modified to satisfy the demands of a changing environment

---

Adaptation and organization are functional invariants that operate at all levels of development.

The two processes of accommodation and assimilation are constantly in action.

Egocentrism

In Piaget's theory, egocentrism is defined as the individual's inability to differentiate between subject and object. Depending on the specific stage of development, this lack of differentiation assumes different forms. As I discuss the major stages in

Egocentrism, or the individual's preoccupation with his or her own point of view, takes a different form at each stage of development.

Piaget's theory below, I will address the form that egocentrism takes in each. For now, some general observations about egocentrism will serve as a useful orientation.

The child's failure to differentiate between subject and object involves varying elements of the child's life space at different developmental levels. Whether it is the inability to differentiate the self from surrounding objects (a type of early infantile egocentrism) or reality from fantasy (a type of adolescent egocentrism), egocentrism encourages assimilation rather than accommodation, because the child focuses on his or her own thoughts or feelings and uses his or her own knowledge as a base of operation (Flavell, 1963). The egocentric child cannot take the perspective of another person (this is especially characteristic of the young child) and "assimilates experiences from the world at large into schemas derived from his own immediate world, seeing everything in relation to himself" (Beard, 1969, p. 25).

Egocentrism take different forms at different developmental levels.

Egocentrism should not be confused with selfishness. The selfish child is aware of other people's feelings; the egocentric child is not. Furthermore, the type of behavior shown by egocentric adults (preoccupation with the self) should not be confused with the construct that egocentrism represents. Egocentric adults focus on their own needs. Some scholars, such as Elkind (1974), believe that the study of egocentrism may help us to understand the link between the cognitive (or thinking) and affective (or feeling and attitudinal) elements of development.

Egocentrism is a powerful construct that has particular significance in each of the developmental periods that Piaget describes. It affects the way the developing child approaches the world and what he or she constructs from the information taken in, influencing development in such areas as interpersonal relations, attitude formation, and social adjustment.

THE SEQUENTIAL COMPONENT

The sequential component of Piaget's theory emphasizes the importance of four qualitatively distinct stages: the sensorimotor stage, the preoperational stage, the concrete operational stage, and the formal operational stage.

One of Piaget's most outstanding contributions to our understanding of cognitive development is his description of a set of qualitatively distinct yet interrelated developmental stages. As we have seen, the notion of stages in development is not unique to Piaget. Many models of development use stages as organizing units (infant, teenager, and so on) to reflect the most important developmental changes that occur during certain periods in an individual's life. Gesell, Freud, and Erikson are excellent examples of theorists whose models incorporate stages, and in many ways their use of this kind of framework is not different from Piaget's. Piaget's notion of stages differs from those of some other theorists on one critical point, however: Whereas Gesell's and Freud's theories employ the concept of stages in a descriptive sense (using the organizing units of stages to give detailed accounts of what occurs when), in Piaget's theory the notion of stages is closely related to the concept of structural change (as it is in Erikson's theory). Hence Piaget's stages are models, not just descriptions.

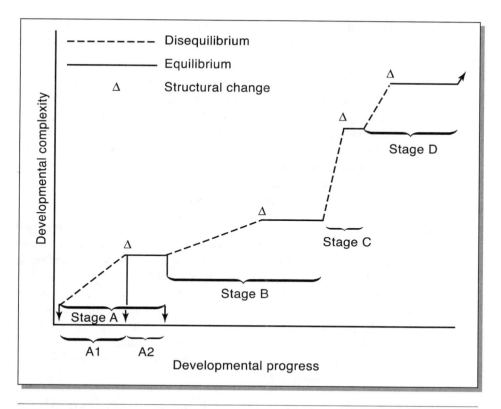

FIGURE 9.2   The Transition From Disequilibrium to Equilibrium

In Gesell's theory, stages serve as a way to organize descriptions of behavior. In Piaget's theory, in contrast, the process that goes on during a stage is what is important. As a biologist, Piaget believed strongly that cognitive mechanisms are an extension of already existing biological systems. Hence he found the parallel between physical stages of growth and psychological or structural change to be a plausible and attractive way of conceptualizing development.

Before we move into a discussion of Piaget's four stages of intellectual development, a brief clarification of the assumptions of the stage notion of development is in order. Figure 9.2 illustrates the progress that an individual might make as he or she advances from one developmental stage to the next. The horizontal axis in the figure represents the degree of developmental progress, which in most cases roughly corresponds to age. The general form of the curve within the graph suggests that developmental complexity is positively related to developmental progress. As development progresses, the process tends to be accompanied by (to subsume) increasingly complex structural change.

The basic premise of Piaget's theory is that the organism is continually striving for a state of equilibrium.

Although our focus here is on Piaget's theory in particular, the following eight statements are characteristic of the cognitive-developmental approach in general:

1. *The organism begins in a state of disequilibrium.* The dashed lines in Figure 9.2 represent periods of disequilibrium, during which a sharp discrepancy exists between the internal organization of the organism and the environmental demands on the organism; that is, there is a conflict between what the organism can do and what it is expected or needs to do. In Piaget's theory, disequilibrium is the most important motivational factor; it is absolutely necessary if development is to proceed.

2. *States of equilibrium do not last as long as states of disequilibrium.* This is illustrated in Figure 9.2 by the shortness of the solid lines representing equilibrium (projected onto the developmental progress axis) in relation to the dashed lines, which represent disequilibrium (compare the lengths of lines A1 and A2, for example). If the process of equilibration is the primary motivator, one might theorize that the organism spends more time in a state of imbalance than in a state of stability. Certain periods of growth (such as adolescence) are characterized by abrupt changes (e.g., in physical appearance and attitude). These changes, however, are usually preceded by periods of some stability.

3. *The organism does not remain in states of equilibrium and disequilibrium for equal amounts of time at each stage, nor is the rate of progress from stage to stage constant.* Individual variability is an important factor in the developmental process. As Figure 9.2 illustrates, not only are the periods of disequilibrium and equilibrium (represented by the dashed and solid lines) within any one stage different in length (as noted in Statement 2), but the rates of disequilibrium (represented by the slopes of the dashed lines) are different as well.

4. *Disequilibrium terminates in structural change.* This structural change places the organism in a position of stability, but the stability lasts for only a short period. The delta (Δ) that appears at the end of the positively accelerating slope of each dashed line in Figure 9.2 represents this structural change. How long this period of equilibrium lasts (and how long the next period of disequilibrium lasts) depends on a host of related influences that will be discussed below.

5. *From the beginning of structural change through the end of the next period of disequilibrium, there is a trend from maximum stability to*

maximum growth. The general progression of development is from disequilibrium to structural change to equilibrium, and then the cycle begins anew. Within this cycle, the maximum amount of change, or development, that can take place does take place. The cycle repeats itself in an effort to satisfy the changing structural needs of the organism.

6. *The order of the stages is fixed.* That is, Stage A always precedes Stage B, Stage B always precedes Stage C, and so on. Piaget uses the word *invariant* (meaning uniform or lacking variability) to emphasize that the same stages occur in all individuals in a fixed sequence. Piaget stresses the order, and not the rate, of progress.

7. *Individual stages of development cannot be skipped, or omitted from the sequence.* That is, an individual cannot progress from an earlier stage of development to a later one without going through any intermediate stages. As Figure 9.2 illustrates, each stage leads into the one that follows; no irregular jumps (from Stage A to Stage C, for instance) are possible. This does not mean, however, that once an individual passes through a certain stage he or she no longer possesses the structural characteristics that define that stage.

According to Piaget's theory, development is a discontinuous process characterized by abrupt changes from stage to stage.

8. *Successive stages are qualitatively different from one another, and later stages are based on the elements and experiences of earlier stages.* Stages of development cannot be skipped because later stages depend on earlier ones for a foundation. In the construction of a new house, pouring the foundation and laying the flooring are separate steps, but it is impossible to put down a floor without first laying the foundation to support it. In much the same way, the individual proceeds through a set of developmental stages that are interrelated. Each successive stage encompasses all of the characteristics of the earlier stages, plus new additional components.

As Figure 9.2 illustrates (and as noted above), each stage of development is characterized by a cycle of disequilibrium, some degree of structural change, and equilibrium. The length of time that each part of this cycle takes varies for different individuals. Some children develop relatively sophisticated problem-solving skills earlier than other children, and some develop certain kinds of social skills later than similarly aged children. It is important to note that the demarcations between periods of disequilibrium and equilibrium are not as abrupt or as uneven as Figure 9.2 implies. In reality, the different processes overlap, and some degree of both disequilibrium and equilibrium is present within any stage of development.

According to Piaget, disequilibrium is the motivation for further development.

The four stages of intellectual development that Piaget describes are as follows:

1. The sensorimotor stage (lasting from birth through age 2)

2. The preoperational stage (lasting from age 2 to age 7)

3. The concrete operational stage (lasting from age 7 to age 12)

4. The formal operational stage (lasting from age 12 through adulthood)

The four stages in Piaget's model are qualitatively distinct from one another and always occur in the same order.

Piaget stresses that the normative age ranges shown here are intended for convenience only. He notes that the stages of development are more clearly defined and understood according to their content than according to when they begin. These age ranges are only approximate and should be treated as such.

Piaget's notion of the stages of intellectual development reflects and emphasizes the structural transitions that take place during different developmental periods; in this model, the stages are not used only as convenient organizers, as a way to provide simple descriptions of different behaviors at different times. Throughout each of these stages there is continuous interplay between the functional invariants of organization and adaptation. Table 9.1 presents a summary of the major characteristics of each of Piaget's four stages, including descriptions of the substages of the sensorimotor stage (discussed below).

The Sensorimotor Stage

The sensorimotor stage of development consists of six substages, all of which occur during the first 2 years of a child's life.

The **sensorimotor stage** of development begins at birth (and possibly even conception) with the simple reflexes of the neonate and terminates at around 2 years of age with the onset of symbolic thought, representing early childlike language. Within this stage of development, Piaget documents six independent yet interrelated substages. Through an examination of these individual stages, we can see how the child develops from a relatively passive organism that acts without any systematic goal into a thinking being who shows the beginning elements of intelligence.

Substage 1: The Use of Early Reflexes

The newborn's innate equipment and preparation for the world are limited. The child cannot distinguish between his or her action on an object and the object itself and is dependent on reflexive behaviors such as grasping, sucking, and reactions to loud sounds for acquiring knowledge about the world.

Although the infant's behavior during the first month of life is not entirely random, it is not goal directed. For example, an infant in this substage will use

TABLE 9.1 Piaget's Stages of Intellectual Development

Stage	Approximate Age	Characteristics
Sensorimotor	0–2 years	Intelligence based on perceptual experiences
1. Reflexive	0–1 month	Increased efficiency of reflexes; lack of differentiation
2. Primary circular reactions	1–4 months	Repetition of certain pleasurable behaviors and formation of habits; coordination of reflexes
3. Secondary circular reactions	4–8 months	Intentional repetition of events discovered through chance; notion of cause and effect
4. Coordination of secondary schemata	8–12 months	Application of old schemata to new situations; object permanence; first clear signs of intelligence; instrumental activity
5. Tertiary circular reactions	12–18 months	Discovery of new means and repetition with variation for novelty's sake; experimentation with cause-and-effect situations; hypothesis testing
6. Symbolic representation	18–24 months	Internalization of actions; beginnings of thought before action; representation of objects and images through imagery; invention of new ideas
Preoperational	2–7 years	Onset of sophisticated language system; egocentric reasoning; perception-bound thinking
Concrete operational	7–12 years	Development of reversible thought, logical operations, conservation, ability to solve concrete problems, experience-based thinking
Formal operational	12 years–adulthood	Formulation and testing of hypotheses, abstract thought, hypothetico-deductive reasoning, thought no longer perception bound

the same reflex over and over (demonstrating reproductive assimilation), without any apparent accommodative change in structure. The child will suck on a blanket or a rag toy in the same way he or she sucks at the mother's breast. Similarly, the child may grasp everything within reach, using the same schema (grabbing) again and again.

Two important characteristics are associated with this substage: First, the infant makes no differentiation between the self and the external world; and second, as the infant gains experience using different reflexive schemata, he or she tends to become more adaptive to the increasing demands of the environment. Even at this first substage of sensorimotor development, the basic building blocks of cognitive development—reflexive schemata—are becoming more complex and adaptive.

Substage 2: Primary Circular Reactions

The second substage of sensorimotor development, which lasts from approximately the age of 1 month to 4 months, is characterized by what Piaget calls *circular reactions* (a term borrowed from biology). The circular reactions in this period are called *primary* because the infant's focus is on his or her own body rather than on external objects. The term *circular reaction* refers to the repetition of a sensorimotor act, such as repeated sucking, grasping, or hitting of one object against another. The purpose of any circular reaction is the modification of an existing schema, which is the hallmark of intellectual development.

During this substage, the child is adept at demonstrating different reflexes and begins to be able to coordinate reflexes. For example, the child can track an interesting object with the eyes and reach out to grasp that object. This substage includes a great deal of trial-and-error learning, in which chance is an important factor. At this point, it should be noted, the child is not a conscious learner; intentionality, a hallmark of what Piaget calls intelligence, is not characteristic of the child's behavior at this stage.

Even though the child is relatively non–goal directed at this substage (compared with later stages), the child's coordination of different circular reactions and trial-and-error learning have an important impact on intellectual development: The child develops some notion of causality. The child may not be able to identify specific cause-and-effect relationships, but an understanding of the idea of cause and effect is initiated.

Substage 3: Secondary Circular Reactions

The major characteristic of the third substage of sensorimotor development is the child's preoccupation with events and objects located outside of his or her own body (hence the adjective *secondary* in the name of this substage). The child tries to produce experiences and to make them last. It is as if the child has found out how to do something new and wants to practice it over and over. This may indeed be the case, because this is a time when functional, or reproductive, assimilation is a major operating force. During this period the child's development reflects Piaget's assertion that the child's world is constructed, not given.

The primary distinction between primary and secondary circular reactions is the focus of the child's behavior. During the primary circular reaction substage, the child is concerned with objects and events in and around his or her body, whereas during the secondary circular reaction substage, the child's concern shifts to external objects and events. The child becomes less self-centered (or less egocentric) and more dependent on things other than him- or herself as a source of information about the world. Behavior during this substage can be characterized as a type of early intentionality, in which the child has some awareness of what factors cause particular events to occur. As Flavell (1963) notes, "The accomplishments of this stage . . . constitute the first definite steps towards intentionality or goal orientation" (p. 102). Keep in mind, however, that actual intentional behaviors do not occur at this substage.

> In the primary and secondary circular reaction substages of sensorimotor development, the child is concerned with furthering his or her knowledge of the outside world.

Intentionality is an important component of Piaget's theory because intelligence is equated with intentional or goal-directed behavior. During the third substage of sensorimotor development, the child begins to understand that certain events in the outside world are under the control of the child's own behavior, but true intentionality is not achieved until the next substage. Through a process of trial and error, the child is exposed to a variety of situations that illustrate the relationships between causes and effects. Given the structural changes that are always occurring, these cause-and-effect experiences eventually take on meaning for the child.

Substage 4: Coordination of Secondary Schemata

The child reaches two major milestones during the fourth substage of sensorimotor development, at approximately 8 to 12 months of age. First, the child begins to use already learned (sometimes called *habitual*) behavior patterns and more than one schema at a time to prolong events that are novel or unusual. For example, if the child is faced with a new type of problem, he or she will repeatedly try to solve it, in spite of barriers that may be in the way. In situations where a substage 3 infant, who does not have a clear picture of how causes and effects are related, would not be likely to persevere, a substage 4 child keeps trying, because he or she has a clear concept of what causes things to happen (Piaget refers to this as the "means-end" relationship). According to Piaget, this is the first true sign of intelligence.

The second major milestone the infant reaches at this substage is the realization that objects in the environment are clearly separate from him- or herself and have distinct qualities of their own. This happens, in part, because the infant's increasingly sophisticated motor skills enable him or her to examine objects more intimately and for longer periods of time. Along with this increased perceptual awareness comes the development of the child's awareness of object permanence. That is, prior to this point, anything removed from the child's immediate perceptual field (hidden under a pillow, for example) effectively no longer existed for the child. For the child before substage 4, "out of sight" equates literally with "out of mind." During substage 4, however, the concept of the object becomes developed, and the child is aware that when something is removed from his or her visual field, it does not actually disappear. This is a landmark in the child's cognitive development because it means that the child's actions are no longer tied to the perceptual characteristics of a situation.

Substage 5: Tertiary Circular Reactions

During the fifth substage of sensorimotor development, a reversal of the means-end relationship that characterized substage 4 takes place. Whereas the substage 4 child uses old means in new settings, the substage 5 child (age 12 to 18 months) uses new means to solve new problems. The child begins to examine cause-and-effect relationships through experimentation, sometimes called "groping accommodation" (Flavell, 1963). The child repeats behaviors, but beyond this simple repetition there is a degree of variation and the discovery of new properties and experiences.

In the sensorimotor development substage of tertiary circular reactions, the child's early cause-and-effect thinking develops into experimental thinking.

The circular reactions in this substage are called *tertiary* to distinguish them from the two earlier types of circular reactions. As noted above, during the primary circular reaction substage, the child is concerned with actions in and around his or her own body, and during the secondary circular reaction substage, the child's focus shifts to objects in the external world. In the tertiary circular reaction substage, the child engages in experimental thinking, hypothesizing about the relationships between new causes and their eventual effects.

Again, increases in motor skills are a contributing factor in this more sophisticated relationship between the child and external objects. This is the age at which most children begin to walk, and with the increased mobility that walking brings, the child's opportunities for new experiences are greatly expanded. The child at this substage is in much better control of the environment than previously and demonstrates this control by effectively manipulating the environment to ends that are novel (at least to the child).

Substage 6: Symbolic Representation

During the final substage of sensorimotor development (at about age 18 to 24 months), the child experiences a major breakthrough in his or her ability to understand relationships between objects and the activities associated with the objects without direct experience or experimentation. The child begins to represent events internally, and symbolic thought becomes the primary mode of thinking. This is a time of incredible growth in the child's qualitative capacities, as he or she begins to invent new ideas rather than simply reformulate old ones. Piaget (1952) refers to this period when the individual begins to represent external events internally as the stage of *representational intelligence*. The beginnings of language (a type of symbolic thought) become apparent in this substage. Object permanence is now fully operative, and the child stands at the doorstep of sophisticated linguistic skills.

Egocentrism During the Sensorimotor Stage

If young infants could verbalize their thoughts, they might say something like, "My world is my actions." Children in the sensorimotor stage of development are unable to differentiate themselves from the external objects they encounter. As Elkind (1974) describes it, the primary developmental task at this stage is the "conquest of the object." That is, the child must learn to distinguish between what constitutes the real world and what constitutes the operations and thoughts internal to the child. In some ways, this may be thought of as the distinction between reality and fantasy.

> During the sensorimotor stage, the conquest of the object is the primary developmental task.

The newborn infant is basically a mass of uncoordinated reflexes with basic needs that must be met. Indeed, our society is structured (or should be) so that infants can be fed when they are hungry and have their diapers changed when they are wet and uncomfortable. The infant's helplessness is evidence of the totally egocentric nature of the child during this stage of development. The theme of undifferentiatedness first becomes manifest in the sensorimotor stage with the child's inability to separate his or her own physical self from objects.

Summary Description of the Sensorimotor Stage

The term that Piaget uses to describe the first of the four developmental stages in his theory—*sensorimotor*—communicates the essence of what happens to the child during that stage, which lasts from birth through the second year. Intelligence and action during this period result from the child's perceptual and sensorimotor experiences. The most crucial component of a child's development is the opportunity to act on the environment in an unrestricted way.

During the first month of the infant's life, behavior is characterized by reflexive activity, with no differentiation between "self" and experience and things that are "not self." In the second substage of sensorimotor development, an increased separation between these behaviors becomes apparent (hence the idea of circular reactions). During the third substage of the sensorimotor period, the child focuses on objects and experiences external to his or her own body and repeats certain things over and over, as if to practice them. During substage 4, the child applies already existing schemata to new problems and forms an object concept that enables him or her to realize that objects removed from the child's perceptual field (out of sight, for example) do not actually cease to exist. In substage 5, increased motor skills—such as walking—aid the child in his or her exploration of the world. The child has more control over the environment and begins to experiment with no apparent goal other than the process of experimentation itself. For example, the child might take a mouthful of milk and let it seep out of the mouth at different rates. Such behavior is sure to have some effects on the parents' behavior and is one way for the child to gain control over a previously alien environment. During the final substage of this period of development, the child becomes capable of representing objects internally, without any need for direct experience. This is the beginning of representational intelligence, symbolic thought, and language.

The Preoperational Stage

In the sensorimotor stage, the child develops from the almost entirely reflexive organism that is the newborn infant to an individual who can intentionally manipulate symbols that represent objects in the real world. Imagine the tremendous amount of growth that is possible in the next stage of development, given the new tools the child has for exploring and experiencing the environment. When the child is no longer bound by perceptual experiences and can go beyond what the environment offers, he or she is progressing from a sensorimotor type of intelligence to the symbolic type of intelligence characteristic of the **preoperational stage** of development. Whereas in the first stage the child was limited to direct interactions with the environment, in this second stage the child learns to manipulate symbols that represent the environment: thus the beginnings of language. The onset and development of language are the most significant events during this stage.

A child in the preoperational stage can intentionally manipulate symbols that represent objects in the real world, such as language.

The Importance of Operations in Piaget's Theory

In the context of Piaget's theory, an **operation** is an action that is performed mentally and is reversible (Piaget, 1950b); that is, when an operation transforms an object or experience, that object or experience can be returned to its original form. The primary distinction between a child in the preoperational stage of cognitive development and a child in a more advanced stage is that the preoperational child is incapable of performing operations.

The processes of addition and subtraction are useful for illustrating operation. The fact that the operation "2 plus 4 equals 6" is logically the same as "6 minus 4 equals 2" may seem obvious to us, but it is not obvious to the preoperational child. The preoperational child cannot mentally rearrange a sequence of events into reverse order. One of the primary findings of Piaget's long and intensive research into this stage of development is the preoperational child's inability to conserve the relationship between different dimensions of an event. For example, if the preoperational child sees a piece of clay formed into two different shapes, he or she cannot understand that although the shape is different, the mass or weight of the piece remains the same. (Technically, this is an example of invariance in one dimension while there is a change in another.)

Figure 9.3 illustrates three common **conservation** tasks that researchers in developmental psychology use with children to explore the children's operational or preoperational thinking. In a *conservation of number* task, the researcher presents the child with a row of objects (such as a row of pennies) and asks the child to construct a second row to match the first row exactly. This task shows whether the child is able to establish a type of perceptual equivalence between two sets of objects. After the child completes the task (as illustrated on the left-hand side of Figure 9.3a), the researcher changes the spacing between the objects in one of the rows (while the child is present), so that one row is shorter than the other (as on the right-hand side of Figure 9.3a). The researcher then asks the child which row has more objects in it. If the child is preoperational, he or she will confuse the dimension of length with that of number and say that the row that is longer has more objects in it. Although this is clearly a contradiction of what the child did earlier, when he or she matched each of the objects in his or her own row with those in the initial row, the child now believes that one row has more objects than the other. This is a good example of how the child's use of language at this age reflects an immature level of thought.

A *conservation of mass* task (Figure 9.3b) is similar in design. For example, the researcher may show a child two balls of clay that are exactly the same shape and size. Then, while the child watches, the researcher forms one of the balls into another shape (from a circle to a sausage, for example). The researcher then asks the child whether either of the pieces of clay is "more" than the other. If the child is preoperational, he or she will say that the piece of clay that appears larger (because it is more spread out) is "more" than the other, although the child has seen that nothing was added to or taken away from either piece of clay. The preoperational child cannot mentally reverse the process that has taken place to

One milestone in development, according to Piaget's theory, is the child's ability to perform an operation—that is, a mental action that is reversible.

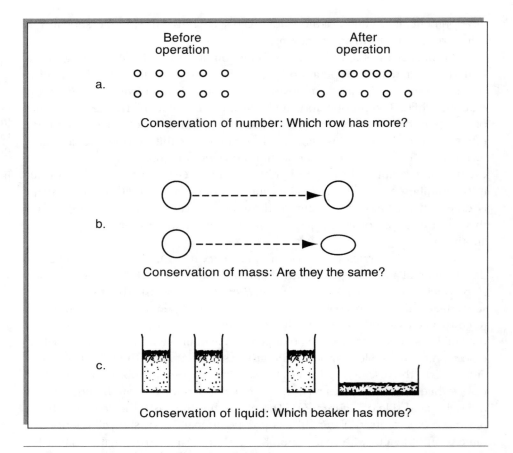

FIGURE 9.3 Examples of Different Kinds of Conservation

make a comparison between the two shapes before and after the manipulation took place.

A *conservation of liquid* task demonstrates dramatically the preoperational child's inability to reverse an event mentally. In such a task (illustrated in Figure 9.3c), the researcher shows the child two identical beakers with the same amount of water in both. The researcher then shows the child two empty beakers of different shapes—a tall, narrow one and a short, wide one. In full view of the child, the researcher pours all the water from one of the original containers into the tall, narrow beaker and all the water from the other original container into the wide, shallow beaker. To the preoperational child, it now appears that there are different amounts of water in the containers. The child's preoperational logic dictates that the difference that is now apparent in the water levels in the two beakers must be a result of water being lost (or gained), not a result of the different shapes of the containers.

The preoperational child cannot conserve—that is, cannot understand that just because one dimension of an experience is changed, other qualities of that experience are not necessarily changed as well. The preoperational child has a difficult time relating two different dimensions of a situation to each other. For example, a preoperational child cannot understand how she can be both a "good girl" and someone's "little sister." The child at this stage of development does not yet possess the cognitive structures necessary to recognize that a change in one dimension of an experience does not necessarily mean a change in others. Because of this, the child is still somewhat perceptually bound and cannot manipulate symbolic elements—that is, reorder them mentally. In essence, the preoperational child believes that what you see is what you get.

Researchers in developmental psychology often investigate children's operational thinking by using conservation tasks.

Egocentrism in the Preoperational Stage

The most important aspect of this phase of intellectual development is the child's increasing use of symbols to represent objects, which is part of the development of a complex and sophisticated system of language. Thus it is no surprise that the child's primary task at this stage in the developmental course of egocentricity is the "conquest of the symbol" (Elkind, 1974). Now that the child has separated from the world of sensorimotor egocentrism and can distinguish between self and external objects, the next task is to learn how to differentiate between symbols and their referents. In other words, the child's world at this stage is a function of the way in which the child chooses to represent the world. The preoperational child cannot assume any perspective other than his or her own; indeed, it is doubtful that the child at this stage even knows that other perspectives exist.

To examine the preoperational child's inability to take another's perspective, Piaget and Inhelder (1956) developed an ingenious method called the *three-mountain task*. Figure 9.4 illustrates this task, showing a physical setup similar to the one Piaget and Inhelder used. The figure depicts the top view and four side views (as seen from seats A, B, C, and D) of a table with a three-dimensional set of "mountains" on it. Each person seated around the table sees a unique view of the three mountains. A child is seated at one of four positions at the table, and a doll is placed at one of the other positions. The child is then asked to choose, from a set of pictures representing all possible views, the picture that represents what the doll sees from its position. If, for example, the doll is sitting in seat D, the correct response is the picture showing view D. When faced with this task, the preoperational child almost invariably chooses the view that represents

During the preoperational phase, egocentrism is represented by the conquest of the symbol.

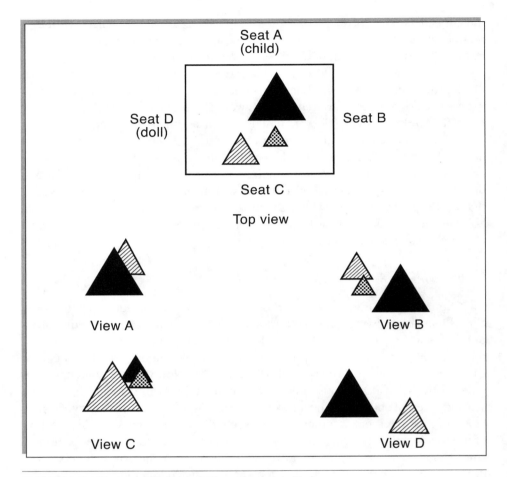

FIGURE 9.4   Piaget and Inhelder's Three-Mountain Task

what the child sees from his or her own position at the table rather than the doll's position. This illustrates the preoperational child's inability to assume a perspective other than his or her own. In contrast, older children almost never fail at this task, and if they do, their errors are nonegocentric rather than egocentric—that is, they may choose the wrong view, but they don't choose their own view.

Another dimension of preoperational egocentrism is the way in which the child at this stage uses language. Although in Piaget's theory language is a necessary prerequisite of the development of adaptive behavior, language alone is not considered to be sufficient. Language has some obvious advantages over sensorimotor functioning, such as the greater speed with which it allows the child to process events. However, without the structural changes that take place at this time, language cannot be a primary component of logical thought. Language serves the important function of enabling the child to manipulate, or rearrange, different symbols (and experiences) without the inefficiency of direct physical activity, but in the preoperational stage language is restricted by the illogical rules the child applies. The preoperational child uses language in an extremely literal way. For example, a child at this stage may be confused by the statement "Johnny has grown a foot," thinking that indeed Johnny has sprouted a third foot.

The preoperational child also exhibits what Piaget calls *egocentric speech,* in which the child does not differentiate between him- or herself and other people. Even though the child at this stage talks with other children, no meaningful transmission of information takes place in such talk; a group of preoperational children talking to each other produces a collection of monologues. Language progresses during this period from being basically egocentric, with the child's verbalizing having no real communicative purpose (that is, the child talks *at* instead of *to* other people), to sociocentric or socialized speech, in which communication takes place (that is, information is transmitted).

Egocentric language parallels preoperational children's conception of following rules when they play games. Even though children at this stage often do not follow whatever rules are supposed to be applied in the games they play, they insist that whatever they do is correct. Given that the only set of rules the preoperational child is aware of is his or her own, it is logical for the child to believe he or she is correctly following the rules. When two preoperational children play a simple game with each other, they change the rules as they go along, each to fit his or her personal needs. Children in the preoperational stage of development have no knowledge that any sets of outside rules might apply to their behavior.

Summary Description of the Preoperational Stage

The preoperational stage is a distinct turning point in the course of cognitive development. For the first time, thought becomes a symbolic process for understanding the world. The most obvious example of this is the development of language.

The world of the preoperational child is bounded by direct contact with concrete objects. The child benefits most from experiences with nonabstract elements and events, because his or her ability to manipulate events or objects that are not directly tied to perceptual experiences is limited. The child cannot mentally reverse an operation and has difficulty understanding the importance of cause-and-effect relationships in solving certain types of problems.

The preoperational child is in a transitional period. Although during this time the child's perspective on the world expands rapidly, there is still some confusion in the child's evaluation of causes and effects. The child makes inappropriate generalizations, attributing the feelings and actions that he or she experiences to inanimate objects (for example, believing that clouds cry to make rain).

The Concrete Operational Stage

Up to the time the child is approximately 7 years old, the child's cognitive capabilities are characterized by three attributes: the inability to assume another perspective (egocentrism), the centering on only one dimension of an experience rooted in perceptual information (centration), and the inability to perform an operation requiring reversibility. During the **concrete operational stage**, these three attributes change in structure, and these changes represent a dramatic transition from illogically based thought to logically based thought. In contrast to the preoperational child, the concrete operational child can conserve, perform certain operations, and conquer a variety of cognitive tasks.

A child who exhibits concrete operational thinking can conserve, perform certain operations, and master a variety of sophisticated cognitive tasks.

The primary reason the adjective *concrete* is part of the name of this stage is that most of the child's operations at this point are still tied to concepts that are bound by the limits of the child's perception (including those concepts with which the child has had some direct experience). For example, the concrete operational child can perform simple operations, such as subtracting one class of objects from another when the materials are available for the child to see and manipulate, but cannot perform operations that are purely verbal without the benefit of previous experience. The latter kinds of problems are too abstract for the child at this stage. Thus, even though the child's cognitive structures are more advanced than they were at an earlier stage, they are still too immature to allow the child to escape the limits of perception.

Classification

The concrete operational child can create hierarchies of different classes and understand the relationships among the members of these classes. For example, the child can understand that there are two major classes of animals and plants that belong to a larger (or supraordinate) class called "living things" and also understand that "living things" can in turn be reduced to two subcategories called "animals" and "plants" (note the reversibility). The child's new ability to understand hierarchies is important because it marks the transition from preoperational to operational thought. The child at this point is beginning to understand the relationship of the elements in a class (e.g., plants and animals) to the class itself (e.g., living things).

Another example of the concrete operational child's ability to understand classifications comes from a task that Piaget frequently used in his research. The task involves two groups of objects that differ in some characteristics, such as color or shape; for our purposes, let's say that a researcher has 20 red wooden blocks and 10 blue wooden blocks. The researcher physically separates the blocks into two groups by color, and then asks the child whether there are more red things or more wooden things. When the preoperational child is faced with this task, he or she cannot perform the logical operation of adding the two subclasses; the child is tied to the perceptual experience associated with the colors of the blocks rather than the general category of blocks (wooden). The concrete operational child, in contrast, performs this task readily.

The abilities to understand sophisticated classifications and to use reversibility are two characteristics of the concrete operational child.

Operations

According to Piaget (1950b), an operation has four properties:

1. *An operation is reversible.* In the example above, the red blocks plus the blue blocks make up the general class of wooden blocks, and if the red blocks are taken away, only the blue blocks will remain. That is, x (red blocks) $-x'$ (blue blocks) $= y$ (all blocks). Here y represents a new class of objects: those that are wooden, are blocks, and are either red or blue. This type of equivalence symbolizes the majority of addition and subtraction problems that the early concrete operational child is expected to be able to solve.

2. *An operation assumes that some type of conservation is taking place.* The primary characteristic of conservation is the maintenance of equivalence between two objects even though one dimension of the object undergoes some change. In this example, regardless of the number of blue blocks versus red blocks, all the blocks are members of the same general class (wooden blocks).

3. *An operation never exists alone.* An operation always includes the reversibility of a process. If it is true that all the blue blocks and all the red blocks equal all of the blocks, then all the blocks minus the red blocks must equal the blue blocks. An operation never exists alone also because it is a component of a structure that consists of many different operations and schemata that are related to one another. This is one reason that the transition from one stage of cognitive development to another is such an exciting aspect of human development.

4. *An operation is an internalized action that can be carried out in thought as well as in action.* Although the concrete operational child can solve problems through the use of mental operations, he or she still has to have some action-oriented referent in order to perform the task successfully. The concrete operational child cannot deal with hypothetical or purely verbal problems without having some perceptual reference point.

Seriation

During the concrete operation stage, the child gains the ability to seriate—that is, to place the events or objects in a series in order according to a particular characteristic.

Another important characteristic of the concrete operational child is the ability to seriate—that is, to place the events or objects in a series in order according to a particular characteristic. For example, if the child is given a set of six cylinders of different heights, he or she can order them according to their height without hands-on examination (but with the cylinders in sight). He or she can also surmise correctly that if the 5-inch canister is larger than the 4-inch canister, and the 4-inch canister is larger than the 3-inch canister, then, by equivalence, the 5-inch canister is larger than the 3-inch one. That is, if $A > B$ and $B > C$, then $A > C$. During the concrete operational stage, for the first time, the child can mentally manipulate the relationships between and among objects. In contrast, the preoperational child cannot successfully order a set of objects along a dimension such as size. The schema for size is simply not yet operative in the preoperational child, let alone the schemata the child needs to understand the relative equivalence between pairs of objects of different heights.

Egocentrism During the Concrete Operational Stage

The outstanding characteristic of the concrete operational child's egocentricity is the "lack of differentiation between assumption and fact" (Elkind, 1974, p. 79). The child at this stage is more likely to alter the facts of a situation than to alter his or her hypotheses about that situation. In this sense, the concrete operational child is rigid and restricted. The child cannot separate the perceptual qualities of an experience from the reality of the situation. This is an interesting type of egocentrism, because the major discrepancy for the preoperational child was between self and others, which now parallels the discrepancy between self and fact. Even though concrete operational children are less self-centered than children in earlier stages, they are concerned about the correctness of their own assumptions in comparison to the demands of the real world.

In his discussion of concrete operational egocentrism, Elkind (1974) describes the strategy of *assumptive reality,* which is the child's way of offsetting the discrepancy that exists between the child's assumption and fact. That is, the child creates a new "reality," changing the facts to fit his or her hypothesis, regardless of the presence of clearly contradictory evidence. For example, if the child has a hypothesis as to why shortening the length of a watch chain will decrease the arc of its swing, and someone demonstrates to the child that the child's hypothesis is incorrect, the child will change his or her perception of the reality of the situation rather than change that hypothesis. One of the most striking types of assumptive reality that Elkind discusses is *cognitive conceit.* Concrete operational egocentrism leads children in this stage to believe that they are smarter than their parents and that their parents are not powerful in the sense of knowing what to do. This cognitive conceit is part of the children's growing awareness that their parents are not superhuman but, rather, have flaws and make mistakes. Children in the concrete operational stage, however, generally assume that they themselves do not make mistakes.

Summary of the Concrete Operational Stage

The concrete operational period in Piaget's theory represents a transition between the preoperational and formal operational stages. Whereas the preoperational child does not yet possess the structures necessary to reverse operations, the concrete operational child's logic allows him or her to do such operations, but only on a concrete level. The child is now a sociocentric (as opposed to egocentric) being who is aware that others have their own perspectives on the world and that those perspectives are different from the child's own. The concrete operational child may not be aware, however, of the content of others' perspectives (this awareness comes during the next stage of cognitive development).

Concrete operational children lack the ability to perform operations that are not tied to perceptual experiences. They do not wonder about abstract issues, such as liberty or the First Amendment, because it is difficult to tie such concepts to concrete experiences. Educational strategies aimed at the concrete operational child should not assume that the child can learn without the benefit of action-oriented experience. Although concrete operational children can solve problems that are somewhat abstract, they are still dependent on perceptual information to formulate and test hypotheses. Finally, the stage of concrete operations—in contrast to the preoperational stage—has the characteristic of reversibility. That is, the concrete operational child understands that the order of an operation can be reversed and the characteristics of an earlier situation recovered.

The Formal Operational Stage

This final stage of intellectual development in Piaget's theory covers the age range from around 11 to 15 years. Cognitive development does not cease after the child reaches 15, but by that time all of the major structural and qualitative changes that are going to take place have hypothetically occurred. After this stage, the individual will add very few new schemata to his or her system; the majority of changes that are likely to take place will be modifications of existing schemata.

The most outstanding difference between children at the concrete operational stage and those at the **formal operational stage** is that the latter are not bound by perceptual experiences in the here and now; they can use past and future deliberations when confronted with new situations. The concrete operational child deals only with problems of the present; the formal operational child can deal with problems in all time frames.

Formal operational thinking is characterized by hypothetico-deductive reasoning.

A second characteristic of children at this stage is that they begin to function like scientists, in that they are capable of (a) accepting assumptions (without needing any physical evidence to validate those assumptions), (b) developing hypotheses ("if . . . then" statements that relate causes and effects), (c) testing these hypotheses, and (d) evaluating the outcomes and restating their hypotheses if the outcomes are not congruent with earlier assumptions. For the first time, systematic scientific thought replaces the variety of other modes of thinking that were present in earlier stages, modes that were minimally effective but limited the child's potential for expanded intellectual awareness.

The following problem is sometimes used to demonstrate how the child's mode of thought differs from one stage of cognitive development to another. Five beakers containing colorless, odorless liquids are placed before the child. The researcher then pours a certain amount of liquid from one beaker into an empty beaker and adds to that a certain amount of liquid from one of the other beakers, whereupon the mixed liquid turns yellow. The researcher then asks the child to reproduce this color, using any combination of the various liquids. The only thing the child knows is that the yellow liquid resulted from a mixture of the liquids in two of the five containers.

There are distinct differences among children in different developmental stages in the ways they approach solving this problem. Infants in the sensorimotor stage (up to 2 years old) pay no attention to the problem situation and merely play with the beakers as toys. Children in the preoperational stage (roughly 2 to 7 years old) randomly combine chemicals and make no attempt to keep track of what they have done. Children in the concrete operational stage, between the ages of 7 and 11, begin to combine chemicals systematically but tend to become confused after several steps. They do not maintain good records of what they have done (the combinations they have tried, and so on). Children in the formal operational stage, however, approach the problem with a logical and complete plan. They take liquids from the containers two at a time and keep records of the combinations that don't work so that they won't repeat themselves. One of the characteristics of this stage of intellectual development is the child's ability to formulate and consider all the possible outcomes of a situation.

During this last stage of cognitive development, there is little differentiation between the organism's structural equipment and the demands of the environment. This does not mean, however, that the child is in a state of equilibrium. In fact, adult thinking and adolescent thinking are characterized by disequilibrium as well as equilibrium, but the pushes, pulls, and transitions that occur are not as extreme as those that characterize the earlier part of life.

The formal operational thinker has the ability to consider many different solutions to a problem before acting. This greatly increases efficiency, because the individual can avoid potentially unsuccessful attempts at solving a problem. The formal operational person considers past experiences, present demands, and future consequences in attempting to maximize the success of his or her adaptation to the world.

Egocentrism During the Formal Operational Stage

The type of egocentrism characteristic of the formal operational stage results from a lack of differentiation between two different elements: the individual's own thoughts and feelings and the thoughts and feelings of others. That is, the formal operational thinker fails to differentiate between his or her own thoughts and what others are thinking. Elkind (1974) asserts that the task here should be called the "conquest of thought," because formal operational children see themselves in the way they think others see them. For example, many adolescents are self-conscious and sensitive to what others think about their clothes and their physical appearance. There is often no reason to believe that others disapprove of a dress style, but it is difficult for the adolescent to separate his or her own thoughts from those of others. This might be one reason teenagers are so susceptible to fads. In addition, this type of egocentrism ensures some degree of social validation, because the child believes that he or she is thinking as others do.

> Egocentrism during the formal operational stage is characterized by a lack of differentiation between the individual's thoughts and feelings and those of others; formal operational children see themselves as they think others see them.

Summary Description of the Formal Operational Stage

Teenagers develop what Piaget calls formal operational thinking, which is the systematic analysis, exploration, and solution of problems. Adolescents can comprehend combinations, rearrangements, and permutations of objects and events, unlike most concrete operational thinkers.

Adolescents differ from younger children in other ways as well. Most of them can deal skillfully with abstract questions or questions about situations that are contrary to fact, such as, What would have happened if the United States had not entered the Vietnam War? The concrete operational child, who is more literal than the formal operational child, insists that questions of this sort are invalid.

During the teenage years, young people realize that thoughts are private and that no one else knows that they are thinking. They value friendship and sincerity highly and spend time trying to understand people's real motives. They are more aware than younger children are that events can be interpreted in many different ways and so there is no definitive form of truth. They are also sensitive to the discrepancy between reality and ideals. Their understanding of politics and attitudes toward arbitrary rules of conduct are different from those of younger children as well. If a teenager believes that a rule is unworkable, he or she is likely to advocate change, whereas a younger child is likely to recommend increasing the punishment for disobedience of the rule, as if it were inviolate or sacred.

In summary, adolescents' thinking is characterized by sensitivity to others, the ability to handle contradictions, and the ability to handle the logic of combinations and permutations. This mature system of thought enables adolescents to master complex systems of literature, mathematics, and science. It also allows them to plan for the future, establish long-range goals, and integrate past and present into a realistic self-identity—all abilities that are necessary for socioemotional adjustment in adulthood.

PIAGET'S MODEL OF DEVELOPMENT

Figure 9.5 illustrates Piaget's model of intellectual development, showing its three basic components: content, structure, and function. The term *content* here refers simply to the overt behaviors that are displayed during a child's intellectual development, such as picking up a toy and putting it down, solving a difficult mathematical problem, or using a spoon to eat. Content is determined by many things and is a reflection of other factors, such as cultural demands, environmental constraints, and the child's current level of development. Content does not stand alone, and it does not determine the level of functioning but only reflects it.

Function here refers to the invariant (never-changing) processes that are characteristic of all levels of development, specifically, the processes of adaptation (assimilation and accommodation) and organization. These functional invariants are universal occurrences that produce changes in content. Content changes with development, but function does not. These are the underlying, ever-present operating forces that guide development.

Finally, the concept of *structure* represents internal schemata and other patterns of behavior. In many ways, structures serve as interpreters or mediators between function and content, and, as Figure 9.5 indicates, both content and function are affected by structural organization.

The three main components of Piaget's model of development are content, structure, and function.

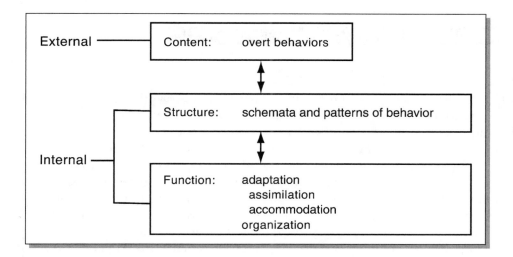

FIGURE 9.5   Piaget's Model of Development

John Flavell (1963, p. 18) presents an excellent explanation of how the three different components of the model differ from one another. He notes, in simple (and somewhat imprecise) capsule definitions, that function is concerned with the manner in which any organism makes cognitive progress, content is the external behavior that tells us that functioning has occurred, and structure is made up of the inferred organizational properties that explain why this content rather than some other content has emerged.

The Developmental Nature of Equilibrium

As the child develops, he or she tends to move from a general state of less equilibrium to more equilibrium, and the child's interactions with the environment become broader, more generalizable, and more stable. In becoming a thinking organism, the child learns how to adjust for changes in the environment even before they occur and how to alter his or her behavior to meet anticipated needs. Thus the child can adapt to new situations with fewer disturbances to existing schemata, and in doing so, he or she forms an increasingly solid foundation for future exploration and growth.

At all stages of development, and in all states of equilibrium, the processes of adaptation and organization operate to seek out new experiences. For this reason, the more active the child is, the more likely it is that he or she will establish a state of coherence and stability. One of the most important educational implications of Piaget's theory is that the action of the child is a primary force.

> Piaget believed strongly that action is the basis for thought and experience is the foundation for intelligence.

Applying Ideas About the Cognitive-Developmental Approach

Examining Egocentrism

In effect, as Flavell (1963) shows, the three components of Piaget's model explain the how (function), what (content), and why (structure) of developmental change. The most important element of the model, however, is the underlying assumption that development results from the child's active participation in and interchange with the environment. Through this interaction, structure and content both undergo dramatic changes and, in concert with forces such as adaptation and organization, produce rich growth and development.

One of the most popular of all the ideas Piaget put forth is the concept of egocentrism, especially as it concerns preoperational children's tendency to view themselves as the center of their activities. To examine this concept, Piaget used the three-mountain task described earlier in this chapter. In the years since, however, there has been some discussion among scholars regarding the appropriateness of the three-mountain task for the examination of egocentrism in very young children. Some have argued that such children cannot understand the demands of the task.

Helen Borke (1975) conducted a study to examine this issue. The subjects were eight 3-year-olds and fourteen 4-year-olds who attended a day-care center. One at a time, each child was presented with a set of four three-dimensional displays that included a fire engine and a Grover doll (Grover is a character on the children's television program *Sesame Street*). The examiner asked the child to predict how the fire engine would look to Grover when he was placed in different positions around the display relative to the fire engine. The four displays were as follows: a practice display (used to familiarize the child with the task), a display similar to Piaget's three-mountain display, a display featuring a small lake and a sailboat, and a display featuring seven miniature animals and people in "natural settings" (including a small house).

When Borke analyzed the children's responses, she found that there were differences in the accuracy of their responses to the different displays, but the differences did not appear to have anything to do with age. The children were most accurate while responding to the displays that included toys, and their error rates increased when they responded to Piaget's original mountain task. Borke's conclusion is interesting and important. She notes that it appears that if children are presented with age-appropriate role-playing tasks, they can demonstrate what she calls "perceptual role-taking ability." Thus there is at least some reason to believe that young children are not always primarily egocentric in their thinking and actions.

TABLE 9.2 Summary of the Characteristics of Circular Reactions

Type of Circular Reaction	Approximate Age	Focus of Activity	Example
Primary	1–4 months	In and around infant's body	Sucking
Secondary	4–8 months	Directed outward toward control of objects in the external world yet no real conscious connection between behavior and result	Repeatedly hitting the bottom of a pot with a stick
Tertiary	8–18 months	Repetition as in secondary reaction, but with some degree of variation; beginnings of real exploration	Playing with food

Equilibrium is a state that the individual actively seeks as part of mastering new parts of the world. It is an underlying theme of all development, and although different stages of development are characterized by differing degrees of equilibration, the process of equilibration is continually going on.

The Developmental Nature of Circular Operations

As noted earlier in this chapter, there are three different types of circular reactions, labeled primary, secondary, and tertiary. A circular reaction is a repetition of sensorimotor acts that facilitates new adaptations. Its purpose is to encourage the individual to experience events (some of which occur by chance) and increase the scope of experience. The individual's scope of experience is a crucial variable in cognitive development, because the more active the individual is, the more likely it is that his or her attempts at adaptation will be successful across a wide range of experiences.

Table 9.2 presents a summary of the characteristics of the three different types of circular reactions. As the table shows, primary circular reactions, which take place when the child is 1 to 4 months old, are sensation oriented and focused entirely on activity in and around the child's own body. Children at this stage cannot differentiate their actions from the experiences or objects involved in those actions. At this stage, the child's world is undifferentiated. Sucking for sucking's sake is a good example of a primary circular reaction.

—— **On the Web** ——

Many different theorists have written about cognitive development, and Jean Piaget's theory is in especially good company when discussion turns to the subject of moral development. At http://tigger.uic.edu/~lnucci/MoralEd/overview.html you will find an article titled "Moral Development and Moral Education: An Overview," which highlights the work of Jean Piaget as well as that of Carol Gilligan and Lawrence Kohlberg, whose work falls within the same general theoretical model. This article can help you see how the principles and ideas addressed in this chapter can be applied to moral development.

> The progression of circular reactions parallels the child's increasing recognition of the importance of his or her social interaction with the world.

The onset of secondary circular reactions (at about age 4 to 8 months) changes the direction of these repetitive acts from a focus entirely on the child's own body to an outward focus, toward control of objects in the external world. The child draws no real connections between what he or she is doing and the outcomes or consequences of that behavior. In other words, the child forms no conscious connection between his or her behavior (cause) and the result of that behavior (effect). (In Piaget's view, the presence of such a connection, which he calls intentionality, is the first real sign of intelligence.) Secondary circular reactions involve the child's direct manipulation of the environment, but the child has little if any cognizance that his or her actions have specific effects on the environment. The child at this age is considered a "naive scientist" who is simply fascinated by the fact that certain things occur again and again, without any real concern for how or why.

At the age of 8 to 18 months, a dramatic change becomes apparent in the child's cognitive apparatus. The child no longer repeats activities simply for repetition's sake; rather, he or she begins to vary repetitions, observe different outcomes, and form a very basic notion of cause and effect. An example of a tertiary circular reaction is a child's repeatedly dropping food to see where it lands. The child varies the amounts and types of food to see what the different results are and uses these experiences to understand what the world represents.

Circular reactions are good examples of the ways in which structural changes provide the foundation for later alterations in cognitive development.

The Developmental Nature of Egocentrism

Table 9.3 shows the developmental course of egocentrism from the sensorimotor stage through the formal operational stage. Although egocentrism takes

TABLE 9.3 The Developmental Course of Egocentrism

Stage	Goal	Accomplishment
Sensorimotor	Conquest of objects	Object permanence
Preoperational	Conquest of symbols	Language
Concrete operational	Conquest of reality	Cause and effect
Formal operational	Conquest of thought	Distinction between reality and fantasy

different forms at different developmental stages (and therefore can be said to be somewhat stage related), it is a pervasive construct throughout development.

The developmental goal of the sensorimotor child, who cannot differentiate between self and physical objects, is the conquest of objects. The goal of the preoperational child, who can clearly separate objects from the activities involved with those objects, is the conquest of the symbol. In conquering the symbol and moving on to useful and productive language, the child begins to differentiate between symbols and what they represent. The child's specific concerns change, but the underlying theme is one of the degree of differentiation that exists between two elements.

For the concrete operational child, the developmental goal is the conquest of reality, or the ability to differentiate between assumptions and facts. This child can understand that cause and effect is a process but is not interested in the relationship between the elements, because he or she does not yet have the ability to function independent of experience. Finally, the formal operational child cannot differentiate between his or her own thoughts and the thoughts of others. A good example of this is adolescents' belief that the way they feel about themselves is the way that others feel about them. The goal of the formal operational child is the conquest of thought, or the differentiation between personal thoughts and the thoughts of others. This progression of increasingly abstract differentiation is considered a developmental phenomenon because it occurs at all stages of development and substantively changes in form yet is still based on the same issue: the degree to which the individual can differentiate between certain elements.

> Egocentrism progresses from a lack of differentiation between self and objects to a lack of differentiation between one's own thoughts and those of others.

JEROME BRUNER'S INFORMATION-PROCESSING APPROACH

The work of Jean Piaget has certainly provided developmental psychologists with a foundation for understanding the nature of intellectual development. Piaget's training

Piaget's work
has provided
the foundation
for the work of
later cognitive-
developmental
theorists.

in biology combined with his strong application of philosophy to lead him to the major contributions he continued to make up to his death in September 1980.

Other cognitive-developmental theorists have used some of Piaget's work as a basis for the development of their own theories regarding how children think and how they learn to think. One such theorist is Oxford University psychologist Jerome Bruner. Bruner is often referred to as a *cognitive structuralist* because, even more than Piaget, he believes that changes in intellectual development result from the modification of internal structures.

Bruner's most outstanding contribution to developmental theory has been his conception that the child's mind operates much like an "information-processing system," or a computer. We'll return to this analogy many times in the following discussion of Bruner's theory, which begins with a description of his theoretical viewpoint.

The Cognitive-Structuralist Viewpoint

One of the major tenets of Piaget's theory of cognitive development is that development results from a combination of strong maturational forces and environmental influences. The end result of the interaction between maturation and environment is qualitative change, such that children at different stages of development have qualitatively different views of the world. For example, as discussed above, the young child lacks the ability to conserve or to reverse operations, whereas the older child is able to perform these mental actions.

Bruner's cognitive-structuralist theory makes a similar assumption, but it differs from Piaget's theory in one major way: Bruner's theory assumes that cognitive growth "occurs as much from the outside in as from the inside out" (Bruner, 1966). This assumption has some profound implications for the way we understand the growth of children's intellectual skills as well as for the way children should be taught (and how they learn) in both informal and formal settings, such as the home and school.

It is interesting to note that some of Bruner's basic assumptions are similar to those of the ethological approach, as discussed in Chapter 4. According to Bruner, the thing that makes development in humans unique—that is, what makes it different from development in other animals—is the cultural context in which human development takes place. Furthermore, in sophisticated cultures (such as that of the United States), the limits of growth depend on how well the culture can assist the process of development. For example, how well does the teaching process bring the challenges and mysteries of the world to the child? In what way, or mode, does it present such material? And what expectations for performance and intellectual growth are present? Given his assumption that intellectual development is

A central aspect
of Bruner's
perspective is
that the unique
thing about human
development is
the cultural
context in which
it takes place.

promoted (or limited) by and reflected in culture, it is no surprise that Bruner also asserts that we have not even begun to tap our potential.

Not only is some of Bruner's theory grounded in part in ethological ideas, but a great deal of his work is based on comparisons of children and animals observed playing in the same habitats yet developing distinctly different skills. For example, Bruner studied films of baboons and of children of the !Kung Bushmen in the Kalahari Desert. He noted that the baboons seemed to focus primarily on their peers for attention and the practice of certain skills, whereas the children maintained almost constant interaction with adults, as they played and danced together. Bruner concluded that in the case of the children, the majority of cultural values, rituals, and customs were transmitted indirectly, with little intentional teaching.

According to Bruner, when teaching occurs in a formal context, such as in schools, rather than through more informal, indirect means, it loses some of its effectiveness, because the children are being asked to understand events outside of the contexts within which they occur. As the discussion below will show, Bruner's thoughts about education have had a great deal of influence; his ideas about intellectual development have been applied extensively in many educational settings.

The Child as a Computer

Bruner views the process of intellectual growth, or development, as one in which the child sees patterns or systems of rules and develops strategies for dealing with those systems when necessary. Thus the child's mind operates in much the same way as a sophisticated computer. Even the most basic computer requires input, does something with that input, and then uses some mechanism to display the resulting output. For example, if a computer is programmed to add two numbers together and we input $4 + 5$, the result, or output, is 9. The computer accomplishes the task of addition by using programming instructions in combination with a set of several different functions that are "internal," or hardwired into the machine—that is, functions that are built into the system.

According to Bruner, the child's mind operates in much the same way. The infant is born with a series of adaptive and well-functioning innate behaviors hardwired in, and the child's mind is in a state of readiness to function if the environment provides sufficiently interesting "programming." Just as we add software to a computer's hardwired functions, parents and teachers provide environmental stimuli that encourage the child to exercise patterns (or programs) of thinking that help expand the child's mind further by introducing new challenges.

Another parallel between the child's intellectual development and the operating of a computer is found in the process of integration. Much as the notion of organization (the tendency for the parts of a system to function together) is important in Piaget's theory, in Bruner's theory integration is crucial to the development of

According to Bruner, an infant is born with a series of innate, or hardwired, behaviors and is ready to be programmed, much like a computer.

cognitive skills. Integration is the process through which the child's mind organizes thoughts and actions into higher-order categories, through the addition and modification of experiences. For example, the very young child becomes a more efficient processor of information when he or she develops the ability to group objects by general attributes or characteristics ("They are all animals") instead of only by singular descriptors ("It's a bear"). Through the process of integration, the mind begins to function in an increasingly efficient manner, so that the child needs less and less information to make decisions or to understand the relationships between objects or events.

The process of integration does not operate in a vacuum. According to Bruner, the way the child represents experiences is influenced by *conventions,* or the social rules established by the child's culture. Part of cognitive development is gaining the ability to use and transmit these conventions through the symbol systems adopted by the culture. Knowledge of our culture's conventions is important, because we cannot deal effectively with our environment without knowing the sets of symbols through which we can communicate with others. For example, in the United States it is conventional to speak English according to a certain set of rules (including rules of grammar and syntax). When we violate those conventions by speaking incorrectly, or by speaking a dialect that few people understand, our speech is not very communicative. Thus the child's opportunity for increased cognitive growth is minimized when he or she does not apply appropriate conventions, because the child cannot receive the input from the environment that is necessary for growth.

Conventions, or social rules, apply to many areas of life aside from the development and use of language. Many classes of behavior, such as how we behave interpersonally, have sets of conventions attached to them. For example, we don't turn our backs on people when they are talking to us, nor do we interrupt them. Such actions violate unwritten social mores, or conventions, associated with the general class of "interaction with other people" behaviors. It is Bruner's contention that we adjust our behavior to fit the conventions of our culture, and through this process we "stretch" our minds to fit new circumstances.

Whereas some of the other theorists discussed in this volume are interested in the content of the child's mind, Bruner's interest is in the rules found in a culture that help shape and develop the child's patterns of thinking and problem solving. In fact, for Bruner, the development of intellectual thinking is the movement of the mind toward more efficient operation. Just as computer programmers try to write efficient programs, using as few instructions as possible, over the course of development the child's mind becomes more sophisticated and efficient in its problem-solving skills. As we will see shortly, this is accomplished through changes in the modes of operation the child uses to represent experiences.

The Child's Representation of the World

Piaget's theory has a great deal to say about the different stages of cognitive development through which all children pass. Although Bruner agrees that children view the world in qualitatively different ways as they develop, he does not attach these different views to stages of development. Rather, Bruner employs the concept of **modes of representation**. His theory is thus somewhat less age bound than Piaget's and reflects his belief about the importance of the influences of culture. However, as Bruner (1966) notes, the modes of representation do occur in a fixed order, "each depending upon the previous one for its development, yet all remaining more or less intact throughout life" (p. 2).

Bruner names three modes of representation: enactive, iconic, and symbolic. When the child is in the first of these, the **enactive mode of representation**, his or her intellectual growth is characterized by action. In this mode, the infant learns to experience the world through direct contact with his or her surroundings. We know from watching young infants that one way they gain knowledge about the world is by acting on it, whether this means putting things in their mouths or developing the kinds of motor skills it takes to explore their immediate surroundings.

During the second year of life, there is a dramatic change in the strategy the child uses to learn about the world. In this new and powerful **iconic mode of representation**, the child uses mental images of objects to acquire knowledge and to increase his or her understanding of the world. This ability to formulate images is a major advance, yet it is most important because it provides the framework for the child's use of symbols, which is characteristic of the **symbolic mode of representation**. In this mode, the child formulates the most efficient symbolic system available, that of language. Language is a very flexible and adaptive tool, and the child uses it to understand and organize patterns of thinking. Instead of simply imagining objects or experiences, the child can now manipulate these images to form new products. Many of these new products increase the child's control over the environment and facilitate further intellectual development.

We can see, then, a progression in the development of the child's operating system, from one in which the child experiences the world through direct action, such as playing (the enactive mode), to one in which the child imagines new things to experiment with (the iconic mode), and then to the most sophisticated level of representation, where the child forms words and concepts to describe what happens (the symbolic mode).

Bruner expresses his view of the development of a child's thinking through the concept of modes of representation rather than stages of development.

The Application of Bruner's Theory to Education

The most widespread application of Bruner's work has been in the area of early childhood education. Before I discuss what Bruner considers to be some of the essential elements of this application, let's look briefly at his view of the role of learning in cognitive development. Keep in mind that, unlike Piaget, Bruner places strong emphasis on the role of the environment and discusses the effects of learning within that context.

Readiness and Bruner's View

Like many cognitive theorists, Bruner believes that we are genetically "wired" with certain basic capabilities, such as the abilities to discriminate sounds and to follow moving objects with our eyes, as well as abilities to respond to other changes in the environment. A primary focus in Bruner's theory of how learning takes place is the concept of readiness. As you recall from Chapter 3, Arnold Gesell also focused on readiness, asserting that children must be biologically ready before they can advance to the next stage of development. Bruner's idea of readiness for learning is similar to Gesell's in that it applies to both learning and development in the young child. Bruner extends the importance of readiness beyond Gesell's application to biological growth, however, by including changes in cognitive functioning as well.

According to Bruner, children are ready to learn different things at different times and, for the most part, anything can be taught to a child of any age as long as it is presented properly.

According to Bruner, as children move along the developmental continuum—from primarily enactive processing of the world to primarily symbolic processing—they are ready for different kinds of learning at different times. Thus it follows that the "task of teaching a subject to a child at any particular age is one of representing the structure of that child's way of viewing things" (Bruner, 1966, p. 33). In other words, rather than expecting the child to adapt to the instructional method, the method needs to be adapted to the child's current developmental level, which dictates how the child relates to the world. When first introduced, this notion gained a lot of attention in the American educational community, where many believed (and some still do) that children must learn certain subject matters when they reach certain ages, regardless of their individual levels of development.

The Role of Teaching

As I have mentioned several times, culture plays a very significant role in Bruner's view of cognitive development. Most American children spend a major part of their lives, from toddlerhood through young adulthood, in school. To understand Bruner's view of the relationship between intellectual growth and formal education, we need to examine the six characteristics of growth that Bruner (1966) describes.

First, Bruner states that intellectual growth is accompanied by increased ability to represent and understand the environment. As noted above, the child must be capable of the highest form of representation, symbolic representation and the use of language, for higher-level intellectual functioning to take place. With more advanced modes of representation, there is more room for additional growth.

Second, intellectual growth depends on the child's use of a "storage system" to remember objects, events, and experiences. The nature of this storage system is in part formed by the demands of the environment. For example, if a child is trying to understand the relationships among objects in a given set, the categories he or she uses to classify the objects will probably be determined by the set of objects itself rather than by some outside criterion. At the least, this means that it is essential to provide children with extensive experiences in a variety of settings. The more experiences children have in different settings, the more adaptable and transferable across settings their developing storage systems will be.

Third, Bruner asserts that the key to increased intellectual growth is the use of language, the most efficient symbolic system available. The child's mind can grow through the use of other symbol systems as well, but above all, these systems must be logically organized so that the child can learn to recognize logical inconsistencies in his or her own thinking. For example, when a toddler sees a cow for the first time and calls it a dog (because it has four legs and a tail, like the dogs the child has seen), the child's parent may respond, "No, that's a cow." In order for this interaction to further the child's intellectual growth, the child needs to understand the parent's correction. By the same token, the parent needs to understand the nature of the child's error in thinking in order to provide meaningful correction.

Fourth, the growth of the child's intellect is a reflection of the interaction between the child and the teacher. (It is important to note that the word *teacher* here refers to anyone who comes in contact with the child as a socializing agent, not only a teacher in a school setting.) The child's level of development should suggest to the teacher ways of organizing the material to be learned to facilitate the child's learning and thus his or her further development.

Fifth, the use of symbol systems (especially language) greatly enhances the effectiveness of teaching and subsequent learning. Symbolic reasoning, the highest form of representation in Bruner's theory, is characterized by the use of sophisticated symbol or language systems. Bruner contends, however, that the development of language does not just parallel cognitive growth; rather, the use of language actually enhances cognitive development. Language is like a set of tools used to build a house, and the final structure represents another step in the development of intellectual competence. For example, the young child uses language to explore the relationships between things. He or she might ask why leaves turn different colors in the fall, and then follow that up with another question of the "what if" type. A child whose use of language tools is more sophisticated might further promote his or her intellectual growth by using an "if . . . then . . . because" progression of statements. Such a progression allows the child to adjust his or her thought system to fit the content of the question to the conditions in the environment.

According to Bruner, the mastery of language is a critical factor in the child's cognitive growth.

Finally, the growing child learns to deal with several alternative events at the same time. To return for a moment to the analogy between the developing child's mind and a computer, we can see that in both, a more efficient way of processing information is accompanied by an ability to process more than one thing at a time. So the mind of the child who can attend to more than one dimension of an event, choose those dimensions that have value for him or her, and use those dimensions to make a decision concerning the event is functioning much more efficiently than the mind of the younger child who can't keep track of simultaneous changes across more than one dimension.

Applying Bruner's Theory to Instruction

Bruner's theory has some clear implications for the design and implementation of instruction. Especially important are the ideas that readiness for learning is crucial to the success of the developmental and learning process and that the environment (that is, the culture, the classroom, and the teacher) must also be suited to the child's level of readiness.

For the teacher applying Bruner's theory, the first task is to identify clearly the concepts that he or she must teach the child. For example, if the child is a second grader, the teacher might need to teach the child the concepts associated with the addition and subtraction of one- and two-digit numbers. (Problems often arise in teaching because teachers themselves are unclear as to exactly what they should be teaching—that is, what their substantive goals should be as far as content is concerned.)

Next, the teacher needs to consider the child's level of readiness, so that he or she can present material to the child that is not beyond the child's ability to learn. At the same time, the teacher needs to be sure the material is different enough from previous work to hold the student's attention. (Perhaps one of the appeals of computer-based instruction for young children is this element of difference combined with a finely tuned system for approximating the level where the child should begin.)

The teacher also needs to present the content to the child in a "spiraling fashion," such that for every new step the child takes toward the teacher-defined goal, the child also reviews previous skills. This redundancy helps to ensure that the groundwork is well established for all subsequent steps.

Finally, perhaps the most important element in Bruner's theory that has been applied to instructional strategies is the practice of giving the child the chance to go "beyond the information given." That is, the teacher gives the child the opportunity to advance beyond what the teacher has offered and explore on his or her own the next logical step in the sequence. According to the tenets of Bruner's theory, the child should be encouraged to create his or her own challenges, to seek out answers through "discovery learning."

Applying Ideas About the Cognitive-Developmental Approach

Paying Attention

A good deal of the discussion of Piaget's and Bruner's theories in this chapter focuses on the active role that the growing child plays in the development of his or her own cognitive and intellectual abilities. In the early 1970s, Jerome Kagan of Harvard University studied infants' attention spans in an attempt to understand the internal operations that occur as infants develop from a sensory orientation to a more operational orientation.

The young infant initially has relatively few schemata (or mental representations of events), but through the processes of organization and adaptation, these schemata change, becoming integrated, modified, and refined. Kagan (1971) indirectly examined the contents of the schemata of infants in his sample (180 firstborn, white children of both sexes) by observing what environmental events caused the infants to habituate (or become bored) and what events attracted them. To accomplish this, he showed the children (at 4, 8, 13, and 27 months of age) a series of four clay faces that were very different from one another: One looked like a "normal" face (with two eyes, a nose, a mouth, and so on,

all in the usual places) whereas the others were in various stages of disarray; in fact, one face had no features, just hair.

Kagan was interested in finding out which kinds of faces would keep the children's attention and which would not. He hypothesized that the children would be most likely to attend to those stimuli that were discrepant from what they already knew, but not so different as to be unrelated to anything they had experienced before. He also hypothesized that the children would be likely to ignore completely any stimulus that was too familiar.

Kagan found that the moderately discrepant faces held the children's interest the longest, an important finding in that it provides evidence that the young infant is capable of formulating and indirectly testing hypotheses. This is a major thesis of cognitive-developmental (and organismic) theorists: that even very young children actively try to understand their world through the interactions between their own perceptions (or schemata) and the reality of the world around them.

The late 1960s and early 1970s saw a great deal of interest among American educators in the application of Piaget's and especially Bruner's theories of cognitive development. The "open classroom" and "free education" concepts were so appealing to some that several programs began privately, and today these concepts are still part of more traditional school systems. Yet many of the practices that theorists such as Bruner would like to see in education have not been implemented. Budget constraints, "back to basics" movements, and teacher education programs lacking in imagination have all hindered progress in this area.

WEB SITES OF INTEREST

- The Jean Piaget Society, at http://www.piaget.org: As is the case for many famous theorists, a scholarly society has been established in Piaget's name. The members of the Jean Piaget Society, which formed in 1970, are interested in exploring the nature of the developmental construction of human knowledge. The society publishes the quarterly journal *Cognitive Development,* which focuses on empirical and theoretical work on the development of perception, memory, language, concepts, and other aspects of cognitive development.
- "Child Psychologist Jean Piaget," by Seymour Papert, at http://www.time.com/time/time100/scientist/profile/piaget.html: Piaget was recently named one of *Time* magazine's 100 most important people of the 20th century. This profile by Papert, who is a professor at MIT, summarizes Piaget's life and work and praises Piaget for finding "the secrets of human learning and knowledge hidden behind the cute and seemingly illogical notions of children." This Web site also includes a timeline and even a quiz.
- "Learning and Teaching: Assimilation and Accommodation," by James S. Atherton, at http://www.dmu.ac.uk/~jamesa/learning/assimacc.htm: Atherton provides thorough explanations of assimilation and accommodation using visual representations. If you want to understand these important concepts more fully, this site is well worth a visit.

FURTHER READINGS ABOUT COGNITIVE-DEVELOPMENTAL APPROACHES

Hsueh, Yeh. (2002). The Hawthorne experiments and the introduction of Jean Piaget in American industrial psychology, 1929–1932. *History of Psychology, 5,* 163–189.

This article discusses an interesting application of Piaget's theory beyond the study of the development of cognition. Hsueh reports on research in which Piaget's clinical method was applied in interviews with thousands of workers in an effort to understand and promote social cooperation.

Nicolopoulou, Ageliki. (1999). Play, cognitive development, and the social world: Piaget, Vygotsky, and beyond. In Peter Lloyd & Charles Fernyhough (Eds.), *Lev Vygotsky: Critical assessments: Vol. 2. Thought and language* (pp. 419–446). Florence, KY: Taylor & Francis/Routledge. (Reprinted from *Human Development,* 1993, *36,* 1–23)

Nicolopoulou is concerned with understanding cognitive development through the sociocultural conception of play, and so explores the role of play in the formation of mind, the shaping of the self, and the definition and reproduction of culture.

Tudge, Jonathan R. H., & Winterhoff, Paul A. (1999). Vygotsky, Piaget, and Bandura: Perspectives on the relations between the social world and cognitive development. In Peter Lloyd & Charles Fernyhough (Eds.), *Lev Vygotsky: Critical assessments: Vol. 1. Vygotsky's theory* (pp. 311–338). Florence, KY: Taylor & Francis/Routledge. (Reprinted from *Human Development,* 1993, *36,* 61–81)

Tudge and Winterhoff examine the views of the diverse theories of Vygotsky, Piaget, and Bandura concerning the relationship between the social world and cognitive development. They discuss the similarities and differences among the theories and note how the narrow focus of theoretical and empirical researchers has obscured the theories' complexity.

Zigler, Edward, & Gilman, Elizabeth. (1998). The legacy of Jean Piaget. In Gregory A. Kimble & Michael Wertheimer (Eds.), *Portraits of pioneers in psychology* (Vol. 3, pp. 145–160). Mahwah, NJ: Lawrence Erlbaum.

Just what is Piaget's legacy? Zigler and Gilman recount Piaget's use of concepts from biology, psychology, philosophy, and mathematics in his examination of how children learn about the world. The topics they cover include Piaget's early life and work, major principles of his theory, and cross-cultural implications of his theory.

CHAPTER **10**

LEV VYGOTSKY'S SOCIOCULTURAL THEORY OF DEVELOPMENT

Where was I when you were born?

—3-year-old boy to his father

Thought is not merely expressed in words; it comes into existence through them.

—Lev Vygotsky

Many theories of development have had important influences on the way we view the growth of cognition in human beings. Piaget's stage-oriented approach may be the most popular (and some might say the most influential) of these, but others are also important, perhaps for different reasons. Developmental psychologist Lev Vygotsky (1896–1934) is responsible for one such theory.

Vygotsky's view emphasizes the importance of the sociocultural matrix of which the individual is a part—that is, according to his theory, social interaction plays a fundamental role in the development of cognition. In addition to genetics and the environment, development is influenced by the mix of social forces that surround the individual. Ongoing qualitative changes in both the environment and the individual produce new developmental accomplishments and mark new developmental milestones. As Vygotsky (1978) puts it, "Every function in the child's cultural development appears twice: first, on the social level, and later, on the individual level; first, between people (interpsychological) and then inside the child (intrapsychological)" (p. 57). For students of history, it should come as no surprise that Marxist social theory finds its way into Vygotsky's approach, given its emphasis first on the culture, and then on the individual.

> Vygotsky believed that children construct their words through activity and interaction with culture and society.

One important distinction between Vygotsky and other cognitive theorists is the relatively direct application of Vygotsky's theory and writings to the process of educating children. As you will read later in this chapter, extensive field trials of educational programs have been based on Vygotsky's sociocultural approach.

THE BASIS OF VYGOTSKY'S THEORY

As with the work of many theorists, it is impossible to separate Vygotsky's thinking and writing from the world in which he lived. Lev Vygotsky was born in western Russia in 1896 (the same year Piaget was born). Although he graduated from Moscow University with a law degree (after trying medical school), he never practiced law; instead, he became a psychologist. His first major work was his doctoral dissertation, *The Psychology of Art,* published in 1925 (Vygotsky, 1925/1971). Vygotsky was under a great deal of pressure to adapt his emerging theories to Marxist ideology, the prevailing political ideology in Russia at the time he was writing—hence the frequent discussion of his work within a Marxist political framework. Some historians believe that it was the rapidly changing social environment in Russia that allowed Vygotsky's work to have the profound influence it had, especially on the Russian educational system. In his short life of only 38 years (he died of tuberculosis), Vygotsky made important and creative contributions to the field of human development.

> Vygotsky's viewpoint on development was heavily influenced by the social and political aftermath of the Russian Revolution.

For most of the years that Vygotsky lectured, taught, and wrote as a psychologist, his ideas went unappreciated in the West. Today, however, Vygotsky's theory is experiencing a revival in the United States, with the recent publication of new translations of many of his works, increased exchanges between Russian and

Western scholars, and, perhaps most important, the direct application of his ideas to education.

Vygotsky's approach is known as a **sociocultural theory,** which means that it emphasizes the influence of social interaction and culture in development. According to Vygotsky, social interaction leads to changes in children's thinking (and then their behavior), and because behavior is rooted in the social context in which it occurs, both thought and behavior vary depending on the cultures in which they take place. Vygotsky suggests that the child's development depends on the child's interactions with other people and with the tools (such as language) that the culture provides to help form the child's view of the world. According to his theory, the fundamental process of learning takes place through the child's interaction with a more knowledgeable person, be that an adult (such as a parent or a teacher) or a peer. It is interesting to note that psychologists working within many different perspectives embrace this view.

> Vygotsky's theory is sociocultural in nature; that is, it emphasizes the social context within which development takes place.

In sum, development always results from internal mental processes (sometimes called *instrumental*), which have their origins in external mental processes (sometimes called *intermental*). That is, for the development of the child's mind to take place, the child must be involved in culture-specific activities (such as education, family rituals, or community activities), which provide a structure within which cognitive and social development can take place.

Although the *sociocultural* label fits Vygotsky's theory well, it is also sometimes referred to as a *cultural-historical* theory or a sociohistorical theory—both labels that further emphasize the theory's view of the comprehensiveness of the relationship between the individual and his or her culture. It should also be noted that Vygotsky is by no means seen only as a cognitive psychologist; for example, learning theory–based developmental psychologists also endorse his views of the learning process.

Four major ideas underlie Vygotsky's theory. First, *children construct their own knowledge.* That is, children are active participants in their own development (this is a notion similar to that expressed by Sandra Scarr [1993], as discussed in Chapter 2). Children are participants not only in shaping their own wants and needs, but even in constructing the kind, type, and quality of knowledge they need to negotiate their everyday existence. For example, given the need to learn how to read, a child will (given the proper environment) seek out opportunities to learn how to read or to improve his or her reading skills.

Second, *development cannot be separated from it social context.* Simply stated, development and social context are one and the same. The process of development relies on maturation and environmental effects, and it always takes place in some social context. According to Vygotsky's view, if two identical children with identical sets of genes are raised in different social contexts, or cultures, their processes of development will be different. The relationship between culture and

> Vygotsky asserts that development cannot be separated from the social context within which it occurs.

thought is crucial—culture influences what and how children think, and different cultures have different kinds of impacts.

Third, *learning can lead development*. As noted in Chapter 7, Robert Gagne (1968) defines development as the cumulative effects of learning. Vygotsky's assumption is somewhat similar. However, Vygotsky does not assert that learning is development (as Gagne and others who support a strict learning theory view of development would say); rather, his view is that learning sets the stage for development. Thus the teacher who sets the stage, or presents the first step—by presenting the child with a task that the child is capable of doing—is leading that child toward increasingly complex levels of development.

Finally, *language plays a central role in mental development*. In Vygotsky's view, language is a cultural tool that allows the child's mind to stretch and grow. It provides labels for the new ideas to which the child is introduced and allows the child to expand already existing ideas into new realms.

> According to Vygotsky, learning can lead development.

The Zone of Proximal Development: What It Is and How It Works

Perhaps the most important and most recognized concept in Vygotsky's theory is the idea that the potential for cognitive development is limited to "the distance between the actual developmental level as determined by independent problem solving and the level of potential development as determined through problem solving under adult guidance or in collaboration with more capable peers" (Vygotsky, 1978, p. 55), an area referred to as the **zone of proximal development**, or ZPD. This concept forms a link between the psychological basis for development and the pedagogical basis for instruction (Hedegaard, 1996).

The ZPD is the "place" where the child and teacher go when it's time to stretch the child's cognitive skills. Working within the ZPD is not as safe as staying where the child knows everything, but it is not as scary or extreme as going to the place where the child knows nothing. In the ZPD the child should be able to maximize his or her development and learning, with tasks that are new enough that the child is not bored, but not so new or so challenging that the child becomes frustrated. The key point is that the concept of such a zone takes into account the dual processes of the child's developmental progress (a naturally occurring phenomenon, according to Vygotsky) and learning (an activity based on practice, with the content of this activity determined by the surrounding culture).

> A critical element of Vygotsky's theory is the concept of the zone of proximal development, or ZPD, which is the distance between the child's potential level of development and what the child can currently do.

Within the ZPD, the child and the teacher work together on different types of (well-thought-out) tasks designed to help the child learn things that he or she could not have learned on his or her own; left to try to accomplish these tasks alone, the child would become increasingly frustrated. This help provided by the

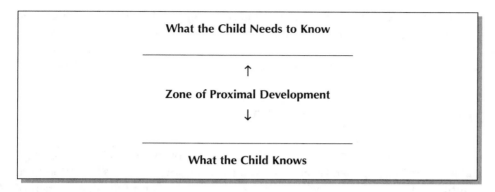

FIGURE 10.1   The Zone of Proximal Development

teacher represents part of the political ideology of the society within which Vygotsky developed his ideas—that is, one in which individuals were expected to look to the state for support and assistance.

The zone of proximal development (illustrated in Figure 10.1) may thus be thought of as the difference between the child's capacity to solve problems on his or her own and the child's capacity to solve problems with assistance (whether from an adult or a peer). The child's current developmental level consists of all the functions and activities that the child can perform on his or her own, without the help of anyone else. The ZPD includes all the functions and activities that the child can perform only with the assistance of someone else. The other person in this process provides structured but not intrusive intervention (this is called *scaffolding*, which I discuss further below); this person may be a schoolteacher, a parent, a peer, or anyone else who knows and understands the material being taught.

The job of the teacher, or "helper," defined broadly, is to move the child away from what he or she already knows and toward what he or she needs to know. The ZPD, is the optimal place for learning to occur, because motivation is maximized in this zone. The child is curious enough to seek out new ideas and is sufficiently grounded in old ones.

The ZPD and the Development of Speech and Language

An example of the process through which a child might learn speech and language will help to illustrate how the concept of the ZPD has direct application to children's development. Tharp and Gallimore (1988) discuss the acquisition of language as a four-stage sequence. The child begins at the level of his or her basic capacity and then progresses through Stage 2, where that capacity is further developed. At Stage 3, the child internalizes his or her understanding of the information, which eventually leads to Stage 4, in which, after the child gains some degree of mastery over the new information, the process begins again with new challenges. At this point, the child relies on help to move forward once again.

THE SEQUENCE OF DEVELOPMENT

Like other developmental psychologists, Vygotsky breaks down the process of development (especially the development of speech and language) into four qualitatively distinct stages: the primitive stage, naive psychology, egocentric speech, and ingrowth.

Like many other developmental psychologists, Vygotsky believed that development occurs in a stagelike fashion. In Vygotsky's theory, the child's transition from external influences to internal thought is broken down into four stages, each of which is characterized by a dialectical relationship—that is, a give-and-take between the qualities of the activity and the qualities of the child's internal thoughts. The results of this interaction are growth and change. Many of the examples Vygotsky gives in his writings about his theoretical perspective concern the development of language, and that is the conceptual framework within which I discuss these stages below. Note the similarities between Vygotsky's four stages and Piaget's (see Chapter 9).

In the first of Vygotsky's stages, the **natural** or **primitive stage** (from birth to about 2 years), the child uses speech for almost purely social reasons; speech at this stage has no significance for the child's intellectual development. Cooing, babbling, social smiles, and easily conditioned behaviors make up the child's social and intellectual repertoire for most of this time. (There are, of course, some 18-month-old children who speak in sentences, if not full paragraphs, but they would be considered to be toward one end of the normal distribution, just as children who don't develop even the most basic language facility would be considered to be at the other end.)

In the second stage (roughly ages 2 to 7 years), the child displays **naive psychology**. In this stage, grammar and syntax become integral parts of the child's speech. Most important, however, is that language at this stage is not a part of the child's thinking process, because it is still symbolic in nature, representing things, not necessarily ideas, and the child is certainly not able to manipulate ideas. The child uses language to communicate needs and ideas, but the way the child thinks is not influenced by language, and the child's thinking does not modify his or her language.

At the third stage of this developmental sequence (which lasts for most of the child's school years, approximately ages 7 to 12), the child uses **egocentric speech**; this is also known as the stage of **external signs**. In this stage, the close interaction between thought and language emerges as a consistently occurring phenomenon. That is, the child constantly talks to him- or herself, maintaining a kind of running dialogue or stream of consciousness. It's as if whatever comes to

━━ **On the Web** ━━

The development of language is an important part of Vygotsky's theory because it is through communication that we get to know the world and the world, in turn, shapes us. Caroline Bowen, a speech and language pathologist, maintains a Web site with links to more than 200 other sites providing information about language and related topics, at http: //members.tripod.com/Caroline_Bowen /home.html. This site is a great place to start if you want to learn more about this almost uniquely human behavior.

the child's mind also comes out of the child's mouth. According to Vygotsky, it is at this stage that language actually begins to influence the child's thinking and, in turn, the child's thinking begins to influence language.

During the fourth stage in this sequence (approximately age 12 and beyond), called **ingrowth**, language takes on its full-blown significance as a mature way for the individual to use symbols in thinking about the world. At this stage, inner speech (thinking about things) influences outer speech (communicating those things to others), and the reverse occurs as well.

EDUCATIONAL APPLICATIONS OF VYGOTSKY'S APPROACH

Given the time in which Vygotsky worked, during which there was a great deal of emphasis on reeducating the Russian people following the revolution, it is no surprise that his primary concern was education. Several fundamental educational practices have grown out of Vygotsky's theoretical viewpoint on child development and learning, some of which are described below.

Scaffolding

The term **scaffolding** refers to techniques an educator uses to build bridges between what the child knows and what the child needs to know (or what the child is being taught), as shown in Figure 10.2. Scaffolding (much like the scaffolding used by builders and renovators working on buildings) serves as a supportive structure that connects the knowing child to the all-knowing child (at least within the realm of what is to be known). The educator (whether a

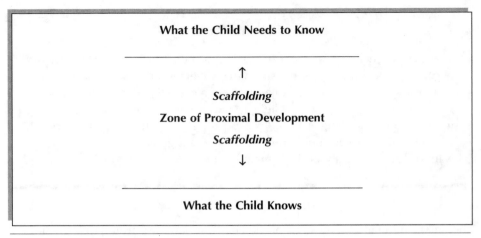

FIGURE 10.2 The Role of Scaffolding in the Zone of Proximal Development

Scaffolding consists of the activities provided by the educator to surround and support the child as he or she is led through the zone of proximal development.

schoolteacher, a parent, or a knowledgeable peer) provides the scaffolding, and then, as the child demonstrates mastery of the material, removes it, leaving the child on his or her own to continue learning. The educator constructs new scaffolding with each new set of tasks presented to the child, again helping to bridge the gap between what the child knows and what he or she needs to knows.

Throughout this process, the educator needs to be sure that the child's zone of proximal development and the scaffolding the educator provides are always congruent with one another. In addition, the educator should think of scaffolding not as a structure, but as a form of support for a structure the child is building, a set of techniques that he or she can use to encourage and reward the child for going beyond his or her current state of experience and reaching out to new ideas and ways of thinking.

Peer Collaboration

We know that interactions with peers have tremendous impacts on children's development. Although we usually think of the influence of peers in relation to the social sphere, peer interactions are no less important in the cognitive arena. One method of instruction based in Vygotsky's theory is that of peer collaboration, in which educators encourage "not-knowing" and "about-to-know" children to work cooperatively with "knowing" peers. Knowing peers can be educators—they can maintain the scaffolding needed until their about-to-know peers learn what they need to learn.

—— On the Web ——

If you're planning on being a teacher (either formal or informal), or you already are one, you should know about how Vygotsky's concept of scaffolding can be applied in the classroom. In their paper "Scaffolding Children's Thinking: Doing Vygotsky in the Classroom With National Curriculum Assessment," at http://www.leeds.ac.uk/educol/documents/000000383.htm, David Leat and Adam Nichol provide a practical example.

Reciprocal Teaching

The idea of reciprocal teaching (the concept that learning goes both ways, from teacher to student and vice versa) is based in the Vygotsky model's emphasis on the importance of social roles when it comes to learning. Constructive and meaningful dialogue between teacher and learner (or learners) is valuable for learners of any age. The teacher (whether a formal teacher, a parent, or a peer) offers a model that the learner imitates (if the conditions are right, as discussed in Chapter 8), and then the learner is reinforced for this behavior through his or her accomplishment (and possibly also through material reinforcers).

> According to Vygotsky, the child's teachers, peers, and parents provide the child with the cultural and social stimulation that enables development to occur.

VYGOTSKY IN THE REAL WORLD

Below are brief descriptions of a few ways in which Vygotsky's theory has been applied in some real-world educational settings, particularly settings that focus on language and mathematics achievement.

Tools of the Mind

Tools of the Mind is a program for teaching reading and writing that is funded by Best Practices in Education, a nonprofit organization devoted to familiarizing teachers in the United States with educational practices that originated in Europe. The important feature of Tools of the Mind is that the program uses a set of teaching techniques that are designed to encourage children to become self-regulating, self-directed learners. When taught by teachers using these techniques, children stay on task longer and learn to learn on their own, which means the teachers can spend less time on classroom management and have more time for teaching. Among other techniques, the Tools of the Mind program employs scaffolding (described above), learning goals, and classroomwide learning plans or menus.

Applying Ideas About Sociocultural Theories of Development

Vygotsky's Theory in the Classroom: What Works?

Any theory, by definition, is a collection of ideas that guide research, and research that tests theories directly is especially interesting. The Metropolitan State College of Denver conducted such research on Vygotsky's theory through an examination of the Tools of the Mind educational program. The researchers focused on testing whether the program could improve the underlying cognitive and early literacy skills of kindergarten students in an urban school district; the sample consisted of 426 kindergartners.

Here's a simple description of the procedure that was followed with each child in the treatment condition in this study (that is, each child who was part of the Tools of the Mind program): The child was asked to "write" on a "menu" his or plans; the child received encouragement to do this as best he or she could, including artwork or scribbles—all the time with the assistance of the teacher. The teacher and the child then discussed and agreed on the child's plan, the idea being that, through this process, the child would begin to learn—for example, about the nature of letters and words, the sounds attached to them, how reading works (e.g., from left to right), and other elements of literacy. According to Vygotsky's theory and the philosophy behind Tools of the Mind, this is a reasonable way to teach a child the tools he or she needs to become a competent reader. Over time, the teacher encouraged the child to expand his or her vocabulary as the program continued. According to Vygotsky's theory, the more the child accomplishes, the more he or she *can* accomplish, because the child learns directly what behaviors are necessary for self-satisfaction—a key element in making further progress.

The results of this research were very positive for the effectiveness of the Tools of the Mind program. The children who participated in the treatment (that is, were part of the program) scored significantly higher on a series of literacy-related and cognitive tasks than did children who did not participate in the program (the control group), particularly in the following areas:

- Sound-symbol correspondence
- Number of words written
- Complexity of the child's written message
- Consistency of use of writing conventions
- Spelling
- Understanding of the concept of a sentence and its importance

Few direct tests of Vygotsky's theory (or, for that matter, the theories of any other cognitive-developmental psychologists) have been conducted in applied settings, but results such as these certainly suggest that cognitive-developmental theoretical perspectives may have some direct and immediate applications.

Learning Goals

Every good teacher knows how important it is for learners to have goals. One way of formulating goals for learners that is consistent with Vygotsky's approach is for the teacher and the student to collaborate. Working together, the teacher and the student decide what skill or behavior needs work and then record the goal in such a way that the student's progress can be tracked through a specific time period. In addition to the goal, the teacher and student develop a set of guidelines for achieving the goal, so that they both know what is expected of them. When appropriate, other children in the classroom (or adults in the school, or parents, or other individuals) are recruited to help as well, and their participation is included as part of the general plan. The key to setting a learning goal is that the goal created must be within the reach of the child's abilities, but not so easily achieved that the child does not have to stretch those abilities to reach the goal. This point is emphasized in many theories of cognitive development, including Vygotsky's: If a task is too easy, the child will become bored; if the task is too hard, the child will give up in frustration.

> Learning goals establish the level of competence the student is to reach so that the teacher and student, working together, can design activities that will help the student reach those goals.

Classroomwide Learning Plans or Menus

A significant goal of any educational program is to teach students how to regulate their own learning behavior—to know what it is they need to learn as well as understand how to go about learning it. In the Tools of the Mind program, educators use classroomwide learning plans or learning menus to give students the tools they need to plan, monitor, and evaluate their own performance, with the eventual goal of their moving away from being monitored by the teacher to being self-monitored. A student might use such a classroomwide menu, for example, to confer with a classmate regarding the completion of assigned work. This kind of interaction helps both individuals involved—the student who is guided and the student who does the guiding. Instead of seeing the teacher as the only reliable source of assistance, the students see one another as such, and the more often they view their peers as primary sources of help, the less they will need the teacher to be there to help them. From this point, it's not a big jump from seeking help from a peer to seeing oneself as the helper, and from there to helping oneself. The goal is the student's self-reliance, a behavior that the student learns as he or she is gradually weaned from dependence on teachers and then from dependence on peers.

Vygotskian Math in Susquehanna, New York

Another example of an application of Vygotsky's approach comes from an educational project led by Jean Schmittau, an associate professor at the State University of New York at Binghamton. Schmittau went to Russia at the invitation of the Russian Academy of Education, where she observed math classes and found that the Russian students' understanding of both basic and advanced math concepts was well beyond the level at which they were instructed—in other words, the Russian students were taught how to learn, not just what they should know. Schmitt adapted the techniques she observed in Russia (which were based on the Vygotsky-related work of Russian psychologist V. V. Davidson) and applied them in a school program in Susquehanna, New York. The project, which is still in place, has proven to make mathematics accessible even to students who have done poorly in math previously (see Kantin, n.d.).

A COMPARISON OF VYGOTSKY AND PIAGET

What interesting works might have resulted if Piaget and Vygotsky could have gotten together over a cup of tea and talked about their respective ideas, given that they had so much in common. Sadly, this never took place, although in one of his books Vygotsky did have a chance to discuss Piaget's work, and Piaget discovered Vygotsky's work many years after the Russian's death. Although these two theorists never had the chance to discuss their work with each other, contemporary developmental psychologists have gained a great deal of knowledge and generated many new ideas as a result of comparing and contrasting their theories.

Piaget emphasized the child's contribution to thinking and cognition, whereas Vygotsky emphasized the contribution of the child's culture.

For both Piaget and Vygotsky, thought and language play predominant roles in the development of cognition. Perhaps the most significant difference between the two is that whereas Piaget believed that the child him- or herself is the most important source of cognition (and development), Vygotsky believed that the primary force in the development of the child's thinking ability is the child's social and cultural environment. That is, Piaget believed in the extension of the child's ideas from the child to the world; Vygotsky, in contrast, believed that the child is part of the world and that ideas originate and develop as a dialectical process. In Piaget's view, development results from a natural process, whereas for Vygotsky, the process is social, cultural, and historical. Thus Piaget looked to the invariant sequence of mental development (his four stages) and Vygotsky looked to the unending and orderly patterns of factors in a child's culture.

This is rather a fine distinction. Piaget views the child's world and its development from the perspective of the child, whereas Vygotsky views the world of the child and the child's development from the perspective of the culture in which the child develops. Although these viewpoints differ, when we understand both, we can see that they truly complement each other: They are two sides of the same coin, and any student of development needs to be well acquainted with both.

WEB SITES OF INTEREST

- "Vygotsky Resources," compiled by Siobhan Kolar and Lisa D'Ambrosio, at http://www.kolar.org/vygotsky: You can learn everything you want to know about Lev Vygotsky by exploring the Web links provided here, which cover everything from an extensive biography to a discussion of Vygotsky's theories to information for teachers. This list of resources is very comprehensive.
- "Lev Vygotsky Archive: 1896–1934," at http://www.marxists.org/archive/vygotsky: This site focuses especially on the Marxist roots of Vygotsky's work and on his writings that reflect that orientation. It includes a photo archive and reproductions of some of his original writings.
- "Vygotsky and Language Acquisition," by Ricardo Schütz, at http://www.sk.com.br/sk-vygot.html: Schütz reviews many of Vygotsky's central ideas concerning the importance of language for the development of cognition. He covers topics such as word meaning, social construction, and the origins of thought.

FURTHER READINGS ABOUT LEV VYGOTSKY AND THE SOCIAL COMPONENT OF COGNITION

Bark, Laura E., & Winkler, Adam. (1999). *Scaffolding children's learning: Vygotsky and early childhood education.* Washington, DC: National Association for the Education of Young Children.

This book is an excellent introduction to Vygotsky's perspective for early childhood educators. Bark and Winkler show how Vygotsky's theory can be applied to educational practices.

DeVries, Rheta. (2000). Vygotsky, Piaget, and education: A reciprocal assimilation of theories and educational practices. *New Ideas in Psychology, 18,* 187–213.

This article provides a comparison of the theories of Piaget and Vygotsky as well as a discussion of the two theorists' followers. Some of the similarities that DeVries mentions are the role that social factors play in child development and the transformative nature of thinking. Among the differences between the theories are their views on the nature of the stimulus and the role of self-regulation and novelty in development.

Matusov, Eugene, & Hayes, Renee. (2000). Sociocultural critique of Piaget and Vygotsky. *New Ideas in Psychology, 18,* 215–239.

Much of what Vygotsky has to say has been evaluated within the historical context of Piaget's theory. Matusov and Hayes discuss Piaget's and Vygotsky's ideas from a sociocultural viewpoint. Among several interesting points they make is their conclusion that there are historical reasons for similarities between the developmental approaches of these two theorists.

Vygodskaya, Gita L. (1999). Vygotsky and problems of special education. *Remedial and Special Education, 20,* 330–332.

It is noteworthy that theories of development are often applied across many different disciplines. In this article, Vygodskaya discusses Vygotsky's contributions to the study, upbringing, and education of disabled children. Vygotsky rejected the idea that such children should be treated as charity cases; instead, he saw them as being ready for integration into "normal" life.

PART VI

A COMPARATIVE ANALYSIS

CHAPTER **11**

COMPARING THEORIES OF HUMAN DEVELOPMENT

In every child who is born, under no matter what circumstances, and of no matter what parents, the potentiality of the human race is born again.

—James Agee

The most powerful factors in the world are clear ideas in the minds of energetic men of good will.

—J. Arthur Thomson

The best ideas are common property.

—Seneca

We are prisoners of ideas.

—Ralph Waldo Emerson

The preceding 10 chapters have introduced you to some of the major theories of human development and to the theorists responsible for them. As you have seen, the diversity of ideas about and approaches to the study of development are as varied as human behavior itself.

This closing chapter has three purposes. The first is to present an overview of the current status of developmental theory. This discussion covers several areas: the comparability of different theories, how effectively various theories explain or predict future outcomes, the differences in the language used by different theorists to describe similar theoretical assumptions, and the issue of whether any theory is "superior" to any other. The second purpose of this chapter is to provide a review of the general approaches to understanding development by evaluating each against Sidman's (1960) six criteria (first discussed in Chapter 1): inclusiveness, consistency, accuracy, relevance, fruitfulness, and simplicity. Finally, we return to the seven questions listed in Chapter 2, which we have used throughout the book as tools for examining the different approaches, and compare the perspectives presented here in light of those questions.

THE STATUS OF DEVELOPMENTAL THEORY

Comparability of Theories

Regardless of theoretical orientation, all theories of development advance from the subject matter of behavior. However, even though different theories of development describe similar phenomena (such as the development of language), the theories are not necessarily comparable with one another. It is difficult to compare theories (and the more general models from which they are derived) when they are based on radically different worldviews, or sets of basic assumptions. For example, theories of development that are based in the behavioral model view the individual as a passive participant who simply reacts to changes in the environment, whereas theories based in the organismic model view the individual as an active participant in the developmental process. There are fundamental differences among theories concerning other issues as well, such as the influence of heredity versus environment and whether the process of development is continuous or discontinuous.

Each developmental theory has its own unique focus as well. For many people, Freud's psychoanalytic theory represents the most valid approach to understanding the development of personality and abnormal behavior. These same people may at the same time believe that Piaget's theory represents a bold and innovative analysis of the way cognitive development takes place. This may be the case even though Freud's and Piaget's views of development are clearly quite different, not only in their central foci, but in their philosophical assumptions.

Developmental psychologists frequently attempt to combine what they consider to be the best qualities of different theories to produce eclectic models that have little philosophical or theoretical rationale of their own. They usually end up with a little bit of everything and not much of anything—which is the problem with many "pop psychology" movements. An eclectic model of development, one that borrows ideas and concepts from different theories, may be useful for understanding a behavior in isolation, but it is unlikely to provide a reliable theoretical account of how development occurs. As noted in Chapter 1, at least one purpose of a theory is to examine relationships among different facts or ideas.

Although the lack of any underlying rationale may prevent eclectic models from being fully successful as theory, many practitioners who work with children are interested primarily in what works best for given purposes. For example, a pediatrician who is treating a child who wets the bed is usually more interested in how techniques based in operant psychology can be used to change the child's behavior than in the philosophical foundations of behaviorism.

In sum, it may be questionable whether it is worthwhile to try to compare different theories of human development, given that the substantive foci of these theories vary so widely. One good reason for comparing theories, however, is to shed light on how they operate; in addition, the focus of one theory might suggest directions worth pursuing within the guidelines of another.

Explanation and Prediction

An effective theory must include specific mechanisms to explain past outcomes and predict future ones (two important purposes of any theory, as noted in Chapter 1). Most of the theoretical descriptions of behavior discussed in the preceding chapters include mechanisms for understanding what has happened and for predicting what will happen.

For example, a great deal of Freud's developmental theory is based on the importance of past experiences and how these experiences form the foundation for later behavior. Freud calls these early predictors of behavior "prototypes," which may be defined as "the original mode[s] of adjusting to a painful or disturbing state" (Hall, 1954, p. 104). In other words, a prototype serves as a model for later adaptations. The individual who sought a reduction in tension, and thus satisfaction, through aggressive acts when very young is likely to use a similar strategy later on in life when placed in a similar set of circumstances. This notion of a prototype may be an effective conceptual tool for understanding the relationship between early and later behaviors, or continuity. Within the psychodynamic model, the only mechanism for predicting future outcomes is past behavior. Historically, researchers working within this model have used case studies; although such studies provide rich detail, they are also highly subjective, and so do not lend themselves to reliable replication over extended periods.

The behavioral perspective focuses on the history of the individual as well as on the current set of environmental influences. For example, we know that if we want to understand the fears a child has about the dark, we should examine the experiences the child has had during the nighttime in the past as well as the child's current nighttime experiences. We might also operate on the assumption that if the conditions are similar from one point in time to another, then the same set of responses might be expected to occur. This assumption grants individual passivity a somewhat extreme role, given that people bring different sets of experiences to the same environmental settings at different times. This might be one reason that behavioral approaches that stress the importance of intervening or mediating variables (such as the theories of Sears and Bandura) have been met with some degree of acceptance by a large number of developmentalists.

Differences in Language

Different theories of development tend to use different terms to describe very similar phenomena, and these phenomena, although similar, assume different positions of importance within particular theories. As noted in Chapter 2, one of the hallmarks of science is that it is a process of building on the work of others. Thus, even though different theorists might not work during the same period, they are generally familiar with the work done by others in their own fields as well as in other fields. Just as Freud borrowed the principle of the conservation of energy from physics, many theorists have found that elements within the work of others serve them well.

As noted in Chapter 2, there are a number of developmental trends that all humans share. Although there are unquestionably some universals in development, as we have seen throughout this book, specific theories address these universals within language frames that best fit the theories' assumptions. Thus, as noted above, different theories may address similar phenomena, but the language they use to describe those phenomena might be very different.

For example, certain theories of development describe forces that oppose each other ("push and pull") and the organism's constant need to seek some kind of balance or resolution (equilibrium, homeostasis, synthesis). Freud's theory addresses such conflicts (the Oedipus and Electra complexes, for example), and Piaget's posits a similar kind of mechanism through the functional invariants of organization and adaptation. Within both these theoretical perspectives, the individual is understood to be continually reorganizing structural mechanisms in response to changes in the environment. Although there is always some pressure to remain at a level that conserves energy and does not demand additional output, the motivation to reach out and explore is often very strong. Gesell's theory includes the concept of reciprocal interweaving, which is the process through which oppositional forces reach some level of physical equilibrium, or balance. Although all of these concepts are similar, they do not represent equally important constructs within the different theories, and the language attached to them differs as well, reflecting the basic assumptions of the theories. It is a mistake to assume that because these different phenomena are comparable to one another the language used to describe them is purely ornamental. Rather, the differences in language reflect the fundamentally different worldviews represented by these theories.

Superiority of Theories

In general, given that theories of human development are based on different assumptions and have historically assumed different roles in the study of human behavior, it is not fruitful to assert that any one is superior to any other (although individual scientists certainly have their favorites). Certainly, one theory might do a better job of explaining certain kinds of outcomes than another; a theory that focuses on a particular outcome probably has the best tools to describe and explain that outcome. For example, Gesell's detailed descriptions of child growth and development have been useful to millions of parents, but his writings don't provide a detailed analysis of unacceptable behavior in children and how parents might handle it. Similarly, ethological approaches give us valuable insight into the formation of parenting behaviors early in the infant's development, but they don't address other phenomena as thoroughly.

Bijou and Baer's functional analysis approach and Piaget's genetic epistemology have similar advantages and disadvantages. Bijou and Baer's most significant contribution to the study of developmental psychology is their detailed and systematic analysis of the environment and of the way in which stimulus events establish and maintain control over the developmental process. But because of the behavioral philosophy that their theory follows, it may exclude an important source of information by ignoring certain internal changes in the individual ("How I feel").

Piaget's theory of cognitive development is best recognized for its detailed description of the different stages of cognitive development and for its theoretical explanation of the transitions between these stages. Many people have called Piaget an interactionist because he places great importance on the biological and environmental influences that surround the developmental process. One criticism of Piaget's theory focuses on its preoccupation with structural changes, represented by overt behaviors, and its relative lack of description of experiences that might help us to understand different behavioral outcomes. This criticism has encouraged some developmental psychologists to look more closely at the role of the ecology of human development—that is, the events surrounding developmental change.

EVALUATING THEORIES OF DEVELOPMENT

Chapter 1 introduced Sidman's (1960) six criteria against which any theory can be evaluated: inclusiveness, consistency, accuracy, relevance, fruitfulness, and simplicity. If we assume that these are all qualities a good developmental theory should have, it is useful to discuss how the different theoretical viewpoints discussed in this book rate on each of these qualities.

Table 11.1 presents absolute ratings (not relative rankings) for each of the four general kinds of theories addressed in this volume on each of Sidman's six criteria. The ratings shown in the table are based on a 3-point scale as follows:

1 = The theory meets the criterion very well.

2 = The theory meets the criterion.

3 = The theory probably does not meet the criterion very well.

The scale has only three points because the task is such a difficult one. Clearly, if the scale had only two points ("meets the criterion" and "does not meet the criterion"), the rating task would be easier, but it would not be more accurate; more gradations in the scale allow for more discrimination between theories. We could use a 6-, 8-, or 10-point scale instead of a scale with only 3 points, but then it would be far too difficult to rate the theoretical perspectives, because each rating would require very fine discriminations. We would become bogged down in minutiae and lose our focus on bigger issues.

Inclusiveness

When we evaluate the inclusiveness of a theory, we are interested in how comprehensive the theory is. In other words, how many and what kinds of events can the theory explain? Does it represent a narrow view of the world, or does it cover a broad, far-reaching arena of possible outcomes?

It is also important to recognize that there are two different types of inclusiveness. First, a theory may be quantitatively inclusive; that is, it may explain (or attempt to explain) many different kinds of events. Second, a theory may be inclusive in that it is content free; that is, it can stand independent of any specific content. For example, the theory of relativity, which assumes that a hypothesis can be tested regardless of the nature of the content, is highly inclusive. Developmental theories that are highly inclusive are not tied to specific content; rather, they make statements about the general nature of behavior.

TABLE 11.1 Ratings of Four Kinds of Theories on Sidman's Criteria

| The Criterion and the Question It Asks | Model of Development | | | |
	Biological	Psychodynamic	Behavioral	Cognitive
Inclusiveness: How many different phenomena does the theory address?	3	3	1	1
Consistency: How well can the theory explain new things without having its basic assumptions changed?	3	1	1	2
Accuracy: How well can the theory predict future outcomes and explain past ones?	1	3	1	2
Relevance: How closely is the theory related to the information collected within that theory? That is, how well does it reflect the facts?	3	2	1	2
Fruitfulness: How well does the theory generate new ideas and directions for inquiry?	3	1	2	2
Simplicity: How simple or unencumbered is the theory? That is, how easy is it to understand?	2	3	1	2

NOTE: 1 = theory meets criterion well; 2 = theory meets criterion; 3 = theory does not meet criterion well.

The behavioral model of development is probably the most comprehensive and inclusive of any of the models discussed in this book: It addresses the process of development with little concern for the type of content or behavior that characterizes that process. The fact that so many of the principles of operant psychology are applicable to animals as well as to humans (remember, the emphasis is on behaviors, not organisms) demonstrates this lack of emphasis on the content of behavior. One criticism directed at the behavioral model, however, is that because its only focus is process, additional theorizing within this model cannot lead to anything new. In other words, if we understand how reinforcement works, no future use of the technique is likely to generate new knowledge or new questions. This is not entirely the case, however; in recent years, behaviorists have been working to extend the model, especially in areas such as cognitive behavior modification and social learning theory, where new questions are being generated.

The cognitive-developmental and organismic theories share some characteristics with theories based on the behavioral model in terms of inclusiveness. They are relatively content free (although they do deal with content areas such as cognition and moral development), but they are best represented by the dual processes of organization and adaptation.

In contrast to these two models, psychodynamic and biological or maturational models tend to be highly content specific. For example, the psychodynamic model provides a very comprehensive perspective on human development, yet it is also the most highly content specific. It leaves little room for a distinction between the process of development and the outcomes that result from that process. For example, conflicts such as those that occur during the phallic stage of development (the Oedipus and Electra complexes) are clearly defined on the basis of content. For Gesell's maturational theory, the case seems to be similar: It is highly content specific and more comprehensive than either behavioral or organismic models. Gesell's description of development is less inclusive than that offered by the psychodynamic model; it concentrates primarily on physical development and deals only peripherally with issues such as emotional and social development. Gesell's five principles of maturational development have never been applied to other dimensions of development, although the potential for such application exists.

Consistency

When a theory is consistent, it is capable of explaining new phenomena without changing its basic assumptions. In other words, in rating a theory on consistency, we want to look at how effectively it can explain new events without those explanations requiring the alteration of the theory's basic framework. For example, say that a developmental psychologist discovers that infant girls can recognize the sound of their mothers' voices during the first 6 hours after birth but infant boys cannot. If the theory within which the psychologist is working can explain this difference easily, the theory is consistent. If the theory's basic assumptions must change to allow the theory to explain the difference, it is not consistent.

Consistency is an important quality in a theory. As noted in Chapter 1, a crucial part of theory development is the reassessment of ideas and hypotheses—an ongoing attempt to improve consistency. A "good" theory can incorporate new events with minimal alteration.

The psychodynamic model is probably the most consistent of all the models we have examined. It can be applied easily and efficiently to aspects of behavior outside of those on which the model was originally based. This does not mean that psychoanalytic theory can describe all these events with the same degree of validity, however. Indeed, many critics of the psychodynamic model believe that because the assumptions of the model are basically untestable (for example, there is no operational definition of the id), the issue of consistency is not relevant to this model. That is, the theory may explain a lot of events, but the explanations are questionable. Because the basic assumptions of the theory are not open to examination, whether the model is consistent or not depends on the evaluator's point of view.

The contrast in consistency between the behavioral and psychodynamic models is very interesting. The psychodynamic model is consistent because it is highly inclusive, whereas the behavioral model is consistent because it is relatively content free. Both models attempt to explain and can explain many different things.

The cognitive-developmental and maturational, or biological, models seem to be somewhat less consistent. For example, the maturational model focuses on biological change, and few attempts (beyond writings in the mass literature) have been made to apply it to social, emotional, and psychological development. Historically, it has been very important, but it has not been successful at explaining behaviors outside of its basic formulation. The cognitive-developmental and organismic models are more consistent than the maturational model, but are also somewhat limited. They focus generally on the areas of cognitive and moral development, with little application to other areas of development. Currently, some work is being done within these models as they apply to imitation and other variables, but to date this work has been focused in a few specific areas.

Lack of consistency is not necessarily a serious fault in a theory. If a theory is largely content specific, then perhaps it should not be judged as a theory of human development, but rather as a theory of personality, or maturation, or sex differences. Perhaps one of the reasons some theories are so vulnerable to criticism is that they have been applied to too many settings or to inappropriate ones.

Accuracy

A theory is accurate if it can predict outcomes with a relatively high degree of success. In other words, a theory's accuracy is determined by how well it predicts certain relationships between variables.

The least predictive of all the models discussed in this volume is probably the psychodynamic model. This is true only because no real criterion for accuracy is defined within the model. In effect, most of the predictions are done ex post facto—that is, after the fact. Freud's theory places little if any emphasis on the manipulation of variables in a true experimental sense, and it is very difficult to conclude, based on this theory, exactly what influences in the individual's life are responsible for what kinds of changes. Similarly, the cognitive-developmental model is not highly accurate. It does do a good job of predicting the sequence and content of stages (global predictions), but it is limited by its lack of operationality in definitions of crucial terms (such as *schema* and *structure*). It is often difficult to predict or evaluate outcomes when the criteria are not clearly operationalized and in some cases are artificial.

On the other hand, both biological and behavioral theories provide a high degree of accuracy. The primary focus of Gesell's theory is normative behavior, and the large body of norms that Gesell assembled has high predictive validity in terms of what behaviors can be expected at what ages (as far as biological growth is concerned). Under controlled conditions, behavioral theories can accurately predict certain outcomes as well. In fact, the behaviorist would say the only reason we cannot predict all behaviors is that no one has yet developed a technology that is sufficiently sensitive to allow us to study all the dimensions of development, including emotion, cognition, and the complete consequences of our actions.

Relevance

A theory is relevant if it represents the data collected within it; that is, it reflects the facts. This criterion is difficult to apply, because it is not always clear what comes first, theory or data. As noted in Chapter 1, the development of a theory is an ongoing process between confirmation (or disconfirmation) of hypotheses and reevaluation of the theoretical assumptions that generated the hypotheses in the first place.

It is difficult to measure the relevance of the psychodynamic model, for example, because it is hard to tell (given the vague definitions that accompany the model) what variables are important. If a hypothesis concerns conflicts that occur during the Oedipal period, for instance, the variables should be tied as logically as possible to the underlying structure of the theory. In psychoanalytic theory this is often very difficult. The same may be true for the cognitive-developmental model, which dictates that the data collected represent some underlying operation. Some critics of the organismic and psychodynamic models raise the question of whether it is reasonable to proceed based on the assumption that the data you collect represent the phenomenon you are interested in studying.

The behavioral and biological models, in contrast, seem to have relatively high degrees of relevance. The foci of both models (and the behaviors of interest) are explicitly defined, in part because the behaviors almost directly represent the theory. For example, Gesell based his principle of developmental direction on the cephalocaudal (head-to-tail) and proximodistal (near-to-far) trends he observed in all the infants he studied. In the behavioral approach, behaviors are defined in a highly operational way, and those definitions give development an almost one-to-one relationship with behavior.

Fruitfulness

Fruitfulness may be the most important quality a theory can have when it comes to the value of the theory to the overall goal of understanding the developmental process. When a theory generates new questions for future research, it is fruitful. Fruitful theories are also sometimes described as *heuristic* or *generative*.

The theories that tend to be most fruitful are those that are least accurate and least relevant. Psychoanalytic theory continues to produce a rich legacy of new questions about human development, in part because this theory is extremely complex. Often, the more multifaceted the theory, the more potential it has for providing new directions. Many of the theories of psychological development that are popularized through the mass media are heuristic in the sense that they generate additional questions.

On the other extreme, the biological or maturational view does not seem very fruitful at all. It has had widespread influence on child-rearing and parenting practices, but it has not generated many new directions for further study.

Finally, the behavioral and cognitive-developmental models seem comparatively fruitful. Both have recently been the subjects of a great deal of controversy, in large part because they have been applied in educational settings. The social importance of extending these theories into applied settings acts as a catalyst for generating new ideas and future directions. Perhaps these two viewpoints are the most fruitful in their usefulness to applied settings.

Simplicity

A simple theory is economical, or parsimonious. When we evaluate the simplicity of a theory, we look at how complex it needs to be to explain behavior. A good example of a simple theory is the germ theory of disease, which needs only one or two postulates to refute the idea of the spontaneous generation of disease.

The psychodynamic model of development is not simple at all; on the contrary, it is very cumbersome. It does not make many basic assumptions about human development, but for the theory to be workable, the assumptions it does make must be accompanied by a great deal of detail.

The biological or maturational and cognitive-developmental models are somewhat simple, but they still require more elaboration than the behavioral model to be effective according to this criterion. Gesell's theory includes only five principles, but it is limited in its applicability. The organismic theory also presents relatively few principles (organization and adaptation), but it includes a detailed group of laws and axioms. It seems that the more content free a theory is, the simpler it is as well.

TABLE 11.2   Important Issues in Development

The Issue	The Question We Ask
The nature of development	What is the major force that influences the course of development?
The process that guides development	What is the underlying process primarily responsible for changes in development?
The importance of age	What role does age play as a general marker of changes in development?
The rate of development	Are there certain sensitive or critical periods during development, and, if so, how are they related to the rate of change?
The shape of development	Is development smooth and continuous, or do changes occur in abrupt stages?
The origins of individual differences	How does the theory explain differences in development between individuals of the same chronological age?
The method used to study development	What methods are used to study development, and how do they affect the content of the theory?

A SUMMARY

At various points throughout this book, summaries of the theoretical viewpoints have been presented through discussions of the differences among them on such important issues as the roles played in development by heredity, environment, and age. A major portion of Chapter 2 is devoted to these differences, because you cannot fully appreciate the theoretical orientations presented without understanding how they differ from one another.

In this final section, we return to six of the seven questions first presented in Chapter 2 (reproduced here in Table 11.2) to gain a better understanding of the substantive differences among the theories discussed in this book. This review does not address the final question in the list, concerning the methodologies used by researchers working within the different perspectives, because methodologies are determined by the research questions being asked, and researchers with very different viewpoints often ask very similar questions.

- *Question 1:* What is the major force that influences the course of development?

Developmental theories point to two primary influences on development: genetic, or hereditary, influences and forces located in the environment. The focus of this question is, Which one of these is the greater influence? Although certain theoretical views are aligned with one side or the other in the heredity/environment debate, it should be clear to you by now that most theoretical stances on this issue are not black-and-white.

Within biologically based views of development, such as that offered by Gesell as well as ethologists and sociobiologists, heredity influences are considered to be paramount. Even though the "recapitulation" argument made in the early years of the 20th century has been disputed, the notion that our ancestors contributed genes that control major dimensions of our behavior has had a profound influence on the formulation of developmental theory. As the work of the Human Genome Project progresses, we will learn more about the relationships between genes (and maturation) and behavior.

A variety of theorists, especially those with strong behavioral orientations, view heredity as contributing only the basic building blocks of behavior, which are then acted on and shaped by the environment. Different behaviorists endorse the importance of the environment to differing degrees, but all believe that the environment is the primary influence on development.

- *Question 2:* What is the underlying process primarily responsible for changes in development?

Two distinct yet overlapping processes combine to produce the developmental outcomes that psychologists study: maturation and learning. Whereas Question 1, above, focuses on *what* influences development, Question 2 is concerned with the mechanism, or the "how," of development.

The strongest proponents of the viewpoint that maturation is the guiding force in development are the biological or maturational theorists, as represented by Gesell. Sociobiologists would argue for maturation just as strongly, but they are unable to back up such arguments with data; too little information is available on humans within a sociobiological context because of the impractical nature of testing these theorists' ideas. As you might expect, the strongest proponents of the idea that the process of learning is the paramount influence in development are theorists who take the behavioral viewpoint, such as Skinner, Bijou, and Baer.

What is most interesting about the maturation/learning question is how theorists who fall somewhere between the two "extremes" incorporate the influences of both into their theoretical formulations. For example, Piaget is often viewed as an "interactionist," that is, a theorist who emphasizes the importance for development of the interaction between the organism and the environment. He does, however, assert that maturational processes set the stage for structural changes to take place in the developing organism. Vygotsky also certainly emphasizes the notion that the child must be ready for learning before an outside social agent can have any impact.

- *Question 3:* What role does age play as a general marker of changes in development?

As you have seen in the discussions presented in the preceding chapters, the importance placed on age varies widely among different theories of development: the variable of age can assume a preeminent position, or it may be of little importance, or it may have no importance at all. Some theorists even imply that there is some danger in relying on age as a marker of development.

On one extreme is Gesell's theory, in which age assumes the important role of an organizing variable. What is interesting, however, is that the idea that age has "predictive" powers (e.g., the "terrible twos") probably did not gain prominence until Gesell's work was popularized through its direct application to child-rearing problems. It's difficult to know, but it is possible that Gesell himself did not mean to imply that age plays any kind of causal role, despite what some proponents of his theory believe.

At the other extreme, age is relatively unimportant for cognitive-developmental and organismic theorists, as well as for those working within the psychodynamic model. Although age ranges are mentioned within each of these approaches in relation to the notion of stages of development, the theorists emphasize that the stages occur concurrently with changes in age, but not necessarily as a direct result of aging. This is evidenced by the fact that the different stages are understood to occur over a great range of ages.

Finally, some theorists, especially certain behaviorists, point out that there are times when considering age can distract attention from variables that are far more important to development. From the functional analysis perspective, for example, including age in an analysis of what kinds of behaviors occur when might just confuse matters, because age may be an irrelevant factor.

- *Question 4:* Are there certain sensitive or critical periods during development?

The answer to this question has particularly significant implications for real-world applications of what we know about human development. For example, one of the major questions that developmental psychologists ask is, What are the effects of early experience on later behavior? This topic has particular importance for the design of intervention programs aimed at improving the lives of developmentally disadvantaged children. Yet the critical question of when such interventions should be offered so that they have the greatest impact is very difficult to answer.

From the point of view of those theoretical approaches that emphasize the importance of heredity and biological operations, there may be particular times when the organism is most receptive to factors that can influence development. For example, the absence of one parent might have little impact on a newborn, but a great deal of impact on a 3-year-old. On the other hand, some theorists believe that any child of any age can learn any subject if it is taught in an "intellectually honest" way; this viewpoint clearly de-emphasizes the importance of critical or sensitive periods. From this perspective, which is endorsed by many behaviorists, the developing organism is seen as being untied to the constraints of nature in terms of potential for change.

- *Question 5:* Is development smooth and continuous, or do changes occur in abrupt stages?

If you meet a child when he is a month old and then don't see him again until he is 6 months old, one of your reactions on that second visit is undoubtedly going to be, "What a change!" If you had seen that child every day from the age of 1 month to 6 months, however, it is likely that you would be much less impressed by the same degree of change. The two views of the process of development contrasted in this question can be compared with your two possible perceptions of the changes in this hypothetical child. On one hand, development may be understood to take place very smoothly, with day-to-day changes barely noticeable. On the other hand, development may perceived as taking place through changes that are so abrupt it is sometimes difficult to see how one level of development relates to the next.

In the past, theorists who saw developmental change as a smooth process, in which what comes later is more of what was there before, tended to be relatively behavioral in their orientation. Behaviorists believe that the changes that occur throughout development are not structural in nature and, hence, not qualitative. The opposite viewpoint, favoring the abrupt quality associated with qualitative change, characterizes many psychoanalytic and cognitive-developmental theorists. These theorists' concept of development as occurring in stages lends itself to the idea that transitions are abrupt, and the very nature of these transitions often provides the most important and provocative information about development.

Keep in mind, however, that the process of development may seem to be discontinuous (or jagged) or continuous (or smooth) in shape depending on the way we look at it, and not because either discontinuity or continuity is the nature of the phenomenon itself. If you look at the process too closely, you see only a small part, and if you look from too far away, you miss the detail.

- *Question 6:* How does the theory explain differences in development between individuals of the same chronological age?

It is almost startling to think that all of the 60,000 people in a stadium watching a football game look very different from one another. And just as they differ in physical appearance, they differ in patterns of behavior, likes and dislikes, and attitudes.

Most theories of development would dismiss the hypothesis that we are born with certain attitudes, beliefs, and abilities. Although some theories may base certain views on the philosophical premise that some abilities are inborn, this is not a major assumption of any of the perspectives discussed in this book. In order to understand the differences among people, most theories focus on individuals' histories and present environments as these interact with some biological givens. Perhaps the most interesting thing about the different theories' answers to this question is that they exhibit more overlap concerning the influence of heredity versus environment and maturation versus learning than do answers to any of the other questions.

Although those who take a behavioral view would no doubt stress the importance of a history of reinforcement, whereas those who take a psychodynamic approach would focus on the important early years, neither group can ignore the importance of all potential factors as they relate to individual differences. The primary reason for this is that psychologists are still not very good at understanding the degree of correspondence between the cause of a behavior (whether it is the resolution of a conflict or the frequency with which a reinforcer is delivered) and the behavior itself. Even if we view behavior as being independent of any underlying structure, we are still somewhat ambivalent as to what we might call covert, or underlying, behaviors and the role they play in development. It's easy enough to recognize hitting a baseball for what it is, but it is much more difficult to understand complex interactions between people or personal feelings.

Individual differences are the essence of what makes the study of behavior so fascinating. By understanding the viewpoints of the various developmental theories discussed in this volume, we can better understand these differences and, in turn, gain some new insights into people's behaviors.

GLOSSARY

Accommodation　The process of modifying existing schemes to satisfy the requirements of a new experience

Accuracy　A theory's ability to predict future events or explain past ones correctly; one of Sidman's six criteria against which a theory should be measured

Action-specific energy　The energy associated with a signed stimulus

Adaptation　The process through which an individual adjusts to the environment

Assimilation　The process through which an individual incorporates new experiences into already existing schemata or structures

Attachment　The process of forming a bond with another individual

Baseline period　A period during which a researcher observes a subject's behavior without regard to reinforcing or punishing stimulus events

Behaviorism　A perspective on development that has as its basis the laws of different types of learning

Bioecological model　A theoretical model that emphasizes the unique contribution that the individual and the environment, working together, make to development

Castration anxiety　The anxiety associated with the castration complex

Castration complex　Within Freudian theory, the fear on the part of a young male that his father will punish him (through castration) for having incestuous feelings about his mother

Cephalocaudal trend　The tendency of development to progress in a head-to-toe direction

Chaining　The process through which a stimulus that acts as a reinforcer for one event becomes a discriminative stimulus for the next

Chemical event   An environmental stimulus that acts at a distance from the organism

Chronological age   The length of time an individual has been alive; a simplistic measure of development

Classical conditioning   The process through which an unconditioned response become paired with a previously neutral stimulus

Concrete operational stage   The third of Piaget's four stages of cognitive development, characterized by the individual's use of operations

Conditioned response (or **conditioned reflex**)   The process through which an originally neutral stimulus takes on the qualities of an unconditioned response

Conditioned stimulus   A stimulus event that takes on the qualities of an unconditioned stimulus after multiple pairings

Confounding   Lack of clarity about which of two or more variables is responsible for observed outcomes

Conscience   What the child thinks his or her parents think is right or wrong

Conservation   The cognitive operation of being able to consider more than one dimension of an experience simultaneously

Conservative quality of instincts   Instincts' tendency to use the least amount of energy necessary to move toward the goal object

Consistency   A theory's ability to explain new discoveries without a need for changes in the assumptions on which the theory is based; one of Sidman's six criteria against which a theory should be measured

Construct   A group of variables that are related to each other

Continuous process view of development   A view of developmental change as occurring in small, gradual steps, with outcomes that are not qualitatively different from what was present earlier, and in which the same general laws underlie the process at all points along the developmental continuum

Continuous reinforcement   The reinforcement of a behavior every time it occurs

Co-twin control research method   A research method in which one of two identical twins is trained on a physical task and then both twins are tested on the task when they are maturationally ready for it; used by Gesell to study the importance of maturation

Cross-sectional sequential design A research design used in studies of development in which different subjects are observed from one testing time to the next

Cross-sectional study A research design used in studies of development in which subjects from different age groups are observed at one point in time

Defense mechanism In Freudian theory, a technique the ego uses to distort reality when the individual faces situations that pose a danger to healthy psychological development

Development A progressive series of changes that occur in a predictable pattern as the result of interactions between biological and environmental factors

Developmental task A psychological task that an individual must complete at a given point in his or her development to progress to the next stage of development and thus, eventually, reach happiness and satisfaction

Differentiation The selective reinforcement of certain associations and the lack of reinforcement of others

Discontinuous process view of development A view of developmental change as occurring in abrupt shifts, in which outcomes are qualitatively different from what existed before and different general laws characterize developmental changes

Discriminative stimulus An event that signals that a behavior will be followed by some type of reinforcer or punisher

Ecological pressure Aspects of the environment that place pressure on the organism to change

Ecology of human development The study of the interaction between a growing organism and the changing immediate environment in which it lives

Ego In Freudian theory, the executor of the individual's conscious wishes

Ego ideal What the child thinks is right or wrong

Egocentric speech Speech that is focused on the individual's worldview

Egocentrism In general, a trend toward seeing (and thinking about) oneself as the center of one's everyday life

Electra complex In Freudian theory, the group of feelings and unconscious desires that occurs in females during the development of the superego, when daughters experience uncomfortable feelings toward their fathers

Enactive mode of representation A stage in Bruner's theory of intellectual growth that is characterized by action

Epigenesis   The concept that each mental event has a unique time of ascendancy, the plan for which is contained in the organism's genes

Ethogram   An inventory or description created by an ethologist as he or she observes and tracks a subject's behavior over time

Ethology   The study of behaviors that are rooted in evolutionary and biological backgrounds

Evolution   The process through which organisms change and adapt as a result of forces in the environment; also referred to as *natural selection*

Evolutionary psychology   The study of the influence of biology on behavior

External signs   Vygotsky's third stage of development, formulated particularly as it applies to the development of language

Extinction   The result on an operant behavior of the lack of reward for that behavior

Fixed action pattern   A series of connected behaviors that form a pattern as a response to an individual stimulus or a set of stimuli

Fixed schedule of reinforcement   A schedule of support in which reinforcements are delivered based on the number or frequency of behaviors

Formal operational stage   The fourth of Piaget's four stages of cognitive development, characterized by hypothetico-deductive thinking

Fruitfulness   A theory's ability to generate new questions; one of Sidman's six criteria against which a theory should be measured

Generalization   A conditioned response to a conditioned stimulus

Genotype   An organism's genetic endowment

Hypothesis   An educated guess that posits an "if . . . then" relationship between variables

Iconic mode of representation   The stage in Bruner's theory of development in which the child uses mental images of objects or pictures to represent the acquisition of knowledge and to foster understanding of the world

Id   In Freud's psychosexual theory, the structural component that is fueled by libidinal energy and is directed at satisfying the individual's basic instincts

Identification   In Freudian theory, the course through which the organism begins to employ ego processes to achieve gratification

Inclusiveness   A theory's ability to address a wide variety of phenomena; one of Sidman's six criteria against which a theory should be measured

Ingrowth   Vygotsky's fourth stage of development, formulated particularly as it applies to the development of language

Innate releasing mechanism   An internal mechanism that precipitates a host of complex behaviors

Instinct   An unlearned psychological drive

Interactional model   A theoretical model in which heredity and environment are considered to interact 100% of the time; that is, as influences on the developing human, the two cannot be separated

Intermittent reinforcement   The reinforcement of a behavior based on a random schedule of responses

Interval schedule of reinforcement   A schedule of support in which reinforcements are delivered based on the passage of time between responses

Law of frequency   A law that states that as the frequency of an S-R connection occurs, the stronger it will become

Law of recency   A law that states that the more recently a particular stimulus has been associated with a particular response, the more likely it is the association will occur again

Learning   A change in behavior as a result of direct or indirect experience

Longitudinal sequential design   A study design used in developmental research in which subjects from different cohorts are compared when they have reached the same ages

Longitudinal study   A study design in which participants are observed over more than one point in time

Maturation   A biological process in which developmental changes are controlled by internal (or endogenous) factors

Mode of representation   In Bruner's theory, one of three ways in which knowledge can be represented

Naive psychology   Vygotsky's second stage of development, formulated particularly as it applies to the development of language

Nativist model   A theoretical model in which hereditary factors are considered to be the primary influence on development

Natural selection The term Darwin initially used to describe species' adaptation and change; later called *evolution* or *descent with modification*

Natural stage (or **primitive stage**) Vygotsky's first stage of development, formulated particularly as it applies to the development of language

Negative reinforcer A stimulus that, on its withdrawal, results in an increase in the probability that a behavior will occur again

Nurturist model A model of development in which environmental factors are considered to be the primary influence on developmental changes

Oedipus complex In Freudian theory, the uncomfortable group of feelings and unconscious desires that young males feel toward their mothers during the development of the superego

Ontogeny The development of an individual

Operant learning Learning that is controlled by the consequences of behaviors

Operation In Piaget's theory, an action that is performed mentally and is reversible

Oral stage of development The first stage in Freud's model of development, during which psychic energy focuses on and is invested in and around the mouth

Organ pleasure Physical sensation associated with the reduction of tension

Organismic event A biological or maturational event that provides stimulation for the organism

Organization The tendency to combine physical and/or psychological processes into a coherent whole

Overlap Categorization of a research subject in one group on the basis of one variable (such as age) when that subject is also at one extreme on another variable relative to that group

Penis envy In Freudian theory, anxiety associated with the Electra complex

Phenotype The physical expression of an individual's genetic endowment

Phylogenetic inertia The tendency of an organism to remain genetically unchanged

Phylogeny The development of a species

Physical event A stimulus event that is produced by humans or occurs naturally

Pleasure principle In Freudian theory, the principle that states that the individual's primary goal is the achievement of pleasure through gratification

Positive reinforcer A stimulus event that, on its presentation, increases the likelihood of a behavior occurring again

Preformationist A person who takes the theoretical viewpoint that all characteristics and qualities of humans are preformed at birth

Preoperational stage The second of Piaget's four stages of cognitive development, characterized by language and egocentric thought

Primary process thinking Thinking that has as its purpose the fulfillment of basic needs and instincts

Principle of developmental direction The principle that states that development is not random but follows occurs in predetermined directions (cephalocaudal and proximodistal)

Principle of functional asymmetry The principle that states that the organism goes through periods of asymmetric or unbalanced development in order to achieve a measure of maturity at later stages

Principle of individuating maturation The principle that states that an internal growth matrix acts as a mechanism to establish the direction and pattern of development of the individual

Principle of reciprocal interweaving The principle that states that inhibition and excitation of different muscles operate in complementary fashion to produce efficient movement

Principle of self-regulatory fluctuation The principle that states that developmental progress fluctuates between periods of instability and stability, or active growth and consolidation

Proximodistal trend The tendency of development to progress from near to far

Psychic energy In Freudian theory, the unconscious energy behind, and driving, the psychodynamic system

Psychosexual stages The stages of development within Freud's psychosexual theory, each of which is based on, but qualitatively distinct from, the others and invariant in its appearance

Psychosocial theory Erikson's model of psychodynamic development, which emphasizes the resolution of psychosocial conflicts at different stages across the life span

Punisher A stimulus event that follows a behavior and decreases the likelihood of its occurring again

Punishment   The act of presenting a stimulus event that decreases the likelihood that a given behavior will occur again

Qualitative developmental research   Research that examines developmental phenomena within the social and political contexts within which they occur

Ratio schedule of reinforcement   A schedule of reinforcement based on number of responses

Reaction potential   The potential that a specific event in the environment will elicit a particular response

Reality principle   In Freudian theory, the principle that states that ego pleasure is realized through adherence to external realities

Recapitulation theory   The theory that in the development (or ontogenesis) of the individual, a sequence of stages occurs that recapitulates the evolutionary history of the development of the individual's species

Reciprocal determinism   A bidirectional process characterized by a reciprocity between the individual and the environment (including other individuals)

Reflex   An unlearned physical response

Reinforcer   Any stimulus that follows a behavior that increases the likelihood that the behavior will occur again

Reinforcing stimulus   A stimulus event following a behavior that increases the likelihood that the behavior will occur again

Relevance   How closely a theory is related to the information collected within that theory; one of Sidman's six criteria against which a theory should be measured

Repetitive quality of instincts   Instincts' tendency to be cyclical in nature, with needs satisfied only temporarily and the system eventually returning to its original state of tension

Respondent learning   Learning that is subject to the laws of classical conditioning, automatic in nature, and not under voluntary control

Response   A measurable reaction to a stimulus event

Response generalization   A process in which the response to a stimulus changes although the stimulus remains the same

Scaffolding   In Vygotsky's theory, a teaching process aimed at bridging the gap between what the child knows and what the child needs to know (or what the child is being taught)

Schedule of reinforcement (or **punishment**)   The timing of patterns of stimuli following operant behaviors

Schema   The primary unit of mental organization; the structure through which a person adapts to the environment

Science   The activity of finding order in nature

Secondary process thinking   Thinking that is associated with cognitive processes and is goal oriented and intentional

Sensorimotor stage   The first of Piaget's four stages of cognitive development, characterized by repetition and the development of early social behaviors

Sequential component (or **stage component**)   The component of a theory that addresses the pattern or progression of the organism through different and increasingly adaptive developmental stages

Setting event   A stimulus event accompanied by a certain response

Shaping   The process through which a behavior is gradually changed

Signed stimulus   A stimulus that has a value to the organism that other stimuli do not have

Simplicity   A theory's parsimony, or lack of complexity; one of Sidman's six criteria against which a theory should be measured

Social event   An interaction between living organisms

Sociobiology   The study of the impact of genes on social behavior

Sociocultural theory   A theory of development in which social interaction is understood to lead to changes in thinking and associated behaviors

Stimulus   An event that causes a change in behavior

Stimulus control   The process through which experiences become valuable to an individual and through which the individual associates particular stimuli with certain outcomes

Stimulus event   A change in the environment that has a measurable impact on behavior

Stimulus function   The functional relationship between a stimulus and a response

Stimulus generalization   A process in which the response to a new stimulus is similar to the response to an earlier, similar stimulus

Stimulus-response connection   The basis of all behavior, influenced by the laws of classical conditioning

Stimulus-response unit   The basic component of behavior

Strange Situation Procedure   A technique developed by Ainsworth to study attachment; consists of a set of brief episodes during which the child is observed while interacting with a parent (usually the mother) and a stranger

Superego   In Freudian theory, the psychological structure that represents moral and ethical standards, such as the ego ideal

Symbolic mode of representation   In Bruner's theory of development, the mode in which the child uses the most efficient symbolic system available, that of language

Taxis   An orienting or locomotor response

Theory   A group of logically related statements that explains events that happened in the past and predicts what events will occur in the future

Unconditioned response   A behavior triggered by an unconditioned stimulus

Unconditioned stimulus   A stimulus that results in behavior without previous experience or learning

Unconscious   The part of the human psyche that is not conscious, or aware

Variable   Anything that can take on more than one label or value

Variable schedule of reinforcement   A schedule of reinforcement in which deliveries of reinforcement vary based on responses over time

Vicarious learning   Indirect learning that takes place without direct reinforcement or direct imitation

Zone of proximal development (ZPD)   In Vygotsky's theory, the distance between the child's actual level of development and the child's potential level of development, or the distance between what the child knows and what the child needs to know

REFERENCES

Ainsworth, M. D. S. (1973). The development of infant-mother attachment. In B. Caldwell & H. Ricciuti (Eds.), *Review of child development research* (Vol. 3, pp. 1–99). Chicago: University of Chicago Press.

Ainsworth, M. D. S., Blehar, M. C., Waters, E., & Wall, S. (1978). *Patterns of attachment: A psychological study of the strange situation.* Hillsdale, NJ: Lawrence Erlbaum.

Allen, K. E., Hart, B., Buell, J. S., Harris, F. R., & Wolf, M. M. (1964). Effects of social reinforcement on isolate behavior of a nursery school child. *Child Development, 35,* 511–518.

Ames, L. B., & Ilg, F. L. (1964). Gesell behavior tests as predictive of later grade placement. *Perceptual and Motor Skills, 19,* 719–722.

Anastasi, A. (1958). Heredity, environment, and the question "how?" *Psychological Review, 65,* 197–208.

Arnett, J. J. (1999). Adolescent storm and stress reconsidered. *American Psychologist, 54,* 317–326.

Ausubel, D., & Sullivan, E. (1970). *Theory and problems of child development.* New York: Grune & Stratton.

Baer, D. M. (1970). An age-irrelevant concept of development. *Merrill-Palmer Quarterly, 16,* 238–245.

Baltes, P. B., & Nesselroade, J. (1974). Adolescent personality development and historical change: 1970–1972. *Monographs of the Society for Research in Child Development, 39*(1, Serial No. 154).

Bandura, A. (1971). Vicarious and self-reinforcement processes. In R. Glaser (Ed.), *The nature of reinforcement* (pp. 228–278). New York: Academic Press.

Bandura, A. (1977). *Social learning theory.* Englewood Cliffs, NJ: Prentice Hall.

Bandura, A. (1982). The psychology of chance encounters and life paths. *American Psychologist, 37,* 747–755.

Bandura, A. (1986). *Social foundations of thought and action: A social cognitive theory.* Englewood Cliffs, NJ: Prentice Hall.

Bandura, A., Ross, D., & Ross, S. A. (1961). Transmission of aggression through imitation of aggressive models. *Journal of Abnormal and Social Psychology, 63,* 575–582.

Bandura, A., & Walters, R. H. (1963). *Social learning and personality development.* New York: Holt, Rinehart & Winston.

Barash, D. P. (1977). *Sociobiology and behavior.* New York: Elsevier.

Beard, R. (1969). *An outline of Piaget's developmental psychology.* New York: Basic Books.

Belsky, J., Steinberg, L., & Draper, P. (1991). Childhood experience, interpersonal development, and reproductive strategy: An evolutionary theory of socialization. *Child Development, 62,* 647–670.

Bettelheim, B. (1976). *The uses of enchantment: The meaning and importance of fairy tales.* New York: Alfred A. Knopf.

Bijou, S. W. (1968). Ages, stages, and the naturalization of human development. *American Psychologist, 23,* 419–427.

Bijou, S. W., & Baer, D. M. (1961). *Child development 1: A systematic and empirical theory.* Englewood Cliffs, NJ: Prentice Hall.

Bijou, S. W., & Baer, D. M. (1965). *Child development 2: Universal stage of infancy.* Englewood Cliffs, NJ: Prentice Hall.

Bijou, S. W., & Baer, D. M. (1978). *Behavior analysis of child development* (Rev. ed.). Englewood Cliffs, NJ: Prentice Hall.

Bloom, B. S. (1964). *Stability and change in human characteristics.* New York: John Wiley.

Borke, H. (1975). Piaget's mountain revisited: Changes in the egocentric landscape. *Developmental Psychology, 11,* 24–43.

Bowlby, J. (1958). The nature of the child's tie to his mother. *International Journal of Psycho-Analyses, 39,* 350–373.

Bowlby, J. (1969). *Attachment and loss: Vol. 1. Attachment.* New York: Basic Books.

Bradley, S. J., Oliver, G. D., Chernick, A. B., & Zucker, K. J. (1998). Experiment of nurture: Ablatio penis at 2 months, sex reassignment at 7 months, and a psychosexual follow-up in young adulthood. *Pediatrics, 102*(1). Retrieved September 19, 2003, from http://www.pediatrics.org/cgi/content/full/102/1/e9

Bronfenbrenner, U. (1977). Toward an experimental psychology of human development. *American Psychologist, 32,* 513–531.

Bronfenbrenner, U., & Morris, P. A. (2000). The ecology of developmental processes. In W. Damon (Series Ed.) & R. M. Lerner (Vol. Ed.), *Handbook of child psychology: Vol. 1. Theoretical models of human development* (5th ed., pp. 993–1028). New York: John Wiley.

Bronowski, J. (1977). *A sense of the future: Essays on natural philosophy* (P. Ariotti, Ed., with R. Bronowski). Cambridge: MIT Press.

Brown, D. (2002). The relationship between attachment styles, interpersonal trust, and the marital attitudes of college students. *Dissertation Abstracts International, 62*(12), 6021B.

Bruner, J. S. (1966). *Toward a theory of instruction.* Cambridge, MA: Belknap.

Byck, R. (1974). *The cocaine papers.* New York: Stonehill.

Cardon, P. L. (2000). At-risk students and technology education: A qualitative study. *Journal of Technology Studies, 26*(1). Retrieved August 26, 2003, from http://scholar.lib.vt.edu/ejournals/JTS/Winter-Spring-2000/cardon.html

Carlton, M. P. (2000). Motivation and school readiness in kindergarten children. *Dissertation Abstracts International, 60*(11), 3899A.

Center for Media Education. (1997). *Children and television: Frequently asked questions.* Retrieved September 2, 2003, from http://www.cme.org/children/kids_tv/c_and_t.html

Chess, S., & Thomas, A. (1977). *Annual progress in child psychiatry and child development* (Vol. 10). New York: Brunner/Mazel.

Coghill, G. E. (1929). *Anatomy and the problem of behavior.* New York: Macmillan.

Colapinto, J. (2001). *As nature made him: The boy who was raised as a girl.* New York: Harper Perennial.

Columbia County Longitudinal Study. (2000). *Progress report.* Retrieved September 2, 2003, from http://www.rcgd.isr.umich.edu/aggr/ccls.html#y2000progress

Darwin, C. (1859). *On the origin of species by means of natural selection.* London: John Murray.

Dewey, J. (1899). *The school and society.* Chicago: University of Chicago Press.

Dollard, J., & Miller, N. E. (1950). *Personality and psychotherapy.* New York: McGraw-Hill.

Elkind, D. (1974). *Children and adolescents.* New York: Oxford University Press.

Erikson, E. H. (1950a). *Childhood and society.* New York: W. W. Norton.

Erikson, E. H. (1950b). Growth and crisis of the healthy personality. In M. J. E. Senn (Ed.), *Symposium on the healthy personality: Suppl. 2. Transactions of the Fourth Conference on Problems of Infancy and Childhood* (pp. 91–146). New York: Josiah Macy Jr. Foundation.

Escalona, S. K. (1968). *The roots of individuality.* Chicago: Aldine.

Ferster, C. B., & Skinner, B. F. (1957). *Schedules of reinforcement.* New York: Appleton-Century-Crofts.

Festinger, L. (1957). *A theory of cognitive dissonance.* Stanford, CA: Stanford University Press.

Fisher, S., & Greenberg, R. P. (1977). *The scientific credibility of Freud's theories and therapy.* New York: Basic Books.

Flavell, J. (1963). *The developmental psychology of Jean Piaget.* New York: D. Van Nostrand.

Frankenburg, W. K., & Dodds, J. B. (1992). Denver Developmental Screening Test (Denver II). In M. Stanhope & R. N. Knollmueller (Eds.), *Handbook of community and home health nursing: Tools for assessment intervention and education* (pp. 317–319). St. Louis, MO: C. V. Mosby.

Freud, S. (1920). *A general introduction to psychoanalysis.* New York: Simon & Schuster.

Freud, S. (1955). Beyond the pleasure principle. In J. Strachey (Ed. & Trans.), *The standard edition of the complete psychological works of Sigmund Freud* (Vol. 18, pp. 3–64). London: Hogarth. (Original work published 1920)

Freud, S. (1957). Character and anal eroticism. In J. Strachey (Ed. & Trans.), *The standard edition of the complete psychological works of Sigmund Freud* (Vol. 11, pp. 21–28). London: Hogarth. (Original work published 1908)

Freud, S. (1959). Three essays on sexuality. In J. Strachey (Ed. & Trans.), *The standard edition of the complete psychological works of Sigmund Freud* (Vol. 9, pp. 169–175). London: Hogarth. (Original work published 1905)

Freud, S. (1961). The ego and the id. In J. Strachey (Ed. & Trans.), *The standard edition of the complete psychological works of Sigmund Freud* (Vol. 19, pp. 3–66). London: Hogarth. (Original work published 1923)

Freud, S. (1964). New introductory lectures on psychoanalysis. In J. Strachey (Ed. & Trans.), *The standard edition of the complete psychological works of Sigmund Freud* (Vol. 22, pp. 3–182). London: Hogarth. (Original work published 1933)

Gagne, R. (1968). Contributions of learning to human development. *Psychological Review, 75,* 177–191.

Gesell, A. (1954). The ontogenesis of infant behavior. In L. Carmichael (Ed.), *Manual of child psychology* (2nd ed., pp. 335–373). New York: John Wiley.

Gesell, A. (1956). *Youth: Years from ten to sixteen.* New York: Harper & Row.

Gesell, A., Ames, L. B., & Bullis, G. E. (1946). *The child from five to ten.* New York: Harper & Row.

Gesell, A., Ilg, F. L., & Ames, L. B. (1940). *The first five years of life.* New York: Harper & Brothers.

Gesell, A., & Thompson, H. (1929). Learning and growth in identical infant twins: An experimental study of individual differences by the method of co-twin control. *Genetic Psychology Monographs, 6,* 1–124.

Gesell, A., & Thompson, H. (1941). Twins T and C from infancy to adolescence: A biogenetic study of individual differences by the method of co-twin control. *Genetic Psychology Monographs, 24,* 3–121.

Gould, R. L. (1979). *Transformations: Growth and change in adult life.* New York: Simon & Schuster.

Gould, S. J. (1977). *Ever since Darwin: Reflections in natural history.* New York: W. W. Norton.

Gould, S. J. (1980). *The panda's thumb: More reflections in natural history.* New York: W. W. Norton.

Grusec, J. (1992). Social learning theory and developmental psychology: The legacies of Robert Sears and Albert Bandura. *Developmental Psychology, 28,* 776–786.

Haj-Yahia, M., & Dawud-Noursi, S. (1998). Predicting the use of different conflict tactics among Arab siblings: I. Israel: A study based on social learning theory. *Journal of Family Violence, 13,* 81–103.

Hall, C. (1954). *Primer of Freudian psychology.* New York: Mentor.

Hall, G. S. (1904). *Adolescence: Its psychology and its relations to physiology, anthropology, sociology, sex, crime, religion, and education* (2 vols.). New York: Appleton.

Harris, J. R. (1998). *The nurture assumption: Why children turn out the way they do.* New York: Free Press.

Havighurst, R. J. (1952). *Developmental tasks and education* (2nd ed.). New York: Longman, Green.

Hebb, D. O. (1947). The effects of early experience on problem solving at maturity. *American Psychologist, 2,* 306–307.

Hebb, D. O. (1949). *Organization of behavior.* New York: John Wiley.

Hedegaard, M. (1996). The zone of proximal development as basis for instruction. In H. Daniels (Ed.), *An introduction to Vygotsky* (pp. 171–195). New York: Routledge.

Hunt, J. M. (1961). *Intelligence and experience.* New York: Ronald.

Ilg, F. L., & Ames, L. B. (1955). *Child behavior: From birth to ten.* New York: Harper & Row.

Jones, E. (1953–1957). *The life and work of Sigmund Freud* (3 vols.). New York: Basic Books.

Kagan, J. (1971). *Continuity and change in infancy.* New York: John Wiley.

Kitchener, R. F. (1978). Epigenesis: The role of biological models in developmental psychology. *Human Development, 21,* 141–160.

Kuhn, T. S. (1962). *The structure of scientific revolutions.* Chicago: University of Chicago Press.

Lamb-Parker, F., Boak, A. Y., Griffin, K. W., Ripple, C., & Peay, L. (1999). Parent-child relationship, home learning environment, and school readiness. *School Psychology Review, 28,* 413–425.

Lampl, M., Veldhuis, J. D., & Johnson, M. L. (1992). Saltation and stasis: A model of human growth. *Science, 258,* 801–803.

Lane, H. (1976). *The wild boy of Aveyron.* Cambridge, MA: Harvard University Press.

Lenneberg, E. H. (1967). *Biological foundations of language.* New York: John Wiley.

Levine, S. (1957). Infantile experience and resistance to physiological stress. *Science, 126,* 405.

Lorenz, K. (1965). *Evolution and modification of behavior.* Chicago: University of Chicago Press.

Maslow, A. (1968). *Toward a psychology of being.* New York: D. Van Nostrand.

Mayer, J. D. (1999). A framework for the study of individual differences in personality formations. In J. A. Singer & P. Salovey (Eds.), *At play in the fields of consciousness: Essays in honor of Jerome L. Singer* (pp. 143–173). Mahwah, NJ: Lawrence Erlbaum.

McGraw, M. B. (1935). *Growth: A study of Johnny and Jimmy.* New York: Appleton-Century-Crofts.

Miller, L., & Gur, M. (2002). Religiosity, depression, and physical maturation in adolescent girls. *Journal of the American Academy of Child and Adolescent Psychiatry, 41,* 206–214.

Money, J., & Ehrhardt, A. A. (1973). *Man and woman, boy and girl: Gender identity from conception to maturity.* Baltimore: Johns Hopkins University Press.

Montessori, M. (1936). *The secret of childhood.* New York: Longman.

Munroe, R. (1955). *Schools of psychoanalytic thought.* New York: Holt, Rinehart & Winston.

National Institute of Mental Health. (1982). *Television and behavior: Ten years of scientific progress and implications for the eighties* (Vol. 1). Rockville, MD: U.S. Department of Health and Human Services.

Overton, W. F. (2000). Developmental psychology: Philosophy, concepts, and methodology. In W. Damon (Series Ed.) & R. M. Lerner (Vol. Ed.), *Handbook of child psychology: Vol. 1. Theoretical models of human development* (5th ed., pp. 107–188). New York: John Wiley.

Pavlov, I. (1927). *Conditioned reflexes.* London: Oxford University Press.

Pawlik, K. (1998). The psychology of individual differences: The personality puzzle. In J. G. Adair, D. Belanger, & K. L. Dion (Eds.), *Advances in psychological science: Vol. 1. Social, personal, and cultural aspects* (pp. 1–30). Hove, Eng.: Psychology Press.

Piaget, J. (1950a). *Introduction to genetic epistemology.* Paris: University Presses.

Piaget, J. (1950b). *The psychology of intelligence.* New York: Harcourt, Brace.

Piaget, J. (1952). *The origins of intelligence in children.* New York: International Universities Press.

Piaget, J. (1970). *Science and education and the psychology of the child.* New York: Orion.

Piaget, J., & Inhelder, B. (1956). *The child's conception of space.* London: Routledge & Kegan Paul.

Ramey, C. T., & Landesman Ramey, S. (1998). Early intervention and early experience. *American Psychologist, 53,* 109–120.

Scarr, S. (1993). Genes, experience and development. In D. Magnusson & P. Casaer (Eds.), *Longitudinal research on individual development: Present status and future perspectives* (pp. 26–50). Cambridge: Cambridge University Press.

Schaie, K. W. (1965). A general model for the study of developmental problems. *Psychological Bulletin, 64,* 92–107.

Schmidt, S., Nachtigall, C., Wuethrich-Martone, O., & Strauss, B. (2002). Attachment and coping with chronic disease. *Journal of Psychosomatic Research, 53,* 763–773.

Sears, E. R., Maccoby, E. E., & Levin, H. (1957). *Patterns of child rearing.* Stanford, CA: Stanford University Press.

Sheehy, G. (1976). *Passages: Predictable crises in adult life.* New York: Bantam.

Sheehy, G. (1995). *New passages: Mapping your life across time.* New York: Random House.

Sheehy, G. (1999). *Understanding men's passages: Discovering the new map of men's lives.* New York: Ballantine.

Sidman, M. (1960). *Tactics of scientific research.* New York: Basic Books.

Skeels, H. M. (1966). Adult status of children with contrasting early life experiences: A follow-up study. *Monographs of the Society for Research in Child Development, 31*(3, Serial No. 105).

Skeels, H. M., & Dye, H. (1939). A study of the effects of differential stimulation on mentally retarded children. *Proceedings of the American Association on Mental Deficiency, 44,* 114–136.

Skinner, B. F. (1938). *The behavior of organisms: An experimental analysis.* New York: Appleton-Century-Crofts.

Skinner, B. F. (1976a). *Particulars of my life.* New York: Alfred A. Knopf.

Skinner, B. F. (1976b). *Walden Two.* New York: Macmillan. (Original work published 1948)

Skinner, B. F. (1989). *Recent issues in the analysis of behavior.* Columbus, OH: Merrill.

Stevenson, H. (1983). How children learn: The quest for a theory. In P. H. Mussen (Series Ed.) & W. Kessen (Vol. Ed.), *Handbook of child psychology, Vol. 1: History, theory, and methods* (4th ed., pp. 213–236). New York: John Wiley.

Strauss, M. A. (1979). Measuring interfamily conflict and violence: The Conflict Tactics (CT) Scales. *Journal of Marriage and the Family, 41,* 75–88.

Tharp, R. G., & Gallimore, R. (1988). *Rousing minds to life: Teaching, learning, and schooling in social context.* Cambridge: Cambridge University Press.

Thorndike, E. L. (1898). Animal intelligence: An experimental study of the associative processes in animals. *Psychological Review Monographs Supplement, 2*(8).

Thorndike, E. L. (1903). *Educational psychology.* New York: Lenicke & Buechner.

van der Mark, I. L., Bakermans-Kranenburg, M. J., & van Ijzendoorn, M. H. (2002). The role of parenting, attachment, and temperamental fearfulness in the prediction of compliance in toddler girls. *British Journal of Developmental Psychology, 20,* 361–378.

Ventura, S. J., Curtin, S. C., & Mathews, T. J. (2000). Variations in teenage birth rates, 1991–98: National and state trends. *National Vital Statistics Reports, 48*(6).

Vygotsky, L. S. (1971). *The psychology of art* (Scripta Technica Inc., Trans.). Cambridge: MIT Press. (Original work published 1925)

Vygotsky, L. S. (1978). *Mind in society: The development of higher psychological processes* (M. Cole, V. John-Steiner, S. Scribner, & E. Souberman, Eds.). Cambridge, MA: Harvard University Press.

Waber, D. B. (1976). Sex differences in cognition: A function of maturation rate. *Science, 192,* 572–574.

Wapner, S. (1964). Some aspects of a research program based on an organismic-developmental approach to cognition: Experiments and theory. *Journal of the American Academy of Child Psychology, 3,* 193–230.

Wapner, S., & Werner, H. (Eds.). (1957). *Perceptual development.* Worcester, MA: Clark University Press.

Watson, J. B. (1925). *Behaviorism.* New York: W. W. Norton.

Werner, H. (1948). *Comparative psychology of mental development.* New York: International Universities Press.

Werner, H. (1957). The concept of development from a comparative and organismic point of view. In D. B. Harris (Ed.), *The concept of development* (pp. 125–148). Minneapolis: University of Minnesota Press.

Wilson, E. O. (1975). *Sociobiology: The new synthesis.* Cambridge, MA: Harvard University Press.

Witkin, H., Dye, R. B., Faterson, H. F., Goodenough, D. R., & Karp, S. A. (1962). *Psychological differentiation.* New York: John Wiley.

Wright, J. C., Huston, A. C., Murphy, K. C., St. Peters, M., Pinon, M., Scantlin, R., & Kotler, J. (2001). The relations of early television viewing to school readiness and vocabulary of children from low income families: The Early Window Project. *Child Development, 72,* 1347–1366.

SUGGESTED READINGS
ON HUMAN DEVELOPMENT

Chapter 1. The Study of Human Development

Achenbach, T. (1978). *Research in developmental psychology: Concepts, strategies, methods.* Riverside, NJ: Free Press.

Adolph, K. E. (2002). Babies' steps make giant strides toward a science of development. *Infant Behavior and Development, 25*(1), 86–90.

Appelbaum, M. I., & McCall, R. B. (1983). Design and analysis in developmental psychology. In P. H. Mussen (Series Ed.) & W. Kessen (Vol. Ed.), *Handbook of child psychology: Vol. 1. History, theory, and methods* (4th ed., pp. 415–476). New York: John Wiley.

Azuma, H., & Imada, H. (1994). Origins and development of psychology in Japan: The interaction between Western science and the Japanese cultural heritage. *International Journal of Psychology, 29,* 707–715.

Bailer-Jones, D. M. (1999). Tracing the development of models in the philosophy of science. In L. Magnani & N. J. Nersessian (Eds.), *Model-based reasoning in scientific discovery* (pp. 23–40). Dordrecht, Netherlands: Kluwer Academic.

Brim, O., & Kagan, J. (Eds.). (1980). *Constancy and change in human development.* Cambridge, MA: Harvard University Press.

Bronowski, J. (1972). *The origins of knowledge and imagination.* New Haven, CT: Yale University Press.

Faucher, L., Mallon, R., Nazer, D., Nichols, S., Ruby, A., Stich, S., et al. (2002). The baby in the lab-coat: Why child development is not an adequate model for understanding the development of science. In P. Carruthers, S. Stich, & M. Siegal (Eds.), *The cognitive basis of science* (pp. 335–362). New York: Cambridge University Press.

Howe, A. C. (1996). Development of science concepts within a Vygotskian framework. *Science Education, 80*(1), 35–51.

Klahr, D. (2000). *Exploring science: The cognition and development of discovery processes.* Cambridge, MA: MIT Press.

Kluger, J., & Lemonick, M. D. (1999, March 29). Putting science to work. *Time,* pp. 198–199.

Langer, J. (1969). *Theories of development.* New York: Holt, Rinehart & Winston.

Lemonick, M. D. (2002, May 20). How everything works. *Time,* p. 67.

Lerner, R. M. (1995). The integration of levels and human development: A developmental contextual view of the synthesis of science and outreach in the enhancement of human lives. In K. Hood & G. Greenberg (Eds.), *Behavioral development: Concepts of approach/withdrawal and integrative levels* (pp. 421–446). New York: Garland.

Masten, A. S., & Curtis, W. J. (2000). Integrating competence and psychopathology: Pathways toward a comprehensive science of adaptation in development. *Development and Psychopathology, 12,* 529–550.

Mehler, J., Dupoux, E., & Southgate, P. (1994). *What infants know: The new cognitive science of early development.* Malden, MA: Blackwell.

Osika, M. J. (1996). Philosophy of science, psychology, and world hypotheses: Development and validation of a world view scale. *Dissertation Abstracts International, 56*(8), 4567B.

Powles, W. E. (1992). *Human development and homeostasis: The science of psychiatry.* Madison, CT: International Universities Press.

Roth, W., & Roychoudhury, A. (1993). The development of science process skills in authentic contexts. *Journal of Research in Science Teaching, 30,* 127–152.

Rousseau, J. J. (1979). *Emile.* New York: Basic Books.

Rubinstein, E. (2000). An interview with the president: "I'd like to see America used as a global lab." *Science, 290,* 2236–2239.

Rutter, M. (2002). Nature, nurture, and development: From evangelism through science toward policy and practice. *Child Development, 73,* 1–21.

Shonkoff, J. P., & Phillips, D. A. (Eds.). (2000). *From neurons to neighborhoods: The science of early childhood development.* Washington, DC: National Academy Press.

Skinner, B. F. (1953). *Science and human behavior.* New York: Macmillan.

Swerdlow, J. L. (1999, October). Science: Asking infinite questions. *National Geographic,* pp. 2–7.

Thompson, R. A., & Nelson, C. A. (2001). Developmental science and the media: Early brain development. *American Psychologist, 56,* 5–15.

Chapter 2. Trends and Issues in Human Development

Berardi, N., Pizzorusso, T., & Maffei, L. (2000). Critical periods during sensory development. *Current Opinion in Neurobiology, 10*(1), 138–145.

Bronfenbrenner, U., & Crouter, A. C. (1982). Work and family through time and space. In S. B. Kamerman & C. D. Hayes (Eds.), *Families that work: Children in a changing world* (pp. 39–83). Washington, DC: National Academy Press.

Cho, K. C. (1994). Investigation of the development of six English grammatical structures in Korean children, in light of the critical period hypothesis. *Dissertation Abstracts International, 54*(7), 2495A.

Dennenberg, V. H. (1964). Critical periods, stimulus input and emotional reactivity: A theory of infantile stimulation. *Psychological Review, 71,* 335–351.

Ekstrand, L. H. (1979). *Replacing the critical period and optimum age theories of second language acquisition with a theory of ontogenetic development beyond puberty.* Lund, Sweden: Lund University.

Grimshaw, G. M., Adelstein, A., Bryden, M. P., & MacKinnon, G. E. (1998). First-language acquisition in adolescence: Evidence for a critical period for verbal language development. *Brain and Language, 63,* 237–255.

Harlow, H. F. (1958). The nature of love. *American Psychologist, 13,* 673–685.

Holmbeck, G. N., Crossman, R. E., Wandrei, M. L., & Gasiewski, E. (1994). Cognitive development, egocentrism, self-esteem, and adolescent contraceptive knowledge, attitudes, and behavior. *Journal of Youth and Adolescence, 23,* 169–193.

Hook, S. (1957). Dialectical materialism and scientific method [Special suppl.]. *Bulletin of the Committee on Science and Freedom.*

Huttenlocher, P. R. (1999). Dendritic synaptic development in human cerebral cortex: Time course and critical periods. *Developmental Neuropsychology, 16,* 347–349.

Kim, I., & Yoon, G. (1988). Adolescent egocentrism and its relationship with cognitive development and parental childrearing practices. *Korean Journal of Psychology, 7*(1), 54–62.

Lapsley, D. K. (1993). Toward an integrated theory of adolescent ego development: The "new look" at adolescent egocentrism. *American Journal of Orthopsychiatry, 63,* 562–571.

O'Connor, B. P., & Nikolic, J. (1990). Identity development and formal operations as sources of adolescent egocentrism. *Journal of Youth and Adolescence, 19,* 149–158.

Riley, T., Adams, G. R., & Nielsen, E. (1984). Adolescent egocentrism: The association among imaginary audience behavior, cognitive development, and parental support and rejection. *Journal of Youth and Adolescence, 13,* 401–417.

Schindler, R. M., & Holbrook, M. B. (1993). Critical periods in the development of men's and women's tastes in personal appearance. *Psychology and Marketing, 10,* 549–564.

Senn, M. J. E. (1975). Insights on the child development movement in the United States. *Monographs of the Society for Research in Child Development, 40*(3–4, Serial No. 161).

Sternklar, S. (1986). Cognitive development and separation anxiety as predictors of ego identity status and egocentrism. *Dissertation Abstracts International, 46*(11), 4030B.

Thompson, R. A., & Nelson, C. A. (2001). Developmental science and the media: Early brain development. *American Psychologist, 56,* 5–15.

Westman, A. S., & Lewandowski, L. M. (1991). How empathy, egocentrism, Kohlberg's moral development, and Erikson's psychosocial development are related to attitudes toward war. *Psychological Reports, 69*(3, Pt. 2), 1123–1127.

Williams, S., & Harper, J. (1974). A study of etiological factors at critical periods of development in autistic children. *International Journal of Mental Health, 3*(1), 90–99.

Chapter 3. Arnold Gesell and the Maturational Model

Ball, R. S. (1977). The Gesell developmental schedules: Arnold Gesell (1880–1961). *Journal of Abnormal Child Psychology, 5,* 233–239.

Bingen, K. M. (2002). Individual differences in infant response to the still-face paradigm and prediction of later attachment. *Dissertation Abstracts International, 62*(12), 5993B.

Dyl, J. (2002). Individual differences in traumatic experiences: Antecedents of ego development in adulthood. *Dissertation Abstracts International, 62*(11), 5370B.

Fagan, T. K. (1987). Gesell: The first school psychologist: I. The road to Connecticut. *School Psychology Review, 16,* 103–107.

Fagan, T. K. (1987). Gesell: The first school psychologist: II. Practice and significance. *School Psychology Review, 16,* 399–409.

Gesell, A. (1928). *Infancy and human growth.* New York: Macmillan.

Gesell, A., & Amatruda, C. S. (1947). *Developmental diagnosis: Normal and abnormal child development: Clinical methods and pediatric evaluations* (2nd ed.). New York: Hoeber.

Gesell Institute. (1987). "Uses and abuses of developmental screening and school readiness training": The Gesell Institute responds. *Young Children, 42*(2), 7–8.

Karrass, J. (2002). Individual differences in temperament, joint attention, and early language. *Dissertation Abstracts International, 63*(1), 566B.

Krause, I. B., Jr. (1968). A comparison of the psychological views of Piaget and Gesell. *Journal of Thought, 3*(3), 168–176.

Lindley, P. G. (1992). Dr. Arnold Lucius Gesell: Philosopher, child psychologist, pediatrician, clinical researcher. *Dissertation Abstracts International, 52*(10), 3521–3522A.

Luoma, J. B. (2002). Individual differences in event clustering in autobiographical memory. *Dissertation Abstracts International, 62*(12), 5971B.

Poon, C. S. K. (2002). Lay personality knowledge and confidence in social inferences: Individual differences, temporal change, and momentary activation. *Dissertation Abstracts International, 62*(12), 6025B.

Sherrington, C. S. (1906). *The integrative action of the nervous system.* New York: Scribners.

Skeels, H. M., Updegraff, R., Wellman, B., & Williams, H. M. A. (1938). A study of environmental stimulation: An orphanage preschool project. *University of Iowa Studies in Child Welfare, 15*(4).

Streff, J. W. (1998). The Gesell years. *Journal of Optometric Vision Development, 29*(1), 13–22.

Thelen, E., & Adolph, K. E. (1992). Arnold L. Gesell: The paradox of nature and nurture. *Developmental Psychology, 28,* 368–380.

Zargarpour, S. (2002). Individual differences in children's group perceptions and peer preferences as a function of prejudice level. *Dissertation Abstracts International, 62*(11), 5436B.

Chapter 4. The Importance of Biology: Ethology and Sociobiology

Archer, J. (1992). *Ethology and human development.* Preston, England: Lancashire Polytechnic Press.

Ardrey, R. (1968). *The territorial imperative.* New York: Delta.

Bowlby, J. (1969). *Attachment and loss: Vol. 1. Attachment.* London: Hogarth.

Bowlby, J. (1973). *Attachment and loss: Vol. 2. Separation.* London: Hogarth.

Bowlby, J. (1980). *Attachment and loss: Vol. 3. Loss.* London: Hogarth.

Chisholm, J. S. (1979). Developmental ethology of the Navajo. *Dissertation Abstracts International, 39*(7), 4363A.

Dawkins, R. (1976). *The selfish gene.* Oxford: Oxford University Press.

Freedman, D. (1979). *Human sociobiology: A holistic approach.* New York: Free Press.

Haviland, J. M., & Walker-Andrews, A. S. (1992). Emotion socialization: A view from development and ethology. In V. B. Van Hasselt & M. Hersen (Eds.), *Handbook of social development: A lifespan perspective* (pp. 29–49). New York: Plenum.

Konner, M. J. (1972). Aspects of the developmental ethology of a foraging people. In N. B. Jones (Ed.), *Ethological studies of child behaviour.* Oxford: Cambridge University Press.

Lerner, R. M., & Von Eye, A. (1992). Sociobiology and human development: Arguments and evidence. *Human Development, 35,* 12–33.

Lorenz, K. (1958). The evolution of behavior. *Scientific American, 199*(6), 67–78.

MacDonald, K. (1984). An ethological-social learning theory of the development of altruism: Implications for human sociobiology. *Ethology and Sociobiology, 5*(2), 97–109.

Nordtvedt, E. L. (1984). The heuristic value of sociobiology for the nature-nurture issue in child development. *Dissertation Abstracts International, 44*(12), 3956B.

Parker, S. T. (2002). Comparative developmental evolutionary psychology and cognitive ethology: Contrasting but compatible research programs. In M. Bekoff, C. Allen, & G. M. Burghardt (Eds.), *The cognitive animal: Empirical and theoretical perspectives on animal cognition* (pp. 59–67). Cambridge, MA: MIT Press.

Roeder, K. D. (1963). Ethology and neurophysiology. *Zeitschrift für Tierpsychologie, 20,* 434–440.

Rosenblatt, J. S. (1989). Ethology in the laboratory: Behavioral development in selective altricial newborn among the mammals. In R. J. Blanchard, P. F. Brain, D. C. Blanchard, & S. Parmigiani (Eds.), *Ethoexperimental approaches to the study of behavior* (pp. 659–673). New York: Kluwer/Plenum.

Sameroff, A. J. (1965). Early influences on development: Fact or fancy? *Merrill-Palmer Quarterly, 21,* 267–294.

Sameroff, A. J. (1983). Developmental systems: Contexts and evolution. In P. H. Mussen (Series Ed.) & W. Kessen (Vol. Ed.), *Handbook of child psychology: Vol. 1. History, theory, and methods.* (pp. 237–294). New York: John Wiley.

Slater, P. (1990). Causes of development in ethology. In G. Butterworth & P. Bryant (Eds.), *Causes of development: Interdisciplinary perspectives* (pp. 64–81). Hillsdale, NJ: Lawrence Erlbaum.

Smith, P. K. (1990). Ethology, sociobiology and developmental psychology: In memory of Niko Tinbergen and Konrad Lorenz. *British Journal of Developmental Psychology, 8,* 187–200.

Sokolov, V. E., & Baskin, L. M. (1992). Development of ethology in the U.S.S.R. *International Journal of Comparative Psychology, 6*(1), 75–78.

Wright, R. (1995). *The moral animal: Evolutionary psychology and everyday life.* New York: Vintage.

Chapter 5. Sigmund Freud's Psychosexual Theory

Abend, S. M. (1991). Freud and his successors: The major developmental stages in the evolution of psychoanalytic theory and technique. In A. Rothstein (Ed.), *The Moscow lectures on psychoanalysis* (pp. 21–43). Madison, CT: International Universities Press.

Benton, R. L. (1995). The prophetic voice of Karen Horney in the evolution of psychoanalytic female developmental theory: From Freud to contemporary revisionists. *Dissertation Abstracts International, 55*(12), 3990A.

Colonna, A. B. (1996). Anna Freud: Observation and development. *Psychoanalytic Study of the Child, 51,* 217–234.

Edgcumbe, R. (2000). *Anna Freud: A view of development, disturbance and therapeutic techniques.* Florence, KY: Taylor & Francis/Routledge.

Emde, R. N. (1992). Individual meaning and increasing complexity: Contributions of Sigmund Freud and Rene Spitz to developmental psychology. *Developmental Psychology, 28,* 347–359.

Jacobs, J. L. (1997). Freud as other: Anti-Semitism and the development of psychoanalysis. In J. L. Jacobs & D. Capps (Eds.), *Religion, society, and psychoanalysis: Readings in contemporary theory* (pp. 28–41). Boulder, CO: Westview.

King, P. (1991). Background and development of the Freud-Klein controversies in the British Psycho-Analytical Society. In P. King & R. Steiner (Eds.), *The Freud-Klein controversies 1941–45* (pp. 9–36). New York: Tavistock/Routledge.

Mayes, L. C., & Cohen, D. J. (1996). Anna Freud and developmental psychoanalytic psychology. *Psychoanalytic Study of the Child, 51,* 117–141.

Muller, J. P. (1996). *Beyond the psychoanalytic dyad: Developmental semiotics in Freud, Peirce and Lacan.* Florence, KY: Taylor & Francis/Routledge.

Nass, M. L. (1966). The superego and moral development in the theories of Freud and Piaget. *Psychoanalytic Study of the Child, 21,* 51–68.

Reisner, S. (2001). Freud and developmental theory: A 21st-century look at the origin myth of psychoanalysis. *Studies in Gender and Sexuality, 2*(2), 97–128.

Sayers, J. (1987). Freud revisited: On gender, moral development, and androgyny. *New Ideas in Psychology, 5,* 197–206.

Silverstein, S. M., & Silverstein, B. R. (1990). Freud and hypnosis: The development of an interactionist perspective. In Chicago Institute for Psychoanalysis (Ed.), *The annual of psychoanalysis* (Vol. 18, pp. 175–194). Hillsdale, NJ: Analytic Press.

Tourney, G. (1965). Freud and the Greeks: A study of the influence of classical Greek mythology and philosophy upon the development of Freudian thought. *Journal of the History of the Behavioral Sciences, 1,* 67–85.

Young-Bruehl, E. (1991). Rereading Freud on female development. *Psychoanalytic Inquiry, 11,* 427–440.

Chapter 6. Erik Erikson's Focus on Psychosocial Development

Bernhardt, A. (1976). Synthesis of the developmental frameworks of Erik H. Erikson and analytical psychology: Ego and self development. *Dissertation Abstracts International, 37*(6), 3061–3062B.

Brichacek, G. B. (1996). Psychosocial development and religious orientation in later life: An empirical study of Erikson and Allport. *Dissertation Abstracts International, 57*(6), 2525A.

Brito, I. (2001). A program for homeless children ages two to five based on Erikson's theory of psychosocial development. *Dissertation Abstracts International, 62*(4), 2048B.

Darling-Fisher, C. S., & Leidy, N. K. (1988). Measuring Eriksonian development in the adult: The Modified Erikson Psychosocial Stage Inventory. *Psychological Reports, 62,* 747–754.

Dusek, J. B., & Flaherty, J. F. (1981). The development of the self-concept during the adolescent years. *Monographs of the Society for Research in Child Development, 46*(4, Serial No. 191).

Erikson, E. H. (1968). *Identity, youth and crisis.* New York: W. W. Norton.

Gross, T. P. (1981). Developmental counseling and psychotherapy: Applying the theories of Piaget, Perry, Kohlberg and Erikson. *Dissertation Abstracts International, 42*(2), 768–769B.

Hoare, C. H. (2002). *Erikson on development in adulthood: New insights from the unpublished papers.* London: Oxford University Press.

Knowles, R. T. (1986). *Human development and human possibility: Erikson in the light of Heidegger.* Lanham, MD: University Press of America.

Maier, H. W. (1959). Three current child development theories applied to child caring tasks: A study of three child development theories as postulated by Jean Piaget, Erik H. Erikson and Robert R. Sears for the purpose of applying principles derived from these theories to child caring tasks in children's institutions. *Dissertation Abstracts, 20,* 1432–1433.

Mayer, E. L. (1998). Erik H. Erikson on bodies, gender, and development. In R. S. Wallerstein & L. Goldberger (Eds.), *Ideas and identities: The life and work of Erik Erikson* (pp. 79–98). Madison, CT: International Universities Press.

Miller, J. P. (1978). Piaget, Kohlberg, and Erikson: Developmental implications for secondary education. *Adolescence, 13,* 237–250.

Murphy, L. B., & Moriarty, A. E. (1976). *Vulnerability, coping and growth: From infancy to adolescence.* New Haven, CT: Yale University Press.

Piers, M. W. (1972). *Play and development: A symposium with contributions by Jean Piaget, Peter H. Wolff, Rene A. Spitz, Konrad Lorenz, Lois Barclay Murphy, Erik H. Erikson.* Oxford: W. W. Norton.

Shoulberg, D. J. (1976). Erik H. Erikson: A developmental view of the rhetorical self. *Dissertation Abstracts International, 37*(2), 696A.

Wallace, D. (1974). An exploration of the latent structure of prosocial student-defined problems and its relationship to the developmental theories about youth of Erik Erikson and Kenneth Keniston. *Dissertation Abstracts International, 34*(11), 7011–7012A.

Chapter 7. Behavioral Models of Development

Akita, K., & Mutou, T. (1993). A developmental study of reading conceptions: Correlational analysis of behavioral and evaluative measures. *Japanese Journal of Educational Psychology, 41,* 462–469.

Baer, D. M. (1976). The organism as host. *Human Development, 19,* 87–98.

Barker, D. B. (1991). The behavioral analysis of interpersonal intimacy in group development. *Small Group Research, 22*(1), 76–91.

Bijou, S. (1968). Child behavior and development: A behavioral analysis. *International Journal of Psychology, 3,* 221–238.

Brooker, B. H. (1981). The development of selective attention in learning disabled and normal boys: An auditory evoked potential and behavioral analysis. *Dissertation Abstracts International, 41*(11), 4301B.

Dekovic, M., & Gerris, J. R. M. (1994). Developmental analysis of social cognitive and behavioral differences between popular and rejected children. *Journal of Applied Developmental Psychology, 15,* 367–386.

Fowler, P. C. (1980). Family environment and early behavioral development: A structural analysis of dependencies. *Psychological Reports, 47,* 611–617.

Kerlinger, F. (1973). *Foundations of behavioral research: Educational, psychological, and sociological inquiry.* New York: Holt, Rinehart & Winston.

Leon, G. R., Fulkerson, J. A., Perry, C. L., & Early-Zald, M. B. (1995). Prospective analysis of personality and behavioral vulnerabilities and gender influences in the later development of disordered eating. *Journal of Abnormal Psychology, 104*(1), 140–149.

Logan, C. A. (1992). Developmental analysis in behavioral systems: The case of bird song. In G. Turkewitz (Ed.), *Developmental psychobiology* (pp. 102–117). New York: New York Academy of Sciences.

Molm, L. D. (1977). The development and maintenance of social exchange: A behavioral analysis. *Dissertation Abstracts International, 38*(2), 1061A.

Rosales-Ruiz, J., & Baer, D. M. (1997). Behavioral cusps: A developmental and pragmatic concept for behavior analysis. *Journal of Applied Behavior Analysis, 30,* 533–544.

Sepehri, M. (1983). A mathematical analysis of behavioral pattern, behavioral change, and cognitive development of Moslem students in academic organizations. *Dissertation Abstracts International, 43*(8), 2571–2572A.

Skinner, B. F. (1957). *Verbal behavior.* New York: Appleton-Century-Crofts.

Standley, J. M., & Hughes, J. E. (1996). Documenting developmentally appropriate objectives and benefits of a music therapy program for early intervention: A behavioral analysis. *Music Therapy Perspectives, 14*(2), 87–94.

Turkheimer, E., & Waldron, M. (2000). Statistical analysis, experimental method, and causal inference in developmental behavioral genetics. *Human Development, 43,* 51–52.

Weiner, L. B. (1990). A developmental analysis of children's sex role self-concept and selected personality, developmental and behavioral measures. *Dissertation Abstracts International, 50*(8), 2439A.

Wilson, K. G., & Blackledge, J. T. (2000). Recent developments in the behavioral analysis of language: Making sense of clinical phenomena. In M. J. Dougher (Ed.), *Clinical behavior analysis* (pp. 27–46). Reno, NV: Context.

Chapter 8. Social Learning Theory

Bandura, A. (1977). Self-efficacy: Toward a unifying theory of behavioral change. *Psychological Review, 84,* 191–215.

Bandura, A. (1978). Social learning theory of aggression. *Journal of Communication, 28*(3), 12–29.

Bandura, A. (1979). *Principles of behavior modification.* New York: Holt, Rinehart & Winston.

Bandura, A. (1997). *Self-efficacy: The exercise of control.* New York: W. H. Freeman.

Bernadett-Shapiro, S. T. (1994). Object relations theory vs. social learning theory: Predictive validity for the development of empathy in first-grade boys. *Dissertation Abstracts International, 54*(12), 4388A.

Burnett, P. C. (1996). An investigation of the social learning and symbolic interaction models for the development of self-concepts and self-esteem. *Journal of Family Studies, 2*(1), 57–64.

Burns, K. L. (1979). Social learning theory and behavioral health care. *Psychotherapy and Psychosomatics, 32,* 6–15.

Carmody, T. P., Istvan, J., Matarazzo, J. D., Connor, S. L., & Connor, W. E.(1986). Applications of social learning theory in the promotion of heart-healthy diets: The Family Heart Study dietary intervention model. *Health Education Research, 1*(1), 13–27.

Chien, C. Y. A. (1995). Developmental adaptation of social learning theory: The etiology of crime and delinquency. *Dissertation Abstracts International, 55*(10), 3319A.

Clawson, H. J. (1999). Testing a social learning theory model of wife abuse among Air Force active duty service members: Does abuse in the family of origin predict spouse abuse later in life? *Dissertation Abstracts International, 60*(6), 3014B.

Curran, G. M. (1997). Developmental pathways to problem alcohol and drug use: A longitudinal analysis of an interactive social learning model. *Dissertation Abstracts International, 57*(11), 4945A.

Decker, P. J. (1986). Social learning theory and leadership. *Journal of Management Development, 5*(3), 46–58.

De Souza, J. M. (1992). An explanatory study of criminal violence among male and female offenders from a social learning and developmental perspective. *Dissertation Abstracts International, 52*(12, Pt. 1), 6645B.

Dickinson, J. A. (1989). Experiential social learning and management for social transformation: A case study of a community development project in Lima, Peru: I and II. *Dissertation Abstracts International, 50*(3), 597A.

Edwards, H. C. (1989). On the development of mathematics teaching skills: A study of theories of cognitive behavior and social learning as applied to education. *Dissertation Abstracts International, 50*(3), 641–642A.

Eisen, M., Zellman, G. L., & McAlister, A. L. (1992). A health belief model-social learning theory approach to adolescents' fertility control: Findings from a controlled field trial. *Health Education Quarterly, 19,* 249–262.

Gagne, E. D., & Middlebrooks, M. S. (1977). Encouraging generosity: A perspective from social learning theory and research. *Elementary School Journal, 77,* 281–291.

Green, B. C. (1997). A social learning approach to youth sport motivation: Initial scale development and validation. *Dissertation Abstracts International, 57*(9), 4128A.

Hawkins, W. E., Clarke, G. N., & Seeley, J. R. (1993). Application of social learning theory to the primary prevention of depression in adolescents. *Health Values, 17*(6), 31–39.

Herbert, M. (1991). *Clinical child psychology: Social learning, development and behaviour.* Oxford: John Wiley.

Hillman, E. R. (1993). Adolescent sexual behavior: A developmental social learning model. *Dissertation Abstracts International, 53*(11), 5977–5978B.

Klein, N. A., Sondag, K. A., & Drolet, J. C. (1994). Understanding volunteer peer health educators' motivations: Applying social learning theory. *Journal of American College Health, 43*(3), 126–130.

Krumboltz, J. D. (1994). Improving career development theory from a social learning perspective. In M. L. Savikas & R. W. Lent (Eds.), *Convergence in career development theories: Implications for science and practice* (pp. 9–31). Palo Alto, CA: CPP.

Krumboltz, J. D., Mitchell, A. M., & Jones, G. B. (1976). A social learning theory of career selection. *Counseling Psychologist, 6,* 71–81.

Krumboltz, J. D., & Nichols, C. W. (1990). Integrating the social learning theory of career decision making. In W. B. Walsh & S. H. Osipow (Eds.), *Career counseling: Contemporary topics in vocational psychology* (pp. 159–192). Hillsdale, NJ: Lawrence Erlbaum.

Lange, D. N. (1971). An application of social learning theory in effecting change in a group of student teachers using video modeling techniques. *Journal of Educational Research, 65*(4), 151–154.

Lunz, J. (1983). Applying social learning theory to advertising. *South African Journal of Psychology, 13*(1), 13–17.

MacDonald, K. (1984). An ethological-social learning theory of the development of altruism: Implications for human sociobiology. *Ethology and Sociobiology, 5*(2), 97–109.

Mallick, S. D., & McCandless, B. R. (1966). A study of catharsis of aggression. *Journal of Personality and Social Psychology, 4,* 591–596.

Meltzoff, A., & Moore, M. K. (1977). Imitation of facial and manual gestures by human neonates. *Science, 198,* 75–78.

Miller, N. E. (1944). Experimental studies in conflict. In J. M. Hunt (Ed.), *Personality and the behavior disorders* (pp. 431–465). New York: Ronald.

Miller, N. E. (1971). Liberalization of basic S-R concepts: Extensions to conflict behavior, motivation and social learning. In N. E. Miller (Ed.), *Neal E. Miller: Selected papers.* Chicago: Aldine & Atherton.

Miller, N. E., & Dollard, J. (1941). *Social learning and imitation.* New Haven, CT: Yale University Press.

Muuss, R. E. (1976). The implications of social learning theory for an understanding of adolescent development. *Adolescence, 11*(41), 61–85.

Nakazawa, J., Ohnogi, H., Itoh, H., & Sakano, Y. (1988). From social learning theory to social cognitive theory: Recent advances in Bandura's theory and related research. *Japanese Psychological Review, 31,* 229–251.

Perry, D. G., & Bussey, K. (1979). The social learning theory of sex differences: Imitation is alive and well. *Journal of Personality and Social Psychology, 37,* 1699–1712.

Propst, D. B., & Koesler, R. A. (1998). Bandura goes outdoors: Role of self-efficacy in the outdoor leadership development process. *Leisure Sciences, 20,* 319–344.

Rottschaefer, W., & Knowlton, W. (1979). A cognitive social learning theory perspective on human freedom. *Behaviorism, 7*(1), 17–22.

Scherer, R. F. (1988). A social learning explanation for the development of entrepreneurial characteristics and career selection. *Dissertation Abstracts International, 49*(3), 554–555A.

Schuster, C., & Petosa, R. (1993). Using social learning theory to assess the exercise related health education needs of post-retirement adults. *International Quarterly of Community Health Education, 14,*(2), 191–205.

Shermack, C. R. (1996). Rotter's social learning theory: Prediction of school achievement in Mexican-Americans. *Dissertation Abstracts International, 57*(3), 2141B.

Sims, H. P., & Manz, C. C. (1981). Social learning theory: The role of modeling in the exercise of leadership. *Journal of Organizational Behavior Management, 3*(4), 55–63.

Skinner, W. F., & Fream, A. M. (1997). A social learning theory analysis of computer crime among college students. *Journal of Research in Crime and Delinquency, 34,* 495–518.

Stuart, R. B. (1989). Social learning theory: A vanishing or expanding presence? *Psychology, 26*(1), 35–50.

Tremblay, R. E., Japel, C., Perusse, D., McDuff, P., Boivin, M., Zoccolillo, M., & Montplaisir, J. (1999). The search for the age of "onset" of physical aggression: Rousseau and Bandura revisited. *Criminal Behaviour and Mental Health, 9*(1), 8–23.

Chapter 9. Jean Piaget's Cognitive Model

Archambaud, N. (1975). The role of language in cognitive development according to J. S. Bruner. *Bulletin de Psychologie, 29*(1–3), 45–55.

Bjorklund, D. F. (1997). In search of a metatheory for cognitive development (or, Piaget is dead and I don't feel so good myself). *Child Development, 68,* 144–148.

Bruner, J. S. (1966). Growth of the mind. *American Psychologist, 21,* 1007–1017.

Bruner, J. S., Goodnow, J. J., & Austin, G. A. (1956). *A study of thinking.* New York: John Wiley.

Bruner, J. S., & Kennedy, H. (1966). The development of the concepts of order and proportion in children. In J. S. Bruner, R. R. Oliver, & P. M. Greenfield (Eds.), *Studies in cognitive growth.* New York: John Wiley.

Buss, A. R. (1977). Piaget, Marx, and Buck-Morss on cognitive development: A critique and reinterpretation. *Human Development, 20,* 118–128.

Dalrymple, A. T. (1971). The role of modeling contingencies in the learning of pre-operational concepts by disadvantaged children. *Dissertation Abstracts, 32*(6), 3616–17B.

El-Gosbi, A. M. (1982). A study of the understanding of science processes in relation to Piaget cognitive development at the formal level, and other variables among prospective teachers and college science majors. *Dissertation Abstracts International, 43*(6), 1914A.

Kagan, J. (1970). The determinants of attention in the infant. *American Scientist, 58,* 298–306.

Kagan, J., & Moss, H. (1962). *Birth to maturity: A study in psychological development.* New York: John Wiley.

Morss, J. R. (1991). After Piaget: Rethinking "cognitive development." In J. R. Morss & T. Linzey (Eds.), *Growing up: The politics of human learning* (pp. 9–29). Auckland, New Zealand: Longman Paul.

Mottet, G. (1975). Relationships of language and of cognitive development in the work of Piaget. *Bulletin de Psychologie, 29*(1–3), 36–44.

Piaget, J. (1957). *Logic and psychology.* New York: Basic Books.

Pollack, R. H. (1971). Binet on perceptual-cognitive development or Piaget-come-lately. *Journal of the History of the Behavioral Sciences, 7,* 370–374.

Russell, J. (1999). Cognitive development as an executive process—in part: A homeopathic dose of Piaget. *Developmental Science, 2,* 247–295.

Silverman, H. J. (1979). Biographical situations, cognitive structures and human development: Confronting Sartre and Piaget. *Journal of Phenomenological Psychology, 10*(2), 119–137.

Srivastava, G. P. (1982). Jean Piaget on cognitive development of children. *Asian Journal of Psychology and Education, 10*(1–4), 40–48.

Chapter 10. Lev Vygotsky's
Sociocultural Theory of Development

Adams, G. R., Day, T., Dyk, P. H., Frede, E., & Rogers, D. R. B. (1992). On the dialectics of pubescence and psychosocial development. *Journal of Early Adolescence, 12,* 348–365.

Baltes, P. B., & Cornelius, S. W. (1977). The status of dialectics in developmental psychology: Theoretical orientation versus scientific method. In N. Datan & H. W. Reese (Eds.), *Life-span developmental psychology: Dialectical perspectives on experimental research* (pp. 121–134). New York: Academic Press.

Eastman, M. (1940). *Marxism: Is it science?* New York: W. W. Norton.

Evans, D. W. (1998). Development of the self-concept in children with mental retardation: Organismic and contextual factors. In J. A. Burack, R. M. Hodapp, & E. F. Zigler (Eds.), *Handbook of mental retardation and development* (pp. 462–480). New York: Cambridge University Press.

Freysinger, V. J. (1995). The dialectics of leisure and development for women and men in mid-life: An interpretive study. *Journal of Leisure Research, 27*(1), 61–84.

Glassman, M. (2000). Negation through history: Dialectics and human development. *New Ideas in Psychology, 18,* 1–22.

Hinde, R. A. (2000). Dialectics in development and everyday life. In L. R. Bergman, R. B. Cairns, L.-G. Nilsson, & L. Nystedt (Eds.), *Developmental science and the holistic approach* (pp. 99–120). Mahwah, NJ: Lawrence Erlbaum.

Hook, D., & Parker, I. (2002). Deconstruction, psychopathology and dialectics. *South African Journal of Psychology, 32*(2), 49–54.

Kantin, K. (no date). Theory unravels math mysteries. Binghamton University, http://inside.binghamton.edu/January-February/25FEB99/math.html.

Lerner, R. M. (1992). Dialectics, developmental contextualism, and the further enhancement of theory about puberty and psychosocial development. *Journal of Early Adolescence, 12,* 366–388.

Lerner, R. M., Lerner, J. V., & Tubman, J. (1989). Organismic and contextual bases of development in adolescence: A developmental contextual view. In G. R. Adams,

R. Montemayor, & T. P. Gullotta (Eds.), *Biology of adolescent behavior and development* (pp. 11–37). Newbury Park, CA: Sage.

Molenaar, P., & Oppenheimer, L. (1985). Dynamic models of development and the mechanistic-organismic controversy. *New Ideas in Psychology, 3,* 233–242.

Niemczynski, A. (1981). Dialectics of continuity/discontinuity in behavioral development. *Polish Psychological Bulletin, 12*(3), 149–158.

Pascual-Leone, J. (1987). Organismic processes for neo-Piagetian theories: A dialectical causal account of cognitive development. *International Journal of Psychology, 22,* 531–570.

Reese, H. W. (1977). Discriminative learning and transfer: Dialectical perspectives. In N. Datan & H. W. Reese (Eds.), *Life-span developmental psychology: Dialectical perspectives on experimental research.* New York: Academic Press.

Reese, H. W. (1982). A comment on the meanings of "dialectics." *Human Development, 25,* 423–429.

Riegel, K. (1976). The dialectics of human development. *American Psychologist, 10,* 689–701.

Riegel, K. (1977). The dialectics of time. In N. Datan & H. W. Reese (Eds.), *Life-span developmental psychology: Dialectical perspectives on experimental research* (pp. 3–45). New York: Academic Press.

Roberts, L. R. (1991). The development of conflict between academic adjustment and social adjustment in early adolescence: Effects of organismic and environmental factors. *Dissertation Abstracts International, 52*(4), 2354B.

Stein, D. G. (1989). Development and plasticity in the central nervous system: Organismic and environmental influences. In A. Ardila & F. Ostrosky-Solis (Eds.), *Brain organization of language and cognitive processes. Critical issues in neuropsychology* (pp. 229–252). New York: Plenum.

Tolman, C. (1981). The metaphysic of relations in Klaus Riegel's "dialectics" of human development. *Human Development, 24,* 33–51.

Wachs, T. D., & Gandour, M. J. (1984). Temperament, environment, and six-month cognitive-intellectual development: A test of the organismic specificity hypothesis. In A. Thomas & S. Chess (Eds.), *Annual progress in child psychiatry and child development* (pp. 191–208). New York: Taylor & Francis.

Wozniak, R. H. (1975). A dialectical paradigm for psychological research: Implications drawn from the history of psychology in the Soviet Union. *Human Development, 18,* 18–34.

Chapter 11. Comparing Theories of Human Development

Abdoo, F. B. (1980). A comparison of the effects of Gestalt and associationist learning theories on the musical development of elementary school beginning wind and percussion instrument students. *Dissertation Abstracts International, 41*(4), 1268A.

Bacalarski, M. C. (1996). Vygotsky's developmental theories and the adulthood of computer-mediated communication: A comparison and an illumination. *Journal of Russian and East European Psychology, 34*(1), 57–63.

Commons, M. L. (1991). A comparison and synthesis of Kohlberg's cognitive-developmental and Gewirtz's learning-developmental attachment theories. In J. L. Gewirtz &

W. M. Kurtines (Eds.), *Intersections with attachment* (pp. 257–291). Hillsdale, NJ: Lawrence Erlbaum.

Cowden, M. A. (1992). Faith development in women: A comparison of the moral development theories of Carol Gilligan and Lawrence Kohlberg and the faith development theory of James Fowler. *Dissertation Abstracts International, 53*(1), 581B.

Gallagher, M. J. (1975). A comparison of Hogan's and Kohlberg's theories of moral development. *Dissertation Abstracts International, 36*(5), 2446–2447B.

Halpen, T. L. (1994). A constructive-developmental approach to women's identity formation in early adulthood: A comparison of two developmental theories. *Dissertation Abstracts International, 55*(3), 1201B.

Lambert, H. (1972). A comparison of cognitive developmental theories of ego and moral development. *Proceedings of the Annual Convention of the American Psychological Association, 7*(Pt. 1), 115–116.

Maxwell, E. (1992). Self as phoenix: A comparison of Assagioli's and Dabrowski's developmental theories. *Advanced Development, 4,* 31–48.

Moglia, R. J. (1976). A comparison of observed behaviors of four year olds with theory-predicted behaviors extrapolated from Freud's and Kohlberg's theories of psychosexual development. *Dissertation Abstracts International, 37*(4), 1614–1615B.

Palisi, A. T., & Ruzicka, M. F. (1974). Panel analysis, comparison of theories of group development. *Interpersonal Development, 5,* 234–244.

Sharabany, R., & Bar-Tal, D. (1982). Theories of the development of altruism: Review, comparison and integration. *International Journal of Behavioral Development, 5*(1), 49–80.

Stotsky, S. (1987). A comparison of the two theories about development in written language: Implications for pedagogy and research. In R. Horowitz & S. J. Samuels (Eds.), *Comprehending oral and written language* (pp. 371–395). San Diego, CA: Academic Press.

Tsujimoto, R. N., & Nardi, P. M. (1978). A comparison of Kohlberg's and Hogan's theories of moral development. *Social Psychology, 41,* 235–245.

Wren, D. J. (1993). A comparison of the theories of adolescent moral development of Lawrence Kohlberg and Carol Gilligan: Alternative views of the hidden curriculum. *Dissertation Abstracts International, 54*(4), 2245B.

NAME INDEX

SUBJECT INDEX

ABOUT THE AUTHOR

Neil J. Salkind has been teaching at the University of Kansas for 30 years, in the Department of Psychology and Research in Education with a courtesy appointment in the Department of Human Development and Family Life. He regularly teaches courses in developmental theories, life-span development, statistics, and research methods. He received his Ph.D. in human development from the University of Maryland. He has published more than 80 professional papers and is the author of several college-level textbooks, including *Child Development, Exploring Research,* and *Statistics for People Who (Think They) Hate Statistics* (Sage; second edition, 2004). He was editor of *Child Development Abstracts and Bibliography* from 1989 through 2002. He is active in the Society for Research in Child Development and is an active writer in the trade area. He lives in Lawrence, Kansas, in a big old house that always needs attention. His hobbies include cooking, masters swimming, restoring an ancient Volvo P1800, and collecting books and reading them.